--------------------

Copyright © 2021

All rights reserved

Cover Design by Karen Warburton
Book Design by Russ Warburton

No part of this book can be reproduced in any form or by written,
electronic or mechanical, including photocopying, recording or by any
information retrieval system without written permission by the Author.

Although every precaution has been taken in the preperation of this book,
the Publisher and Author assume no responsibilty for errors or
ommissions. Neither is any liability assumed for damages resulting from
the use of information contained herein.

Foreword

When we started the Great War Group, we had two major goals in mind – one was to diversify coverage of the war in the English language so that it was not always about our own. The second was to encourage and support members and enthusiasts who wanted to do more than just read the latest book about the First World War. In this respect, Russ is one of our success stories.

For those of us that did not arrive at the First World War via an academic track, our passion for learning and remembering usually manifested itself with a desire to find out more about a single individual, or perhaps, a group with whom we felt an affinity. Often, those people are family members. The stories of everyday men and women are why we do what we do. It is an overwhelming source of pride for us that members like Russ feel empowered and supported enough to ask questions, to investigate their stories and then put the results of their hard work, their passion and their respect for these relatives and persons of interest, into print. This will leave an honourable legacy for future generations to remember their own family's contribution to the war.

Not only that, but in this case, invaluable information about the 10th Royal Welsh Fusiliers is now available to others who might like to follow his example.

That Russ has done this at such a difficult time only makes us more proud of him, and we know that his Grandfather would echo that sentiment.

Alex Churchill
Author, Researcher & Historian

Preface

My Taid (Welsh for Grandad) was a grumpy old man who spent his days sitting on the garden wall watching the world go by, or sitting in the armchair chewing tobacco and spitting it into the electric fire and poking the very same electric fire with a poker because he said he was cold, much to the utter dispair of my Mother and Father.

My Taid had lived with my family for a few years. Myself, my older Brother Steve and my older Sister Linda all remember him with fondness, if a little warilly.

He used to eat condensed milk out of the tin, spill most of it and then deny all knowledge of even eating it!

He would only have a bath in the front room in front of the electric fire, in an old tin bath that my Mother would have to fill with hot water boiled in the kettle, even though we had a perfectly modern bathroom upstairs!

He would always wear a shirt and a trilby and called everyone Joe, because he couldn't remember names, but he was our Taid and we loved him.

My Taid never talked much about 'The War' and on the rare occasions he did, he mentioned that he was wounded and that the conditions were terrible, and that was it.

He passed away in 1970 at the age of 90, when I was only 8 years old. I would love to have the chance to ask him more question about his life, but like many of us, we leave it too late and before you know it, they are gone.

I have always had a keen interest in The Great War and after many years, decided to research **'My Taid's War'**. He served with the 10th (Service) Battalion Royal Welsh Fusiliers until 1918 then joined the 8th Entrenching Battalion and then the Hood Battalion of the 63rd Royal Naval Division until the end of the War.

So this is 'His', and the 10th (Service) Battalion Royal Welsh Fusilier's story.

I hope you enjoy it as much as I have enjoyed researching it?

Acknowledgements

This book could not have been written without the help from the following:-

- Flintshire War Memorials Project
- Chris Baker & his website "The Long Long Trail"
- The Staff at Hawarden Record Office
- The Great War Forum
- The Great War Group

- Thank you Alex Churchill for the Foreword

- Thank you to my family and friends for the support offered and given

Dedication

This book is dedicated to my Wife Karen, who has not only typed all of this book and put it into some kind of order, but has been my rock over the last few years, through some very dark days.

She is always there for me.

Love you loads, my Girl!

Contents

Glossary	- Terms & Abbreviations
Chapter 1	- The Early Years
Chapter 2	- Call To Arms
Chapter 3	- Training
Chapter 4	- 1915 - To The Front
Chapter 5	- 1916 - The Grinding War
Chapter 6	- 1917 - Through Mud & Bullets
Chapter 7	- 1918 & Disbandment
Chapter 8	- 8th Entrenching Battalion & 63rd Royal Naval Division (R. N. D.)
Chapter 9	- Battalion Honours
Chapter 10	- Edwin's War In Map Form
Chapter 11	- The Later Years
Glossary	- Sources & Permissions

Glossary of Terms and Abbreviations

A.D.S.	ADVANCE DRESSING STATION
A.S.C.	ARMY SERVICE CORPS
B.E.F.	BRITISH EXPEDITIONARY FORCE
BATT.	BATTALION
C.O.	COMMANDING OFFICER
C.O.Y.	COMPANY
C.S.M.	COMPANY SERGEANT MAJOR
D.S.M.	DISTINGUISHED SERVICE MEDAL
D.S.O.	DISTINGUISHED SERVICE ORDER
F.A.	FIELD AMBULANCE
F. G. C. M.	FIELD GENERAL COURT MARTIAL
G.H.Q.	GENERAL HEAD QUARTERS
G. O. C.	GENERAL OFFICER COMMANDING
H. E.	HIGH EXPLOSIVES
H.Q.	HEAD QUARTERS
I.W.M.	IMPERIAL WAR MUSEUM
K. O. Y. L. I.	KINGS OWN YORKSHIRE LIGHT INFANTRY
M.C.	MILITARY CROSS
M.G.C.	MACHINE GUN COMPANY
M.M.	MILITARY MEDAL
M.O.	MEDICAL OFFICER
N.C.O.	NON COMMISSIONED OFFICER
O.P.	OBSERVATION POST
O.R.	OTHER RANKS
R.A.	ROYAL ARTILLERY
R.A.M.C.	ROYAL ARMY MEDICAL CORPS
R.E.	ROYAL ENGINEERS
R.F.C.	ROYAL FLYING CORPS
R.G.A.	ROYAL GARRISON ARTILLERY
R. I. R.	RESERVE INFANTRY REGIMENT (GERMAN)
R. M.	ROYAL MARINE
R.N.D.	ROYAL NAVAL DIVISION
R. N. V. R.	ROYAL NAVAL VOLUNTEER RESERVE
R.W.F.	ROYAL WELSH FUSILIERS
S. A. A.	SMALL ARMS AMMUNITION
SUB/LIEUT	SUB LIEUTENANT
T. M.	TRENCH MORTAR
Q. M.	QUARTER MASTER

Chapter 1
<u>The Early Years</u>

My Taid Edwin Roberts, was born on Monday 23rd June 1879 at 14 Beaumaris Street, Kirkdale, West Derby, Liverpool to Thomas Roberts and his Wife Margaret Roberts (formally Davies).

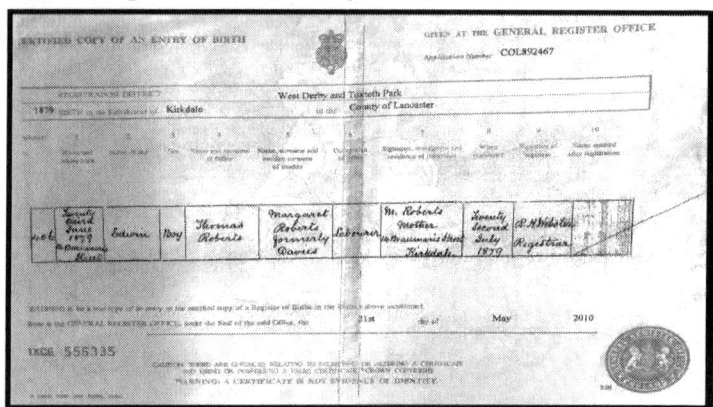

Edwin Roberts Birth Certificate

At the time of the 1881 census, Edwin's Father Thomas was a labourer and the family were living at 40 Haddocks Street, Kirkdale, West Derby.

Haddock Street shown in the centre of the photograph where the family lived

Marriage Certificate of Thomas and Margaret Roberts Edwin's Parents

The household consisted of the following:-

NAME	RELATIONSHIP TO HEAD OF FAMILY	AGE	OCCUPATION
THOMAS ROBERTS	HEAD	27	STEAMSHIP STOKER
MARGARET ROBERTS	WIFE	27	-
EDWIN ROBERTS (MY TAID)	SON	2	-
WILLIAM T. ROBERTS	SON	1	-

Thomas and his Wife Margaret both state on the 1881 census that they were born in Bagillt, Flintshire, North Wales but moved to Liverpool, like many families at that time, to find work.

At the time of the 1891 census, the family had moved back to North Wales and were living at Top Hill, Holywell, Flintshire.

Sadly, Margaret, Thomas' Wife & Edwin's Mother, had died in 1889 at the age of 35 and was buried at Bagillt Cemetery on October 22nd 1889.

Death Certificate of Margaret Roberts, Edwin's Mother

Thomas remarried on October 27th 1890 to Hannah Eliza Davies, who was 29 years old. They married at Holywell Parish Church. Thomas was a bricklayer and 36 years old. Hannah was illiterate and signed the wedding certificate with a "X."

Marriage Certificate of Thomas and Hannah, Edwin's Father and Step-Mother

The 1891 census tells us that the family consisted of the following:-

NAME	RELATIONSHIP TO HEAD OF FAMILY	AGE	OCCUPATION
THOMAS ROBERTS	HEAD	36	BRICKLAYER
HANNAH ELIZA ROBERTS	WIFE	29	-
EDWIN ROBERTS (MY TAID)	SON	11	SCHOLAR
WILLIAM T. ROBERTS	SON	10	SCHOLAR
CHARLES ROBERTS	SON	7	SCHOLAR
SARAH C. GITTINS	DAUGHTER	5	SCHOLAR

Charles and Sarah were born in Bagillt, Flintshire, North Wales to Thomas and his first Wife Margaret before she died in 1889.

Edwin joined "Bagillt Board Boys School" on 28th September 1889 aged 10 years old with his Brother William.

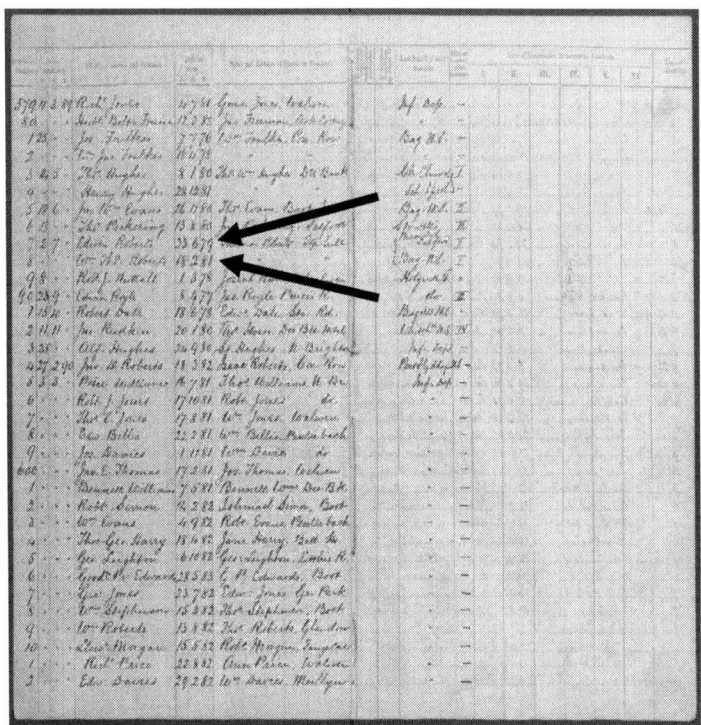

Edwin and William shown on the 9th and 10th lines on the School's National Register

At the time of the 1901 census the family had moved to 11 Brooklyn Terrace, Bagillt, Flintshire, North Wales and the census shows the following:-

NAME	RELATIONSHIP TO HEAD OF FAMILY	AGE	OCCUPATION
THOMAS ROBERTS	HEAD	46	BRICKLAYER
HANNAH ELIZA ROBERTS	WIFE	40	-
EDWIN ROBERTS (MY TAID)	SON	21	COAL MINER
WILLIAM T. ROBERTS	SON	20	BRICKLAYER
CHARLES ROBERTS	SON	18	BRICKLAYER
SARAH C. ROBERTS	DAUGHTER	15	-
JOHN D. ROBERTS	SON	9	SCHOLAR
PETER ROBERTS	SON	7	SCHOLAR
EDWARD ROBERTS	SON	4	-
ELIAS ROBERTS	SON	2	-

Edwin was working as a Coal Miner, possibly at Bettisfield Colliery in Bagillt. His other Brothers William and Charles had followed in their Father's footsteps and became Bricklayers. Thomas and Hannah, by this time, had had 4 more children.

Bettisfield Colliery

Bettisfield Colliery opened in 1872. In 1896 there were 538 men employed there, including 100 "Surface Workers" producing house and steam coal.

The two shafts sunk to a depth of 290 yards. One shaft was 17ft diameter and the other was 10ft 6 inches diameter.

By 1908, it was in the hands of the Bagillt Coal Company Ltd and they employed 641 men.

On 10th of June 1905, my Taid Edwin, married Mary Parry at Bethel Chapel, Pen-y-Ball Street, Holywell. Edwin was 25 years old, and he was employed as a "Coal Cutter". Mary was 22 years old and a Spinster.

Bethel Chapel, Pen-y-Ball Street, Holywell

Marriage Certificate of Edwin and Mary Roberts

Edwin was living at Hope Cottages, Bagillt, Flintshire, North Wales and Mary was living in Pen-y-Ball Street, Holywell, Flintshire, North Wales at the time of the wedding.

The happy couple moved into 20 Pierce's Row, Bagillt and by the time of the 1911 census Mary had given birth to two Sons, John D. Roberts, aged 4 and William Thomas Roberts aged 1.

Edwin's younger brother William Thomas Roberts was sadly killed in a mining accident on 11th of December 1909 at Bettisfield Colliery where they both worked.

FATAL COLLIERY ACCIDENT.

A terrible accident occurred on Saturday afternoon at Bettisfield Colliery, Bagillt, Flintshire. A tub-load of coal became unhooked and ran down a decline in the underground workings. Three men at the bottom of the hill were struck by the tub, and two of them, named Jones and Roberts, were killed outright, while the third, a man named Wright, was badly crushed. He was removed to Holywell Cottage Hospital, this being the first case treated in that institution, which was the gift of a Londoner, Mr. Edwin Jones.

Newspaper Article from Cannock Chase Courier - Saturday 18th December 1909

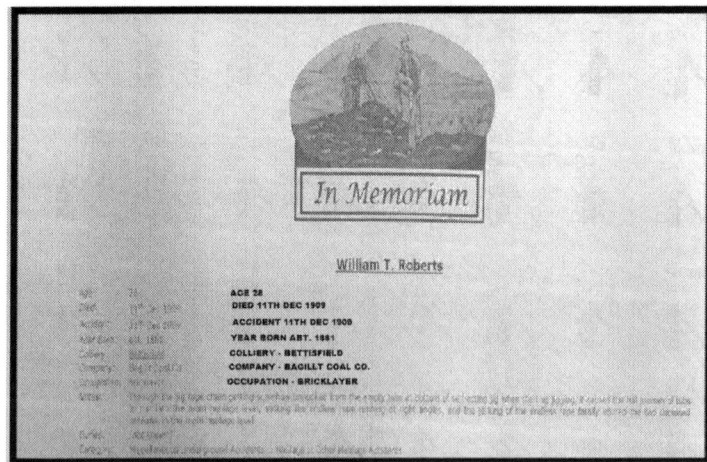

Durham Mining Museum Individual In Memoriam Tribute

Edwin named his second Son after the Brother he lost.

Edwin and Mary had another child in 1914, a daughter named Katie Roberts and they had moved to 17 Primrose Hill, Holywell, Flintshire, North Wales.

Chapter 2
Call to Arms

The *"Call to Arms"* in and around the Holywell area was the same as across the whole of the country. Everyone, it seems, were keen to **"Do Their Bit"**. Many joined the ranks very quickly just in case they missed out, as rumour was it, that the War would be over by Christmas and the British Empire would prevail in the fight against an evil aggressor. Recruiting drives and numerous meetings were held across the length and breadth of the country.

An example of these meetings was held in the Local Assembly Hall, an article appeared in The County Herald on 11th September 1914 entitled: -

"Holywell and the War, an enthusiastic Meeting"

There was a crowded attendance at the Assembly Hall on the Tuesday evening when a meeting was held for the purpose of inducting the men of the district to join Lord Kitchener's Army. The Chair was occupied by Hon-Major J. Lloyd Price, who was supported on the platform by Col. Howard, the Vicar J. W. Thomas, Dr. H. W. S. Williams, Alderman Joseph Jones, Messer D. F. Pennant, H. A. Tilby (Clerk of Flintshire County Council), Thomas Waterhouse, Captain James Ayer, J. Kerfoot Roberts, Frank Jones, Rhyl. In the course of the opening remarks, The Chairman, alluded to the valiant manner in which the British Army was fighting in France and stated nothing like it had ever been recorded in history, but the Army wanted reinforcements and "Where were they to come from?" It was for the young able-bodied men of the country, to come to their assistance, because it would be a shame to leave them alone to fight their Country's battles in France *(hear, hear)*. He had hoped Lord Mostyn would have been able to attend this meeting, but he was not well enough to do so. He referred to the ex-Officer of that district Mr Ayer, who had done excellent work, proving himself one of the best in the Country in recruiting and sent an excellent lot of men to Wrexham and Chester.

Colonel Howard then addressed the meeting. He said that the recent performance of the British Army was the most remarkable Military feat ever recorded in history *(hear, hear)*, they had beaten the Germans who were five to one against them *(applause)*, but General French had sent home to say, he must have more men in order to maintain their position in the field and in Europe, and to the men of Holywell, he *(The Speaker)* appealed that night, Lord Kitchener has asked for 500,000 more men and had already 300,000, so 200,000 were still required.

These new troops would be put into training as soon as possible and as soon as the Inspecting Officer was satisfied as to their fitness, they would be sent to the front, and not before. During the past few days, he had been with his friend, Mr Herbert Lewis, speaking at meetings of this character *(hear, hear)* there was no distinction of politics now. They all stood on one common platform *(hear, hear)*.

The Speaker then referred to the numbers raised in Flintshire at the time of the Napoleonic Wars and said at that time, the loyal Holywell volunteers, were 140 strong *(hear, hear)*. Proceeding to refer to the prospects of the great struggle, Colonel Howard described what would happen if Germany won. They had, he said, to deal with a powerful and unscrupulous enemy, and they wanted to be in a position to deal with him in such a way, as to crush his power forever *(hear, hear)*. War was Hell, there is no other word for it. Lord Kitchener's objective, in raising his New Army, was to keep the War out of this Country.

He appealed to the young men of the good old town of Holywell, to come forward, your men between the ages of 19-35, should do their duty to their Country, which was in such terrible danger at the present moment. Mr H. A. Tilby then delivered a forceful and inspiring address.

He said that if Britain were beaten in this fight, they would have to abandon all those high ideals of freedom and liberty for which they now stood, and they would be governed by brute force, might against right.

He hoped and believed they were going to win, but that would have to come by fighting, not by shouting *(hear, hear)*. They wanted to show by their deeds, that they had men who were determined. Their ideals should continue to live. He appealed to the young men, if they wanted to end it, this is the way to stop the awful devastation and to roll up and roll up at once, to go and fight side by side, shoulder to shoulder, with those who were upholding the 'Flag of this Country' so valiantly at the front *(hear, hear)*.

Life in Britain just before the War was not easy for my Taid Edwin, as it was for so many others. Many children died young and male life expectancy was only 50 years of age. Health and safety laws were non existant and thousands of men, like Edwin's younger Brother William, died each year in industrial and agricultural accidents. So when the *"Call to Arms"* came, no wonder so many men were eager to escape their dull and drab lives for the chance of an adventure that the Army were offering. They were promised a guaranteed wage, were clothed and housed, had decent food (far better and more regular from what they received at home) and probably, for the first time in their lives had adventure beckoning them in foreign fields. Their country also needed them!

The raising of the **'New Armies'** was one of the most important and far reaching decisions taken by the British throughout the War. Kitchener's plan of raising a massive *"Force of Soldiers to fight on The Western Front"* remains his claim to fame. Kitchener, in his new role; Secretary of State of War, requested, without delay, the raising of 500,000 men, with the opening of the first 100,000 known as simply "K1" was announced on 8th August 1914.

Kitchener fought off opposition to his plan for the New Armies, many wanted them to be merged with the already established Territorial Army. This was also the view of Field Marshall French, the Commander in Chief of the British Expeditionary Force (B. E. F.).

Kitchener had great concerns about the idea of merging the two together, as many of the Territorials had volunteered for Home Service only and Kitchener was worried about the poor performance of French's Territorials in the Franco-Prussian War of 1860-1871.

Eventually, five New Armies were raised and were numbered "K1 to K5". These Armies mostly contained six Divisions. K5 had seven, each of twelve Battalions.

In Lord Kitchener's first morning at The War Office on 6th August 1914, his Private Secretary, Sir George Arthur, handed him a pen with which to give his signature for the official stamp. The pen did not work. *"Dear Me"* muttered Kitchener, *"What a War Office, not a scarp of Army and not a pen that will write."*

Kitchener immediately started work on expanding the Army and later that day he sought parliamentry approval for the size of the Army to be increased by 500,000 men. On the following morning, 7th August, Kitchener's **"Call to Arms"** was published in newspapers across the country under the heading *"Your King and Country needs you"*.

A few hours after the article appeared, Kitchener outlined his proposals to the Cabinet, declaring that the War could not be won solely by sea power and that Britain must be ready to place Armies of millions in the field and sustain them for several years. It was clear to Kitchener, even at this early stage, that conflict would be a long hard struggle.

Recruiting Poster

Recruiting Poster

Many recruits feard they would be rejected on account of poor eyesight or because they were too small.

Private T. H. Merrifield, Service No. 15044, 10th (Service) Battalion Royal Welsh Fusiliers was astonished by the superficial nature of examination in September 1914. The Medical Officer, after finding Private Merrifield's left eye very weak, said *"Ah well, you always shut that eye when you are firing a rifle, so that won't matter as your other eye is 100%"* and passed him "Fit for Duty".

Sixteen year old Lewis Roberts enlisted in the 10th (Service) Battalion Royal Welsh Fusiliers in Llandudno in October 1914, having followed the Sergeants suggestion that he should walk around the table twice before giving a false age!

When War broke out, the flood of volunteers initially overwhelmed the system and short-cuts were taken to help with the process. The recruits had to pass a rudimentary interview by the 'Recruiting Sergeant' and after a basic medical examination, they had to complete a 'Attestation Form' (essentially an oath of allegence to the King and Country) in duplicate. It was the Army Form B111 that committed the soldier to serve until the War was over.

Attestation Form

The recruits then swore an oath of allegiance to the King before an Officer.

The medical was not too demanding and the form B178 was completed by the Medical Officer. It included a physical description of the recruit. Another Officer then certified the form with his approval.

B178 Form

The recruit had to be aged between 19 and 38, my Taid Edwin was 35 years old at the time of his enlistment, at least 5ft 3 inches tall and physically fit.

After this stage, the recruit was deemed to be a soldier, subject to King's regulations. He then received the King's shilling and was sent home to await "Call Up" for training.

The basic rate of pay for a soldier was one shilling per day. This could be increased by earning "Proficiency Pay", such as "Marksmanship" or other skills.

An increase of one penny was paid to the soldier when on "Active Duty".

If a soldier was married, like Edwin was, a compulsory stoppage of six pence per day was to be paid to his Wife. This increase depended on how many children the soldier had.

From 29th September 1917 a further three pence per day was given as a pay increase.

Edwin's service record, like many others, was destroyed during the Blitz in 1940, but according to other records that still exsist, he joined the 10th (Service) Battalion Royal Welsh Fusiliers at Wrexham, having enlisted at the Drill Hall in Holywell as part of Kitchener's 3rd New Army.

The Drill Hall was built in 1914 by John Sibeon & Sons of Holywell, replacing the Drill Hall in Brynford Street, which had been home to the Yeomanry

At the time of his enlistment, my Taid Edwin would have been 35 years old. This must have been a very hard decision for Edwin to make as he was married with three young children and was working as a Coal Miner, a "Reserved Occupation" which meant he did not have to enlist, but he did so anyway. Edwin was issued with service number 15736 and preceded to Wrexham.

Wrexham Barracks

Recruits at Wrexham Barracks

Official Army Orders

XVIII. Augmentation of the Army. With reference to Army Order I of 21st August 1914 (A. O. 324 of 1914), and Army Order XII of 11th September, 1914.

His Majesty the King has been graciously pleased to approve of a further addition to the Army, of Six Divisions and Army Troops.

- 2. These Divisions will be numbered from 21 to 26.
- 3. The new Battalions will be raised as additional Battalions of the Regiments of Infantry of the Line, and will be given numbers following consecutively on the existing Battalions of these Regiments. They will be further distinguished by the word "Service" after the numbers.

Appendix A.

25th DIVISION

76th Brigade
{
10th (Service) Battalion Royal Welsh Fusiliers
6th (Service) Battalion The South Wales Borderers
7th (Service) Battalion The Kings (Shropshire Light Infantry)
10th (Service) Battalion The Welch Regiment
}

Appendix C.

25th Division Commander, Major-General F. Ventris.
76th Brigade Commander, Brig-General H. J. Archdale

In compliance with the above Army Orders, recruiting was commenced at the Regimental Depot, Royal Welsh Fusiliers, Wrexham, during September 1914 and the recruits were formed into Three Companies: 'A', 'B' & 'C' being the nucleus of the 10th (Service) Battalion under Major F. N. Burton (Retired 87th Punjabis Indian Army) and 2nd Lieutenant B. D. John.

Chapter 3
Training

The main problem with training was that at the time, a substaintial influx of men were joining and there was insufficient Officers and N. C. O.'s, with enough experience, to train the new recruits.

Almost one of the first acts of Kitchener becoming Secretary of State for War, was to tell the British Expeditianary Force to leave behind three Officers and fifteen N. C. O.'s from each Battalion to be used to train the new recruits.

Other men that were on the reserve list and senior men who had retired were also called back into service to help train the vast amount of new recruits.

The Government also advertised in the local press around the whole of the country, asking for Junior Officers to join the ranks.

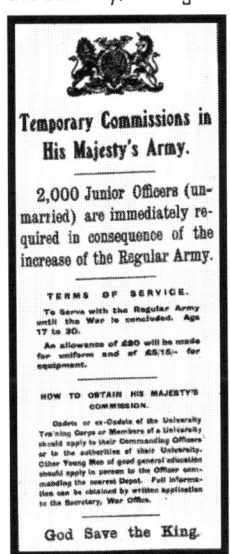

The Boston Guardian & Lincolnshire Independent Newspaper. Saturday August 22nd 1914

Another problem was because of the huge influx of recruits in 1914 it was impossible to clothe and arm them all straight away to the current specifications. The War Office was unsuccessful in obtaining enough khaki uniforms in the opening weeks of the War, so recruits were made to wear replacement uniforms. Around 500,000 recruits wore improvised uniforms during training which were sourced from Post Office stocks and were made from blue serge; popularly known as "Kitchener's Blues".

Blue was used as a substitute for the traditional khaki. The khaki dye came from Germany, whose chemical industry specialised in dyestuffs. This, of course, became unobtainable once War broke out and it took sometime to find a replacement khaki dye to make new uniforms. In November 1914, the new 'Director of Army Contracts' had changed the supply system, and this led to a boom in 'khaki contracts' in the British tailoring trade. Old rifles and other items were found from reserve stores and issued until more could be produced.

My Taid Edwin and the other recruits at Wrexham were formed into three Companies, 'A', 'B' & 'C' being the nucleus of the 10th (Service) Battalion Royal Welsh Fusiliers under the command of Major Frederic Nuthall Burton (Retired, 87th Punjabis Indian Army) & 2nd Lieutenant Bernard Digby Johns. Edwin was placed into 'C' Company.

Frederic Nuthall Burton

Bernard Digby Johns

The Battalion were to stay at Wrexham Barracks until 26th September.

During their short time at Wrexham Barracks food and other supplies were running low due to the influx of new recruits. If the recruits had enough money and were allowed out of the Barracks, they could supplement their poor Army Rations by purchasing food from the local shops, but this also proved difficult, as Private T. H. Merrifield, service number 15044 states:-

"There was so much demand for food that I had to walk miles to get bread as Wrexham was so crowded with new recruits. Most of the local shops sold out of everything edible very quickly so you had no option but to walk to the surrounding villages to buy food." - Private T. H. Merrifield service number 15044

The 10th (Service) Battalion left Wrexham Station on 26th September in two troop trains to Codford St. Mary in Wiltshire, where it went under canvas in the camp of the 76th Brigade. It was under command of Brigadier General Hugh James Archdale (retired Royal Welsh Fusiliers).

Royal Welsh Fusiliers at Wrexham Station 1914

The 10th (Service) Battalion Royal Welsh Fusiliers were based at Camp 12 on the Eastside and close to the Chitterne Road, where the five camps, numbered 8-12, were based.

Whilst the new training camps were being built, tented accommodation was provided. Adequate for a 'Territorial Field Camp', but hardly the perfect setting to train an amateur Army to the peak of Military effect.

Example of a Bell Tent

During the Great War both the twin villages of Codford St. Mary and Codford St. Peter were ideally suited for Military use, with their proximity to the railways and to the training areas of Salisbury Plain. At the outbreak of the War in August 1914 to the end of September 1914, no less than 24,000 soldiers arrived in the vicinity. Codford had fifteen camps whilst the surrounding satellite villages had a further twelve. Almost at once, temporary shops sprung up as villages used all available space to provide for the needs of the ever increasing Military population.

Codford High Street

The men were under canvas whilst the huts were being constructed and in October, and through the Winter months, the weather in Codford took a turn for the worse. The wet and cold conditions turned the roads and fields into a mass of sticky mud, from which there was no escape. Extensive flooding occurred in the village, especially in the area around the railway station.

Trenches around the tents had been dug to try and keep the water away from them. One soldier commentated, *"There are lakes all around the tents"*.

Training was suspended, even the route they marched was deemed impossible during the heavy rains in October and November 1914. The soldiers had no change of clothing and no washing facilities so they went down to the river to wash the mud off their uniforms and themselves. One disillusioned soldier commented, *"I have never seen so much mud in all of my life as I have seen in Codford!"* Mass meetings were held in Codford for the 25th Division and the whole company refused to go on parade unless the living conditions were attended to.

In the mud at Codford

The soldiers referred to Codford as "**Mudford**" or "**Codford on the mud**". Poems were written about the conditions.

Here is an extract from one called "Codford Camp":-

"There are lots of little huts, all dotted here and there
For those who have to live inside, I've offered many a prayer
Inside the huts, there's RATS as big as any nanny goat
Last night a soldier saw one trying on his overcoat
It's slutch up to the eyeballs, you get it in your ears
But into it you've got to go without a sign of fear
And when you've had a bath of slutch, you just set to and groom
And get cleaned up for next Parade, or else, its order room"

The following Officers joined the Battalion for duty on **September 26th**:-

- Major C. H. Lord
- Captain E. W. Maples
- Captain E. Freeman
- Lieutenant & Quarter Master. E. H. Chapman
- 2nd Lieutenant G. C. Lloyd
- 2nd Lieutenant W. P. Griffiths
- 2nd Lieutenant G. E. Taylor
- 2nd Lieutenant J. P. Carrington
- 2nd Lieutenant C. A. R. Follitt
- 2nd Lieutenant A. W. Spence
- 2nd Lieutenant H. V. Piercy

These Officers were to help with the training and organisation of the Battalion. Recruitment of more Officers continued throughout the Battalions training.

October 1st Captain E. Freeman was appointed Adjutant.

Captain E. Freeman

On **October 3rd**, Colonel Sergeant J. Hill was appointed Regimental Sergeant Major (R. S. M.).

On **October 7th**, Major Henry Cornwall Cotton Gibbings joined the Battalion. Gibbings was a retired Major from the Royal Inniskilling Fusiliers. Appointments like this showed the need for experienced Officers to train the Battalion.

On **October 10th**, the Battalion had their **'First Major Inspection'**, carried out by Lieutenant General Pitcairn Campbell, C. B., General Commander in Chief, Southern Command, on behalf of the Secretary of State for War. (Kitchener).

Lieutenant General Pitcairn Campbell

Report of the inspection was noted as **"Satisfactory"**

On **October 13th**, Brevet-Colonel W. R. H. Beresford Ash, (retired pay), Royal Welsh Fusiliers, joined the Battalion and assumed command. Major F. N. Burton assumed the position of Second in Command.

Brevet-Colonel W. R. H. Beresford Ash

More Officers continued to join the Battalion between **October 13th & November 11th**.

- **2nd Lieutenant F. C. G. Larkworthy**
- **2nd Lieutenant R. W. Phillipps**
- **2nd Lieutenant H. A. V. Maynard**
- **Lieutenant R. S. Renton (R. A. M. C.)**

On **November 11th 1914** the Battalion left Codford, in two troop trains from Wylye Station to Bournemouth Hampshire and marched into its alloted billets in the Winton-Moordown district, two miles North of Bournemouth.

Wylye Station

By the middle of November 1914 it was announced that the 10th (Service) Battalion Royal Welsh Fusiliers were to be billeted in Bournemouth for the Winter with many other Battalions.

Accommodation was needed for 10,000 to 12,000 soldiers.

'Billeting Officers' were busy arranging accommodation from Branksome to Winton-Moordown, Malmesbury Park, Boscome and Pokesdown but the centre of Bournemouth was to be left out of the areas used for billeting.

The 10th (Service) Battalion Royal Welsh Fusiliers were billetted in the Moordown area.

The Reverend H. Bloomfield, of St. John the Baptist Church Moordown writes: -

"The Winter 1914-1915, the first Winter of the War, will be remembered for it's torrents of rain, which led to the Military Authorities to billet Battalions of The Royal Welsh Fusiliers and The South Wales Borderer's in our Parish; right pleased were the men after their terrible experiences on Salisbury Plain, to find a roof over their heads and a comfortable bed beneath it."

The Armstrong Hut

The 'Design Branch' of the 'Directorate of Fortifications & Works', under Major B. H. O. Armstrong, having already done a great deal of necessary works before the War, produced a complete set of drawings for the typical **"Hut"** within two days of being asked. Armstrong proposed that the **"Huts"** to be 60ft long, by 20ft wide, with an average height of 10ft, allowing space down the centre for the tables and benches. A single **"Hut"** held 32 men plus a Junior N.C.O.

Forty such **"Huts"** would be provided for each Battalion and were to be constructed on a wooden framework with corrugated iron on the roof and external surfaces and an asbestos lining inside.

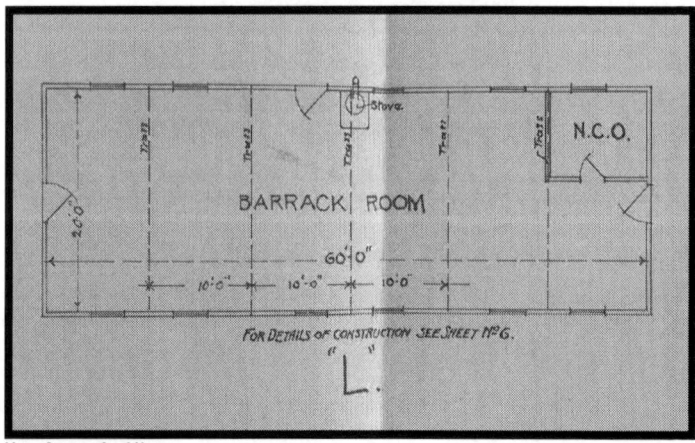

Map of a standard Hut

A Great War Hut

Soldiers inside a Hut

Due to the vast number of recruits, existing facilities were not big enough, so new training camps were constructed. Some recruits had to be billeted with local families until the accommodation could be provided.

3 Soldiers billeted with a local family at 82 Ensbury Park Road

There was a steady intake of Officers joining the Battalion during **November & December 1914:-**

- 2nd Lieutenant J. A. Walker
- 2nd Lieutenant T. A. Oliver
- 2nd Lieutenant H. A. Davies
- 2nd Lieutenant H. J. K. Lewis
- 2nd Lieutenant A. W. Fish
- 2nd Lieutenant C. E. L. Locke
- 2nd Lieutenant G. D. Scale
- 2nd Lieutenant A. G. W. Buchanan
- 2nd Lieutenant J. L. T. Davies
- 2nd Lieutenant E. W. Bell
- 2nd Lieutenant A. V. Cree
- 2nd Lieutenant H. E. Wynne-Williams
- 2nd Lieutenant W. B. Morgan

On **December 30th** Major Charles Henry Lord, dropped dead from a heart attack when on parade with 'B' Coy. Major Lord, aged 65, offered his services again to his Country at their time of need, thereby setting an example to all when serving His King and Country.

OFFICER'S SUDDEN DEATH ON PARADE.

A MAJOR'S TRAGIC END AT MOORDOWN.

The death occurred very suddenly and under tragic circumstances at Moordown on Wednesday morning whilst on parade, of Major Charles Henry Lord, aged 64 years, of the 10th Battalion Royal Welch Fusiliers, stationed at Moordown, whose home address is 9, Moreton Avenue, Harpenden, Hertfordshire. The deceased came to the district on November 11th, and had followed his duties regularly since. About fourteen days ago he was examined by Dr. R. S. Renton, who found him suffering from degenerate disease of the arteries. On December 24th he went to his home for six days' leave, and returned to his duties at 9.15 a.m. on Wednesday, when he appeared in good health and told his commanding officer that he felt much better. At 10.30 a.m. on Wednesday he was on parade at Moordown, when he was seen to fall to the ground in the presence of Thomas Reginald Lee, a sergeant of the 10th Battalion Royal Welch Fusiliers. Dr. Renton, of the R.A.M.C., was at once called, but could only pronounce life extinct.

THE INQUEST.

Mr. F. G. Lefroy (the Bournemouth borough coroner) conducted the inquiry into the circumstances surrounding the death of Major Lord yesterday (Friday) at half an hour after noon, in the Littledown Road Coroner's Court.

Councillor W. Taylor was the foreman of the jury.

The Coroner, in opening the inquest, said that that was a perfectly formal inquiry.

Ralph Stuart Renton, M.D., of the R.A.M.C., stationed in Bournemouth, said that on the 30th ult. deceased was on the parade at Red Hill Common at about 10.45 a.m. Major Lord fell down and witness, on being called to see him, found him dead. Some three weeks ago witness attended the Major with reference to service abroad and he then discovered on examination that his arteries were affected. The cause of death was primarily arterial schlerosis and cerebral hemorrhage. Dr. Renton also gave evidence of identification. The cause of death was a natural one.

Mr. Lefroy said that there was a sergeant of the regiment present who actually saw the deceased fall down. But as they knew the facts he did not know whether the jury wanted to hear him.

The jury decided that there was no need to call this sergeant, and returned a verdict in accordance with the medical evidence.

The Guardian, Saturday January 2nd 1915

There was another intake of Officers to the Battalion in **January 1915:-**

- 2nd Lieutenant R. A. Adamson
- 2nd Lieutenant D. S. Hughes
- 2nd Lieutenant M. Murray
- 2nd Lieutenant W. Hughes
- 2nd Lieutenant R. D. Stanley
- 2nd Lieutenant A. Nevitt
- 2nd Lieutenant A. J. S. James
- 2nd Lieutenant J. D. W. Candy
- 2nd Lieutenant B. J. Stedman
- 2nd Lieutenant W. T. Lyons
- Captain G. P. Blake

During February the Battalion received the sad news that Major General Sir Luke O'Connor V. C. K. C. B. Colonel of the Royal Welsh Fusiliers had died aged 84. Major General O'Connor was the first soldier to receive the Victoria Cross (V. C.) Britain's highest award for gallantry in the face of the enemy. He received this whilst serving with the 23rd Regiment of Foot (later The Royal Welsh Fusiliers), during the Crimean War.

He was appointed Major General of his old Regiment on 3rd June 1914.

His Victoria Cross is displayed at The Royal Welsh Fusiliers Museum in Caernarfon Castle Gwynedd.

Major General Sir Luke O'Connor V.C. K.C.B.

Major General O'Connor was replaced by Major General Sir Francis Lloyd K. C. B. C. V. O. D. S. O. on **March 3rd 1915**.

Major General Sir Francis Lloyd K.C.B. C.V.O. D.S.O.

During the Battalion's time at Bournemouth, one Officer, 2nd Lieutenant (later Captain) John A. Walker who was billeted at The Conservative Club, Moordown, knocked down a cyclist whilst driving his motorcar on Sunday 14th February 1915.

The local paper, The Western Gazette, reported the incident on Friday 19th February, see the article below: -

2nd Lieutenant (later Captain) John A. Walker

> **MOTOR AND CYCLE COLLISION.**—On Sunday afternoon, almost at the exact spot where a recent fatal accident occurred, a collision took place between a motor-car, driven by Lieutenant John Walker, of the 10th Battalion Royal Welsh Fusiliers, and a bicycle ridden by Mr. R. B. Badeley, secretary of the Bournemouth Club, who resides at Hothfield, Milton-road, Bournemouth. The motor-car was proceeding along the Christchurch-road in the direction of Boscombe, and the cyclist was coming from St. Swithun's-road into the main road when the collision occurred. The driver of the car endeavoured to pull up in order to avoid an accident, with the result that the car skidded round on to the footpath, the side of the car striking the front wheel of the bicycle. Mr. Badeley had a nasty fall, and was taken to the Royal Boscombe Hospital, where he was found to be suffering from cuts on the head and bruises. After receiving attention he was able to proceed home. The bicycle was badly damaged.

The Western Gazette, Friday February 19th 1915

On March 1st, in accordance with Regimental custom, (a custom which still remains to this day), a telegram was sent to His Majesty, The Colonel in Chief, sending *"Best Wishes on Saint David's Day"*.

The following reply received was: *-"Buckingham Palace – His Majesty, thanks the Officers, Non-Commissioned Officers, and men, of the 10th Battalion Royal Welsh Fusiliers for their Loyal and Dutiful Greetings on Saint David's Day."*

One Officer joined the Battalion On **March 19th 1915**:-

- 2nd Lieutenant F. A. Samuel

On **April 29th** the Battalion left Moordown and marched the eleven miles to temporary billets at Ringwood, Hants.

Soldiers marching from Moordown to Ringwood

On **April 30th 1915** the 10th (Service) Battalion Royal Welsh Fusiliers marched almost nineteen miles to Romsey, Hants and stayed under canvas with the three other Battalions of the 76th Brigade. Whilst at Romsey the 10th Battalion R. W. F. made quite an impression on the locals.

Local newspapers "The Romsey Advertiser" and "The Hampshire Advertiser" reported on the 7th May that the streets were lined with people to welcome the Battalions and on the 15th & 21st May, that the local Church was celebrating their 253rd Anniversary with a service in which the 10th (Service) Battalion Royal Welsh Fusilier Choir performed.

> TROOPS. — Romsey was very lively last week end, bodies of soldiers with fife, drum, and bugle bands playing, coming from their billets at Bournemouth and elsewhere to the neighbourhood of Romsey. On Thursday in last week the streets were lined as the 8th (Service) Battalion King's Own Lancasters passed through, on Friday came the 10th Batt. Royal Welsh Fusiliers, and on Saturday the King's Shropshire Light Infantry. The inhabitants have also had the pleasure of witnessing a fine show of horses coming and going from the Remount Camp. Some members of the H.L.I. on leave have shown their preference for Romsey by paying it a visit.

Romsey Advertiser 7th May 1915

ABBEY CONGREGATIONAL CHURCH ANNIVERSARY.—The 253rd anniversary of this church was celebrated on Sunday, the Rev. D. J. Nicholas, B.D., of Sydenham, preaching morning and evening. At the 3 o'clock afternoon service there was a very large congregation. The service opened with the hymn, "All Hail the Power," the Rev. D. J. Nicholas prayed, and the choir of the Royal Welsh Fusiliers, now under canvas at Woodley, sang "The Sweet By-and-bye." Madame Anna Shergold, Queen's Hall, London, sang "Angels Guard Thee" in fine soprano voice. The Welsh choir sang "The Pardoning God," Mr. G. C. Ely (deacon) made the announcements, Corpl. Roberts sang "Lead, Kindly Light," and the congregation sang "Jesus, Lover of my Soul." Rev. J. D. Nicholas said that when he consented to preach in that church he did not know that he should have the pleasure of listening to the choir of the Royal Welsh Fusiliers, and probably the secretary of the church (Mr. G. C. Ely) did not know when he invited him that he was a Welshman. He thought he might venture to say that there was a quality about the Welsh singing that was not commonly to be found elsewhere in the United Kingdom, and whilst most people could not tell what that quality was, there was no doubt they appreciated the efforts put forth. He might say that nothing was really to be found at its best unless the whole soul was thrown into it.

Hampshire Advertiser County Newspaper 15th May 1915

SOLDIERS' CHOIR AT ROMSEY.

In connection with the Royal Welsh Fusiliers, in camp at Woodley, there is a fine choir, the members of which were on Sunday induced by the Rev. E. F. M. Vokes to assist at a largely attended afternoon service at the Baptist Chapel, and again at the evening service. In the afternoon Mr. Vokes said it was a tremendous privilege to have the soldiers with them. During the last few months they had thousands upon thousands of soldiers upon their premises, and had been glad to welcome them, but that day they were having what might be called an adequate return, and perhaps it was the first time in the history of Romsey that any church in the town had had a soldiers' choir with them. The singing of the men was very fine and quite thrilling. Among the items, which are most popular with Welsh people, were "All Hail the power of Jesus's Name," "Jesu, Lover of my soul," "Lead, kindly Light," "Land of my Fathers" (in Welsh and English), "The Crusaders," and "Valiant Warriors."

Romsey Advertiser 21st May 1915

In Romsey, tented camps had sprung up in the Woodley and Abbotswood areas. The 10th (Service) Battalion R. W. F. would have been one of the first units to occupy these camps and were based at the Woodley Camp.

The camps at Woodley and Abbotswood were only ever intended as temporary transit camps and were only made semi-permanent but in 1918, when large numbers of 'American Troops' arrived, there was a greater necessity so construction and reconstruction was undertaken.

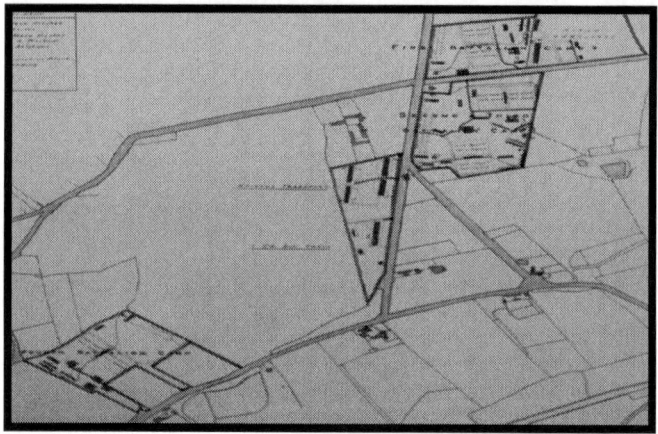

Map of Romsey Camp

The Battalion was inspected on 14th May by Lieutenant Colonel Archibald James Murry K. B. C. C. V. O. D. S. O. of the Army Council. The report of the inspection was **"Satisfactory"**

Lieutenant Colonel Archibald James Murry K.B.C. C.V.O. D.S.O.

Major General Beauchamp John Colclough Doran assumed command of the 25th Division on the 26th May replacing Major General F. Ventris.

Major-General Beauchamp
John Colclough Doran

Major-General Francis Ventris

On the **27th May 1915** the 10th (Service) Battalion R. W. F. marched from their camp in Romsey to Flowerdown Camp in Winchester, a distance of 19.3km (12 miles). The Battalion only stayed for one night before moving on. Flowerdown Camp was another camp with a problem of flooding and was known to the soldiers as **"Mud Down Camp."**

A postcard showing WWI soldiers at "Mud Down Camp" Flowerdown Camp

Comical postcard showing life at "Mud Down Camp" Flowerdown Camp!

On the **28th May 1915** the Battalion marched from Flowerdown Camp to temporary billets at Alresford, known as Morn Hill Camp, a distance of 20.9km (13 miles). During the Great War, Winchester became a major transit location for troops destined for the Western Front. Vast numbers of 'Barrack Huts' were built and it is reported that Morn Hill Camp could accommodate more than 50,000 troops at one time during the latter part of the War.

Troops arriving at Morn Hill Camp, Alresford

Morn Hill Camp Alresford

On **29th May 1915** the Battalion marched to temporary billets in Odiham Camp in Hampshire, a distance of 30km (19 miles).

Hampshire Regiment marching through Odiham

On **June 3rd 1915**, the Battalion left Odiham and marched the 16km (10 miles) to Aldershot and occupied the Barrossa Barracks with the Kings Own Royal Lancaster Regiment. The 10th (Service) Battalion Royal Welsh Fusiliers would remain at Aldershot carrying out their final training until embarkment for France.

Aldershot Command Head Quarters

1 Officer joined the Battalion On **June 3rd 1915**:-

- 2nd Lieutenant P. T. Dale

On **June 8th** the Battalion was inspected by General Sir A. Hunter G.C.B. G.C.M.G D.S.O., Commanding Aldershot Training Centre.

Gerneral Sir A. Hunter
G.C.B. G.C.M.G D.S.O.

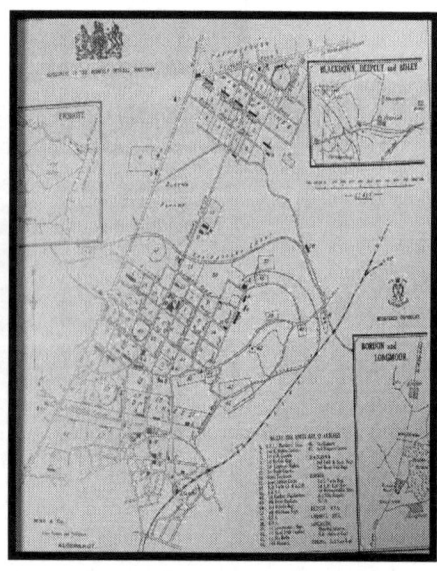

Map of Aldershot Training Centre

On **June 9th** The Commanding Officer announced with regret, the death of Lieutenant C. G. Lloyd. Lieutenant Charles Gordon Lloyd, aged 30, sadly took his own life by drinking carbolic acid. The Liverpool Echo reported the incident on Thursday, June 10th 1915.

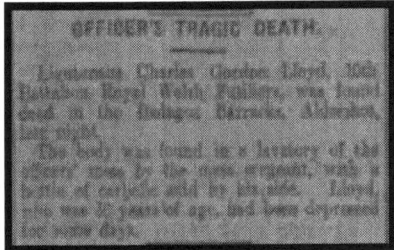

"OFFICER'S TRAGIC DEATH - Lieutenant Charles Gorden Lloyd, 10th Battalion Royal Welsh Fusiliers, was found dead in the Barrossa Barracks, Aldershot, last night. The body was found in the lavatory of the Officer's mess by the mess Sergeant, with a bottle of carbolic acid by his side. Lloyd, who was 30 years of age, had been depressed for some days."

Liverpool Echo Thursday 10th June 1915

Throughout July 1915, the Company, Battalion, Brigade and Division were steadily engaged in every form of training, including long marches and night and day operations in the vicinity of Aldershot and Farnborough. 'Service Rifles' and 'Lewis Guns' were also issued and intense 'Musketry Training' commenced. All training was to show that the long expected move overseas would soon take place.

My Taid, Edwin was training at Aldershot when an article appeared in the local newspaper, The Flintshire County Herald - Dated 30th June 1915, regarding him.

Article about my Taid, Edwin - The Flintshire Herald 30th June 1915 -

Soldier with a bogus pass - At the Court House, last Friday morning, before Messrs John Carman (in the chair) and H V Lloyd, Edwin Roberts (Primrose Hill) was charged with absenting himself from his regiment at Aldershot - P. C. Chesters stated that in consequence of a telegraphic message received the previous day, he made enquiries with regard to the prisoner, at 11.30 he found him in High Street. He told him he should arrest him for being an absentee from the 10th Battalion of the Royal Welsh Fusilier at Aldershot. He said he had got a pass, and that it expired that day, and that he was going back that day. He showed the witness the pass, which he found to be a bogus one, and he thereupon brought him to the Police Station - The Magistrates Clerk - Was it signed by the Commanding Officer? - It was signed by someone - Inspector Hill hereupon handed the pass to the Bench. The Clerk: How did you find out it was a bogus pass? The Inspector: He admitted it. The pass is in proper form, but has been filled in by someone else - The Clerk suggested to the inspector he should send the pass to the Commanding Officer; and he said he would do so - The Bench remanded the prisoner to do custody of the military escort which the Inspector intimated was already there.

So my Taid Edwin went absent without leave. Why did he do this? Maybe it was to go back and see his Wife and three young children? Or maybe Edwin, who was now 35 years old, had just had enough of the younger Officers and N. C. O.'s telling him what to do. Maybe he just wanted to go back home to familiar surroundings including his local pub?
Alas, we shall never know.

I would like to think it would have been for the first reason, to see his Wife and children, but having heard stories from other members of my family, I think it was probably the latter – to go to the pub!

In August the Battalion was inspected by Field Marshall the Earl Kitchener of Khartoum K.C. K.P. G.C.B. O.M. G.C.S.I. G.C.M.G G.C.I.E. Secretary of State for War. The report for the inspection was **"Satisfactory"**

Field-Marshall The Earl Kitchener of Khartoum Secretary of State for War inspecting Troops

Later in the same month the Battalion was inspected on the line of march near Aldershot by His Majesty the King, who was accompanied by Her Majesty & Her Royal Highness the Princess Mary.

The King and Lord Kitchener inspecting The Troops at Aldershot August 1915 before the 10th Battalion Royal Welsh Fusiliers embarked for France

Also, in August 1915 a visit by Rudyard Kipling to Aldershot showed an expressed concern about the gulf now beginning to develop between those who volunteered and those still not under arms.

He listened to the complaints of the men in the camp about the way those still not in uniform were prospering at home in the absence of the men in training at Aldershot.

Like many others, Kipling was puzzled why underage recruits were not spotted by the professional soldiers responsible for their training.

Rudyard Kipling

Throughout the War, Aldershot Camp provided a constant supply of trained men for the fighting on many fronts.

The lack of general supervision and co-ordination of training, the delays in revising existing tactical doctrine and the over dependence of Commanding Officers on out-of-date manuals all conspired to give training an air of amateur out-of-date practice, which only began to improve when the first of the New Armies had already gone overseas.

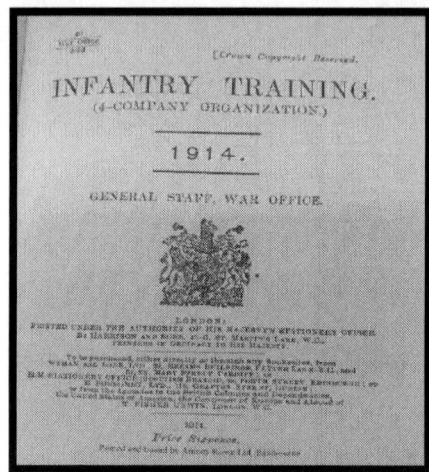

Infantry Training Book 1914

The main job of the instructions was to create a fit and efficient fighting force, attend to discipline and remain steadfast under fire.

As the Infantry Books states:-

"The object to be aimed at in the training of an Infantry Soldier is to make him mentally and physically a better man than his adversary on the field of battle."

Basic training for the new recruits was divided into two equal parts. The soldier had to become fit and learn about his equipment and be taught how to shoot and fight with gun and bayonet, as well as learning the basic skills, he would need to prepare himself for War.

Initially, however, the most important and intensive part of his training was designed to instill unquestioned disipline and to build up his physique.

It was in the manual **"Infantry Training (1914)"** that set out the syllabus, which would turn the raw recruit into a trained fighter soldier. There were eleven components to this: -

1. THE DEVELOPMENT OF SOLDIERLY SPIRIT
2. INSTRUCTION IN BARRACK & CAMP DUTIES
3. PHYSICAL TRAINING
4. INFANTRY TRAINING
5. ROUTE MARCHING
6. MUSKETRY INSTRUCTION
7. MOVEMENTS AT NIGHT
8. GUARDS & OUTPOSTS
9. DUTIES OF SOLDIERS IN THE FIELD
10. USE OF ENTRENCHING EQUIPMENT
11. BAYONET FIGHTING

1. THE DEVELOPMENT OF SOLDIERLY SPIRIT

The objects of developing a soldierly spirit was to help the soldier to bear fatigue, privation and danger cheerfully. To imbue him with a sense of honour. To give him confidence in his superiors and comrades. To increase his powers of initiative, self confidence and self restraint. To train the soldier to obey orders or to act in the absence of orders for the advantage of his Regiment under all conditions. To produce such a high degree of courage and disregard of self, that in the stress of battle, he will use his brains and his weapons cooly and to the best advantage. To impress upon him that, so long as he is physically capable of fighting, that surrender to the enemy is a disgraceful act.

The soldier should be instructed in the deeds which have made the British Army and his Regiment famous, and, as his intelligence develops, the instruction should be extended to simple lessons drawn from Military history in general, illustrating how success depends on the above qualities.

The privileges which he inherits as a citizen of the Great Empire should be explained to him and he should be taught to appreciate the honour which is his, as a soldier, of serving his King and Country.

2. INSTRUCTION IN BARRACK & CAMP DUTIES

The new recruits would be taught the basics about life in the barracks and what their general everyday duties were.

A typical day started with 'Reveille' (A bugle or trumpet call to wake the soldiers and call them to duty) at 5.30am after tidying and cleaning their quarters. At 6.30am recruits would parade for an hour and a half. After breakfast which was at 8am, the morning was spent drilling on the parade ground learning to march. Between 12.15pm and 2pm the recruits took lunch before returning to the parade ground for more drills. Once this had finished, around 4.30pm, the recruits would spend time cleaning kit and shining boots and generally getting used to Army life.

3. PHYSICAL TRAINING

The object of physical training is the production of a state of health and general fitness in order that the body may be enabled to withstand the strains of daily life and to perform the work required of it without injury to the system.

Physical training was based on the Swedish Drill System of "**Physical Jerks.**" Gymnastics, competitive sports and running formed a large part of the physical training routine.

Physical Training

4. INFANTRY TRAINING

Infantry Training would consist of training the recruits in general principals of defence, for example;

*Choice of position
*Distribution of Troops detailed to defend the position

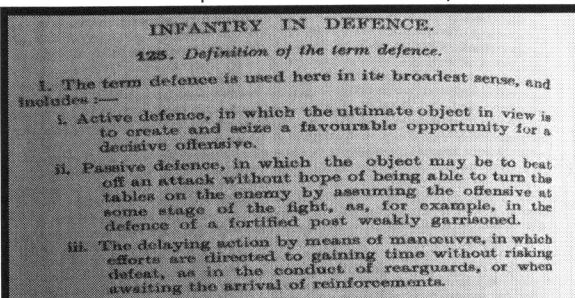

Defence definition from the Infantry Training 1914 book

Infantry Training would consist of training the recruits in general principals of attack, for example;

*Infantry in attack
*Assault & pursuit of the enemy

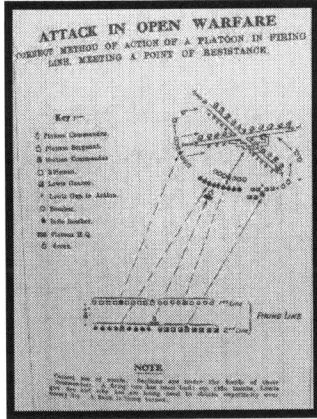 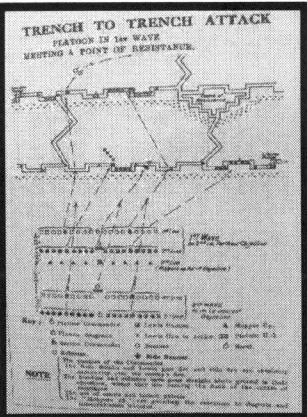

Diagrams from An Officers Manual of The Western Front 1914-1918

The new recruit would also atttend lectures on subjects of attack & defence.

5. ROUTE MARCHING

The first few weeks of training provided a severe test of the resolution and stamina of all ranks. Hours were long and hard. Once the recruits became used to the drills, fitness increased and **"Route Marches"** became longer and longer. Initially, the marches were for about five or six miles, with a halt for ten minutes every hour. However, the marches were extended to twelve or thirteen miles and then to more than twenty miles in some cases. As well as getting recruits into a high level of fitness, the importance of looking after one's feet became equally as important to the recruits and the Officers in charge.

For all the technology of modern warfare and the widespread use of mechanical transport in everyday life, the Army were desperately short of motor transport in 1914 and the abilities of the soldiers to march long distances was still considered to be of the upmost importance.

Royal Welsh Fusiliers "Route Marching"

6. MUSKETRY INSTRUCTION

The Standard Service Rifle of the Great War was the **"Short Magazine Lee Enfield"**, or **"SMLE"** as it was known.

The weight of the SMLE was 8lbs 10oz. unloaded and without bayonet.

The rifles magazine held 10 cartridges (also known as rounds). They were loaded from above using disposable clips which each held 5 rounds. The rifle was a **"Bolt Action System."** To shoot, each round had to be fed into the part of the barrel known as a **"Chamber"** using the bolt. It was opened and closed in somewhat similar fashion to a common door bolt. The bolt was lifted, thus, unlocking it, and then pulled to the rear and the fired cartridge was ejected. Simultaneously a fresh cartridge was pushed up by the spring from the magazine beneath it and the bolt was then pushed forward feeding the cartridge into the chamber. Finally, before the rifle could be fired, the bolt was pushed down to lock it safely in place.

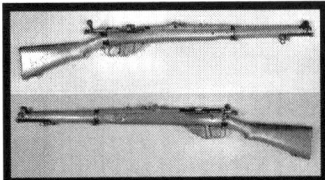
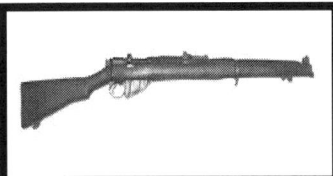

SMLE Mark 1   SMLE Mark 3

Musketry Training

Owing to the general lack of rifles in the first year of the War, my Taid Edwin and his Battalion would have been forced to carry out much of their 'Arms & Musketry Training' with obsolete or dummy weapons. At the end of November 1914, it was calculated that the New Armies possessed only 30% of the required number of modern service rifles, the remaining 70% being made up of old Lee Enfields and wooden drill purpose rifles.

7. MOVEMENTS AT NIGHT

The main objective of this training is to prepare the soldier to become accustomed to moving in the dark, so that the soldiers and his Battalion can act with the same freedom by night as they would have by day.

Ability to see in the dark increases with practice, objects became more visible when the moon is behind the soldier rather than in front of him.

Training the soldier's hearing was another objective. It is easier to hear sounds on soft ground when standing, or hard ground, when flat. Marching as quietly as possible was also essential at night.

Other training that was carried out was learning to carry entrenching tools and weapons without making a noise.

8. GUARDS & OUTPOSTS

According to the Infantry Training Manual 1914, the importance of **"Outposts"** is stated as:-

1. Every body of troops when halted will be protected by outposts
2. The duty of outposts is to give warnings of any threatened attacks and observe the enemy lines
3. Resistence will consist of delaying the enemy on a prepared defensive line, called the outpost of resistance!

The Outpost - A British Soldier watching the enemy through his periscope

9. DUTIES OF SOLDIERS IN THE FIELD

The training in 'Field Operations' will take in all the training methods the soldier has learnt and combine them into 'Field Operations', 'Methods of Attack', and 'Defence Training' will be implicated. Conditions of the ground and local areas will be then taken into consideration before applying the lessons learnt. Training will be given to the 'Platoon and Sector Commanders' in grasping the situations rapidly, and issuing clear and suitable orders quickly to their men. Training will be given to the continuance of operations after the units have become mixed and commanders killed or wounded. Village and wood fighting with practical illustrations are given. Training will be given on 'Carrying Out an Attack or Defence of a certain position'.

The soldiers will be taught the importance of the relationship between fire and movement, with special attention to the various methods of advancing under different conditions of fire and ground.

The soldier will be taught that the most important requirement in cover when firing, is that he can use his rifle to the best advantage.

Instruction will be given in the 'Occupation and Preperation of Quarters' including, billets, camps and bivouacs and the importance of sanitation, how to prepare food and look after their own comfort in circumstances, resembling as closely as possible, those of active service.

10. USE OF ENTRENCHING EQUIPMENT

The **"Entrenching Tool"** became extremely important with the Introduction of 'Trench Warfare'. The British Entrenching Tool of this period was a two-part design, with a metal head and wooden handle. The metal head consisted of an 'Adze Spade Blade' and a 'Pick Spike' with the pick spike serving as a handle. Between the blade and the spike there was a ring into which the handle could be inserted at right angles to the head. When the handle inserted the tool could be used as a pick mattlock.

Besides being used for digging defensive fighting positions **(known as**

"**Digging In**"), the entrenching tool was also used for digging latrines and graves.

The tool could also be used as a weapon in close quarter fighting. Soldiers routinely sharpened the edges for use as weapons.

Entrenching Tools

11. BAYONET FIGHTING

The Infantry Training Manual reads:-

"The rifle and bayonet are the principal weapons of the individual Infantry soldier. The first requirement of the Infantry soldier is confidence in these weapons based on his skill in their use. The bayonet is a weapon for hand-to-hand fighting and it's use, or the threat of it's use, finally drives the enemy 'from his position' or causes him to surrender."

The Training Pamphlet, on the use of the bayonet, issued in 1918 states:-

"If possible, the point of the bayonet should be directed against the opponents throat, especially in 'Corps-v-Corps' fighting as the point will enter easily and make a fatal wound when penetrating a few inches. Another area to use the bayonet is near the eyes which makes an apponent 'funk other' and vulnerable. Other usually exposed parts to aim for are the face, chest, lower abdomen and thighs and the region of the kidneys when the back is turned.

Four to six inches penetration is sufficient to incapacitate an apponent and allows a quick withdrawal, whereas, if the bayonet is driven home too far, it is impossible to withdraw it. In such a case as not being able to withdraw, a round should be fired to break up the obstruction".

Bayonet Training

The SMLE accepted a sword bayonet patten in 1907 that had a blade length of 17 inches. It had wooden grips and weighed, with scabbard, 1 ½ lbs (750g). It was attached to a circular protuberance just below the muzzle of the rifle and cupped into place on a lug beneath the barrel. The scabbard was simplified to meet 'Wartime Production Quotas' and the bayonet was soon made without the upturned hook to it's quillon as this was deemed unnecessary.

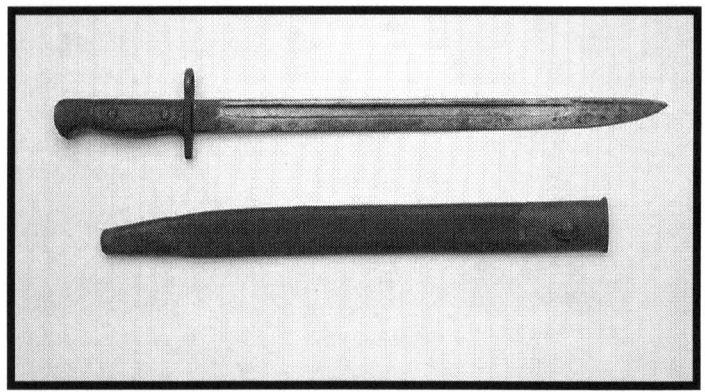

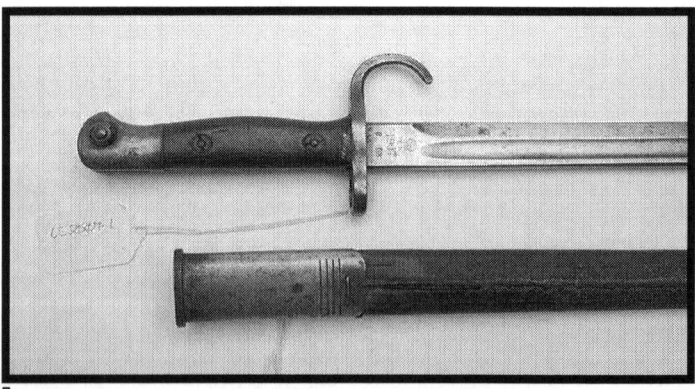

Bayonets

Due to the continuing need for improvement and for the soldiers to be ready for the front, a new training schedule was devised from October 1917 and was for the new recruits, who had been conscripted under the terms of the 1916 Military Service Act.

The schedule is shown below; –

FIRST TWO WEEKS

TRAINING	HOURS	INCLUDING
PHYSICAL	6 HOURS	PHYSICAL EXERCISE CONNECTED WITH BOMB (GRANADE) THROWING
SQUAD DRILL WITHOUT ARMS	16 HOURS	
MUSKETRY	10 HOURS	
INTERIOR ECONOMY	12 HOURS	KIT INSPECTION, CARE OF EQUIPMENT, MARCHING ORDERS, ETC.
ANTI GAS	2 HOURS	
SPECIAL LECTURES	6 HOURS	CAMOUFLAGE, CO-OPERATION WITH OTHERS, ARMS, TRENCH WARFARE ETC.
ORGANISED GAMES & SCHOOL EDUCATION	12 HOURS	FOOTBALL, BOXING, ETC. TO 2ND CLASS CERTIFICATE LEVEL
	TOTAL 64 HOURS	

WEEKS 3 & 4

TRAINING	HOURS	INCLUDING
PHYSICAL	10 HOURS	PHYSICAL EXERCISE CONNECTED WITH BOMB (GRANADE) THROWING
BAYONET	6 HOURS	
SQUAD DRILL WITHOUT ARMS	9 HOURS	
SQUAD DRILL WITH ARMS	9 HOURS	
MUSKETRY	16 HOURS	
INTERIOR ECONOMY	4 HOURS	KIT INSPECTION, CARE OF EQUIPMENT, MARCHING ORDERS, ETC.
ANTI GAS	2 HOURS	
SPECIAL LECTURES	2 HOURS	CAMOUFLAGE, CO-OPERATION WITH OTHERS, ARMS, TRENCH WARFARE ETC.
ORGANISED GAMES & SCHOOL EDUCATION	14 HOURS	FOOTBALL, BOXING, ETC. TO 2ND CLASS CERTIFICATE LEVEL
	TOTAL 72	

WEEKS 5 & 6

TRAINING	HOURS	INCLUDING
PHYSICAL	10 HOURS	PHYSICAL EXERCISE CONNECTED WITH BOMB (GRANADE) THROWING
BAYONET	6 HOURS	
SQUAD DRILL	20 HOURS	
MUSKETRY & MINIATURE RANGE PRACTICE	16 HOURS	
INTERIOR ECONOMY	3 HOURS	KIT INSPECTION, CARE OF EQUIPMENT, MARCHING ORDERS, ETC.
NIGHT WORK	3 HOURS	
GUARDS	3 HOURS	
ANTI GAS	2 HOURS	
SPECIAL LECTURES	3 HOURS	CAMOUFLAGE, CO-OPERATION WITH OTHERS, ARMS, TRENCH WARFARE ETC.
ORGANISED GAMES & SCHOOL EDUCATION	14 HOURS	FOOTBALL, BOXING, ETC. TO 2ND CLASS CERTIFICATE LEVEL
	TOTAL 84	

WEEKS 7 & 8

TRAINING	HOURS	INCLUDING
PHYSICAL & RUNING	10 HOURS	PHYSICAL EXERCISE CONNECTED WITH BOMB (GRANADE) THROWING
BAYONET	6 HOURS	
SQUAD DRILL	18 HOURS	
MUSKETRY & MINIATURE RANGE PRACTICE	18 HOURS	
INTERIOR ECONOMY	2 HOURS	KIT INSPECTION, CARE OF EQUIPMENT, MARCHING ORDERS, ETC.
NIGHT WORK	3 HOURS	
ANTI GAS	2 HOURS	
BOMBING	3 HOURS	
SPECIAL LECTURES	3 HOURS	CAMOUFLAGE, CO-OPERATION WITH OTHERS, ARMS, TRENCH WARFARE ETC.
ORGANISED GAMES & SCHOOL EDUCATION	14 HOURS	FOOTBALL, BOXING, ETC. TO 2ND CLASS CERTIFICATE LEVEL
	TOTAL 84	

WEEKS 9 & 10

TRAINING	HOURS	INCLUDING
PHYSICAL & RUNING	10 HOURS	PHYSICAL EXERCISE CONNECTED WITH BOMB (GRANADE) THROWING
BAYONET	6 HOURS	
SQUAD DRILL	12 HOURS	
MUSKETRY	20 HOURS	PART ONE MUSKETRY COURSE
INTERIOR ECONOMY	2 HOURS	KIT INSPECTION, CARE OF EQUIPMENT, MARCHING ORDERS, ETC.
NIGHT WORK	3 HOURS	
GUARDS	5 HOURS	
FIELD ENGINEERING	2 HOURS	
ANTI GAS	2 HOURS	
BOMBING	3 HOURS	
ROUTE MARCHING WITHOUT PACKS	3 HOURS	
SPECIAL LECTURES	2 HOURS	CAMOUFLAGE, CO-OPERATION WITH OTHERS, ARMS, TRENCH WARFARE ETC.
ORGANISED GAMES & SCHOOL ED.	14 HOURS	FOOTBALL, BOXING, ETC. TO 2ND CLASS CERTIFICATE LEVEL
	TOTAL 84	

WEEKS 11 & 12

TRAINING	HOURS	INCLUDING
PHYSICAL & RUNING	10 HOURS	PHYSICAL EXERCISE CONNECTED WITH BOMB (GRANADE) THROWING
BAYONET	6 HOURS	
SQUAD DRILL	12 HOURS	
MUSKETRY	20 HOURS	FIRING PART 2 MUSKETRY COURSE
INTERIOR ECONOMY	2 HOURS	KIT INSPECTION, CARE OF EQUIPMENT, MARCHING ORDERS, ETC.
NIGHT WORK	3 HOURS	
FIELD ENGINEERING	4 HOURS	
ANTI GAS	2 HOURS	
BOMBING	6 HOURS	
ROUTE MARCHING WITHOUT PACKS	3 HOURS	
SPECIAL LECTURES	2 HOURS	CAMOUFLAGE, CO-OPERATION WITH OTHERS, ARMS, TRENCH WARFARE ETC.
ORGANISED GAMES & SCHOOL ED.	14 HOURS	FOOTBALL, BOXING, ETC. TO 2ND CLASS CERTIFICATE LEVEL
	TOTAL 84	

WEEKS 13 & 14

TRAINING	HOURS	INCLUDING
PHYSICAL & RUNING	10 HOURS	PHYSICAL EXERCISE CONNECTED WITH BOMB (GRANADE) THROWING
BAYONET	6 HOURS	
SQUAD PLATOON & COMP. DRILL	12 HOURS	
MUSKETRY	20 HOURS	FIRING PART 3 & 4 MUSKETRY COURSE
FIELD WORK & ENGINEERING	15 HOURS	
ANTI GAS	1 HOUR	
BOMBING	6 HOURS	
ROUTE MARCHING WITHOUT PACKS	4 HOURS	
SPECIAL LECTURES	2 HOURS	CAMOUFLAGE, CO-OPERATION WITH OTHERS, ARMS, TRENCH WARFARE ETC.
ORGANISED GAMES & SCHOOL ED.	14 HOURS	FOOTBALL, BOXING, ETC. TO 2ND CLASS CERTIFICATE LEVEL
	TOTAL 84	

WEEKS 15 & 16

TRAINING	HOURS	INCLUDING
PHYSICAL & RUNING	10 HOURS	PHYSICAL EXERCISE CONNECTED WITH BOMB (GRANADE) THROWING
BAYONET	6 HOURS	
SQUAD PLATOON & COMP. DRILL	8 HOURS	
MUSKETRY	16 HOURS	FIRING PART 3 & 4 MUSKETRY COURSE
FIELD WORK & ENGINEERING	21 HOURS	
ANTI GAS	1 HOUR	
BOMBING	6 HOURS	
ROUTE MARCHING IN MARCHING ORDER	2 HOURS	
SPECIAL LECTURES	2 HOURS	CAMOUFLAGE, CO-OPERATION WITH OTHERS, ARMS, TRENCH WARFARE ETC.
ORGANISED GAMES & SCHOOL ED.	14 HOURS	FOOTBALL, BOXING, ETC. TO 2ND CLASS CERTIFICATE LEVEL
	TOTAL 84	

WEEKS 17 & 18

TRAINING	HOURS	INCLUDING
PHYSICAL & RUNING	10 HOURS	PHYSICAL EXERCISE CONNECTED WITH BOMB (GRANADE) THROWING
BAYONET	6 HOURS	
DRILL & MUSKETRY	12 HOURS	
INTERIOR ECONOMY	2 HOURS	KIT INSPECTION, CARE OF EQUIPMENT, MARCHING ORDERS, ETC.
FIELD WORK & ENGINEERING	24 HOURS	
ANTI GAS	2 HOURS	
BOMBING	6 HOURS	
ROUTE MARCHING IN MARCHING ORDER	6 HOURS	IN CONJUNCTION WITH FIELD WORK
SPECIAL LECTURES	2 HOURS	CAMOUFLAGE, CO-OPERATION WITH OTHERS, ARMS, TRENCH WARFARE ETC.
ORGANISED GAMES & SCHOOL ED.	14 HOURS	FOOTBALL, BOXING, ETC. TO 2ND CLASS CERTIFICATE LEVEL
	TOTAL 84	

WEEKS 19 & 20

TRAINING	HOURS	INCLUDING
PHYSICAL & RUNING	10 HOURS	PHYSICAL EXERCISE CONNECTED WITH BOMB (GRANADE) THROWING
BAYONET	6 HOURS	
DRILL & MUSKETRY	12 HOURS	CEREMONIAL DRILL
INTERIOR ECONOMY	2 HOURS	KIT INSPECTION, CARE OF EQUIPMENT, MARCHING ORDERS, ETC.
FIELD WORK & ENGINEERING	28 HOURS	
ANTI GAS	2 HOURS	
BOMBING	6 HOURS	
ROUTE MARCHING IN MARCHING ORDER	2 HOURS	IN CONJUNCTION WITH FIELD WORK
SPECIAL LECTURES	2 HOURS	CAMOUFLAGE, CO-OPERATION WITH OTHERS, ARMS, TRENCH WARFARE ETC.
ORGANISED GAMES & SCHOOL ED.	14 HOURS	FOOTBALL, BOXING, ETC. TO 2ND CLASS CERTIFICATE LEVEL
	TOTAL 84	

WEEKS 21 & 22

TRAINING	HOURS	INCLUDING
PHYSICAL & RUNING	10 HOURS	PHYSICAL EXERCISE CONNECTED WITH BOMB (GRANADE) THROWING
BAYONET	6 HOURS	
DRILL & MUSKETRY	8 HOURS	CEREMONIAL DRILL
INTERIOR ECONOMY	2 HOURS	KIT INSPECTION, CARE OF EQUIPMENT, MARCHING ORDERS, ETC.
FIELD WORK & ENGINEERING	32 HOURS	
ANTI GAS	2 HOURS	
BOMBING	6 HOURS	
ROUTE MARCHING IN MARCHING ORDER	2 HOURS	
SPECIAL LECTURES	2 HOURS	CAMOUFLAGE, CO-OPERATION WITH OTHERS, ARMS, TRENCH WARFARE ETC.
ORGANISED GAMES & SCHOOL ED.	14 HOURS	FOOTBALL, BOXING, ETC. TO 2ND CLASS CERTIFICATE LEVEL
	TOTAL 84	

WEEKS 23 & 24

TRAINING	HOURS	INCLUDING
PHYSICAL & RUNING	8 HOURS	PHYSICAL EXERCISE CONNECTED WITH BOMB (GRANADE) THROWING
DRILL & MUSKETRY	8 HOURS	CEREMONIAL DRILL
INTERIOR ECONOMY	2 HOURS	KIT INSPECTION, CARE OF EQUIPMENT, MARCHING ORDERS, ETC.
FIELD WORK & ENGINEERING	32 HOURS	
ANTI GAS	2 HOURS	
BOMBING	6 HOURS	
ROUTE MARCHING IN MARCHING ORDER	8 HOURS	
SPECIAL LECTURES	2 HOURS	CAMOUFLAGE, CO-OPERATION WITH OTHERS, ARMS, TRENCH WARFARE ETC.
ORGANISED GAMES & SCHOOL ED.	14 HOURS	FOOTBALL, BOXING, ETC. TO 2ND CLASS CERTIFICATE LEVEL
	TOTAL 84	

On conclusion of this training, the recruits would become available for overseas postings unless medically classified as **"A4"** which means men who were not at the minimum age for overseas service.

Chapter 4
1915 - To The Front

Message from His Majesty the King to the Division leaving for France: –

"Officers, Non Commissioned Officers and men: you are about to join your comrades at the front in bringing to a successful end this relentless War of nearly a year's duration. Your prompt patriotic answer to the Nation's Call-to-Arms will never be forgotton.

The Keen exertions of all ranks during the period of training have brought you to a state of efficiency not unworthy of my regular Army, I am confident that, in the field, you will uphold the traditions of the fine Regiments whose name you bear. Ever since your enrollment, I have watched the growth, and steady progress of all units.

I shall continue to follow with interest the fortunes of your Division.

In bidding you "Farewell" I pray God may bless you in all your undertakings."

Aldershot 1915

SEPTEMBER

The 'Musketry & Machine Gun Training' was completed and all the necessary transport and equipment was issued, and orders to be in readiness for service overseas have been received, all ranks of the Battalion were given leave to spend at home before leaving for France. My Taid Edwin, would have been given a **"Pass"** *(a genuine one this time!)*, to travel back to his home in North Wales to spend time with his young family before travelling back to Aldershot.

On return to Aldershot, the following Officers were transferred to the 12th (Reserve) Battalion Royal Welsh Fusiliers.

NAME & RANK
MAJOR H. C. C. GIBBINGS
MAJOR E. W. MAPLES
2ND LIEUTENANT H. A. DAVIES
2ND LIEUTENANT R. O. STANLEY
2ND LIEUTENANT J. P. CARRINGTON
2ND LIEUTENANT H. V. PIERCY
2ND LIEUTENANT T. A. OLIVER
2ND LIEUTENANT J. O. CANDY
2ND LIEUTENANT B. J. STEADMAN

Captain W. T. Lyons was appointed Adjutant.

Major E. Freeman who on promotion from Captain was appointed to Command 'C' Coy in place of Major E. W. Maples, who was transferred to 12th (Reserve) Battalion.

Regimental Sergeant Major J. Hill left the Battalion on promotion to Lieutenant and Quarter Master of the 20th Battalion Royal Welsh Fusiliers. Company Sergeant Major J. Robinson was appointed Regimental Sergeant Major in his place.

The list of Regimental and Company Staff embarking for France are shown below: -

STAFF	NAME & RANK
COMMANDING OFFICER	BREVET-COLONEL W. R. H. BERESFORD-ASH
SECOND IN COMMAND	MAJOR F. N. BURTON
ADJUTANT	CAPTAIN W. T. LYONS
QUARTER MASTER	LIEUTENANT E. H. CHAPMAN
SIGNALLING OFFICER	CAPTAIN E. W. BELL
MACHINE GUN OFFICER	LIEUTENANT G. D. SCALE
BOMBING OFFICER	LIEUTENANT W. B. MORGAN
MEDICAL OFFICER	CAPTAIN B. GRELLIER
CHAPLAIN	CAPTAIN THE REV. D. C. WILLIAMS

Company Commanders

STAFF	NAME & RANK
'A' COY.	CAPTAIN R. A. ADAMSON
'B' COY.	CAPTAIN G. P. BLAKE
'C' COY.	MAJOR E. FREEMAN
'D' COY.	CAPTAIN F. A. SAMUEL

Company Second in Command

STAFF	NAME & RANK
'A' COY.	CAPTAIN E. W. BELL
'B' COY.	CAPTAIN W. P. GRIFFITHS
'C' COY.	CAPTAIN B. D. JOHNS
'D' COY.	CAPTAIN J. A. WALKER

Platoon Commanders

STAFF	NAME & RANK
NO. 1	LIEUTENANT W. B. MORGAN
NO. 2	2ND LIEUTENANT W. HUGHES
NO. 3	2ND LIEUTENANT H. J. K. LEWIS
NO. 4	2ND LIEUTENANT H. E. G
NO. 5	2ND LIEUTENANT A. V. CREE
NO. 6	2ND LIEUTENANT F. C. G. LARKWORTHY
NO. 7	2ND LIEUTENANT C. A. R. FOLLITT
NO. 8	2ND LIEUTENANT A. G. BUCHANAN
NO. 9	LIEUTENANT A. J. S. JAMES
NO. 10	LIEUTENANT M. MURRAY
NO. 11	2ND LIEUTENANT A. W. FISH
NO. 12	LIEUTENANT H. A. V. MAYNARD
NO. 13	2ND LIEUTENANT A. NEVITT
NO. 14	2ND LIEUTENANT J. L. T. DAVIES
NO. 15	2ND LIEUTENANT C. L. LOCKE
NO. 16	2ND LIEUTENANT O. S. HUGHES

STAFF	NAME & RANK
REGIMENTAL SERGEANT	MAJOR J. ROBERTSON
REGIMENTAL QR.-MR	SERGEANT E. JONES
ORDERLY ROOM QR.-MR	SERGEANT H. GURREY
ORDERLY ROOM	SERGEANT J. EATON
REGIMENTAL TRANSPORT	SERGEANT H. TAYLOR
OFFICER'S MESS	SERGEANT T. H. KILLINGBECK

Company Sergeant Major

STAFF	NAME & RANK
'A' COY.	COMPANY SERGEANT MAJOR E. PETERS
'B' COY.	COMPANY SERGEANT MAJOR W. H. REYNOLDS
'C' COY.	COMPANY SERGEANT MAJOR E. FISHER
'D' COY.	COMPANY SERGEANT MAJOR C. OWEN

Company Quarter Master Sergeant

STAFF	NAME & RANK
'A' COY.	COMPANY QR.-MR.- SERGEANT A. CLARKE
'B' COY.	COMPANY QR.-MR.- SERGEANT T. PATON
'C' COY.	COMPANY QR.-MR.- SERGEANT A. SOUTHBY
'D' COY.	COMPANY QR.-MR.- SERGEANT G. JONES

SEPTEMBER 26th – EMBARKMENT FOR FRANCE

The 'Advance Party' was under the command of Major F. N. Burton, and consisted of the Regimental Machine Gun Sections under Lieutenant G. D. Scale and Transport Personel/Animals and Vehicles under Lieutenant A. J. S. James. They left Aldershot by troop train for Folkestone and embarked for France on the transport ship S. S. Victoria, or the S. S. City of Benares *(there is some confusion over which ship the advance party left for France on)*.

The written 'War Diary' states it was the S. S. Victoria, whilst the published Diary by F. N. Burton, Officer in Command of the Advance Party, states it was the S. S. City of Benares that they left on.

The 'Advance Party' left from Folkestone and arrived at Le Havre with 8 Officers, 108 other ranks (O. R.) and 76 animals and marched into rest camp.

SEPTEMBER 27th
The remaining Battalion under the command of Brevet-Colonel W. R. H. Beresford-Ash left Aldershot by troop train for Dover and embarked on the S. S. Onward, for Bologne with 27 Officers and 888 other ranks (O. R.) on board.

There is again, some confusion with the exact figures of the Battalion as according to the written War Diary, it states 27 Officers and only 822 other ranks (O. R.) that landed at Bologne, whereas it states 888 other ranks (O. R.) are listed in the published War Diary. The Battalion marched into rest camp.

SEPTEMBER 28th
The 'Advance Party' entrained at La Havre and went by troop train to Pont Des Briques where it rejoined the main Battalion.

SEPTEMBER 29th
At 2am on the 29th September the Battalion proceeded by rail to Caestre where the Battalion detrained and marched into billets at Merris and neighbouring farms a distance of approximately 9km (5 ½ miles). Merris is located 35 kilometers (21.7 miles) from Lillie. The Battalion stayed at Merris for 6 days and time would have been spent training and familiarising themselves with the area.

OCTOBER 5th
The Battalion in Brigade marched into temporary billets at Bailleui , a distance of 8km (4.9 miles).

OCTOBER 7th

The Battalion in Brigade marched to Ploegstreet Trench area, a total of 15km (9.3 miles) and formed the support to the 8th Kings Own Royal Lancashire Regiment occupying trenches in front of the Ploegstreet Wood Trench lines.

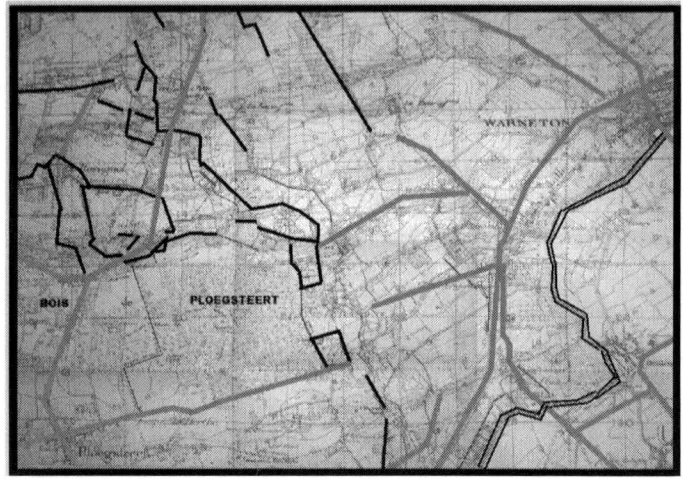

Ploegstreet village and wood is 12km (8 miles) South of Ypres and not far from the French border. It became known as **"Plugstreet"** to the British troops and over the two days my Taid Edwin and his Battalion would have been taken in detachments to the Front-Line for familiarisation purposes and tutroridge.

OCTOBER 9th

The Battalion, with the 7th Kings Shropshire Light Infantry marched back to the temporary billets at Bailleul. With a population of over 13,000 inhabitants in 1914, Bailleul became an important centre behind British lines and once the Front-Line had settled down in October 1914, not only was it an important railway location, it was also useful for billeting the troops due to the many houses and farms in the area.

OCTOBER 10th

The Battalion left Bailleul and marched 16km (9.9 miles) to a Belgium farm located 2.4km (2 ½ miles) South East of Poperinghe and 5.6km (3 ½ miles) West of Ypres. Map reference: Map 28: Grid reference: G18B, which indicates that the farm in question is **"Line Farm"** which still exists today.

Line Farm 2023

The 76th Brigade had now been transferred from the 25th Division to the 3rd Division commanded by Major General Sir James Aylmer Lowthorpe Haldane C.B. D. S. O.

The 76th Brigade were based at Branhoek near Line Farm.

OCTOBER 11th

The Battalion were temporarily attached to 8th Brigade, 'A' & 'B' Companies (COY) and marched into Ypres Salient Trenches and were attached to the 2nd Battalion Royal Scots for 48 hours instruction in 'Trench Duties'.

OCTOBER 13th

The Battalion Head Quarters and 'C' & 'D' Companies marched into Ypres Salient Trenches for instruction in 'Trench Duties' by the 2nd Battalion Royal Scots and 'A' & 'B' Companies (COY) returned to reserve camp on complition of their training.

TRENCH LIFE

no-man's-land
enemy
barbed wire
parapet
elbow rest
sandbags
ammunition shelf
2.0 m
firestep
duckboards
sump
0.5 m
dugout

Forward listening post (sap)
Communication trench
No Man's Land
Parados for protection from explosions from behind the trench
Front-line trench
Firebay
To reserve trench
Support trench
Company HQ dugout

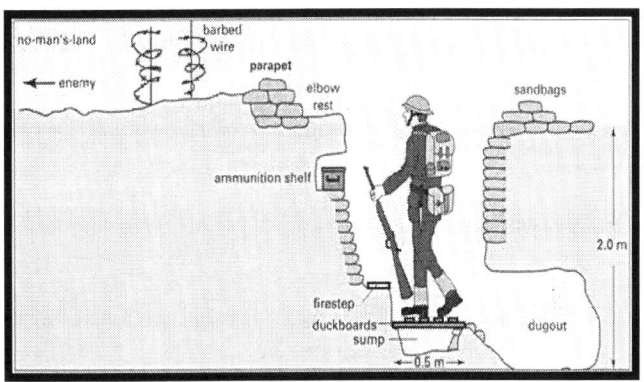

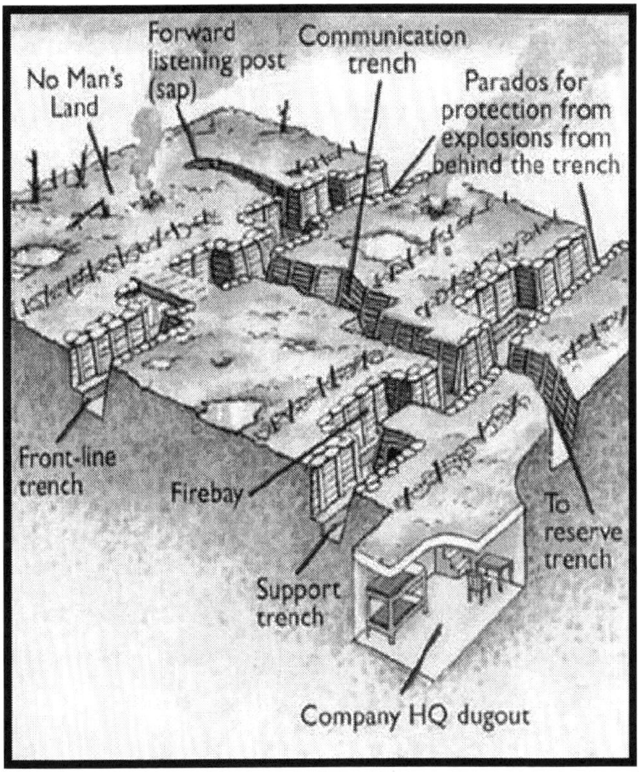

A general pattern for trench routine was for a soldier and his section to spend **4 days** in the **Front-Line Trench**, then **4 days** in **Close Reserve** (support trench) and then finally **4 days Rest** but this could vary depending on the conditions, the availablity of enough troops to rotate them and the men in reserve may be needed to reinforce the Front-Line at short notice. The rotation of the troops was a very tense time as the noise and activity increased the risk of attracting enemy shell fire, machine gun fire or even a trench raid.

Once the incoming relief had replaced the outgoing sections, various precautionary actions would be taken, at least one man in every four at night and at least one man in every ten, during the day, were posted as Sentries, on look-out duty, often in 'Saps', dug a little way ahead of the main Front-Line Trench. They would listen intently for any sounds that might indicate enemy activity and observe any such activity across no mans land.

The other men of the section would be posted in the Front-Line Trench or Support Trench, unless they were a specialist, such as a Signaller or a Machine Gunner. Men would be assigned to carry out repairs on the trenches or could be in 'Digging Parties' and under cover of darkness would be sent to repair barbed wire defences.

Unless a major offensive or enemy attack was taking place, **"Trench Life"** was usually very tedious.

The Officers in charge had to balance between the need to work and the need for rest and sleep for his men.

The main enemies for **"Trench Life"** were the weather and boredom. The loss of concentration by the soldiers could be fatal. One mistake and the soldier could become another victim of the enemy sniper, who were always watching the line, waiting for the unfortunate soldier to make a mistake.

At dawn and dusk, the whole British line was ordered to **"Stand To"**, which meant a period of manning the trench in preperation for any enemy attack.

All men serving in the Front-Line Trench or Support Trench had to wear their equipment at all times. Men in the Front-Line Trench had to keep their bayonets fixed during the hours of darkness, or just in case there had been an alert of a possible enemy attack.

A soldier must not leave his post without the permission of his immediate Officer. There was 1 Officer per Company on trench duty at all times. The Officer had his N. C. O.'s report to him hourly, the Officer moved continually up and down the line checking that all equipment was in good order and that the Sentries were alert and awake and that they were as comfortable as can be.

The N. C. O.'s had to inspect the men's rifles twice daily and ensure that the fighting equipment and ammunition was in good order.

From mid 1915 every trench had to have a **"Gas Attack Warning System"** in place. Often, this would be an empty shell casing held up by string or wire that would be hit with a piece of wood or metal to sound the alarm of the gas attack and all men should then put on their gas masks.

Every day, the Battalion holding the Front-Line Trench would request from the Brigade a list of equipment needed to carry out their day to day work and duties and men would be sent back to Brigade to ask a 'Carrying Party' to fetch it.

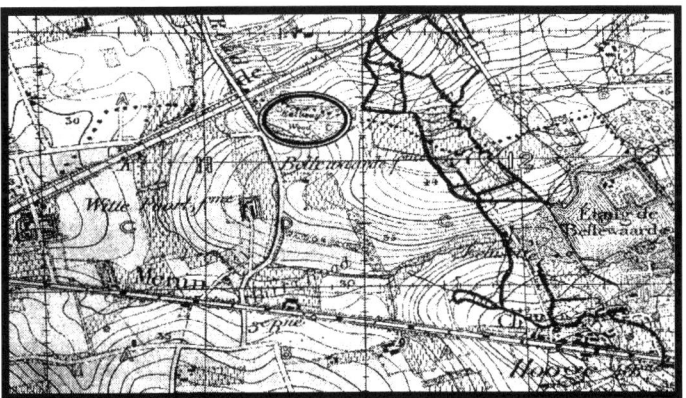

Map showing the trenches around Railway Wood – where my Taid, Edwin & his Battalion were based

OCTOBER 15th

On the 15th October 'A' & 'B' Companies rejoined the Battalion Head Quarters and then the whole of the Battalion took over the trenches in the Hooge/Railway Wood sector; trench sections A11 to A4. Held by the 2nd Battalion Royal Scots, who on relief, marched back to the rest billets.

The Battalion distribution was as follows:-

- 'C' & 'D' Coys in the **First Line (Fire) Trenches**
- 'B' Coy in **Reserve Trenches**
- 'A' Coy in **Redoubts 2 & 3**

During this time, the 10th Battalion had it's first casualties. **Private Lawrence Henry Eede**, service number 15002, was killed by a rifle bullet to the head, probably shot by a sniper. Lawrence was born in 1888 in New Cross, London and when enlisting in Colwyn Bay, North Wales, he gave his place of residence as Westcliffe on Sea. Lawrence is remembered on the Southend War Memorial and also on the Menin Gate Memorial as sadly, his grave was lost during later fighting around the area. Also wounded that day was **Private Thomas Roberts**, service number 23185, who received a rifle bullet to the arm and hand. The wound was quite severe and Thomas was sent home on the Hospital Ship Calais, for further treatment.

OCTOBER 16th

The Battalion continued to occupy the trenches and the casualties continued to increase.

Private W. H. Williams, service number 15318 received a rifle bullet to the neck and **Private L. Broadhurst**, service number 23305 received a rifle bullet to the arm.

I often wonder about the first casualties that the Battalion received; was it because the soldiers wanted to **"look over"** the parapet to see the German Front-Line and were picked off by a keen German Sniper? The wounds would suggest that this was the case, but we will never know for certain.

OCTOBER 17th

At 7pm 'B' & 'D' Coys exchanged positions. Casualties killed were **Private Samuel Gam,** service number 27288 from Ratcliffe, Middlesex and **Private Joseph Parry**, service number 16025 from Mold, Flintshire, North Wales who had been listed as wounded but had then died seven days later on the 24th October. Both soldiers died from shrapnel wounds. It was reported that Private Parry had sixty-three distinct wounds from the shrapnel shell which had burst in the front bay of his section of 'D' Coy. Private Parry is buried at Etaples Military Cemetery, France and Private Gam is buried at Divisional Cemetery, Belgium.

OCTOBER 18th

At 6pm 'A' & 'C' Coys changed positions. Casualties included my Taid, **Private Edwin Roberts, service number 15736. He received shrapnel wounds to the shoulder, chest and forearm.**

RANK	NAME	SERVICE NO.	WOUND
COMPANY QUARTER M. SGT.	ANTHONY G. SOUTHBY	15430	RIFLE BULLET - FRACTURED JAW
SERGEANT	JOHN HUGHES	15336	RIFLE BULLET - HAND
CORPORAL	GEORGE PEMBERTON	14655	RIFLE BULLET - RIGHT ARM
LANCE CORPORAL	SAMUEL C. BRUCE	14256	RIFLE BULLET - RIGHT ARM
CORPORAL	WILLIAM T. JONES	15722	SHRAPNEL - NOSE & EYE
PRIVATE	SAMUEL HOLLINGSWORTH	15731	SHRAPNEL - FACE & LEFT THUMB

My Taid, Edwin would have been sent to a Casualty Clearing Station (C.C.S.) with the other wounded soldiers to be treated and sent to a base hospital if the wounds were severe enough.

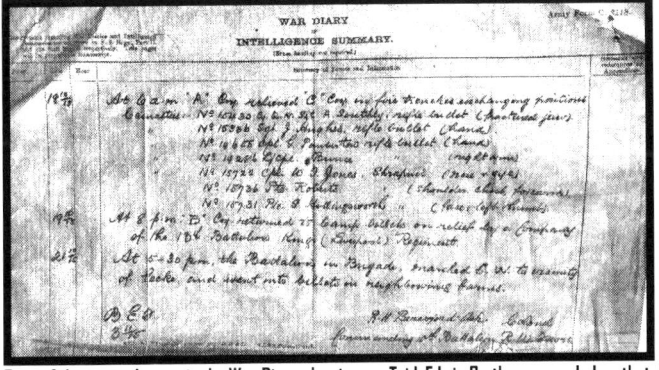

Copy of the original entry in the War Diary showing my Taid, Edwin & others wounded on that day

I researched the other soldiers wounded in the same incident as my Taid, Edwin, and found that the **Company Quarter Master Sergeant Southby**, service number 15430 recovered from his wounds to the jaw and returned back to the Battalion, later gaining a commission as a Second Lieutenant and then later Captain with the Royal Berkshire Regiment and survived the War.

Sergeant Hughes, service number 15336 also recovered from his wounds and returned to the Battalion, later transferring to The Royal Flying Corps (R. F. C.) and survived the War.

Corporal George Pemberton, service number 14655 received what is known as **"Blighty Wounds"** to the hand and was invalided out of the Army due to his wounds.

Lance Corporal Samuel C. Bruce, service number 14286 also recovered from his wounds and returned to his Battalion. Bruce was wounded again in April 1918, receiveing a gunshot wound (G. S. W.) to the thigh and ankle whilst serving with the 9th Battalion Royal Welsh Fusiliers.

Corporal William T. Jones, service number 15722 recovered and returned to his Battalion. Sadly Corporal Jones was killed in action on the 16th August 1916 and is remembered on the Thiepval Memorial. He was awarded (posthumously) The Distinguished Conduct Medal on 20th October 1916. *See chapter 9 – Battalion Honours – for details of his Citation*

Private Samuel Hollingsworth, service number 15731 recovered from his wounds but he too, was sadly killed in action on the 19th February 1916 and has no known grave so is remembered on the Menin Gate Memorial in Ypres, Belgium.

Photograph of Private Samuel Hollingsworth

My Taid, Edwin, returned to his Battalion after his wounds had healed.

OCTOBER 19th

At 8pm 'B' Coy marched back to rest camp (map reference G18B – Line Farm) on relief by a Company of the 13th Battalion Kings Liverpool Regiment.

OCTOBER 20th

The Battalion, Head Quarters, 'A', 'C' & 'D' Coys on relief by the 13th Battalion Kings Liverpool Regiment marched out of the Ypres Salient Trenches (Hooge) into temporary billets at Poperinge.

OCTOBER 21st

'B' Coy, the Battalion transport and the Head Quartermaster's establishment marched from rest camp (Line Farm), 3.21km (2 miles) East of Poperinghe and rejoined the Battalion in billets there.

During October 1915, 76th Brigade were transferred to the 3rd Division from the 25th Division and the composition of the Brigade underwent some changes. The 13th Kings Liverpool Regiment and the 7th Kings Shropshire Light Infantry were transferred to the 8th Brigade, The 2nd Suffolk Regiment, the 1st Gordon Highlanders and the 4th Gordon Highlanders were transferred to the 76th Brigade from the 8th Brigade.

The composition of the 76th Brigade was now as follows:-

- 2nd Suffolk Regiment
- 1st Gordon Highlanders
- 4th Gordon Highlanders
- 8th Kings Own Royal Lancaster Regiment
- 10th Battalion Royal Welsh Fusiliers

At 5pm the Battalion in Brigade marched to Eecke, a distance of 16km (10 miles) and went into rest billets in the neighbouring farm.

OCTOBER 25th

A class of instruction in 'Trench Digging', 'Revetting, Draining and Sandbagging' under The East Riding Field Company R. E. commenced. Ten Officers and ten N. C. O.'s from the Battalion attended the course with other Battalions in the Brigade.

OCTOBER 27th

A representative detachment of N. C. O.'s and men of the Battalion which included an Officer and twenty men marched to Reningelst, 16.2km (10 miles) and joined a Battalion (formed from representative detatchments of all the Battalions in the 3rd Division), under the command of Colonel W. R. H. Beresford-Ash, 10th Battalion Royal Welsh Fusiliers, and with other representative Battalions of the remaining Divisions of the Second Army, were inspected by His Majesty the King, who was accompanied by the President of the French Republic, Monsieur Raymond Poincare and Field Marshall Sir J. P. French G.C.B. G.M. G.C.V.O. K.C.M.G.

The Battalion remained at Eecke billets for the next three weeks, being fully occupied in route marching, entrenching and bombing practice, and in all general Company and Battalion training.

NOVEMBER

On **November 3rd** it was noted in the Battalion's War Diary that **Private A. Edwards**, service number 15461 was accidentally killed and that **Private A. B. Poffley**, service number 24637 was wounded, both of 'C' Coy (my Taid, Edwin's Company).

No further explanation was given. How did this happen?

After further investigation, I found that Private Edwards was killed by Private Charles William Knight, service number 15437 and Private Poffley was wounded in the same incident.

Charles William Knight faced Court-Martial for murder. The report of the incident states:-

"On the 3rd November 1915, Private Knight entered his billet of C. Coy in a drunken state and started shooting indiscriminantly at members of his platoon. He killed Private Alfred Edwards, service number 15461 and wounded Private Alfred Bernard Poffley, service number 24637, Company Sergeant Major Edward Fisher showed great courage in apprehending Knight and promptly arrested him."

Private Knight was tried by Field Court-Martial three days later on the 6th November 1915. The Court-Martial agreed that Private Knight had been very drunk and not acting in a responsible manner and that the court should have considered whether Knight was in such a drunken state that he would not have realised what he was doing, but the question wasn't asked. Private Knight's previous record would not have helped him either, he already had five charges of drunkenness levied against him in just over a year and there was also a report (shown below) from his Commanding Officer, Lieutenant Colonel Beresford-Ash which also did not help his case.

"No. 15437 Private Charles William Knight of the Battalion under my command is a man of apparently very low origin, though of considerable personality. He had great influence amongst the other men and was more than once recommended to me for promotion. He is a man who is addicted to drink and when under it's influence, appears to lose control over his actions. He joined the B. E. F. on 28th September last."

So Private Knight was a very popular soldier amongst his fellow soldiers but when he drank too much, the drink took hold and changed him for the worse.

Private Knight defended himself during the trial. The heated atmosphere of the Court-Martial, when his very life was on the line, required the mind of a trained lawyer, not a soldier serving in the terrible conditions of the trenches and trench warfare.

The Commanding Officer of the 76th Infantry Brigade, Brigadier E. St G. Pratt said:-

"In my opinion, it is a clear case of murder and owing to the ease of which men can obtain ammunition on active service, it is necessary, in such cases, to carry out the extreme penalty of the Law."

Concern was also expressed by Major General Haldene, Commanding Officer of the 3rd Division, who asked: -

"Whether anyone else fired at all, or whether all other rifles being examined, showed no trace of being fired? There appears to be no doubt that the accused conduct was such that any 'reasonable man' must have known it was likely to cause grevious bodily harm and that the charge is correct. I recommend that Private C. Knight's offence be treated as murder and not manslaughter."

The case hinged on Private Knights state of mind at the time of the offence and if he would he have started firing his rifle if he had not been drunk?

But there is little doubt that he was very drunk at the time of the offence, but did he really know what he was doing?

If he didn't know what he was doing, then should he have been found guilty of only Manslaughter?

Nevertheless, Private Knight was found guilty of murder and condemned to death. He was shot nine days later on the 15th November 1915 and is buried in Grand Hazard Military Cemetery. Private Knight was only 28 years old and was originally from Fulham, London.

Private Alfred Edwards, service number 15461 was born in Rhos, near Wrexham, North Wales in 1893 and was the Son of Elizabeth Samuels (formerly Edwards) and Edward Samuels (his Step-Father) of Stone Cottages, Avongoch, Ruabon, Denbighshire and was killed by Private Knight on 3rd November 1915, aged 22. He is buried at Eecke Churchyard in France.

Private Alfred B. Poffley, service number 24637 was born in Reading in 1891. He enlisted in the Army on the 12th May 1915 joining the 10th (Service) Battalion Royal Welsh Fusiliers. He left for France with his Battalion in September 1915. He received a gunshot wound (G. S. W.) to his right thigh in the incident with Private Knight on the 3rd November 1915 and was treated at Boulogne Base Hospital before being shipped back to England for further treatment at Huddersfield Military Hospital. Private Poffley remained in England until March 1917 where he joined the Labour Corps and served in Egypt until July 1919 under service number 548546. After the War he applied for a pension due to the wound he received in the incident in November 1915.

Private C. Knight was the only soldier of the 10th (Service) Battalion Royal Welsh Fusiliers to be executed during the War.

The Shot at Dawn Memorial is a monument at the National Memorial Arboretum near Alrewas, in Staffordshire, Great Britain.

It commemorates the 306 British Army and Commonwealth soldiers executed after Court-Martial for desertion and other capital offences during World War I.

It was not all doom and gloom for the Battalion during training and rest periods behind the lines, my Taid Edwin's local Newspaper, "The County Herald" published a letter received from two soldiers from Holywell.

HOLYWELL WAR ITEMS.

10th Royal Welsh Fusiliers in France.

Holywell Boys in a Football Match.

From "Somewhere in France" (dated November 9th) we have received the following very interesting letter, signed by Sergt. J A Jones and Corporal J E Roberts (both of Holywell):—

"We have no doubt that the inhabitants of Holywell and district will be glad to hear of some of the doings of the 10th R.W.F. since we left England. We would be glad, therefore, if you would allow us, through the medium of your valuable paper, to give them a brief outline of our experiences. Shortly after landing we were drafted into the firing line, and received our 'baptism' of fire; and the conduct of the Battalion evoked the unstinted admiration of the Line Regiments who were with it. In spite of the heavy bombardment to which we were subjected, our casualties, we are glad to say, were comparatively slight. At the time of writing we are enjoying a period of inactivity well in rear of the firing line.

Needless to say, these rests are greatly appreciated by all ranks; and last Saturday being a Divisional holiday, a highly interesting football match was played between teams representing the N.C.O's and the men of "A" Company. An element of humour was introduced into the game by the inclusion of several of the "Old School" on the side of the N.C.O's, notably among them being Drummer-Sergt. Hollins, who kept goal; Q.M.S Clarke ("Nobby") and Sergt. Matt Beard. The game was brimful of amusing incidents, some of which are worth recording. Sergt. Beard, despite his age, amazed the spectators by going clean through the opposing defence and scoring the winning goal for his side, whilst Nobby Clark showed some of his old time brilliance by repeatedly clearing his lines, under heavy pressure. During the game both teams had to line up and be counted, as the Referee had received an intimation that the Non-Coms. were playing twelve men. The match resulted in a victory for the Non. Coms by 2 goals to 1. Capt. Adamson officiated as referee, and he performed a difficult task to the satisfaction of all concerned.

The teams were as follows:—N.C.O's:: Goal, Sergt. Hollins (captain); back, Q.M. S. Clarke (Flint) and C.S.M. Peters (Wrexham); half backs, Sergts T C Jones (Ruthin), Bowen (Wrexham) and J A Jones (Holywell); forwards, Sergts Harding (Barry), McSweeney (London), Beard (Flint), Barton (Llanasa) and Dooley (Wrexham).— Privates: Goal, Johnson; backs, Williams and Davies; half backs, Meaden (captain), James and Kendrick; forwards, Davies, Jones, Beechey, Goodwin and Williams; linesmen. Corporal J E Roberts (Holywell) and Private Ben Davies (Flint).

In conclusion, we should like the inhabitants and district to know that all the 'bhoys' are going on well."

Article from The County Herald - Friday November 19th 1915

In 1915, my Taid Edwin's, local Newspaper, The County Herald printed another letter from a soldier serving with the 10th (Service) Battalion Royal Welsh Fusiliers. The letter was from Private Zachariah Pritchard, service number 15635 of Bagillt, (a village next to Holywell), to his Mother from France. It stated:-

"The men have been in the trenches for several weeks. We then left the trenches and were billeted in barns amongst the cattle, even this was a welcome change from the cold trenches. Winter has set in in the district where we are. The people of Bagillt could not realise how the men fared out here and the French people charge double the price for everything. There are several Bagillt men in the Battalion and I am sure the people of Bagillt could help us in some manner, surely they would not begrudge something for the boys who are fighting out here? Our chums must have had a terrible time in the trenches last Winter and I suppose the men of the 10th Battalion were in for a similar experience."

Private Pritchard, like many others, was hoping the people back home would send items of clothing, cigarettes and food, to help them get through their ordeal.

Private Pritchard was wounded on December 18th 1915.

During their time at Eecke, the Battalion was inspected by Major General J. A. L. Haldane, commanding the 3rd Division and General Sir H. Plumer K. C. B. commanding the Second Army.

Major General James Aylmer Lowthorpe Haldane   General Sir Herbert Charles Onslow Plumer K.C.B.

The report of the inspection was **'Satisfactory'**

NOVEMBER 20th

The Battalion, in Brigade, marched from the rest billets at Eecke into a temporary rest camp at Reningelst a distance of 14.3 km (approx 9 miles).

NOVEMBER 21st

The Battalion marched into the trench area North-East of St. Eloi and relieved the 8th Queens (Royal West Surrey) Regiment and the 2nd London Regiment in trench numbers 29, 30 & 31, distribution to 'A' Coy in 29, 'B' Coy in 30 & 'C' Coy in 31.

NOVEMBER 22nd

'D' Coy took over from 'A' Coy of the 8th Queens (Royal West Surrey) Regiment. The Battalion suffered the following:-

RANK	NAME	SERVICE NO.	WOUND
PRIVATE	J. COLDOUGH	23493	RIFLE BULLET TO HEAD - KILLED
CORPORAL	H. FOULKES	15254	RIFLE BULLET TO CHEST

For the next few days the Battalion continued to receive casualties.

NOVEMBER 23rd

RANK	NAME	SERVICE NO.	WOUND
PRIVATE	G. HODSEN	13839	RIFLE BULLET TO BODY - KILLED

NOVEMBER 24th

RANK	NAME	SERVICE NO.	WOUND
CORPORAL	H. STAPLEY	15802	RIFLE BULLET TO RIGHT SHOULDER
PRIVATE	J. BRYANT	27234	RIFLE BULLET TO RIGHT THIGH
PRIVATE	T. H. MANSFIELD	15044	SHRAPNEL (BACK)

Private Bryant was being carried on a stretcher down Trench 28, the Communication Trench by Private Mansfield and three other Stretcher Bearers of the R.A.M.C. when a shrapnel shell burst and wounded Private Bryant again and wounded the Stretcher Bearers too. Sadly Private Bryant died of his wounds the next day having received shrapnel wounds to the head and neck.

'D' Coy (less 25 men and 1 Platoon Officer) handed over ¾ of the trench at 9.30pm to a detatchment of the 1st Battalion of the Northumberland Fusiliers and moved to a reserve post at the rear of Trench 31.

NOVEMBER 25th
2nd Lieutenant P. T. Dale joined the Battalion for duty.

NOVEMBER 26th
The Battalion had the following casualties: -

RANK	NAME	SERVICE NO.	WOUND
PRIVATE	W. WYER (D. COY)	16047	SHRAPNEL TO THE RIGHT ARM
PRIVATE	P. J. SPARKES (A. COY)	15148	SHRAPNEL TO THE BACK
PRIVATE	H. LESTER (C. COY)	20011	SHRAPNEL TO THE HEAD & TOE

NOVEMBER 27th
Private R. Owens ('B' Coy), service number 15251 was killed by a sniper, suffering a rifle bullet to the head. The sniper that shot Private Owens was killed by one of the Battalion's own snipers and another German was also killed by a Sentry on duty.

NOVEMBER 28th
The Battalion were relieved in the trenches by the 2nd Battalion Suffolk Regiment and marched into rest camp A, West of Dicksbusche on the Ouderdoi Road. Again, the Battalion suffered casualties from German snipers before the Battalion was relieved.

RANK	NAME	SERVICE NO.	WOUND
PRIVATE	T. LYNCH (C. COY)	23213	RIFEL BULLET TO HEAD - KILLED
PRIVATE	M. MURPHY (D. COY)	23201	RIFLE BULLET TO SHOULDER & BACK

The weather had really started to change and heavy frost was reported for this day. The Battalion remained at rest camp until early December.

DECEMBER 1915
DECEMBER 4th & 5th
The Battalion marched to the trenches in the evening of the 4th December and took over from the 2nd Suffolk Regiment, who returned to rest camp. 'D' Coy (half of the Platoon) were in Trench 28 (left sub-section), 'A' Coy was in Trench 29, North of Ypres-Comines Canal, 'B' Coy was in Trench 30, 'C' Coy in Trench 31 and the remainder of 'D' Coy and the Specialist Company in reserve dugouts in Trench 31R.

DECEMBER 6th

The Battalion's Snipers claimed two German soldiers.

The practice of **"Sniping"** was not new in 1915. The Germans were exceedingly adapt at it and they had dominated the activity in 1914.

Major Hesketh-Pritchard, a former **'Big Game Hunter'** gradually introduced the art with telescopic-sighted rifles necessary to accomplish sniping. But it was not just the weapon that was important, new skills had to be learnt by the soldier, long range shooting and the art of camouflage had to be practiced.

A skillful sniper not only causes casualties, it also lowers morale considerably among the enemy soldiers in the area where the sniper is operating.

The slightest exposure by the unexpecting soldier would invite a bullet, which invariably struck without warning or chance to avoid.

Several snipers were credited with over 100 kills.

DECEMBER 7th

Casualties recorded were: -

RANK	NAME	SERVICE NO.	WOUND
LANCE CORPORAL	W. STAINTON (C. COY)	15549	KILLED

DECEMBER 8th

It was a very clear day and as a result of this, there was considerable shelling on both sides. The Germans put several 4.2 high explosive shrapnel shells, known as **'Wooly Bears'**, close to 76th Brigades Head Quarters and sent over five 17 inch shells in Ypres. This is known as the **'Ypres Express Shell'** because of the noise it made in the air.

DECEMBER 9th

A Petty Officer, one Seamen and one Marine from the Grand Fleet arrived to spend 24 hours with the Battalion and joined 'A' Coy in Trench 29 (The Bluff). Admiral Jellicoe was anxious that his men should see as much trench life as possible in the little time they were with the Battalion. The sailors were greeted on their arrival with a **'Salute'** from the German trench mortars and as both sides were active throughout the day the *'Guests',* by no means, had a dull day.

The Belgium Artillary shelled the German Front-Line, in front of the Battalion and the Germans replied with *'Howiters and Field Guns'.*

Casualties were: -

RANK	NAME	SERVICE NO.	WOUND
CORPORAL	M. EVANS	15089	KILLED
PRIVATE	E. FRY (A. COY)	14966	WOUNDED
PRIVATE	D. LEWIS	15396	WOUNDED
PRIVATE	T. ROBERTS (A. COY)	15179	WOUNDED

One German soldier was killed by the Battalion sniper.

DECEMBER 10th

The Battalion was relieved in the trenches by the 2nd Battalion Suffolk Regiment and marched back to rest camp A. West of Dickebusche.

DECEMBER 11th TO 17th

During the rest periods the 76th Brigade received intelligence of a possible *'Gas Attack'* by the Germans along the front. The weather was fine but cold. The 2nd Battalion Suffolk Regiment on the night of the 16th December sent out a large 'Wiring Party' of men to put up wire in front of the Bluff Craters. Over 100 yards of wire was erected, using the *'New Iron Corkscrews'.*

The corkscrew picket was screwed into the ground rather than being hammered in, as the timber posts had been.

The hammering had made loud noises which attracked the attention of the enemy, increasing enemy fire.

The corkscrew picket was screwed into the ground by turning it in a clockwise direction using an entrenching tool handle, or a stick inserted into the bottom eye of the picket for leverage, this was quieter to do.

The bottom eye was also used in order to avoid bending the verticle bar of the picket.

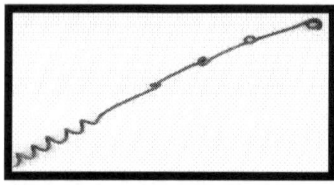
Iron Corkscrew Picket

Wiring Party going forward

Iron Corkscrew Pickets and Barbed Wire Defences

DECEMBER 17th

The Battalion marched out of the rest camp at dusk and took over their former trenches from the 2nd Battalion Suffolk Regiment, who then returned to the rest camp. The Battalion suffered the following casualties: -

RANK	NAME	SERVICE NO.	WOUND
PRIVATE	J. ROBERTS (C. COY)	14986	KILLED
PRIVATE	E. O. WILLIAMS (B. COY)	15340	DIED OF WOUNDS
SERGEANT	S. DILLOW (D. COY)	15725	WOUNDED
PRIVATE	W. DOWNES (A. COY)	28630	WOUNDED

DECEMBER 18th

The Battalion continued to receive casualties: -

RANK	NAME	SERVICE NO.	WOUND
CORPORAL	J. J. WILLIAMS (C. COY)	15618	KILLED
PRIVATE	Z. PRITCHARD (C. COY)	15635	WOUNDED

DECEMBER 19th

According to the 76th Brigade's War Diary for this day, at 5.20am, a very heavy enemy bombardment started. For sometime, it was difficult to fathom where the bombardment was heaviest along the line. The 10th Battalion reported to the Brigade that their Front-Line was being bombarded but there were no signs of the impending gas attack. At 6am, the Brigade received orders from the 3rd Division Head Quarters to **'Stand By'** for immediate attack by the enemy and the 2nd Battalion of the Suffolk's and the 4th Battalion of the Gordon Highlanders, both in reserve, were put on alert. News of the gas attack was reported North of Ypres-Boulers Railway. There was more enemy shelling of the Front-Line than normal and the allied artillery responded by bombing the enemies trenches with good effect. At 5.30pm the enemies artillery commenced with a heavy bombardment on the left sector, both Front-Line and Support Trenches and the Reserve Trenches were heavily shelled which caused considerable damage. The bombardment lasted for over an hour but again, the allied artillery retaliated and caused considerable damage to the enemies Front-Line. The 10th Battalion suffered the following casualties: -

RANK	NAME		WOUND
PRIVATE	H. HOCKAM (A. COY)	15053	KILLED
PRIVATE	T. R. MASON (B. COY)	15249	DIED OF WOUNDS
PRIVATE	J. HIGGINSON (B. COY)	15078	DIED OF WOUNDS
PRIVATE	T. WHEEL (C.COY)	15652	WOUNDED
SERGEANT	R. H. HARDING (A. COY)	15566	WOUNDED
PRIVATE	E. ASHTON (C. COY)	3116	WOUNDED
LANCE CORPORAL	D. SAILSBURY (C. COY)	15548	WOUNDED

DECEMBER 21st

The Battalion sent out a 'Wiring Party' in front of the Loop Trench but work was stopped due to the enemies rifle fire. The following casualties were: -

RANK	NAME	SERVICE NO.	WOUND
PRIVATE	J. HUMPHRIES (C. COY)	15472	KILLED
PRIVATE	W. SMITH (A. COY)	15023	WOUNDED
PRIVATE	F. HUGHES (C. COY)	15492	WOUNDED
PRIVATE	D. GRIFFITHS (B. COY)	15380	WOUNDED

DECEMBER 22nd

A quiet day was reported in the trenches. Heavy rain was falling throughout the day. One casuality was reported as **Private J. Humphries**, service number 15472 ('C' Coy) who was killed.

DECEMBER 23rd

A Zepplin was observed over the trenches about 10.30pm the previous night moving North-East. It was a very clear day on the 23rd with a considerable amount of hostile fire received mostly to the rear areas of the Front-Line. Casualties were: -

RANK	NAME	SERVICE NO.	WOUND
SERGEANT	T. LLOYD (D. COY)	15561	WOUNDED
CORPORAL	J. WRIGHT (D. COY)	15719	WOUNDED
PRIVATE	S. HUGHES (D. COY)	23304	WOUNDED
PRIVATE	W. J. EVANS (C. COY)	15438	WOUNDED
PRIVATE	T. J. OWENS (D. COY)	15699	WOUNDED

DECEMBER 23rd

The Battalion were relieved in the trenches by the 2nd Battalion Suffolk Regiment between 8pm and 10pm and marched into rest camp near Dickebusche. Major E. Freeman assumed temporary appointment of Second in Command as Major F. N. Burton was invalided back to England.

DECEMBER 25th

The 76th Brigade received orders that **'No Action'** was to be taken on Christmas Day which would have likely provoked retaliation on the part of the Germans. The Germans were heard to be singing but nothing else. A quiet day was had by all.

This picture appeared in War Illustrated dated 25th December 1915

CHRISTMAS MESSAGE FROM HIS MAJESTY THE KING.

The following message has been received:-

"Another Christmas finds all the resources of the Empire still engaged in war, and I desire to convey on my own behalf, and on behalf of the Queen, a heartfelt Christmas greeting and our good wishes for the New Year to all who, on Sea and Land, are upholding the honour of the British name. In the officers and men of my Navy, on whom the security of the Empire depends, I repose, in common with all my subjects, a trust that is absolute. On the officers and men of my Armies, whether now in France, in the East, or in other fields, I rely with an equal faith, confident that their devotion, their valour and their self-sacrifice will, under God's guidance, lead to Victory and an Honourable Peace. There are many of their comrades now, alas, in hospital and to those brave fellows, also, I desire, with the Queen, to express our deep gratitude and our earnest prayers for their recovery.

Officers and men of the Navy and Army, another year is drawing to a close, as it began, in toil, bloodshed and suffering; but, I rejoice to know that the goal to which you are striving draws nearer into sight.

MAY GOD BLESS YOU AND ALL YOUR UNDERTAKINGS."

GEORGE, R.I.

The following reply has been despatched:-

To:- HIS MAJESTY THE KING,
Buckingham Palace,
London.

The Army in France under my command desires to be allowed to express its warmest thanks to Your Majesty and to Her Majesty the Queen for the gracious message received. On behalf of the troops I respectfully beg Your Majesties to accept the most heartfelt good wishes of all ranks for X'mas and the New Year and an expression of their firm and lasting determination to prove themselves worthy of the great trust which Your Majesty reposes in us.

From:- SIR DOUGLAS HAIG.

Christmas Day, 1918.

Christmas message from King George V. Sent to 76th Brigade to be passed onto the Battalion

DECEMBER 27th
Colonel W. R. H. Beresford-Ash Commanding Officer was wounded by shrapnel to the right leg when he was near to the 76th Head Quarters and was taken to the Casualty Clearing Station (C. C. S.) for treatment.

DECEMBER 29th
It was decided that Colonel Beresford-Ash was unable to continue as Commanding Officer of the Battalion and was temporary replaced by Major F. L. Makgill-Crichton-Maitland from the 1st Battalion Gordon Highlanders.

Major F. L. Makgill-Crichton-Maitland shown on the right of the photograph

DECEMBER 31st
The Battalion marched out of rest camp and took over it's former trenches from the 2nd Battalion Suffolk Regiment.

During the month of December 1915 the Battalion had suffered the following: -
- **10 KILLED**
- **19 WOUNDED (INCLUDING THEIR COMMANDING OFFICER)**

Casualty figures would increase significantly for the Battalion in the next few months.

Chapter 5
1916 - The Grinding War

JANUARY 1916

JANUARY 1st

The Battalion was in the trenches North-East of St. Eloi on the Ypres-Comines Canal. A new trench off 29 (The Bluff), where 'A' Coy were positioned was started and progressed well. The general conditions of the trench area, where the Battalion was based, was fair but still needed work. The allied artillery bombarded the enemy's dugouts during the night; the enemy did not respond.

JANUARY 2nd

There was very little activity along the Front-Line, it was noted in the War Diary, that the enemy were very cautious now and the Battalions snipers were having difficulty in keeping up their daily average kills.
Unfortunately, the Battalion were still taking casualties; as follows:-

RANK	NAME	SERVICE NO.	WOUND
PRIVATE	W. EVANS (B. COY)	15290	KILLED
PRIVATE	F. BARNETT (D. COY)	23958	KILLED
LANCE CORPORAL	R. JONES (A. COY)	15160	WOUNDED
COMP. QTR MASTER SERGEANT	T. PATON (B. COY)	15332	WOUNDED
PRIVATE	T. EDMUNDS (D. COY)	31318	WOUNDED
PRIVATE	D. MILLS (B. COY)	15264	WOUNDED
PRIVATE	W. ROBINSON (C. COY)	15206	WOUNDED

JANUARY 3rd

Heavy rain was reported on this day. Patrols were sent out at night, no enemy patrols were encountered. Casualties wounded as follows:-

RANK	NAME	SERVICE NO.	WOUND
SERGEANT	W. HAWKINS (B. COY)	8782	WOUNDED
PRIVATE	T. W. JONES (B. COY)	14984	WOUNDED

JANUARY 4th

Another quiet day for the Battalion on the Front-Line. Belgium artillery fired upon and destroyed two of the enemy's saps; this drew retaliation from the enemy firing trench mortars into King's Street and Pear Street Trenches.

This, however, caused little damage but again, the Battalion suffered casualties:-

RANK	NAME	SERVICE NO.	WOUND
PRIVATE	F. HARRHY (C. COY)	24424	WOUNDED
PRIVATE	J. OWEN (C. COY)	15614	WOUNDED
PRIVATE	H. HUMPHRIES (C. COY)	15633	WOUNDED
PRIVATE	H. MILLAN (C. COY)	15466	WOUNDED
PRIVATE	T. NIXON (A. COY)	15056	WOUNDED

JANUARY 6th

The Battalion sent out a 'Wiring Party' to repair wire between the canal and The Bluff.

When assigned as a member of a **'Wiring Party'** you were usually operating under the direction of more experienced N. C. O's. Men would creep into **"No-Man's Land"** under the cover of darkness to repair, replace or place new wire in front of their Front-Line. Casualties on the 6th January were **Lance Corporal R. Jones** service number 15160 and **Private F. Harrhy** service number 24424, wounded on the 2nd and 4th January but died of their wounds.

JANUARY 7th

The Battalion were relieved by the 2nd Battalion Suffolk Regiment and marched back to the rest camp near Dickebusche. While the Battalion were in the rest camp back at the Front-Line, work had started on the **"New Bluff Tunnel"** by 172 Tunnelling Company Royal Engineers, known as **'The Moles'**.

Royal Engineer Tunnelling Companies were specialist units within the British Army. They were formed to dig tunnels under enemy lines.

The stalemate situation in the early part of the War led to the deployment of **'Tunnel Warfare'**. After the first German attacks in December 1914, when they exploded ten mines under the trenches of the Indian Sirhind Brigade, the British began forming suitable units in February 1915. Eight 'Tunnelling Companies' were created and were operational in Flanders from March 1915.

Left:- Founder of the Royal Engineers Tunnelling Companies was **Major Sir John Norton Griffiths MP.**

Mining continued throughout the War and was a vital part of the allied victories.

To read more about the Tunneller's War in Flanders, the *"Beneath Flanders Fields"* book by Peter Barton, Peter Doyle and Johan Vandewalle is an excellent read.

Mine Chamber

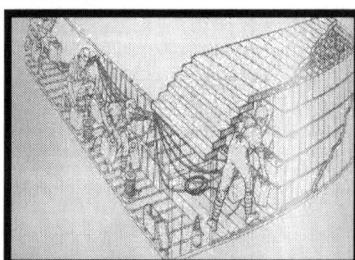

172 Tunnelling Camp

Officer of the 172 Tunnelling Coy

JANUARY 14th

The Battalion marched out of rest camp at Dickesbushe and took over Trenches 29-31 from the 2nd Suffolk Regiment, who marched back to the rest camp. Good progress had been made on The Bluff Tunnel by 172 T. C. The length of the tunnel would be approximately 80 yards. One casualty wounded this day was **Private W. Evans** (B. Coy) service number 14195.

JANUARY 17th

The 6th Belgian artillery battery was withdrawn and replaced by 23rd battery R. F. A. Before the Belgian artillery left, they fired a farewell blast at the enemy in the front of our 31 Trench.

Eight Threlfallite Bombs (a mixture of phosphorous and petrol) were thrown into the enemy trenches. One enemy dugout was on fire and Germans could be heard screaming. The Bluff defences are nearly complete after work carried out to rebuild them.

The Battalion had the following casualties: -

RANK	NAME	SERVICE NO.	WOUND
SERGEANT	R. J. LOFTUS (C. COY)	3167	KILLED
PRIVATE	C. W. JONES (A. COY)	18316	WOUNDED
PRIVATE	P. KYNASTON (A. COY)	24915	WOUNDED

A reinforcing draft of three men from 3rd (Reserve) Battalion Royal Welsh Fusiliers arrived.

JANUARY 20th

Orders were received from 3rd Division via 76th Brigade that ammunition allowance has been still further reduced and are only to call for artillery fire in an emergency.

JANUARY 21st

The Battalion were relieved by the 2nd Suffolk Regiment and marched into rest camp at Dickesbusche.

JANUARY 22nd

At 2.15am the Germans exploded a very large mine at the South-East corner of The Bluff under no. 29 Trench (occupied up until yesterday by the Battalion). The damage was considerable and at least 250 yards of the Front-Line Trench was destroyed. Casualties to the 2nd Suffolk were considerable, over 100 men were killed, wounded or missing.

A crater measuring roughly 125 yards long, 50 yards wide and 60 foot deep was created by this mine. The crater was quickly occupied by the 2nd Suffolks and they prepared themselves to face the expected enemy attack which fortunately did not come.

JANUARY 23rd
The 2nd Suffolks were still holding the crater until the trench behind could be repaired.

JANUARY 24th
A party of three Officers and 100 other ranks (O. R.) from the 10th (Service) Battalion Royal Welsh Fusiliers, led by Captain R. A. Adamson marched from rest camp at Dickebusche to the trench area damaged by the enemy mine to assist in repairing and defending it. The Battalion did excellent work and two new trenches were completed and the Suffolks holding the crater were withdrawn to the new trenches.

The 10th Battalion R. W. F. suffered the following casualties: -

RANK	NAME	SERVICE NO.	WOUND
CAPTAIN	R. A. ADAMSON		WOUNDED (SLIGHTLY IN ARM)
COMPANY SERGEANT MAJOR	E. PETERS (A. COY)	15066	WOUNDED
PRIVATE	S. M. EVANS (A. COY)	15095	WOUNDED
PRIVATE	E. JOHNSON (E. COY)	27227	WOUNDED
PRIVATE	A. G. SAMSON (B. COY)	11944	WOUNDED
PRIVATE	E. GRIFFITHS (A. COY)	23430	WOUNDED
PRIVATE	B. O'BRIAN (B. COY)	5131	KILLED

JANUARY 26th
Private S. Johnson service number 27227 died of his wounds received on 24th January.

JANUARY 27th
Major F. L. Makgill-Crichton-Maitland (1st Gordon Highlanders) was appointed to command The Battalion, with acting rank of Lieutenant Colonel.

JANUARY 28th
The Battalion left rest camp and marched into trenches and relieved the

2nd Battalion Suffolk Regiment who returned to rest camp at Dickebusche. Half of 32 Trench was also taken over from the 1st Battalion Gordon Highlanders.

JANUARY 29th

The Bluff tunnel is now ready for use and a concealed trench has been made from Thames Street Trench to its Southern exit.

The Battalion suffered the following casualties:-

RANK	NAME	SERVICE NO.	WOUND
SERGEANT	W. J. BRIDLE (C. COY)	15413	WOUNDED
PRIVATE	W. WILLIAMS (B. COY)	15000	WOUNDED

JANUARY 30th

Sadly **Private W. Williams** service number 15000 died of his wounds received on the day before 29th January 1916.

FEBRUARY 1916

FEBRUARY 1st

Enemy artillery shelled Trenches 30R to 32R. Little damage was done and no casualties were incurred.

FEBRUARY 2nd

The 4th Gordon Highlanders were transferred from the 76th Brigade with only four Battalions remaining.

FEBRUARY 4th

The Battalion less 'A' & 'B' Coys were relieved by the 2nd Battalion Suffolk Regiment and marched back to rest camp. The 'A' & 'B' Coys, under the command of Major E. Freeman took over the 4th Gordon Highlanders positions.

FEBRUARY 5th

Major Stuart Scott Binny assumed command of the 10th (Service) Battalion Royal Welsh Fusiliers from Major Makgill-Crichton-Maitland.

FEBRUARY 6th

The Battalion, less two Companies ('A' & 'B') marched to Poperinghe where it entrained for Audruicq a distance of 65km (40 miles) and then marched into temporary billets at Hellebrouck a distance of 13km (8 miles). 'A' & 'B' Companies in trenches, were relieved by the 10th Battalion Notts & Derby Regiment (Sherwood Foresters) and marched back to rest camp.

FEBRUARY 7th

The Battalion less two Companies ('A' & 'B') marched to Granspette and took over rest billets from the 7th Battalion Border Regiment.

FEBRUARY 8th

'A' & 'B' Coys, under the command of Major E. Freeman marched to Ganspette and rejoined the Battalion.

FEBRUARY 9th & 10th

During the 9th and 10th February, the 10th Battalion billets were inspected by the General Officer Commanding (G. O. C.). It was noted that the 10th Battalion billets were **'Rather Scattered'**

FEBRUARY 10th, 11th, 12th & 13th

The Battalion continued with their training. Musketry training was able to be carried out due to the availability of several ranges in the area.

FEBRUARY 14th

It was reported to the 76th Brigade that the enemy have attacked and captured the Front-Line Trenches between Ypres-Comines Canal and the Railway.

FEBRUARY 15th

The enemy were still in occupation of the trenches captured on February 14th. The 3rd Division ordered the 76th Brigade, including the 10th (Service) Battalion Royal Welsh Fusiliers to return to Poperinghe immediately by train. When the Battalion arrived, they marched into billets near Vlamertinghe.

FEBRUARY 16th

The 76th Brigade was placed at the disposal of the 17th Division who had taken over the area from the 3rd Division earlier in the month. The Battalion marched to the trench area North-East of St. Eloi and took over what remained of the old trenches, from the 7th Battalion East Yorks Regiment. Distribution was, 'D' Coy in Trench 32, 'C' Coy in Trench 31, 'B' Coy in Trench 30, 'A' Coy in Trench 29 (The Bluff) and 30R. It was very clear that the enemy have obtained a foot-hold and an advantage in the vicinity of The Bluff. It was clear that the 76th Brigade, including the 10th Battalion will have to undertake the recapture of the lost trenches.

FEBRUARY 17th

At 5.30am the enemy heavily bombarded the Battalions trenches. The bombardment lasted for over half an hour. There was nothing the Battalion could do except sit and wait until it ended. The Battalion received it's heaviest casualties since arriving on the Western Front:-

RANK	NAME	SERVICE NO.	WOUND
PRIVATE	A. BASSETT	15201	KILLED
PRIVATE	E. CAPEY	18300	KILLED
PRIVATE	W. MILLINGTON	16291	KILLED
PRIVATE	D. JONES	15119	KILLED
PRIVATE	T. MARSTON	12781	KILLED
LANCE CORPORAL	J. E. ROBERTS	23754	KILLED
PRIVATE	W. V. ROBERTS	23452	KILLED
LIEUTENANT	A. V. CREE		KILLED
LANCE SERGEANT	E. CATHERALL	15787	KILLED

RANK	NAME	SERVICE NO.	WOUND
PRIVATE	H. L. COCKER	12476	KILLED
PRIVATE	L. FALLOWS	31159	KILLED
PRIVATE	D. LINDLEY	23358	KILLED
PRIVATE	R. ROBERTS	15670	KILLED
SERGEANT	R. ROWLANDS	15088	KILLED
PRIVATE	H. STOOKS	13956	KILLED
PRIVATE	T. EVANS	15529	KILLED
PRIVATE	T. STEWART	15416	KILLED
PRIVATE	H. TIMMS	23211	KILLED
PRIVATE	J. CAMPBELL	16238	KILLED
PRIVATE	J. PARR	15572	KILLED
CAPTAIN	B. D. JOHNS		KILLED

RANK	NAME	SERVICE NO.	WOUND
PRIVATE	T. JOHN	15142	DIED OF WOUNDS
PRIVATE	C. NORTHWOOD	23687	DIED OF WOUNDS
PRIVATE	T. O. DAVIES	15502	DIED OF WOUNDS
LANCE CORPORAL	H. T. DAVIES	16203	DIED OF WOUNDS
PRIVATE	C. JONES	15338	DIED OF WOUNDS

RANK	NAME	SERVICE NO.	WOUND
CAPTAIN	G. P. BLAKE		WOUNDED
LIEUTENANT	M. MURRAY		WOUNDED
2ND LIEUTENANT	A. G. W. BUCHANAN		WOUNDED
CORPORAL	J. ROBINSON	23281	WOUNDED
PRIVATE	T. ROGERS	15179	WOUNDED
PRIVATE	W. R. MORGAN	15041	WOUNDED
PRIVATE	S. P. PARRY	14915	WOUNDED
PRIVATE	J. S. VINE	24913	WOUNDED
PRIVATE	H. THOMAS	15046	WOUNDED
PRIVATE	A. ABEL	23447	WOUNDED
PRIVATE	J. ROBERTS	15369	WOUNDED
PRIVATE	E. JONES	15537	WOUNDED
PRIVATE	J. GRIFFIN	23488	WOUNDED
PRIVATE	J. F. MIDDLETON	23205	WOUNDED
PRIVATE	D. INGRAM	15323	WOUNDED
PRIVATE	J. DADE	15459	WOUNDED
PRIVATE	J. MARLOW	23659	WOUNDED
PRIVATE	R. RICHARDS	15609	WOUNDED
PRIVATE	D. STOKES	15557	WOUNDED
PRIVATE	F. SPENCER	15648	WOUNDED
PRIVATE	T. GRAY	15626	WOUNDED
PRIVATE	F. W. PRITCHARD	2337	WOUNDED
PRIVATE	T. JONES	15640	WOUNDED
PRIVATE	W. T. WILLIAMS	15475	WOUNDED
PRIVATE	D. OWENS	15491	WOUNDED

RANK	NAME	SERVICE NO.	WOUND
PRIVATE	W. GREEN	19126	WOUNDED
PRIVATE	A. JONES	25339	WOUNDED
PRIVATE	S. HILL	23299	WOUNDED
PRIVATE	A. HOLDEN	15556	WOUNDED
PRIVATE	S. MCCARTHY	13731	WOUNDED
PRIVATE	W. ROBERTS	15399	WOUNDED
PRIVATE	W. J. JONES	15025	WOUNDED
PRIVATE	W. H. WILLIAMS	15377	WOUNDED
PRIVATE	D. L. JONES	15349	WOUNDED
PRIVATE	D. PARRY	15102	WOUNDED
PRIVATE	G. W. BIRCHALL	24779	WOUNDED
PRIVATE	H. HUGHES	15501	WOUNDED
COY SERGEANT-MAJOR	E. FISHER	15790	WOUNDED
SERGEANT	J. P. WRIGHT	15753	WOUNDED
CORPORAL	J. ROBERTS	24793	WOUNDED
PRIVATE	T. MARSTON	15388	WOUNDED
PRIVATE	P. ROGERS	24828	WOUNDED
LANCE CORPORAL	B. HAPWOOD	16101	WOUNDED
LANCE CORPORAL	T. JENKINS	16102	WOUNDED
PRIVATE	J. BROWN	15697	WOUNDED
PRIVATE	B. BENSON	4724	WOUNDED
PRIVATE	J. H. LULLINH	12261	WOUNDED
PRIVATE	B. DAVIES	16112	WOUNDED
PRIVATE	A. PURVIS	23311	WOUNDED
PRIVATE	E. PRICE	16055	WOUNDED

Captain Johns was the son of Mr A. C. John of Carrickfergus. He was educated at Hatfield Grange, Repton and Oriel College, Oxford. He was commissioned in the 10th (Service) Battalion Royal Welsh Fusiliers. He had only just returned to the Battalion after a week on leave when he was killed on 17th February 1916.

FEBRUARY 18th
Work on the assembly positions for the attack started, the weather was fine.

FEBRUARY 19th

The Battalion continued to receive heavy artillery fire and casualties were heavy:-

RANK	NAME	SERVICE NO.	WOUND
CAPTAIN	J. A. WALKER		KILLED IN ACTION
PRIVATE	B. DAVIES	15183	KILLED IN ACTION
PRIVATE	E. PRICE	16055	KILLED IN ACTION
PRIVATE	T. SPENCER	23276	KILLED IN ACTION
LANCE CORPORAL	A. E. WILKES	16259	KILLED IN ACTION
PRIVATE	J. J. THOMAS	24404	KILLED IN ACTION
PRIVATE	C. A. WILLIAMS	15301	KILLED IN ACTION
PRIVATE	S. HOLLINGSWORTH	15731	KILLED IN ACTION
PRIVATE	M. REARDON	16199	KILLED IN ACTION

RANK	NAME	SERVICE NO.	WOUND
LANCE CORPORAL	D. D. JONES	16176	WOUNDED
PRIVATE	T. R. GREGORY	27229	WOUNDED
PRIVATE	W. J. HEWITT	15393	WOUNDED
PRIVATE	J. C. BUTLER	23428	WOUNDED
PRIVATE	R. M. WILLIAMS	15079	WOUNDED
PRIVATE	D. J. WILLIAMS	15373	WOUNDED
PRIVATE	J. SHAW	9983	WOUNDED
PRIVATE	V. EVANS	24890	WOUNDED
PRIVATE	J. WILLIAMS	15203	WOUNDED
PRIVATE	S. EVANS	15334	WOUNDED
PRIVATE	T. J. CONNAH	13697	WOUNDED
PRIVATE	J. MALKIN	23151	WOUNDED
PRIVATE	J. ELLIS	10005	WOUNDED

Captain John Arthur Walker was killed along with nine of his men while moving to trenches at Gordon Terrace, near St. Eloi. He was the only Son of John & Margaret Walker from Osbourne House, Llandudno. He was educated at Shrewsbury and at the out-break of War, he was at Trinity Hall, Cambridge. He joined the Officer Training Corps (O. T. C.) and was commissioned on November 13th 1914. He is buried at Reninghelst New Cemetery, Belgium. There is a three-light stained-glass window Memorial to him in St. George's Church Llandudno and he is also commemorated on the Llandudno War Memorial.

FEBRUARY 20th

Work continued on the assembly positions and repairing the worst of the damage to the trenches.

FEBRUARY 21st

Considerable activity by both allied and German artillery continued. Reserve Wood was heavily shelled. British artillery retaliated with heavy shell fire.

FEBRUARY 22nd

The Battalion were relieved in Trenches 32, 31, 30 and 29 by 2nd Battalion Suffolk Regiment and took over trenches and dugouts R9, R10 and Gordon Terrace.

FEBRUARY 23rd

The Battalion were relieved in the Trenches R9 and R10 by the 9th Battalion West Riding Regiment and marched into temporary rest camp J.

FEBRUARY 24th

The weather took a turn for the worst, it was very cold and snowing. Officers of the Battalion joined others at Head Quarters to discuss the ongoing situation. It was decided that a raid is to be made on the supposed German mine shaft opposite The Bluff.

FEBRUARY 25th

A reinforcing draft of 19 rank and file arrived from base camp and joined the Battalion.

FEBRUARY 28th

The Battalion received the following casualties: -

RANK	NAME	SERVICE NO.	WOUND
SERGEANT	F. COLE	6080	WOUNDED
PRIVATE	E. T. ROBERTS	15824	WOUNDED
PRIVATE	T. J. DACKINS	15695	WOUNDED
PRIVATE	T. SHACKLEY	15755	WOUNDED
PRIVATE	E. H. WROE	15637	MISSING

During the Battalions rest time around the Poperinghe area, the Officers would have spent some time in Talbot House.

Talbot House "Toc H" - Poperinghe

When Talbot House opened its doors in December 1915, it was not only set up as an **'Everyman's Club'** but also as an **'Inn'**. Officers on leave got bed and breakfast here, whilst waiting for a train that was to take them home, or take them back to the Front-Line.

From the very first day, the accommodation was in great demand, so much so, that five months later, the accommodation facilities were moved further down the road to a building to be known as **'Skindles Hotel'.**

During the early period of Talbot House, a visitors book was kept, in which, almost 1,300 signatures (mainly in pencil) were recorded. Officers from nearly all units active in the area, at that time, seemed to have found their way to Talbot House.

Officers of the 10th (Service) Battalion Royal Welsh Fusiliers were visitors to this wonderful place of peace and tranquility, amid the horrors of War that surrounded them. According to their visitor book, the following Officers visited Talbot House between January and April 1916:-

- 2nd Lieutenant Albert Nevitt – Officers Book - page 25 (26/01/1916) & page 33 (06/02/1916)
- 2nd Lieutenant William Sniddons – Officers Book – page 62 (24/03/1916)
- Captain George Penderell Blake – Officers Book – page 25 (27/01/1916)
- Captain John Arthur Walker – Officers Book – page 25 (26/01/1916)
- Captain Bernard Grellier – Officers Book – page 51 (23/02/1916)
- Lieutenant Algernon William Fish – Officers Book – page 57 (08/03/1916) & page 66 (02/04/1916)
- Lieutenant George Devereux Scale – Officers Book – page 50 (22/02/1916)
- Major Edward Freeman – Officers Book – page 16 (09/01/1916) & page 21 (20/01/1916)
- Lieutenant Albert John Stanley James – Officers Book – page 50 (22/02/1916)

Out of the nine Officers listed above, five would later be killed in action (Freeman, Walker, James, Scale & Blake).

Men swarmed about the house from 10am to 8pm and Officers flowed in from 7pm. The charge for Officers bed and breakfast was 5 francs; the **'Robin Hood Principle'** taking from the rich to give to the poor.

The house provided rest and recreation to all soldiers visiting, regardless of their rank.

"ALL RANK ABANDON YE WHO ENTER HERE"

This sentence became one of the pillars of the house.

Rev. **'Tubby'** Clayton the founder of Talbot House insisted that the house had to be a place where people could forget about the War for just a moment.

I would like to think my Taid Edwin, visited Talbot House, maybe he sat in the gardens or played billiards, or even spent time in the **'Upper Room'** the little chapel in the attic. I would like to think he found peace away from the horrors for just a little while.

You can still visit Talbot House today. And if you ever get chance and want to spend a night or two away and enjoy a comfy bed and a hearty breakfast, and be able to soak up the atmosphere of this wonderful house, it's a must.

Talbot House 2022   Talbot House Gardens(circa 1915-18)

Soldiers in the Music Room

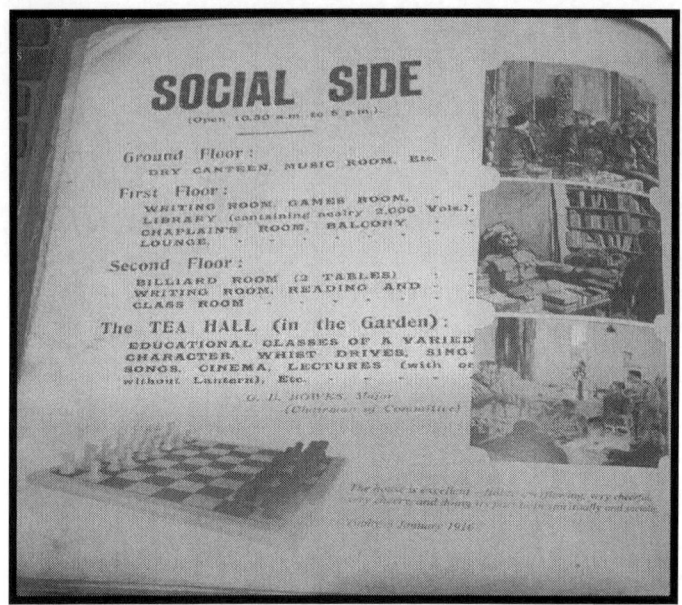

Talbot House Social

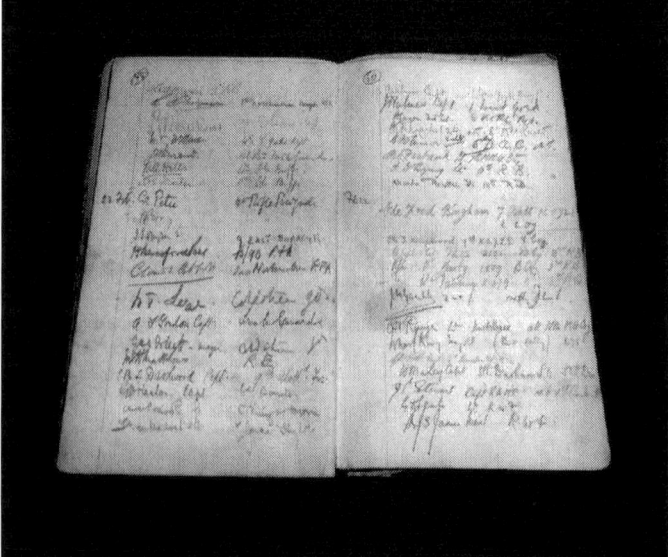

Talbot House Officers Book

MARCH 1916

MARCH 1st

The Battalion in Brigade marched to the trenches where, with the 76th Brigade, relieved the 52nd Brigade, 17th Division, the 10th Battalion moved into trench positions Lnakhup to Gordon Terrace to Duckwalks to Gordon Post. The Battalion received the following orders – *"The Battalion will detail a party to carry out a raid on the German trenches on the canal bank C4 AB7 with the object of discovering and destroying a suspected enemy mine shaft."*

A 'Raiding Party' of 2 Officers and 44 other ranks (O.R.) was assembled for the task. The order continued – *"The rest of the Battalion would be held in support of the Suffolks and will keep in constant communication with them, when Griffiths Trench is left unoccupied owing to the Suffolks advance, the 10th Battalion will move forward with one Platoon and three Grenadiers to occupy it. Griffiths Trench must never be left unoccupied."*

Battalions will assault at 4.30am tomorrow morning, there will be no preparatory artillery bombardment.

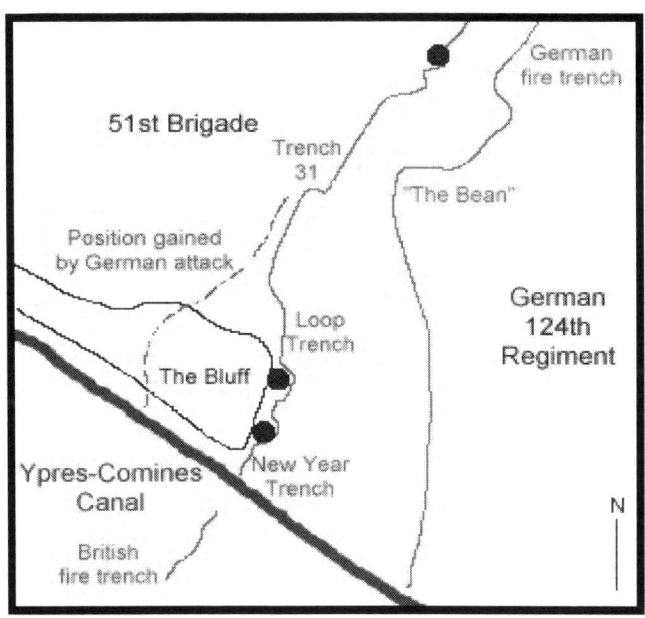

MARCH 2nd

The attack of The Bluff leading the Battalions were; 2 Suffolks, 8 Kings Own and 1 Gordon Highlanders. They began the assault at 4.30am. The British artillery fire began two minutes after the attack had started. The attack achieved complete surprise although an enemy machine gun on the left caused heavy casualties to 1 Gordon Highlanders. The 172nd Tunnelling Company R. E. also suffered casualties, having destroyed a tunnel in no mans land that led to The Bluff, men were cut down by heavy enemy machine gun fire.

By 5.10am the Infantry had captured all objectives. The Battalion took back all of the trenches lost in February and also took a small portion of the German Front-Line Trenches. Finding many of the enemy without equipment, five German Officers and 248 other ranks (O.R.) were taken prisoner. When the attack commenced the 10th (Service) Battalion Royal Welsh Fusiliers, first squad, advanced with the 2nd Suffolks, with the objective to bomb and block the enemies Communication Trench running from the left of the crater until relieved. The second squad was later called up to the crater where they succeeded in dislodging a number of enemy snipers that were causing casualties to the Battalions.

At 4.30pm 'A' Coy 10th (Service) Battalion Royal Welsh Fusiliers moved up to reinforce the 2nd Suffolks and assist in digging the new trenches.

At 8.30pm 'B' Coy moved up to reinforce the 2nd Suffolks and also assisted in digging new trenches. The Battalion held the William and Griffiths Trenches.

The 'Raiding Party' of two Officers and 44 other ranks (O.R.) raid was cancelled and they were employed in clearing and storing grenades and held in support of the 2nd Suffolks.

German artillery was curiously slow to react to this surprise attack and only opened fire at 9.30am, intensifying at 11am, which caused considerable casualties. Some sporadic attempts to counter-attack were made by the enemy, but these attacks were beaten off.

The 10th Battalion had taken part in their first attack on the German Front-Line and had achieved all it's objectives, but sadly with a heavy cost to lives: -

RANK	NAME	SERVICE NO.	WOUND
PRIVATE	D. LLEWELYN (A. COY)	15127	KILLED IN ACTION
PRIVATE	W. H. DAVIES (B. COY)	15136	KILLED IN ACTION
PRIVATE	G. THOMAS (B. COY)	15680	KILLED IN ACTION
PRIVATE	T. BRADY (D. COY)	10636	KILLED IN ACTION
PRIVATE	A. CROWE (D. COY)	9804	KILLED IN ACTION
PRIVATE	L. DEVEREUX (A. COY)	15131	KILLED IN ACTION
PRIVATE	M. B. MORRIS (B. COY)	23486	KILLED IN ACTION
PRIVATE	G. HORNBY (B. COY)	15334	KILLED IN ACTION
CORPORAL	C. J. REED (D. COY)	15700	KILLED IN ACTION
PRIVATE	T. J. LLEWELYN (D. COY)	16277	KILLED IN ACTION
PRIVATE	H. BEVAN (D. COY)	15715	KILLED IN ACTION
PRIVATE	J. P. JONES (C. COY)	15243	KILLED IN ACTION
PRIVATE	T. D. EVANS	15578	DIED OF WOUNDS IN ACTION
PRIVATE	J. OWEN (D. COY)	17521	MISSING REPORTED KILLED
PRIVATE	T. GRIFFITHS (C. COY)	15115	MISSING REPORTED KILLED
PRIVATE	R. PRITCHARD	14934	MISSING

RANK	NAME	SERVICE NO.	WOUND
CAPTAIN	W. P. GRIFFITHS		WOUNDED
LIEUTENANT	H. J. K. LEWIS		WOUNDED
LIEUTENANT	H. A. V. MAYNARD		WOUNDED
2ND LIEUTENANT	J. L. T. DAVIES		WOUNDED
SERGEANT	R. G. ROBERTS (B. COY)	15386	WOUNDED
LANCE CORPORAL	M. DRISCOLL (B. COY)	15312	WOUNDED
LANCE CORPORAL	F. BRIERLEY (C. COY)	15603	WOUNDED
PRIVATE	R. PUGH (C. COY)	15455	WOUNDED
PRIVATE	H. ,WOODWARD (C. COY)	23297	WOUNDED
PRIVATE	R. WILLIAMS (C. COY)	15443	WOUNDED
PRIVATE	T. JONES (C. COY)	15489	WOUNDED
PRIVATE	J. JONES (C. COY)	24783	WOUNDED

RANK	NAME	SERVICE NO.	WOUND
PRIVATE	J. JONES (C. COY)	15473	WOUNDED
PRIVATE	M. G. BELLINGHAM (C. COY)	15593	WOUNDED
PRIVATE	E. A. MCDONALD (C. COY)	15555	WOUNDED
PRIVATE	J. NESSLING (C. COY)	23270	WOUNDED
PRIVATE	E. WALKER (C. COY)	23157	WOUNDED
PRIVATE	E. THOMAS (C. COY)	15552	WOUNDED
CORPORAL	W. H. MOORE (C. COY)	17319	WOUNDED
PRIVATE	L. PEARSON (D. COY)	23265	WOUNDED
CORPORAL	T. KEAY (A. COY)	15205	WOUNDED
PRIVATE	J. HUGHES (A. COY)	15036	WOUNDED
PRIVATE	E. S. PARRY (A. COY)	15097	WOUNDED
PRIVATE	G. E. JONES (A. COY)	34792	WOUNDED
PRIVATE	E. HOLLAND (A. COY)	23436	WOUNDED
PRIVATE	H. HARRIS (A. COY)	23728	WOUNDED
PRIVATE	A. PETRIE (B. COY)	15105	WOUNDED
LANCE CORPORAL	T. BROWN (B. COY)	23439	WOUNDED
SERGEANT	D. F. DUIGNANT (B. COY)	16197	WOUNDED
SERGEANT	J. HOLL (B. COY)	16027	WOUNDED
LANCE CORPORAL	A. W. FLOOK (C. COY)	15677	WOUNDED
PRIVATE	H. C. WEST (B. COY)	23219	WOUNDED
PRIVATE	G. BRANCH (B. COY)	18351	WOUNDED
PRIVATE	A. E. JAMES (D. COY)	23202	WOUNDED
PRIVATE	W. J. RICHARDS (D. COY)	16284	WOUNDED
PRIVATE	S. WILLIAMS (D. COY)	16247	WOUNDED
PRIVATE	T. GREEN (D. COY)	23220	WOUNDED
PRIVATE	T. WESTERN (D. COY)	6621	WOUNDED
PRIVATE	J. LINHAM (D. COY)	15668	WOUNDED
LANCE CORPORAL	P. C. DANIELS (D. COY)	16242	WOUNDED
PRIVATE	A. C. WEBSTER (D. COY)	16031	WOUNDED
PRIVATE	E. JONES (D. COY)	10487	WOUNDED
PRIVATE	A. E. ECKERSLEY (D. COY)	23204	WOUNDED
PRIVATE	G. LAITY (A. COY)	15685	WOUNDED
SERGEANT	J. A. JONES (A. COY)	14906	WOUNDED
PRIVATE	R. E. MATTHEWS (A. COY)	15410	WOUNDED
PRIVATE	J. MCREADY (A. COY)	23194	WOUNDED
PRIVATE	D. P. WILLIAMS (A. COY)	15008	WOUNDED
PRIVATE	R. ROBERTS (A. COY)	15165	WOUNDED
PRIVATE	T. WILLIAMS (A. COY)	13997	WOUNDED
PRIVATE	E. C. JONES (B. COY)	15311	WOUNDED
PRIVATE	R. HUGHES (B. COY)	14640	WOUNDED
PRIVATE	A. HARRIS (B. COY)	23477	WOUNDED
PRIVATE	R. JONES (B. COY)	14644	WOUNDED
PRIVATE	R. P. JONES (B. COY)	15228	WOUNDED
PRIVATE	J. SIMON (B. COY)	14929	WOUNDED
PRIVATE	T. JONES (B. COY)	15370	WOUNDED
PRIVATE	H. BRAMALL (B. COY)	15343	WOUNDED
PRIVATE	J. HUGHES (B. COY)	1118	WOUNDED
PRIVATE	W. P. MACDONALD (C. COY)	14166	WOUNDED
PRIVATE	J. MCDONAGH (C. COY)	15452	WOUNDED
PRIVATE	J. HUGHES (B. COY)	23371	WOUNDED
SERGEANT	A. BRINDALL (B. COY)	31942	WOUNDED
PRIVATE	W. JONES (B. COY)	14825	WOUNDED

RANK	NAME	SERVICE NO.	WOUND
PRIVATE	R. H. WARHURST (B. COY)	17179	WOUNDED
PRIVATE	T. JONES (B. COY)	14991	WOUNDED
PRIVATE	J. THOMAS (B. COY)	15277	WOUNDED
LANCE CORPORAL	H. SMITH (C. COY)	15585	WOUNDED
PRIVATE	G. ALLCOCK (C. COY)	24788	WOUNDED
PRIVATE	E. J. WILLIAMS (C. COY)	15474	WOUNDED

Private Matthew Benjamin Morris service number 23486

Born in Stafford in 1885 at 22 Bridges Street, Sutton-in-Ashfield. Private Morris enlisted in Nottingham in March 1915, joining the 10th (Service) Battalion Royal Welsh Fusiliers and was killed in action on 2nd March 1916. He left a Wife and four children behind.

A letter to Private Morris's Wife Clara, from his Lieutenant, says- *"I very much regret to say that your Husband was killed in action on the 2nd March. He was hit in the head by a piece of shell and died instantly. He was carried down and buried with a number of other men. I always found him an excellent man in the trenches and one who never showed fear."*

His grave was lost but he is remembered on the Menin Gate Memorial. Clara, his Wife, wrote the following, that appeared in the Notts Free Press on 2nd March 1917, one year on from his death:-

"A loving Husband, a faithful friend
One of the best God could lend
When nights are dark and friends are few
Dear Husband and Dad, how we long for you"

From a sorrowing Wife and little ones.

MARCH 3rd

A heavy howitzer shell made a direct hit on the 10th Battalion Head Quarters dugout at Gordon Post with the following casualties –

RANK	NAME	SERVICE NO.	WOUND
MAJOR (TEMPORARY LIEUT-COL)	S. BINNY COMMANDING OFFICER		KILLED

RANK	NAME	SERVICE NO.	WOUND
MAJOR	EDWARD FREEMAN 2ND IN COMMAND		KILLED
CAPTAIN	W. T. LYONS ADJUTANT		KILLED
2ND LIEUTENANT	W. HUGHES		KILLED
PRIVATE	J. WILLIAMS (A. COY)	15132	KILLED
PRIVATE	H. ROGERS (A. COY)	18328	KILLED
PRIVATE	G. ROBERTS (B. COY)	15371	KILLED
PRIVATE	B. KNIGHT (C. COY)	23303	KILLED
CORPORAL	W. B. DAVEY (A. COY)	15404	KILLED
LANCE CORPORAL	B. DALLISON (D. COY)	15664	KILLED
PRIVATE	W. T. ROBERTS (B. COY)	14971	KILLED
PRIVATE	P. O'BRIEN (C. COY)	15451	KILLED
PRIVATE	W. COLLINS (B. COY)	16114	KILLED

Major Edward Freeman
2nd in Command, 10th (Service) Battalion Royal Welsh Fusiliers

Major Freeman was the Son of Harold and Alice Freeman of Malvern Wells. He was the Husband of Katherine Freeman who was from Gallt-y-Beran, Pwllheli. He is buried in Spoilbank Cemetery, located in the Ypres Salient on the Western Front.

The 76th Brigade was relieved by the 8th Battalion in the recaptured trenches. The 10th Battalion marched back to billets at Poperinghe under the command of the remaining Senior Officer – Captain F. A. Samuel. The weather was now really bad, with heavy snow falling. The relief was not completed until daylight on the 4th March.

MARCH 5th

The Battalion were resting and cleaning up. The men were exhausted and still shaken up from the heavy enemy artillery received during the last 48 hours.

MARCH 6th

The following Officers joined the Battalion for duty: -

- 2nd Lieutenant D. McBean
- 2nd Lieutenant O. L. Jones
- 2nd Lieutenant W. N. Davies
- 2nd Lieutenant F. A. Lawson

MARCH 7th

The Battalion was inspected by General Sir Herbert Plumer K.C.B. Commanding 2nd Army, who congratulated all of the ranks on their behaviour during the recent operations at The Bluff.

The Battalion received further messages of congratulations via 76th Brigade Head Quarters from G.O.C. 3rd Division which said: *"My congratulations, please convey to all ranks my appreciation of the gallant manner in which the attack was carried out."*

From 17th Division said – *"Very hearty congratulations to all ranks on success gained."*

From 51st Infantry Brigade – *"Hearty congratulations on your complete success."*

From Army Commander – *"I am very pleased to have reports of your operations, please convey my appreciaition to all ranks."*

From Commander in Chief – *"I have heard, with very great pleasure, the good news of the capture of The Bluff and trenches North of the canal. I have been kept informed, from day to day, of the carefully thought-out and methodical preperations which have been devoted to this enterprise. Please convey to all the ranks concerned in the operations, my heartiest congratulations and thanks."*

MARCH 8th

The weather was still bad, with heavy snow falling. Re-equipment of the Battalion was making good progress.

MARCH 9th

Major G. R. Crosfield of the 4th Territorial Battalion South Lancashire Regiment assumed command of the 10th (Service) Battalion Royal Welsh Fusiliers with the temporary rank of Lieutenant Colonel, replacing Lieutenant Colonel Binny who was killed on March 3rd when shellfire hit the Battalion's command post.

G. R. Crosfield pictured in the Belfast Telegraph February 12th 1932

MARCH 10th

Captain D. W. G. Jackson joined the Battalion for duty and assumed post of 2nd in Command replacing Major E. Freeman who was killed on March 3rd.

The weather was still very cold with lying snow. The following Officers also joined the Battalion for duty:-

- Captain T. Hughes
- Lieutenant H. W. Rayner

MARCH 11th & 12th

The Battalion continued training and was re-equipped ready to return to the trenches.

MARCH 13th

The Battalion marched out of the rest billets in Poperinghe and returned to the trenches relieving the 2nd Suffolk Regiment.

The trenches were in a terrible condition and the men were standing in water, knee high in places, and with many of the Battalions men still lying dead on the battlefield from the attacks carried out on 2nd and 3rd March. The Battalion immediately started work in repairing the trenches and draining the system and sending out 'Burial Parties' to remove the dead from the battlefield.

The following Officers joined the Battalion for duty:-

- Captain C. P. C. Daniel
- 2nd Lieutenant S. F. Bancroft
- 2nd Lieutenant W. J. D. Hale

Water in the Trenches

MARCH 14th First Spring Day

Work on repairing the trench and drainage system was progressing well. Enemy snipers were very active in the left sector. The sections opposite The Bluff were quiet. Casualties reported were: -

RANK	NAME	SERVICE NO.	WOUND
PRIVATE	W. J. HAWES	15067	WOUNDED
PRIVATE	W. EVANS	15010	WOUNDED
PRIVATE	W. HUGHES	15135	WOUNDED

Also on this day the Battalion's Captain Chaplain the Reverend David Cynddelw Williams was determined to give a proper burial to Lieutenant W. Hughes who was killed on March 3rd. His body had been roughly located in 'No Mans Land' and Reverend Williams described in his Diary, of the going through the barbed wire into mud so thick and cloying that – *"It was sucking his boots off."*

With enemy star shells constantly bursting around him, Reverend Williams located Lieutenant Hughes's body. He was properly buried and a short service held at the graveside.

The Chaplin Reverend Williams was well liked by the Officers and the men of the Battalion. His steadfast, but sometimes naïve character endeared him to the men, especially as he was willing to share with them the dangers of the trenches. Reverend Williams placed a swear box in the Officers Mess, the proceeds of which he purchased a primus stove. Reverend Williams saw his mission as to try to turn the men away from drink, women and swearing and to turn them to God. He felt that he was more successful on the path to righteousness with the South Walians in the Battalion. He had more trouble trying to convert the North Walians, which my Taid Edwin was included.

Captain Chaplin the Reverend David Cynddelw Williams

MARCH 15th

In the morning the enemy fired trench mortars in the vicinity of The Bluff and also shelled our right sector. In the afternoon, our artillery responded, after which, the enemy stopped. The following casualties were received:-

RANK	NAME	SERVICE NO.	WOUND
LIEUTENANT	D. MCBEAN		KILLED
LANCE SERGEANT	W. J. EVANS	15125	KILLED
LANCE SERGEANT	A. V. RACKSTRAW	15656	DIED OF WOUNDS
PRIVATE	S. F. DAVIES	15147	WOUNDED
PRIVATE	J. JAMESON	15209	WOUNDED
PRIVATE	G. ROBERTS	15077	WOUNDED
SERGEANT	J. LEWIS	16227	WOUNDED
PRIVATE	T. EDWARDS	15163	WOUNDED
PRIVATE	D. J. MANTON	15403	WOUNDED
PRIVATE	W. MORGAN	15139	WOUNDED
CORPORAL	A. COLE	15040	WOUNDED

2nd Lieutenant D. McBean had only been with the Battalion 9 days. He had previously served at Gallipoli with the 8th Battalion Royal Welsh Fusiliers.

MARCH 17th

The Battalion were relieved in the trenches by the 2nd Battalion Suffolk Regiment and marched back to camp A. Casualties were: -

RANK	NAME	SERVICE NO.	WOUND
PRIVATE	T. CROOK	23154	WOUNDED
PRIVATE	E. JACKSON	15533	WOUNDED
PRIVATE	D. J. JONES	16193	WOUNDED

MARCH 21ST

The Battalion marched back to the trenches and relieved the 2nd Battalion Suffolk Regiment and took over the right sector. An enemy aeroplane was continually patrolling his own and our lines between 7.30am and 12.30pm. Although the aeroplane was flying low, our machine gun fire (M.G.) seemed to have no effect.

MARCH 23rd

The 76th Brigade was relieved in the trench area by 59th Brigade (17th Division). The 10th Battalion was relieved in the trenches by a Battalion of the 6th Durham Light Infantry and marched into temporary camp H.

MARCH 24th

The following Officers joined the Battalion for duty: -

- 2nd Lieutenant W. G. Daniel
- 2nd Lieutenant A. E. Capell
- 2nd Lieutenant W. Siddons
- 2nd Lieutenant F. E. Crane
- 2nd Lieutenant J. C. Davies
- 2nd Lieutenant E. H. Bayliss

MARCH 25th

The Battalion was inspected by Major General J. A. L. Haldane C.B. D.S.O. Commanding the 3rd Division, who again, congratulated all ranks for their service and commitment during the recent operations. He also presented the following Officers with ribbons of the respected decorations awarded to them recently:-

- Major (Temporary Lieutenant-Colonel) G. R. Crosfield - The Distinguished Service Order (D.S.O)
- Captain B. Grellier (R.A.M.C) - The Military Cross (M.C.)

He also gave a **'Memorial Card'** respecting the gallant conduct displayed by **Lance Sergeant W. J. Evans**, service number 15125, killed in action on 15th March.

Two of the Battalions Coys went to the trenches in the vicinity of St. Eloi to provide 'Carrying & Working Parties'.

Sergeant T. H. Killingback, service number 15246 was appointed Regimental Quarter Master Sergeant.

MARCH 26th

Two of the Battalions Companies provided 'Carrying & Working Parties' to the trenches. Weather was reported as very cold and wet.

MARCH 27th

2nd Lieutenant E. Vaughan-Jones reported for duty. The Battalion marched from camp H. to Scottish Wood in the vicinity of Voormezele (St. Eloi trench area) and assumed position in reserve to 8th Brigade. The Brigade attacked enemy trenches South of the St. Eloi and was a complete success.

MARCH 28th

The Battalion moved forward and occupied trenches which were captured from the enemy on the 27th March by the 9th Brigade. All the 76th Brigade Battalions were now in the trenches captured by the 9th Brigade. No Battalions of the 76th were in reserve.

MARCH 29th

The Battalion received the following casualties: -

RANK	NAME	SERVICE NO.	WOUND
PRIVATE	J. SPOONER	15069	WOUNDED
PRIVATE	A. MALLETT	23216	WOUNDED
PRIVATE	W. BOWEN	15019	WOUNDED
PRIVATE	J. S. VYNE	24913	WOUNDED

MARCH 30th

The Battalion were ordered to bomb the enemy out of their positions at Crater No. 5, points 77, 85 and 76. With the attack being led by Lieutenant A. Nevitt. The Battalion's Bombing Officer commenced the attack at midday. The attack failed and the survivors of the attack returned to their positions. Heavy shelling by the Germans at this time, caused heavy casualties to the Battalion:-

RANK	NAME	SERVICE NO.	WOUND
MAJOR (TEMP LIEUT/COLONEL) COMMANDING OFFICER	G. R. CROSFIELD		WOUNDED BY ENEMY SHELLFIRE

Captain D. W. G. Jackson assumed temporary command of the Battalion.

RANK	NAME	SERVICE NO.	WOUNDED
CAPTAIN	W. P. GRIFFITHS		KILLED IN ACTION
LANCE CORPORAL	J. EVANS	15039	KILLED IN ACTION
LANCE CORPORAL	M. EVANS	14192	KILLED IN ACTION
PRIVATE	W. J. HOBSON	15532	KILLED IN ACTION
PRIVATE	G. TINSLEY	23496	KILLED IN ACTION
2ND LIEUTENANT	H. E. WYNNE-WILLIAMS		KILLED IN ACTION
PRIVATE	D. J. MORRIS	15275	KILLED IN ACTION
PRIVATE	A. PHILLIPS	15303	KILLED IN ACTION
PRIVATE	E. J. WILLIAMS	15474	KILLED IN ACTION
LANCE CORPORAL	P. C. DANIELS	16242	KILLED IN ACTION
MAJOR (TEMP LIEUT/CORP)	G. R. CROSFIELD		WOUNDED
CAPTAIN	C. P. C. DANIELL		WOUNDED
2ND LIEUTENANT	A. NEVITT		WOUNDED
LANCE CORPORAL	J. JONES	14968	WOUNDED
PRIVATE	R. WILLIAMS	32514	WOUNDED
PRIVATE	J. O. PEARCE	14914	WOUNDED
PRIVATE	T. ALSOP	15358	WOUNDED
PRIVATE	S. CRAVEN	15476	WOUNDED
PRIVATE	W. JONES	16311	WOUNDED
PRIVATE	D. DAVIES	15520	WOUNDED
PRIVATE	A. C. JONES	25339	WOUNDED
LANCE CORPORAL	J. DOYLE	15449	WOUNDED
CORPORAL	S. ASTILL	9233	WOUNDED
PRIVATE	A. EDMONDS	15673	WOUNDED
PRIVATE	J. W. JONES	15587	WOUNDED
LANCE CORPORAL	J. BROADBENT	19626	WOUNDED
PRIVATE	H. FRANCIS	13338	WOUNDED
PRIVATE	W. J. RICHARDS	16284	WOUNDED
SERGEANT	R. W. BARKER	15110	WOUNDED
PRIVATE	R. BILLINGHURST	18412	WOUNDED
PRIVATE	A. MELIA	15329	WOUNDED
PRIVATE	J. CONWAY	5552	WOUNDED
PRIVATE	D. T. PIERCE	15375	WOUNDED
PRIVATE	R. HUGHES	24488	WOUNDED
PRIVATE	H. ROCK	23206	WOUNDED
PRIVATE	E. GWILT	15434	WOUNDED
PRIVATE	H. J. ROBERTS	15477	WOUNDED
PRIVATE	F. CARPENTER	11082	WOUNDED
LANCE CORPORAL	F. WEGG	15590	WOUNDED
PRIVATE	T. GLOVER	23499	WOUNDED
PRIVATE	R. WILLIAMS	15443	WOUNDED
PRIVATE	T. WHITE	16317	WOUNDED
PRIVATE	H. WALTERS	15764	WOUNDED

Private William James Hobson, service number 15532 was born in Llandudno on 26th June 1896 and is one of six children. He had two Sisters Elizabeth & Louisa and three Brothers Anthony, William & Hugh. He attended St. Georges National (mixed) School. He lived with his Father, Joseph who was a Stone Mason and his Mother Ellen and siblings at Tan-y-Craig, Great Orme. On the 1911 census he is 15 and listed as an Errand Boy. He enlisted in Llandudno and entered France on 27th September 1915. He was killed in action, shot through the head, aged 19 but has no known grave. He is remembered on the Menin Gate Memorial, panel 22 & the Llandudno War Memorial.

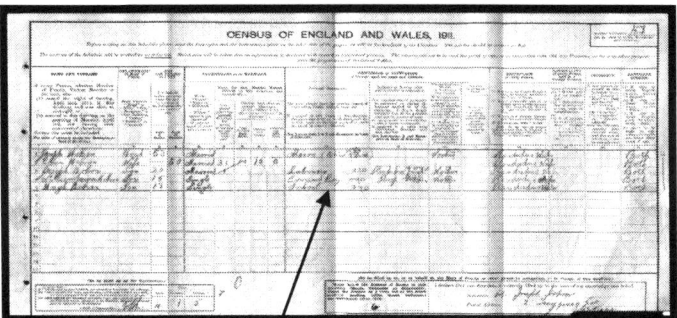

National School Register (4th name on the list)

1911 census showing William as a Grocer's Errand Boy

Llandudno War Memorial

MARCH 31st

Captain D. W. G. Jackson who assumed temporary command of the Battalion yesterday 30th March was wounded and Captain F. A. Samuel assumed temporary command of the Battalion. During the month of March, the Battalion were still holding the enemy trenches captured on 27th of March. It was noted in the Brigade Diary that *"The 10th (Service) Battalion Royal Welsh Fusiliers and the 2nd Suffolk Regiment are not physically capable of doing anything more."* But they held the trench.

APRIL 1916

APRIL 1st

The Battalion repulsed three counter attacks from the enemy in the early morning. The Battalion held it's ground but suffered the following casualties: -

RANK	NAME	SERVICE NO.	WOUND
CAPTAIN	T. HUGHES		KILLED
LANCE CORPORAL	P.C. DANIELS	16242	KILLED
2ND LIEUTENANT	W. SIDDONS		WOUNDED
2ND LIEUTENANT	E. H. BAYLISS		WOUNDED

The Battalion were finally relieved in the advance trenches by 1st Gordon Highlanders. Lieutenant A. J. S. James was appointed Acting Adjutant.

The following Battalion Officers were posted to Companies as follows: -

- 2nd Lieutenant A. W. Fish to take over command of 'C' Coy
- 2nd Lieutenant S. F. Bancroft to take over command of 'D' Coy
- 2nd Lieutenant F. A. Lawson from 'A' Coy to 'D' Coy
- 2nd Lieutenant F. E. Crane from 'C' Coy to 'D' Coy

Lieutenant Albert John Stanley James

Lieutenant James had been with the Battalion since they arrived in France in September 1915 and was originally the **'Transport Officer'** during the battle to retake The Bluff on March 3rd.

Lieutenant James wrote to his friend Percy on 23rd March 1916 offering his condolences to him about his friend Jack who had been killed whilst serving with the Dorsets.

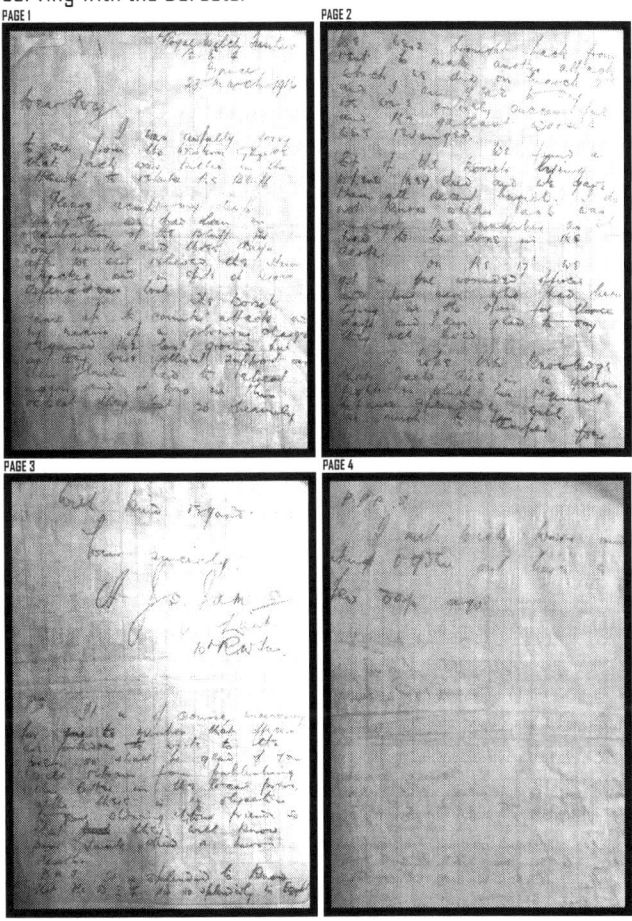

4 Page Letter from Lieutenant James to Percy

PAGE 1

                                        Royal Welch Fusiliers
                                        B.E.F.
                                        France
                                        23 March 1916

Dear Percy

I was awfully sorry to see from the Western Gazette that Jack was killed in the attempt to retake the Bluff.

Please accept my deep sympathy. We had been in occupation of the Bluff for some months and three days after we were relieved the Hun attacked and in spite of heroic defence it was lost.

The Dorsets came up to counter attack and by means of a glorious charge regained the lost ground but as they were without support on their flanks had to retreat again and it was in this retreat they lost so heavily.

PAGE 2

We were brought back from rest to make another attack which we did on March 2nd and I am glad to say we were entirly successful and the gallant Dorsets were revenged. We found a lot of the Dorsets lying where they died and we gave them all decent burial. I do not know wether Jack was amoung the number as it had to be done in the dark.

On the 17th we got in one wounded Officer and four men who had been lying in the open for three days and I am glad to say they all lived.

I hope the knowledge that Jack died in a glorious fight in which his regiment behaved splendidly will do much to comfort your

PAGE 3

grief.
With kind regards
Yours sincerely
A, J, S, James
Lieut.
10th R.W.Fus.

P.S.

It is with course unnessesary for you to mention that Officers are forbidden to write in person, so I shall be glad if you will rerfrain from publishing this letter in the local press altho there is no objection to you showing it to your friends, so that ~~Jack~~ they will know poor Jack died a heroic death.

P. P. S.
If it splendid to know that the D.I.V. did so splendidly in Egypt

PAGE 4

P. P. P. S.
I met Dick Ware and Hugh O'Quine out here a few days ago.

It tells Percy not to take the letter to the Press Office as it is forbidden to write to family and friends telling them where and what happened to their relatives before official news of deaths had been received.

APRIL 2nd

The Battalion marched into rest billets one mile west of Bailleul.

APRIL 4th

The Battalion received a letter from commanding Officer G. R. Crosfield D.S.O. who had been wounded on March 3rd saying: –

"It had been a great pleasure for me to command the 10th Battalion R. W. F. and I was awfully pleased with the spirit they showed in the crater trenches."

APRIL 5th

The Battalion marched into rest billets at Thieushock a distance of 8.5km (5.28 miles) in the vicinity of Caestre. It was noted that the Battalion were in **'good'** billets.

APRIL 6th

Captain A. De. L. Long of the 1st Gordon Highlanders assumed command of the 10th Battalion with the temporary rank of Lieutenant Colonel.

Weather was noted as fine and the Battalion was resting and refitting. Captain A. Bles joined the Battalion and was posted to 'D' Coy and appointed as 'Sniping & Intelligence Officer'. 2nd Lieutenant D. S. Hughes was evacuated sick to England.

The following congratulatory message was issued from the General Officer Commanding (G. O. C.) 3rd Division concerning the action in March:- *"The G. O. C. 3rd Division has observed with satisfaction what a large amount of hard work the 76th Brigade, Pioneer Battalion, 17th Division and Royal Engineers have carried out during the past few days on the left sector of the* *front held by the Division which has just been handed over. Thanks to the ready response which has been made to his appeal. The defences have been restored to an extent exceeding his expectations and the ground has been largely cleared of the debris resulting from the action of 2nd and 3rd March. He congratulates all ranks on their successful efforts as well as those Officers of Engineers and Infantry who organised and superintended the work in question."*

Another message concerning these actions were received from Brigadier General M. Powel Commanding Artillery 3rd Division:-

"The 3rd Division Artillery wish to congratulate the 76th Brigade on their success and to express their admiration for the way 76th Brigade hung on in the trenches under adverse conditions."

The holding action carried out during the actions of March by the 10th Battalion proved vital to the 3rd Division's success in this operation.

APRIL 9th

The following message was received from Brigadier General E. St. G. Pratt D.S.O on relinquishing command of the 76th Brigade due to ill health:-

"In saying goodbye to the Brigade, Brigadier-Gerneral Pratt wishes to thank all ranks for the ready support they have always given him during the recent operations at the Bluff, one and all showed their determination to win this was the keynote to success and when then time comes, will again ensure fresh honors being won by the Brigade."

Brigadier General Pratt also expressed his sincere regret at being unable to personally visit the Battalion and expressed his determination to visit them at the first opportunity he may have.

Brigadier General R. J. Kentish D.S.O. assumed command of 76th Brigade.

APRIL 10th

2nd Lieutenant W. J. D. Hale was appointed 'Transport Officer'. Lieutenant G. O. Scale returned to duty and was appointed 'Officer Commanding' (O.C.) of 'C' Coy. The Machine Gunners and Snipers visited the School of Instruction at Mont Des Cats. 'B' Coy were having baths whilst 'C' Coy were innoculated by the Medical Team. Training for the Battalion continued.

APRIL 11th

Brigadier General R. J. Kentish D.S.O. 76th Brigade visited the Battalion. Owing to heavy rain, the route march planned for today was cancelled.

APRIL 12th

Weather was reported as very bad with heavy rain. Training was disrupted but lectures and inspections of kit etc. were carried out.

APRIL 13th

Weather had improved, training continued. There was a lecture given to the Battalions N. C. O.'s. A conference was held for all the Battalion's Commanding Officers (C. O.) at Brigade Head Quarters.
There was a football match between 'A' Coy and 'B' Coy in the afternoon.

APRIL 14th

Lieutenant W. B. Morgan and 2nd Lieutenant A. B. Capel were evacuated to England.

The Battalion were inspected by Lieutenant Colonel A. De. L. Long Commanding Officer of 10th Battalion.

APRIL 15th

In the morning the Battalion were again inspected by Brigadier General R. J. Kentish D.S.O. The report on the inspection stated – *"Turn out left much to be desired."* In the afternoon there was a football match between the 10th (Service) Battalion Royal Welsh Fusiliers and the 1st Gordon Highlanders for the '**Brigade Cup**'. The 10th Battalion were the winners.

APRIL 18th

The Battalion received orders to march to La Clytte via Bailleul to help with the digging of the trenches on the Vierstraat Switch, under the command of 56th Coy Royal Engineers. The Battalion stayed under tents that night.

APRIL 19th

During the day the Battalion visited Reningelst Cinema where special programmes of entertainment had been arranged. The Battalion again worked on the trenches during the cover of darkness.

Reningelst was a small village behind the lines of the Ypres-Salient. It was a frequent base for soldiers between stints in the trenches. It was away from the direct threats of the Front-Line, about 5km but close enough to quickly return to the Front-Line if needed. Concerts and cinemas were provided by the Y. M. C. A. to entertain the troops.

APRIL 20th

The Battalion, after finishing their fatigue work, marched back to billets at Thieushouk under the command of the Adjutant. The Battalion's Commanding Officer, Company Commanders and Company Sergeant Majors visited the new line of trenches that the Battalion had been working on at Vierstraat Switch.

APRIL 21st - Good Friday

The Battalion were given a days holiday from duties by Brigadier General R. J. Kentish Commanding Officer of the 76th Brigade. In the afternoon, the Battalion's football team drew 0-0 against the team from the 3rd Division.

APRIL 22nd

Brigadier General R. J. Kentish Commanding Officer of the 76th Brigade visited the Battalion and spoke about leadership and the importance of inspections of the Battalion. There was also a 'Trench Mortar Demonstration' held at Berthen at which the Battalion's 'Trench Mortar Teams' attended.

Lieutenant V. H. Parry reported for duty and was posted to 'B' Coy.

APRIL 23rd – Easter Sunday

Church Parade was held in the morning and the Battalion received the following message: –

"The Commander in Chief has awarded 2nd Lieutenant A. Nevitt 'The Military Cross'. Please convey to Lieutenant Nevitt, the Brigadier's and the Brigade's staff's hearty congratulations."

These congratulations, together with those of the Battalion were immediately wired to 2nd Lieutenant Nevitt, who was being treated for his wounds received on 30th March, in a hospital bed in London.

*(To read more about 2nd Lieutenant Nevitt's award – see chapter 9 in this book)

The following Officers from the 12th Reserve Battalion Royal Welsh Fusiliers joined the Battalion for duty:-

- 2nd Lieutenant W. Macaulay to 'A' Coy
- 2nd Lieutenant L. P. Vernon to 'C' Coy
- 2nd Lieutenant S. G. Shute to 'B' Coy
- 2nd Lieutenant D. T. Williams to 'D' Coy
- 2nd Lieutenant E. W. Edwards appointed Assistant Machine Gun Officer
- 2nd Lieutenant H. Page to 'D' Coy (from Inniskilling Dragoons)

APRIL 24th

A representative detachment of 50 other ranks (O. R.) under the command of Captain C. A. R. Follit marched to Fletre to attend a Ceremonial Parade for the presentation of **'The Ribbon of the Victoria Cross'** to **Captain the Reverend Edward Noel Mellish**, the Royal Army Chaplain's Department, attached to the Royal Fusiliers. Captain Mellish was awarded the Victoria Cross for showing conspicuous bravery during heavy fighting. He moved between trenches at St. Eloi for over 3 days, tending to and rescuing the wounded from the battle, despite being swept by heavy machine gun fire.

Captain the Reverend Edward Noel Mellish

In the afternoon the Battalion took part in the **'Cross Country Race'** which the 2nd Battalion Suffolk Regiment won, the 1st Gordon Highlanders came second and the Machine Gun Company finished third.

In the evening a **'Brigade Concert and Boxing Tournament'** was held at Eccke. Lance Corporal Michael Driscoll, service number 15312 won the **'Lightweight Boxing Competition.'**

Private Griffiths was beaten in the semi-final of the heavyweight competition. The Battalion also contributed four very successful songs at the concert.

Michael Driscoll, service number 15312 won the 'Lightweight Boxing Competition.'

The Battalion received the following communication from Brigadier General R. J. Kentish D.S.O. C.O.C. 76th Brigade: –

"The Brigadier wishes to inform all ranks of the 10th Battalion R. W. F. that he considers that the turnout and appearance of the men on parade, on the occasion of his inspection on April 22nd was, in view of what the Battalion had been through recently, highly creditable to all concerned. There are certain matters that need attention and these have been brought to the notice of the Commanding Officer, Lieutenant Colonel Long. When these have been attended to, the Brigadier is confident that the Battalion will rival in smartness and soldierly training the parent Battalions of the Distinguished Regiments of which the 10th Battalion forms part.

The Brigadier being a Fusilier himself, is very proud and appreciaites to the full, the privilege he enjoys in having a Battalion, of one of the oldest and original Fusilier Regiments of the British Army, under him."

APRIL 25th

At 9am the General Officer Commanding (G. O. C.) gave a lecture to the Battalion on '**Drill & the importance of it**'.

At 5pm there was a lecture by General Powell to all Officers and N. C. O.'s on '**Artillery Co-operation**'.

The final of the Brigades football competition was also held today. The 1st Gordon Highlanders beat the 8th Kings Own Royal Lancaster Regiment.

APRIL 27th

The Battalion marched to Kemmel Shelters under Captain Bles and took over from the 4th Battalion East Yorkshire Regiment in Brigade reserve.

The C.O. and Adjutant were at a conference at Brigade Head Quarters.

APRIL 28th

The Battalion moved up into the trenches and took over Trenches 'E1 to E5' from 5th Battalion Yorkshire Regiment. Two platoons of 'B' Coy and 'D' Coy were attached to 'A' and 'C' Coys in the Front-Line Trench with the remainder of the Battalion in the Regent Street Dugouts.

2nd Lieutenant L. G. Godfrey joined the Battalion for duty from the 1st Bedford Regiment and was posted to 'C' Coy.

APRIL 29th

76th Brigade Head Quarters were shelled by the enemy artillery at 9.50am. **2nd Lieutenant Crane** and **Sergeant J. A. Jones**, service number 14906 from the Battalion, who were attending a **'Bayonet Training Course'** were wounded.

At 9.30pm two Polish Deserters came over from the enemy trench and gave themselves up to the Coy occupying **'E5'** Trench. Captain Scale interrogated the prisoners and learnt from them, that a **'Gas Attack'** followed by an **'Infantry Attack'** at 1am was to be undertaken. The prisoners were then taken to the Brigade Head Quarters, which had moved to Locke, and further interrogated and the information about the impending attack was confirmed. All Coys in the Battalion were warned, including, the 1st Gordon Highlanders on the left of the Battalion and the North Staffords on the right of the Battalion, the Machine Gun Section in SP 8 and SP 9 and in Forts Victoria, Edward and Dupree. Also all trench mortar batteries and all other batteries covering the Battalion's front, were on alert. All necessary precautions were taken.

Vermorel Sprayers were filled, this was used to neutralise trenches and dugouts which had been contaminated with chlorine gas, a mixture of chemicals that included sodium hyposulphite, a chemical used in photographic processing.

The men had their gas helmets rolled up on their heads ready to use, two bombs were issued to every man, rifle bolts and Lewis gun actions were greased and extra ammunition was issued.

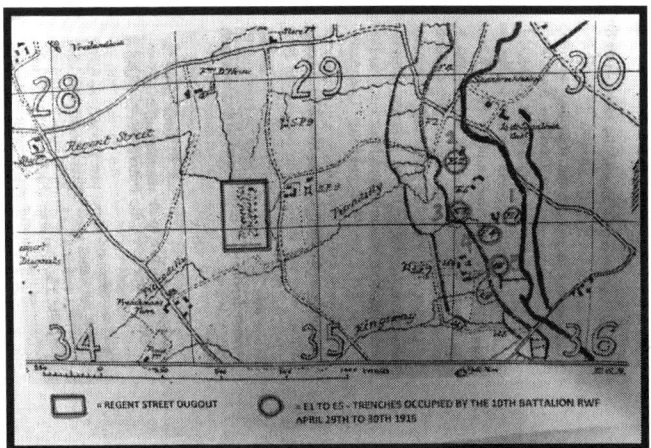

Map showing Regent Street Dugout & Trenches 1 to 5

APRIL 30th

The **'Gas Helmet'** that my Taid Edwin, and the other men in the Battalion would have used, would have been the **'PH Helmet'**. This helmet replaced the **'P Helmet'** in October 1915 and added **'Hexamethylene Tetramine'** to the **'Sodium Penolate & Glycern'** in which the flannel layers of the cloth helmet was dipped in. The PH Helmet had a rubber exhale valve fed from a metal tube which the wearer held in his mouth. The exhale valve was needed because a double layer flannel, one treated or not, was needed because the solution attacked the fabric.

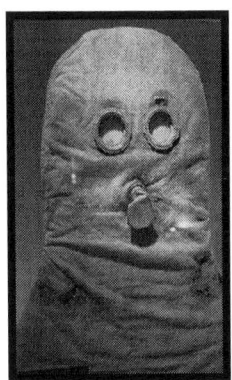
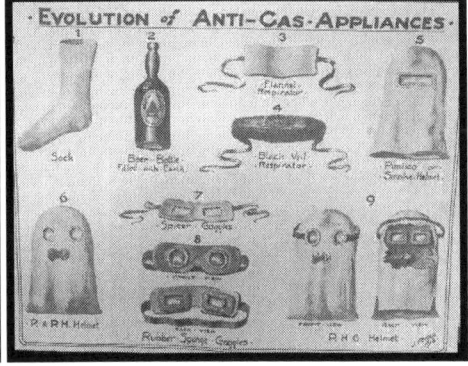

At 12.40am during the early morning of the 30th April, gas was heard hissing from the cylindars in the German trench opposite the Battalions Front-Line and a **'Gas Cloud'** was seen to be approaching the Front-Line Trenches. The **'Gas Alarms'** were immediately sounded. The gas was the thickest opposite trenches **'E1 & E2'** where the enemys trench was only 35 yards away. At this point, some of the men of the Battalion were gassed due to being unable to get **'Their Gas Helmets On and Adjusted Correctly.'**

The enemy had trouble leaving their own trenches due to the rapid fire coming from the Battalions positions. The enemy attacked in **'Three Parties'** between Trench **'E1 & E4'** and some of the enemy succeeded in entering the Battalions **'E3'** Trenches through a gap on the right, but they were soon forced to retreat, when they were met by a platoon of bombers under Lieutenant H. V. Piercy, who forced them back. The supporting platoon moved up from the Regent Street Dugouts under the command of Captain E. W. Bell and Captain Follit.

By 1.20am the gas had cleared and the situation was under control.

The gas came over in two waves. Regent Street Dugout, Piccadilly and Pall Mall Trenches were heavily shelled. The Brigadier General R. J. Kentish, 76th Brigade at Kemmel Shelter was in constant communication with the 10th Battalion during the attack.

Due to the casualties the 10th Battalion received in this attack, 2nd Suffolk Regiment were moved up to support them by reinforcing the Regent Street Dugouts and the Garrison General Head Quarters (G. G. H. Q.), just in case the enemy renewed their attack.

By 3.30am all was quiet along the Front-Line and when dawn broke, some enemy dead were seen near their own parapet. Two wounded prisoners were brought into the Battalions trench, for identification purposes, as it was important to know what enemy Battalion carried out the attack, by Captain Follitt and Lieutenant Piercy and O. L. Jones. The efficient fire of the Brigades artillery had prevented the enemy coming over in any large numbers. The enemys communication trenches had been shelled by the Brigade guns. The rest of the day remained quiet and this gave the Battalion time to rest and reorganise where necessary.

In the evening, at about 10pm, another **'Gas Alarm'** was sounded, but proved to be a **'False Alarm'** due to the clouds of smoke from bursting shells and trench mortar bombs being mistaken for gas. It was noted how extremely difficult it was to know if it was gas that was present or not when wearing their gas helmets.

In order to shorten the Battalions line, Trench **'F5'** was taken over by the 1st Gordon Highlanders. The Battalion suffered the following casualties during the enemy attack on 30th April:-

RANK	NAME	SERVICE NO.	WOUND
SERGEANT	H. HOLLINS	19121	KILLED
PRIVATE	J. FISHER	27397	KILLED
PRIVATE	C. SHEPLEY	36266	KILLED
PRIVATE	J. T. HARRIS	11943	KILLED
PRIVATE	F. HORTON	36238	KILLED

RANK	NAME	SERVICE NO.	WOUND
PRIVATE	F. SIGLEY	23189	KILLED BY GAS
LANCE CORPORAL	H. DUDLEY	23191	KILLED BY GAS
PRIVATE	M. HESTER	15447	KILLED BY GAS

RANK	NAME	SERVICE NO.	WOUND
CORPORAL	D. H. SIMMS	14190	DIED BY GAS
PRIVATE	J. HUGHES	15036	DIED BY GAS
PRIVATE	W. P. MACDONALD	14166	DIED BY GAS
PRIVATE	J. JONES	5031	DIED BY GAS
PRIVATE	A. MELIA	15329	DIED BY GAS
PRIVATE	J. E. GOODWIN	15141	DIED BY GAS
LANCE CORPORAL	G. H. WILLIAMS	15403	DIED BY GAS

RANK	NAME	SERVICE NO.	WOUND
PRIVATE	T. PENNY	15157	DIED OF WOUNDS
PRIVATE	D. MICHAEL	15273	DIED OF WOUNDS (PRISONER OF WAR)

RANK	NAME	SERVICE NO.	WOUND
2ND LIEUTENANT	E. VAUGHAN-JONES		WOUNDED
SERGEANT	J. A. JONES	14906	WOUNDED
PRIVATE	B. WILLIAMS	15050	WOUNDED
PRIVATE	G. SANDERS	15015	WOUNDED
PRIVATE	T. E. EDWARDS	13808	WOUNDED
PRIVATE	LL. JONES	15214	WOUNDED
PRIVATE	D. H. EVANS	33456	WOUNDED
PRIVATE	T. CUFFE	4643	WOUNDED
PRIVATE	J. D. EVANS	15710	WOUNDED
PRIVATE	E. J. EVANS	15693	WOUNDED
PRIVATE	E. REES	15048	WOUNDED
PRIVATE	E. MALONEY	15654	WOUNDED
PRIVATE	E. JONES	15389	WOUNDED
PRIVATE	W. MIDDLETON	24238	WOUNDED
2ND LIEUTENANT	F. E. CRANE		WOUNDED
PRIVATE	J. ROBERTS	14967	WOUNDED
PRIVATE	S. F. DAVIES	23320	WOUNDED
PRIVATE	J. BASSETT	15020	WOUNDED
PRIVATE	S. GROSVENOR	24675	WOUNDED
PRIVATE	R. B. OWEN	5906	WOUNDED
PRIVATE	C. E. EVANS	36320	WOUNDED
PRIVATE	T. OWEN	16285	WOUNDED
PRIVATE	T. PRICE	6610	WOUNDED
PRIVATE	E. GRIFFITHS	16279	WOUNDED
LANCE CORPORAL	F. H. BOWKER	15285	WOUNDED
PRIVATE	W. H. PETERS	15108	WOUNDED
PRIVATE	H. REES	15515	WOUNDED

RANK	NAME	SERVICE NO.	WOUND
CAPTAIN	E. W. BELL		FROM GAS POISON
PRIVATE	T. WILLIAMS	12679	FROM GAS POISON
PRIVATE	A. E. LEWIS	15408	FROM GAS POISON
PRIVATE	T. H. SMITH	15013	FROM GAS POISON
PRIVATE	E. HARRIS	15528	FROM GAS POISON
PRIVATE	H. JONES	14658	FROM GAS POISON
LANCE CORPORAL	W. KNOTT	15281	FROM GAS POISON
PRIVATE	G. W. BIRCHALL	24779	FROM GAS POISON
PRIVATE	L. BOWEN	23442	FROM GAS POISON
PRIVATE	T. HAWKER	7841	FROM GAS POISON
PRIVATE	W. ROBERTS	16282	FROM GAS POISON
PRIVATE	T. CROMPTON	8455	FROM GAS POISON
PRIVATE	W. HART	6620	FROM GAS POISON
PRIVATE	G. EVANS	15792	FROM GAS POISON
PRIVATE	L. PEARSON	23265	FROM GAS POISON
PRIVATE	O. PARRY	15102	FROM GAS POISON
PRIVATE	C. WILLIAMS	14666	FROM GAS POISON
PRIVATE	P. S. TUCKER	5290	FROM GAS POISON
PRIVATE	H. J. ROBERTS	15477	FROM GAS POISON
2ND LIEUTENANT	E. W. EDWARDS		FROM GAS POISON

RANK	NAME	SERVICE NO.	WOUND
SERGEANT	A. SPROSTON	23059	FROM GAS POISON
PRIVATE	P. KYNASTON	24915	FROM GAS POISON
PRIVATE	C. H. TAYLOR	23222	FROM GAS POISON
PRIVATE	D. E. JONES	23171	FROM GAS POISON
PRIVATE	R. ROBERTS	15321	FROM GAS POISON
PRIVATE	R. ROBERTS	15165	FROM GAS POISON
PRIVATE	G. KENNEDY	14910	FROM GAS POISON
PRIVATE	L. DAVIES	15607	FROM GAS POISON
PRIVATE	B. WILLIAMS	15484	FROM GAS POISON
PRIVATE	G. COUDE	14904	FROM GAS POISON
PRIVATE	W. OWEN	15136	FROM GAS POISON
PRIVATE	E. W. BERRY	36552	FROM GAS POISON
PRIVATE	C. SMITH	23427	FROM GAS POISON
PRIVATE	J. STOTT	15592	FROM GAS POISON
PRIVATE	L. N. WISEBECK	23491	FROM GAS POISON
PRIVATE	G. SPENCER	23442	FROM GAS POISON
CORPORAL	A. W. JONES	31841	FROM GAS POISON
PRIVATE	E. C. JONES	31759	FROM GAS POISON

This was not only the first gas attack that my Taid Edwin and the Battalion faced but was the first gas attack that the 3rd Division had encountered.

MAY 1st

It was a very quiet day for the Battalion in the Front-Line. The Battalion received the following messages in reference to the actions of 29th & 30th April: -

"The Brig. wishes to convey to you, to convey to your Battalion, his keen appreciation of the soldierly qualities displayed by all ranks under your command during the action which commenced at 12.45am this morning and finished at 3am. The enemy attempted to penetrate our lines, but failed miserably: their failure must be attributed to the splendid fighting spirit of the 10th Battalion Royal Welsh Fusiliers, The Corps Commander personally visited the Brigade today and expressed his admiration of the conduct of your Battalion. The Brig. is confident that, so long as this spirit exists, the 10th Battalion R. W. F. will continue to add to it's already splendid fighting reputation." - Brig.-General R. J. Kentish D. S. O. 76th Brigade

The Army Commander has just visited Brigade Head Quarters for the express purpose of expressing his satisfaction with the conduct of all ranks of your Battalion on the night of 29th & 30th April. He considers the men withstood their first experience of gas in a manner which was highly creditable to them and he wishes to make known to them his admiration of his conduct.

The Major General commanding, notes with satisfaction, that owing to the careful manner in which the instructions regarding measures to be taken in case of gas attacks were attended to, and also the good discipline of the 10th Battalion Royal Welsh Fusiliers, which was subjected to gas fumes in the early morning of the 30th April.

The casualties suffered were comparitively few. As he frequently pointed out, there is little to fear when the enemy attempts to surprise us in this manner, provided the proper precautions are taken; and that this, was proved, by the 10th Battalion Royal Welsh Fusiliers. The first troops of the Division who have been subjected to a gas attack.

MAY 2nd

Weather was very wet but hot. The Battalion continued to work repairing and building up the parados and parapet in E1 Trench. Also 'Wiring Parties' continued to replace wire lost or damaged during the attack. Work was also started on building the new H. Q. in F2 Trench. The Battalion were having to **'Stand-To'** every night still wearing their gas helmets rolled up on their heads because there was danger of another gas attack as the wind was still in a North-Easterly direction.

MAY 3rd

The enemy artillery fired a few 4.1 shells into the Battalions trenches. No casualties were received and only slight damage was done to a parapet. In the evening, the Battalion was relieved in the Front-Line Trenches by the 2nd Suffolk Regiment and marched back to rest camp.

MAY 4th

The Battalion were resting in the morning. Breakfast was at 10am. Afterward the Battalion were cleaning up and an inspection was carried out on their rifles. A draft of 1 N. C. O. and 16 other ranks (O. R.) joined the Battalion and were inspected by the Commanding Officer. In the afternoon, the Battalion marched down to Lecre for a lecture by Brigadier on **"Esprit De Corps"**. The Brigadier congratulated the Battalion on their appearance.

MAY 5th

A draft of 2 N. C. O.'s and 11 other ranks (O. R.) joined the Battalion and were inspected by the Commanding Officer. New clothing was issued, a rifle inspection was carried out by an Armourer and there was also a 'Gas Helmet Drill'. 'Working Parties' of 5 Officers and 130 other ranks (O. R.) carried out duties in the evening.

MAY 6th

There was a demonstration to the Battalion of 'Guard & Saluting Duties'.

There was a presentation of the **'White Cards'** issued by the General Officer Commanding of the 3rd Division to **Corporal H. Hussey**, service number 24891 and **Private J. Lloyd**, service number 15514 in recognition of their conspicuous gallantry in action. The 'White Cards' (other colours were used depending on the choice of the Division) were used to acknowledge the bravery of a soldier in action against the enemy. Sometimes, this could prelude an award of a medal.

A large calibre-shell fired by the enemy landed within 10 yards of the Battalion Head Quarters. No casualties were reported.

MAY 7th

The Coys of the Battalion took it in turns to have baths and a change of clothes. A gas demonstration in the afternoon was cancelled due to the wet and windy weather. A 'Working Party' of 5 Officers and 150 other ranks (O. R.) carried out duties in the evening.

MAY 8th

The billets were inspected by the Commanding Officer (C. O.) of the Battalion. A football match was played in the afternoon against the 1st Gordon Highlanders. The Battalion were beaten 3-0. Work continued in the evening with 2 Officers and 30 other ranks (O. R.). Captain F. A. Samuel returned to the Battalion from hospital.

MAY 9th

There was a **'Kit Inspection'** held in the morning. A lecture was given at Locre by the Brigadier to all Officers and N. C. O.'s. A message was received from the Army & Corps Commander: -

"The Army Commander has gone carefully into the reports furnished in connection with the recent gas attack on the Front-Line of the 3rd and 24th Divisions, and he wishes Commanders of Formations to convey to the units who were engaged in that area, his appreciaition of the steadiness and courage displayed by all ranks, whereby, the enemy failed to gain any advance from gas emmision. The Corp Commander also wishes to express his appreciaition of the high soldierly qualities shown by all ranks under very trying circumstances."

Captain F. A. Samuel was appointed Second in Command of the Battalion with the rank of Temporary-Major. Captain Black was appointed Officer Commanding (O. C.) of 'D' Coy.

MAY 10th

A demonstration of **'Wire Entanglements'** was given to Officers and N. C. O.'s then the Coys were given time to practice these methods. A lecture was given in the afternoon by the Commanding Officer (C. O.) on **'Trench Orders'**.

MAY 11th & 12th

Training for the Battalion continued in the afternoon of the 12th. The following rewards for gallantry during the actions of 30th April were announced: -

- Captain C. A. R. Follitt – Military Cross (M. C.)
- Private J. Lloyd 15514 – Distinguished Conduct Medal (D. C. M.)
- Acting Company Sergeant Major E. Roberts – Military Medal (M. M.)
- Lance Corporal A. E. Polin – Military Medal (M. M.)

MAY 13th

The Battalion marched out of camp at Kemmel Shelters and moved into trenches, relieveing the 2nd Suffolk Regiment in the right sector. A draft of 106 other ranks (O. R.) joined the Battalion.

Private George John Culpitt service number 35115

One of the O. R.'s that joined 'A' Coy on this day was *Private George John Culpitt, service number 35115*. The hand written Diary started when Private George Culpitt volunteered for the Royal Welsh Fusiliers in 1915. He joined because he had a Welsh friend who was joining up at the same time.

Private George Culpitt, after training at Kimnel Park in North Wales, left for France on April 27th 1916 to continue training, later joining the 10th (Service) Battalion Royal Welsh Fusiliers in May 1916.

*Some of his diary entries will be used during the continuing story of the Battalion.

"After breakfast and a wash in a neighbouring ditch, we fell in for a few words from the C. O. and to be allocated Companies, and I found myself in 'A' Company together with 7 other chaps who had left Kimnel Park with me. In a short address, the C. O. (Temporary Lieut-Col A. De. L. Long) informed us that they had had a rough time in a gas attack which the Germans had made on them at the end of April. We were dismissed and told to be ready to move up the line that evening."

At 6 o'clock, we fell in, we were told we were going to the reserve line. We moved off and entered the C. T. (communication trench) which, after we had travelled for about half an hour, suddenly opened out to a wide space in front of which could be seen piles of sand bags which denoted the trench, this was the second or reserve line and contained a number of dugouts or shelters in which were company head quarters, the dressing station and such like. We were then taken into the trench proper and given our positions in the trench and shown various shelters where we could sleep and put kit on.
I found myself with two men of the original Battalion and from this gained a certain amount of moral courage from the fact that one felt they could be relied on in an emergency." – Private George Culpitt, 35115 10th (Service) Battalion Royal Welsh Fusiliers

Private George Culpitt was obviously relieved he was with two experienced men for his first time in the Front-Line Trench. Experienced soldiers were so important to the newcomers to the Battalion.

MAY 14th

The enemy bombarded the Battalions trenches with trench mortars. The Battalion received the following casualties: -

RANK	NAME	SERVICE NO.	WOUND
PRIVATE	E. PRITCHARD 'B' COY	14930	KILLED
PRIVATE	I. WILLIAMS 'B' COY	11228	WOUNDED
PRIVATE	R. JONES 'B' COY	11932	WOUNDED
PRIVATE	W. LEVER 'B' COY	15170	FROM GAS POISON

MAY 15TH

A very quiet day in the trenches. The enemy artillery had been more active over the past few days without causing too much damage. 1 casualty wounded was **Private A. Liggins**, service number 23327.

MAY 16th

The Battalions Head Quarters were moved to the Regent Street dugouts. An enemy aeroplane dropped four bombs in Locre, causing very little damage. The following Officers joined the Battalion for duty:-

- 2nd Lieutenant W. C. Wells to 'D' Coy
- 2nd Lieutenant W. A. Cowie to 'C' Coy
- 2nd Lieutenant J. E. Hughes to 'B' Coy

Nine cadets were attached to the Battalion from General Head Quarters (G. H. Q.) for instruction in 'Trench Duties'. 1 casualty who died of wounds was **Private T. Bridges**, service number 6323.

Stand-To, Stand-Down

As the favourite and favourable time for attacks by the enemy is in the hours of **'Dusk & Dawn'**. All along the line, the men fixed bayonets and mounted the fire step, keeping a weary eye on the enemys line in case of said attack. If it is a quiet part of the line, **'Stand-To'** is only for an hour, morning or evening, but, if it is a lively part of the line, and an enemy attack is imminent, **'Stand-To'** could last all night. If it is only a short **'Stand-To'**, then Sentries are posted and are changed every hour. Sentries are always posted during the day, with the use of periscopes to view 'No Mans Land' and the 'German Trenches' as generally it is too dangerous to 'Put Ones Head Over The Top' of the trench in daylight.

"Personally I always found the morning 'Stand-To' very trying until one got used to it. After a night's work, this hour always came as a hardship, for one was always so very tired, that very often, one fell asleep as one stood. To be rudely awakened by one's knees giving way, or by feeling one's rifle slipping out of one's hand" – Private George Culpitt, 35115 10th (Service) Battalion Royal Welsh Fusiliers

Private George Culpitt was very lucky he wasn't seen by an Officer or N. C. O. If a soldier was seen to be asleep on duty, serious charges would have been brought against him.

Upon orders to **'Stand-Down'** it was customary while in the trenches to issue some 'Tea & Rum' or sometimes 'Cocoa'. After this, it was best to try and get to sleep again until breakfast time, some two hours later. Breakfast, nearly every morning, consisted of bacon, bread and sometimes butter or margarine.

MAY 17th

The enemy bombarded Trench 'F2' with trench mortars and the enemy artillery shelled the Pall Mall and Wind Street Trenches. A "Gas Alarm" sounded late that night, but proved to be a false alarm.

Private George Culpitt, 35115, wrote in his Diary –

"While we were waiting about in the trench, word came down to get our gas helmets ready as the wind was in Fritz's favour and it was thought likely that he might repeat his attempt of two or three weeks ago and try and gas us. Soon after we heard the gas gongs going further along the line to the right, and of course, at once, got our helmets on and awaited the attack, we thought would inevitably follow. It certainly was a lively first night in the Front-Line, but after wearing our helmets for about 15 minutes, we got orders, to our great relief, to take our helmets off as no gas appeared to be coming over, and it transpired, later, a Battalion further along the line had got the wind up and sounded the alarm for no reason at all." - Private George Culpitt, 35115 10th (Service) Battalion Royal Welsh Fusiliers

MAY 18th

Captain J. A. B. Spencer joined the Battalion for duty. A quiet day in the trenches. 1 Casualty wounded was **Lance Corporal Toohey**, service number 5373.

MAY 19th

The enemy bombarded Trench 'F2', Pall Mall and Piccadilly with trench mortars. The Brigades artillery retaliated and silenced the enemy for the rest of the day.

MAY 20th

The Battalion was relieved in the trenches by the 2nd Suffolk Regiment and marched into billets in the Divisional Reserve at Locre. Captain E. W. Bell returned to the Battalion and was posted to 'C' Coy.

MAY 22nd

The following messages were received by the Battalion: -

"We are all very proud of the splendid record of the 10th Battalion, which has, in every way, maintained the great record of the Regiment, your Division Commander, a little time ago, told me the 10th Battalion had done splendidly at the 'Bluff'. All good wishes from us all, and may the two Battalions meet soon." - Officer Commanding (O. C.) 1st Battalion R. W. F.

"The second Battalion are proud and gratified to know that the 10th Battalion are so worthily upholding the traditions of the Royal Welsh Fusiliers." - Officer Commanding (O. C.) 2nd Battalion R. W. F.

"All ranks of the 12th Battalion send hearty congratulations to all ranks of the 10th Battalion on their recent success at the Front." - Officer Commanding (O.C.) 12th (Reserve) Battalion R. W. F.

MAY 23rd

A lecture was held by the Brigadier General of the 76th Brigade on the attack on the Battalions Front-Line Trenches. A draft of 10 other ranks (O. R.) joined the Battalion for duty.

MAY 26th

The Battalion were relieved by the 4th East Yorks Regiment and marched from Locre to V Corps rest area near Fletre, a distance of 12.4km (7 ½ miles).

MAY 27th

A draft of 100 other ranks (O. R.) joined the Battalion from 1st Garrison Battalion R. W. F. based at Gibraltar.

MAY 29th
A draft of 10 other ranks (O. R.) joined the Battalion for duty.

MAY 31st
A lecture was given to Officers of the Battalion on 'Guard Mounting Duties'. Transfers were made; Captain Blake to 'B' Coy as Commander, Captain Bell to 'D' Coy as Commander, Captain Follitt to 'A' Coy as Temp. Commander and Captain Spencer attached to 'B' Coy.

JUNE 1916

JUNE 1st
A lecture by the Brigadier on **'Esprit De Brigade'** and also a demonstration of **'Drill & Saluting'**. The afternoon saw further training in **'Bayonet Fighting & Bomb Throwing'**. Lieutenant Piercy was transferred to 'D' Coy.

JUNE 3rd
To celebrate the King's Birthday, a Ceremonial March Past Parade was held.

JUNE 4th
Captain A. De. L. Long to be promoted to Brevet Major.

JUNE 5th
The Battalion marched to billets between Meteren and Bailleul a distance of 7.1km (4 ½ miles) and took over from the 13th Battalion Kings Liverpool Regiment. Lieutenant J. W. Blackstone (Welsh Yeomanry T. F.) joined the Battalion for duty and took over the roll as 'Transport Officer'.

JUNE 6th & 7th
Training continued for the Battalion during these two days in Gas Helmet Training, Kit Inspections, Order Drills and there was a lecture to the new drafts by Medical Officer Captain Grellier on 'Gas & the Effects it has on soldiers'. There was also a lecture on 'German Atrocities and Trench Warfare' by Major Long, Company Commander (C. O.).

JUNE 8th

The following messages were published in General Orders by Command of His Majesty the King: -

"The King has learnt, with profound regret, of the disaster which the Secretary of State for War has lost his life while proceeding on a special Mission to the Emperor of Russia.

Field-Marshall Lord Kitchener gave 45 years of distinguished service to the State, and it is largely due to his administrative genius and unswerving energy that the country has been able to create, and place in the Field, the Armies which are to-day upholding the traditional glories of our Empire. Lord Kitchener will be mourned by the Army as a great soldier, who under conditions of unexampled difficulty, rendered supreme and devoted service both to the Army and the State."

Lord Kitchener had devoted personal attention to the deteriorating situation on the Eastern-Front and it was suggested by the Chancellor of the Exchequer; Reginald McKenna, that Kitchener, head to a special and confidential mission to Russia to discuss munition shortages and Military strategy and also the financial difficulties the Imperial Russian Government was having at the time. The Tsar formally invited Lord Kitchener to sail to Archangel with a knowledgeable party to discuss these matters on the 27th May 1916. On 2nd June, Lord Kitchener met the King heading to Scapa Flow Scotland, for the sailing to Archangel on 5th June. He sailed from Thurso on H. M. S. Oak and had lunch with Admiral Sir John Jellico Commander in Chief of the Grand Fleet, on board H. M. S. Iron Duke, later transferring to H. M. S. Hampshire (an armoured cruiser). The sea was very rough and shortly before 7.30pm, H. M. S. Hampshire struck a German mine and sank within minutes. Out of the 600 crew, only 12 survived. Lord Kitchener went down with the ship and his body was never found.

H. M. S. Hampshire

JUNE 9th

There was a demonstration of attack from Fletre to Metern by the Commanding Officer to the Officers and N. C. O.'s. The following promotions were Gazetted:-

- Temporary Lieutenant G. D. Scale to Temporary Captain
- Temporary Lieutenant C. A. R. Follitt to Temporary Captain
- Temporary Lieutenant A. J. S. James to Temporary Captain
- Temporary Captain A. J. S. James to be Adjutant

Private George Culpitt, 35115 wrote in his Diary:-

"There were numerous shops and estaminets in Meteren at which eggs, chips, bread & butter and coffee could be obtained quite cheaply. The Divisional cinema was also stationed in the village and of course, always had a full house. At the time Charlie Chaplin films were the favourite." - Private George Culpitt, 35115 10th (Service) Battalion Royal Welsh Fusiliers

Charlie Chaplin films were always popular with the troops. The appearance of a cut out figure of Charlie with the slogan *'He's Here!'* at the entrance to the cinema, was enough to fill the seats.

There is a story about a detachment of the Highland Light Infantry on the eve of their departure back to the Front, that they pinched one of the Charlie Chaplin cut-outs and carried it with them to the trenches and stood the life-size cut-out on the parapet so the Germans, after seeing Charlie, would *'die laughing!'*

The Battalion were also allowed into the town of Bailleul where there was a Y. M. C. A. cinema where Private George Culpitt enjoyed a concert given by Miss Lena Ashwell's Party.

Miss Lena Ashwell's concert parties toured the Western Front in groups of 6 or 7, to entertain the troops. Miss Ashwell was a well known actress and a worker for 'Womens Rights'. She had enlisted the help of Princess Helena Victoria to set up organised entertainment for the troops. The concert parties consisted of a Soprano, Contralto, Tenor and Base as well as an instrumentalists and an entertainer.

Miss Lena Ashwell   A Poster depicting Miss Lena Ashwell singing to the troops

> **The Powers of Music.**
>
> "Once when a concert was about to begin in a hut crowded with men (they will wait for hours for the 'sing-song,' as they call it), the presiding Colonel announced that there were men outside who were going up to the trenches that night, and he asked that room inside the hut should be made for them. Without a word the entire audience filed out and let the other men in. One lad wrote to me that 'It just made all the difference going into the firing line with that music stirring one's heart.'

Miss Lena Ashwell's Newspaper Article

It was so important for the morale of the men serving on the Front-Line, or lying in a hospital bed, wounded, for the concerts like Lena's to take the men away from all the death and destruction they had seen, and give them a chance to sing and laugh and enjoy themselves for a little while until they had to return to the Front.

"We gave two concerts last night at 5pm and 7pm. I do wish you had been here to have seen the very evident intense enjoyment of the Men." – Frederick Hudson – a member of the concert party

"Our Party came in and sang softly to the men as they were having their wounds dressed, and how great a difference it made to these poor suffering heroes, it could not have been easy for the singers to keep cheerful amid such a gruesome audience." - Lena Ashwell

JUNE 11th

The Battalion in Brigade marched into billets at Hardifort near Cassel a distance of 21.5km (13 ½ miles). This was the start of three days of marching to reach the Divisional Training Ground, where the Battalion would undergo training for the Somme Offensive.

Private George Culpitt, 35115, wrote in his Diary: -

The first day we did about 20 miles, halting for dinner on a field and reached our billets about 5pm. On our way, we had to pass through the town of Cassel which stood all on it's own on the top of a large hill, and from the highest point, looking down on the winding road, it was a fine sight to see the different Battalions stretched out at intervals." - Private George Culpitt, 35115 10th (Service) Battalion Royal Welsh Fusiliers

JUNE 12th

The Battalion marched into billets in the area of Lederzeele a distance of 14.4km (9 miles). The Officers Commanding the Battalion and 1st Gordon Highlanders were taken by the Brigade Commanding Officer to see a practice attack by the Guards Brigade.

JUNE 13th

The Battalion in Brigade marched into billets in the Divisional Training Area at Eperleques at a distance of 13.3km (8 ½ miles).

JUNE 14th

A draft of 14 other ranks (O. R.) and 2nd Lieutenant Williams joined the Battalion for duty and was posted to 'A' Company. Demonstrations of attack to Officers and N. C. O.'s was given and in the afternoon 'Musketry Training' was carried out.

JUNE 15th

A draft of 26 other ranks (O. R.) joined the Battalion for duty. Time was spent practicing the attack of a 'Flagged Course'.

JUNE 16th TO 21st

The Battalion were continuing training and preparing for the **'Big Push'**, working closely with the rest of the Battalions in the Brigade.

JUNE 21st

- **Company Sergeant Major W. Webb of the 2nd Suffolk Regiment was appointed Acting Regimental Sergeant Major for the 10th (Service) Battalion Royal Welsh Fusiliers**

JUNE 23rd

2nd Lieutenant W. A. Bouette and Lieutenant J. F. Dale joined the Battalion and were posted to 'A' and 'B' Companies respectively.

June 23rd was my Taid Edwin's 37th birthday and he was sent a Bible by his sister Catherine, which he carried with him for the rest of the War.

 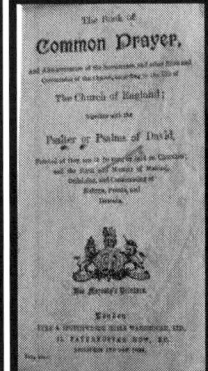 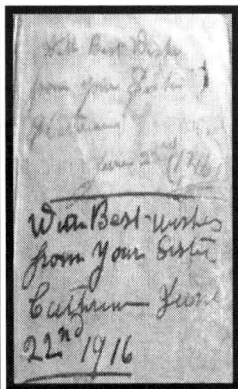

JUNE 24th & 25th

A sports day was held in the morning and a concert in the evening for the entertainment of the Battalion. The following appointments were made:-

- 2nd Lieutenant L. G. Godfrey was appointed Scout Officer
- 2nd Lieutenant L. Williams was appointed Assistant Transport Officer

For the rest of June, training continued for the Battalion to make sure they were ready for the upcoming battle. Weather was reported as wet and had been for the last few days.

JULY 1916

JULY 1st - The Somme Offensive

The Battalion marched to St. Omer a distance of 10.5km (6 ½ miles) and entrained for Doullens.

Private George Culpitt, 35115, wrote in his Diary: -

"We marched to St. Omer which we reached at 4pm and entered the station to entrain for the scene of action. We were put in wagons 25 in each, which proved too many for comfort and travelled all night passing Calais, Boulogne and Abbeville and so on until in the early morning of July 2nd we had landed at Doullens. We continued our journey by road to the village of Gezaincourt, some three miles from Doullens which we reached about 4am, knocking the inhabitants up to find billets. Once the billets were secured, we endeavoured to get some sleep before breakfast, which came up about 10am. We then washed in a stream which ran behind the farm. In the afternoon when it became known that we might do a lot of marching, we had a feet inspection, and then we knew that we were to take part in the offensive that started on July 1st. – Private George Culpitt, 35115 10th (Service) Battalion Royal Welsh Fusiliers

JULY 2nd

The Battalion arrived at Doullens at 2am. The men had coffee and biscuits and then marched to billets at Gezaincourt a distance of 4.5km (2.76 miles). 76th Brigade, 3rd Division were now placed under IV (4th) Army.

Private George Culpitt, 35115 wrote in his Diary: -

"At 10pm on 2nd July 'A' and 'D' Coys were woken and told to be ready at 11pm to go with the Battalion's Medical Officer Captain B. Grellier to assist with the casualties at a Casualty Clearing Station (probably C.C.S. 29th). We made our way to the Clearing Station just outside the village and throughout the night assisted the RAMC Orderlies and Stretcher Bearers in the work of helping the wounded, carrying the stretchers and such like necessary jobs. Never shall I forget the sight of so many wounded men stained with the mud of the battlefields of the Somme, be-spattered with blood, their arms in slings, heads in bandages, all of them living emblems of the War. It is one thing to see the wounded hero in hospital blue, once more clean and civilised, then he is in keeping with his surroundings, but it is another and altogether different thing to see him coming down from 'The Line' unwashed, unshaven and mud soaking through his clothes. It is then that one feels that the War has been brought home to one." – Private George Culpitt, 35115 10th (Service) Battalion Royal Welsh Fusiliers

JULY 3rd

The Battalion received orders at 6.50am to march to Naours a distance of 14.1km (8.76miles). The Battalion left at 8.50am and arrived at the billets at Naours at 1.15pm. The brass bands of the Brigade played in the evening in the village joined by the R. W. F. choir. It rained during the night.

JULY 4th

Orders were received from the Brigade Head Quarters that the Battalion should now march to the next destination under the cover of darkness. The Battalion left their billets at 9pm and marched to Rainneville a distance of 12.5km (7 ½ miles) and arrived at the billets at 1am.

JULY 5th

The following Officers joined the Battalion and were posted to Companies:-

- 2nd Lieutenant D. E. Thomas to 'A' Coy
- 2nd Lieutenant G. H. Jennings to 'C' Coy
- 2nd Lieutenant J. Thompson to 'D' Coy
- 2nd Lieutenant W. S. Wynne-Williams to 'B' Coy
- 2nd Lieutenant A. B. Brotherton to 'B' Coy

Captain Bles was transferred to Intelligence Corps and Captain Spencer detailed for duty as Draft Conducting Officer.

The 3rd Division was now placed under XIII Corps.

The Battalion in Brigade marched out of billets at Franvillers a distance of 13.7km (8 ½ miles). It was deemed better to march at night due to the extreme heat in the day and the Battalion were also getting closer to the 'Front-Line'.

JULY 6th

The Battalions Commanding Officer and other Officers and the Adjutant visited trenches in front of Carnoy. The Battalion left billets at Franvillers at 9pm and marched to billets in **'Bivouacs'** at Bois Celestine near Carnoy a distance of 16.8km (10 ½ miles) arriving at 2am.

A draft of 15 other ranks (O. R.) joined the Battalion for duty.

JULY 7th

Heavy rain had started during the previous night and continued for most of the day. The Battalion remained in their bivouacs. At 4.15pm under the Second in Command, the Battalion marched to their bivouacs at Bronfay Farm, just outside Carney. A meeting of senior Officers was held at the farm. The land around Bronfay Farm had been 'No Mans Land' before the attacks on 1st July.

During the night and early morning of the 8th July a 'Reconnoitring Party', under Lieutenant L. G. Godfrey was sent out.

JULY 9th

The 3rd Division had been ordered to attack and capture the Longueval-Bazentine Ridge on a date to be notified later. The 76th Brigade had been allotted a sector and the work of reconnaissance dumps etc. was well under way. Enemy shell fire was heavy. In the afternoon and early evening the Battalion practiced the attack on a flagged course. During the evening a 'Battalion Carrying Party' suffered the following casualties: -

RANK	NAME	SERVICE NO.	WOUND
CORPORAL	J. H. MULLINS	18267	KILLED
PRIVATE	D. GRIFFITHS	15182	DIED OF WOUNDS

RANK	NAME	SERVICE NO.	WOUND
SERGEANT	R. CARR	14643	WOUNDED
PRIVATE	R. ROBERTS	15231	WOUNDED
PRIVATE	W. ROWLANDS	15293	WOUNDED
PRIVATE	D. JONES	29476	WOUNDED
PRIVATE	J. ROBERTS	14967	WOUNDED
PRIVATE	E. J. THOMAS	34153	WOUNDED
PRIVATE	T. G. HUGHES	12421	WOUNDED
PRIVATE	D. G. J. WATKINS	29584	WOUNDED
PRIVATE	G. E. LEWIS	31014	WOUNDED
PRIVATE	T. A. PROSSER	31401	WOUNDED
PRIVATE	J. MORRIS	23326	WOUNDED
PRIVATE	C. J. WOOD	15037	WOUNDED

RANK	NAME	SERVICE NO.	WOUND
LANCE CORPORAL	D. REES	15159	WOUNDED
LANCE CORPORAL	J. JONES	14968	WOUNDED
LANCE CORPORAL	D. WILLIAMS	15031	WOUNDED
PRIVATE	W. J. BROWN	34054	WOUNDED
PRIVATE	W. O. DAVIES	36831	WOUNDED
PRIVATE	A. EDWARDS	34084	WOUNDED
PRIVATE	W. RYAN	33814	WOUNDED
PRIVATE	W. GREATORIX	23688	WOUNDED
PRIVATE	H. JONES	29583	WOUNDED
PRIVATE	D. WILLIAMS	15024	WOUNDED
PRIVATE	S. R DAVIES	23220	WOUNDED
PRIVATE	D. LLOYD	37456	WOUNDED

Private George Culpitt 35115, explained what happened in his Dairy: -

"We had gone down the road about 2000 yards when we fell out on a grassy plot on the side of the road, and also to await until it got a little darker before we continued our journey. We were all sitting fairly close together when suddenly there was a large explosion near at hand, and a great volume of dust and smoke rose in the air. Thinking that we had been seen by the enemy, we made a dash for cover while the crys and groans of the wounded could be heard, but luckily, this was not the case, we therefore returned to the spot to attend to the chaps who were hit, we found that someone had been playing with a german bomb with the result that it had gone off. Some twenty men were wounded by the explosion, one of them, a Corporal, died some five minutes after by being hit, it was therefore, a much older and wiser party that continued it's way up the dump a half an hour later. – Private George Culpitt 35115 10th (Service) Battalion Royal Welsh Fusiliers

JULY 10th

The Battalion sent out 'Wire Patrols' accompanied by the 2nd Suffolks to examine the enemys wire defences and both reported back stating that the enemys wire was still intact and undamaged which was not a good sign. With the impending attack imminent, the Battalion continued practicing the attack on the flagged course.

The Battalion received the following messages: -

From the Fourth Army – *"The Commander in Chief has directed the Army Commander to express to you his great satisfaction at the way patrols have carried out their work in your Corps during the past few days."*

From the 76th Brigade – *"The Brigadier-General wishes you to convey to the Officers, N. C. O.'s and men forming your permenant Carrying Party, his appreciaition of the good work done, which has been reported to him by his staff. He also wishes you to inform the Officers, N. C. O.'s and men who composed the patrol which went out last night, that he is exceedingly pleased with the information brought in."*

This was in connection to the 'Wiring Patrols' carried out on the night of the 8th and 9th and the morning of the 10th July.

JULY 11th & 12th

During these two days the Battalion continued to practice for the forthcoming attack. The Battalion had to move their bivouacs three times due to the enemy artillery fire.

JULY 13th

Orders were received from Head Quarters instructing 76th Brigade that the disposition had changed, instead of attacking on the right of the position towards Longueval, the Brigade was placed in Divisional reserve in the afternoon of the 13th. The Brigade received orders to take up position in the 'Captured Front and Support Lines in Montauban Valley'. The 10th (Service) Battalion were disposed as folows: -

- 'B' Coy in Front
- 'A' Coy on Right
- 'D' Coy on Left
- 'C' Coy and Specialists – Behind

The Battalion got into position in good order and without casualties.

At 3pm the Battalion was ordered to **'Stand-To'** and to be ready to move at 20 minutes notice.

Private George Culpitt, 35115, wrote in his Diary: -

"Before we shifted the Brigadier paid us a visit and encouraged us to do our best, saying that he thought this ought to be a decisive battle." – Private George Culpitt, 35115 10th (Service) Battalion Royal Welsh Fusiliers

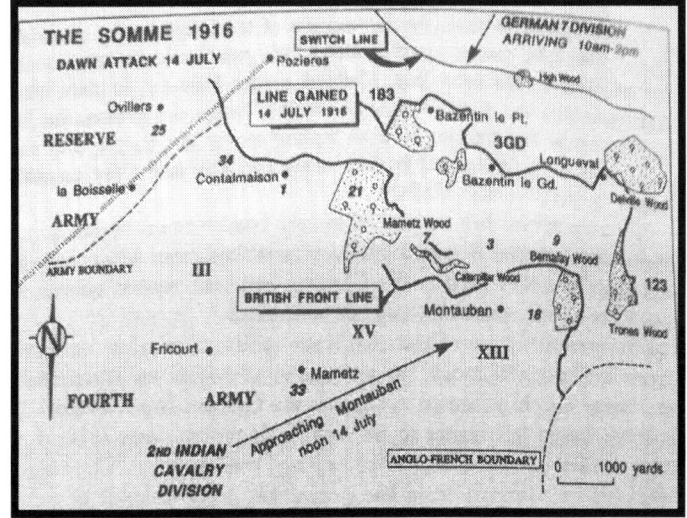

Captured Front and Support Lines in Montauban Valley

JULY 14th

The attack was timed to take place at 3.25am. At 3.20am the bombardment became intense, the whole enemy front being lit up by the bursting shells. At 3.25am, the troops advanced and shortly after it was known that the attack had been successful. At dawn, a steady stream of prisoners and wounded moved down the Carnoy-Montauban Road, all unwounded German prisoners were used as stretcher bearers to carry our wounded soldiers. The Battalion received orders to move forward at 8.45am and take over the section of Montauban Alley, previously held by the 1st Gordon Highlanders, who with the 8th Battalion the Kings Own Royal Lancaster Regiment, advanced to Caterpiller Valley. The 10th Battalion moved across the open area in platoons in single file, at one point, some delay and congestion occurred owing to another Battalion crossing our line, at this point, the Battalion came under hostile enemy shell fire, but the Battalion had to find cover in the Loud Trench. The Battalion managed to reach their position in Montauban Alley, and then by this time the situation was quiet and men of the 8th and 9th Brigades could be seen walking about the captured area. The Battalion had the great satisfaction of seeing the Cavalry pass through their lines and attacking the enemy, inflickting some casualties before they were held up and had to retire. The 1st and 2nd Battalion Royal Welsh Fusiliers were close by to the Battalion. Casualties for this day were two wounded, **Private M. Hughes**, service number 15427 and **Private C. Furnival**, service number 23498.

Private George Culpitt, 35115, wrote in his Diary: -

"Just before dawn the bombardment opened and it was one of the most fierce of the many I had witnessed in France. When we found that there was very little doing in the way of retaliation, we stood on top of the trench and watched the flashes of the guns which lit up the skys seemingly on all sides. The scene was splendid and at the same time, terrible and it must be said that Fritz was getting a little bit of what, for the first year of the War, our lads had to stand." - Private George Culpitt, 35115 10th (Service) Battalion Royal Welsh Fusiliers

JULY 15th

The Battalion remained in Montauban Alley and received the following casualties: -

RANK	NAME	SERVICE NO.	WOUND
PRIVATE	H. BOURNE	36055	WOUNDED
PRIVATE	E. WILKINSON	33057	WOUNDED
PRIVATE	L. STEMBRIDGE	27275	WOUNDED
PRIVATE	T. HAWKER	7841	WOUNDED

'C' Coy provided a 'Working Party' of 100 men to help bury 'Communication Cables'. The Commanding Officer and Captain Blake visited the captured trenches. The Battalion received the following messages that were sent to the 3rd Division and the 76th Brigade from General Furse, 9th Division:-

"I wish to express my thanks for all the excellent arrangements for yesterday's operations handed over by the 76th Infantry Brigade, they are largely responsible for the smooth working of the operations."

General Officer Commanding 3rd Division to General Officer Commanding 76th Division wrote: -

"Although your Brigade was in reserve yesterday, the words of the Corps Commander published in the 3rd Division A/7866 of 15/7/16 apply to all ranks in your Brigade. As it was their energy and forethought in making the preliminary arrangements which made possible the successful deployment and attack of the 27th Brigade."

The A/7866 the General Commanding Officer wrote about, refered to a message received from Lieutenant General W. Congreve V.C. K.C.B. M.V.O. D.L. Commanding the XIII Corps, praising the work, organisation and discipline shown by the Brigade in the lead up to the attack on the 14th July.

JULY 16th

The Battalion were still in Montauban Alley and 'B' Coy provided a 'Working Party' to continue the work of burying the 'Communication Cables'. The Battalion evacuated the trenches near High Wood due to there being an advanced. 1 Casualty was wounded today, **Private T. Murphy**, service number 17331.

JULY 17th

A 'Fatigue Party' from the transport lines was brought up to serve as a 'Burial Party' for the dead that lay out on the battlefield. Some of the Battalion's Officers and men visited the 1st and 2nd Battalion Royal Welsh Fusiliers who were in close proximity to the Battalions trenches.

JULY 18th

The Battalion moved forward to the Sunken Road (leading from Montauban to Caterpiller Valley) and took over the trenches originally started by the 8th Battalion Kings Own Royal Lancaster Regiment and the 1st Gordon Highlanders.

JULY 19th – Delville Wood

The Battalion spent the morning improving the trenches and at 3pm in the afternoon, the Commanding Officer of the 1st Devonshire Battalion came to 'Reconnoitre' the position, which was to be taken over by his Battalion. At 4pm orders received for the Battalion to move immediately to the Battalion's original area in the Breslau Front and Support Trenches. There was a certain amount of enemy shelling and the Battalion received the following casualties: - 1 'Killed' and 4 'Wounded' **(names are included in the list of casualties on the 20th July).**

The Commanding Officer for the Battalion was ordered to report to

Brigade Head Quarters at 8.45pm where he received orders to attack Delville Woods the following morning.

Private George Culpitt, 35115 wrote in his Diary: -

"Our Captain told us to make ourselves comfortable for the night and we therefore began making shelters etc. We were just settling down for the night when word came down our Captain wanted to speak to the Company. We were told that we would go up to the Front-Line that night to prepare to make an attack on Delville Wood. This is a great surprise to us as we thought we were going to be relieved, but it could not be helped and we began to console ourselves with 'What will be, will be' and 'if you are going to get hit, you'll get hit.' "– Private George Culpitt, 35115 10th (Service) Battalion Royal Welsh Fusiliers

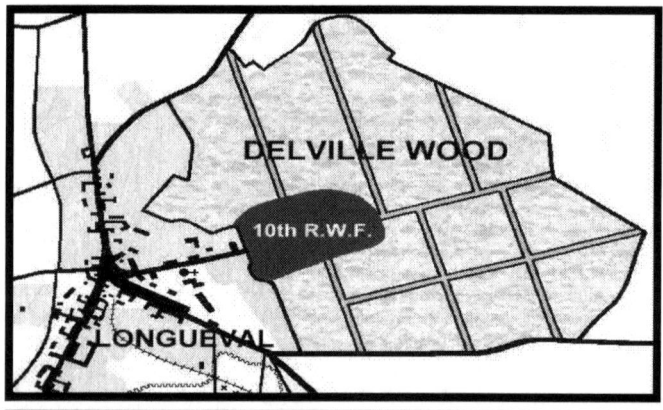

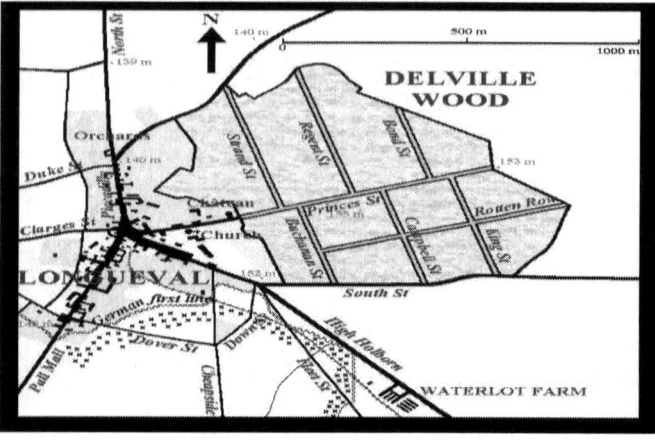

The orders received were that the line was held at Prince's Street. The 2nd Suffolk Regiment were to attack Longueval and sweep the North-East portion of Delville Wood as far as The Strand and meet up with the 10th Battalion R. W. F. The 10th Battalion were to be deployed on Prince's Street and were given a front of 600 yards to attack extending from The Strand to the East edge of Delville Wood, this area was to be consolidated and connections established with the 2nd Suffolk Regiment. Guides would meet the Battalion at S22 D.52 sheet 1 at Montuaban, to lead them to the Southern edge of the wood where other Guides would be available to take the Battalion to the line of deployment ready for the attack to take place. There would be a slow bombardment of Delville Wood all through the night which would become intense at 3.20am with the attack commencing at 3.35am in which the 2nd Suffolk Regiment would attack from the 'West'. It was left to the discretion of the Commanding Officer of the 10th Battalion to attack at 3.45am with his Battalion depending on the progress of the 2nd Suffolk Regiment. The Battalion would be at the rendezvous at 11.30pm.

The following Battalions orders were issued :-

- **Three Coys will deploy behind the line at Prince's Street and each Coy on a 200 yard frontage**
- **'B' Coy (Captain Blake) on the 'Right'**
- **'D' Coy (Lieutenant V. H. Piercy) in the 'Centre'**
- **'C' Coy (Captain G. D. Scale) on the 'Left'**
- **'A' Coy (Captain C. P. C. Daniel) Reserve of Bombers**
- **(Lieutenant D. T. Williams) & 4 Lewis Guns**
- **(Lieutenant W. G. Daniel) Being in Reserve**
- **1 Vickers Gun & 76th Brigade Machine Gun Company (M. C. G.) were attached to 'B' Coy to protect the 'Right Flank'**
- **Remaining in Reserve to be used as the situation demanded**

There was a Parade at 10pm and they then moved off in columns of fours arriving at the first rendezvous point without casualties.

JULY 20th

From this point the Battalion moved across country by 'Compass Bearing' whilst still below the last crest. Heavy machine gun fire opened on the Battalion's front and they also received a certain amount of shell fire. It was decided not to get 'Artillery Formation' because of the risk of losing connection in the darkness and endangering the success of the whole operation, as this was deemed too great.

Private George Culpitt, 35115 wrote in his Diary: -

"As we lay there, with the continual explosion and concussion of Fritz's shells all around us, never knowing whether the next moment would be our last ones, thoughts could never be described as pleasant and many a man has prayed to be preserved, who at any ordinary time, has never thought of God. At such time as this one, is brought face to face with death and although there is no fear, one feels very curious as to what may take place should one be fatally hit." - Private George Culpitt, 35115 10th (Service) Battalion Royal Welsh Fusiliers

During the enemys machine gun and artillery fire, and then 20 minutes later the Battalion suffered two Officers and several other ranks wounded. When the enemy fire had diminished to a certain extent, the Battalion moved forward, and although experiencing some difficulties owing to shell holes and a trench and some old French barbwire, met the Guides at a point close to the South-Western corner of the woods. They were led East along South Street in single file, then North-by-West up the side of Buchanan Street, which was held by the South Africans. At this point, the Battalion's troubles commenced. It was very clear that the Battalion was nowhere near the position on Prince's Street where they needed to be. The Battalion were met by a considerable amount of enemy rifle fire and short bursts of machine gun fire. 'Vary Lights' were sent up a short distance to the Battalions front and the Germans were heard shouting all over the wood. The Guide maintained that the Battalion was close to Prince's Street, but evidently, that was not the case, as the Battalion was at the most, only 150 yards from the South edge of the wood. The only option for the Battalion was to deploy. A compass bearing was taken and a star selected due East for the leader of the deployment to march upon. Captain Blake, Captain Follitt and 2nd Lieutenant Godfrey

'Advanced on the Compass Point' with 'B' Coy following. The intention being that 2nd Lieutenant Godfrey should halt after 200 yards to mark the 'Right Flank' of 'C' Coy. Captain Follitt was to halt after 400 yards to mark the 'Right Flank' of 'D' Coy and Captain Blake to advance to the Eastern edge of the wood. Companies would then halt, turn to their 'Left' and extend back to the Officers marking their flanks. The 'Left Flank' was on Buchanan Street and 'B' Coy had moved out along the line of deployment to a distance of 100 yards, when the German were seen advancing. The Battalion sent up 'Vary Lights' and shouting to 'B' Coy to fire steadily. They then managed to lie down under cover for sometime, to avoid the heavy machine gun fire being received. The men remained steady in spite of very trying circumstances. It was evident that the enemy were 'Attacking in Force' or were aware that our troops were being deployed for an attack. A further deployment of 200 yards was made, the progress of which was checked by machine gun fire to the 'Right & Rear'. At this point, another attack was again repulsed. In order to avoid machine gun fire the direction of deployment was changed to South-East. During this action the Battalion came under fierce fire from 'A' Coy 11th Essex Regiment, who were unaware of the 10th Battalion's positions and had not been informed of the impending attack. 'Vary Lights' went up a short distance in front of the 10th Battalion's Front-Line and on Captain Follitt's challenging, no reply was given, and machine gun and rifle fire commenced. This stopped all further deployment of the Battalion and orders were given for the Battalion to 'Dig In' and the impending attack would take place from where the Battalion was, on a restricted front. At 3.30am, further orders were received for the attack to take place at 3.45am, not 3.35am as originally planned. This was done in the hope that the development of the attack, by the 2nd Suffolks, would relieve some of the pressure on the 10th Battalion Royal Welsh Fusiliers.

At 3.45am the attack commenced. 'C' Coy on the 'Left Flank' met with heavy machine gun fire and bombs and were held up, but rallied by Captain G. D. Scale, they continued forward until they were level with the rest of the Battalion.

Owing to heavy casualties in Officers and men, it was impossible for the Battalion to continue with the attack and the line had to be withdrawn, with fighting continuing in isolated groups on returning to the line. The more advanced groups of the Battalion reported that large German reinforcements were seen entering the rear of the woods.

Delville Wood after the attack

After daylight, the 'Advanced Parties' suffered heavily from snipers and were eventually compelled to withdraw to the 'Line Party' held by the Berks & Essex Regiments and the Machine Gun Company of the 53rd Brigade. The remaining guns of the 76th Brigade Machine Gun Company were placed in position along the side. From this time onwards, the Battalions were on the defensive and 'Dug-In' the best they could.

Private George Culpitt, 35115 wrote in his Diary: -

"I was digging energetically to join up if possible with these on the right but hearing a row behind, looked back to see the three chaps getting out of a hole, to run back to the next line. Without any more hesitation, I quickly grasped my rifle and bayonet and followed suit. Directly, I got on the top, the sniper started paying me his attention but dodging and running round various shell holes and falling over tree trunks and such like. I did not give him much chance to get aim at me. At length, sweating and out of breath, I spied the trench in front and utterly exhausted by my efforts, fell into it glad of even the very slight cover it afforded. Here I stayed for about three hours where we underwent a very heavy strafing from Fritz, every shell seeming to fall very near the trench, so terrible was the force of some of the explosions. When the bombardment had abated, I made my way again to the trench where I had dug in first thing that morning and here coming across some fellows of my own Company, got in with them. Out of the many sets of equipment I succeeded in salvaging a pack to replace the one I had left in the shell hole in front and also some rations for which I was grateful for as we had not had anything to eat since 9 o'clock the nigh previous, and now there was a lull and one began to feel hungry. So we partook of some bread and cheese and a little of our precious water and feeling refreshed began to settle down and dig a bit deeper, clean our rifles and do sundry odd jobs of this sort to prepare for a counter attack from Fritz, which was anticipated." – Private George Culpitt, 35115 10th (Service) Battalion Royal Welsh Fusiliers

A mixed platoon under Sergeant Pettifer were sent to the Battalion's 'Right' to reinforce the Essex Regiment. At 2pm the Commanding Officer (C. O.) was sent for by Brigade Head Quarters to report on the situation and after this meeting, returned at 8.30pm having received orders to make arrangements for relief of all fractions of the Battalion holding the wood by the 4th Battalion Royal Fusiliers. The relief was carried out by 3.26am on 21st July. The 4th Battalion Royal Fusiliers suffering heavy casualties in the process. The 10th Battalion R. W. F. returned to their original quarters in the Breslau Trenches.

The Battalion suffered the following casualties at Delville Wood: -

RANK	NAME	SERVICE NO.	WOUND
CAPTAIN	G. P. BLAKE		KILLED IN ACTION
2ND LIEUTENANT	L. G. GODFREY		KILLED IN ACTION
SERGEANT	R. J. ROBERTS	15372	KILLED IN ACTION
SERGEANT	F. DIVER	15516	KILLED IN ACTION
CORPORAL	T. F. ELLIS	15226	KILLED IN ACTION
CORPORAL	R. O. DAVIES	17688	KILLED IN ACTION
LANCE CORPORAL	J. G. EVANS	13009	KILLED IN ACTION
LANCE CORPORAL	J. L. DAVIES	40459	KILLED IN ACTION
LANCE SERGEANT	C. H. DUNFORD	7842	KILLED IN ACTION
PRIVATE	E. HOLLAND	23436	KILLED IN ACTION
PRIVATE	W. J. PRITCHARD	29579	KILLED IN ACTION
PRIVATE	D. J. REES	13188	KILLED IN ACTION
PRIVATE	G. F. PIERCE	15364	KILLED IN ACTION
PRIVATE	H. BURGESS	15342	KILLED IN ACTION
PRIVATE	H. OWEN	14237	KILLED IN ACTION
PRIVATE	P. ROGERS	36663	KILLED IN ACTION
PRIVATE	S. J. ARTHURS	15509	KILLED IN ACTION
PRIVATE	H. BOOKER	12192	KILLED IN ACTION
PRIVATE	J. THOMPSON	6548	KILLED IN ACTION
CAPTAIN	G. O. SCALE		KILLED IN ACTION
2ND LIEUTENANT	H. PAGE		KILLED IN ACTION

RANK	NAME	SERVICE NO.	WOUND
PRIVATE	J. BURGESS	17226	KILLED IN ACTION
PRIVATE	C. BULLOCK	8363	KILLED IN ACTION
PRIVATE	J. CRAVEN	17226	KILLED IN ACTION
PRIVATE	W. JONES	25181	KILLED IN ACTION
PRIVATE	T. A. JONES	31377	KILLED IN ACTION
PRIVATE	J. JOHNSON	5664	KILLED IN ACTION
PRIVATE	E. MALONE	15645	KILLED IN ACTION
PRIVATE	W. NEAVE	16577	KILLED IN ACTION
PRIVATE	E. J. OWEN	26184	KILLED IN ACTION
PRIVATE	J. PUFFER	36664	KILLED IN ACTION
PRIVATE	R. STILTON	34598	KILLED IN ACTION
PRIVATE	J. STOTT	15592	KILLED IN ACTION
PRIVATE	T. WALTERS	15619	KILLED IN ACTION
PRIVATE	P. EVANS	15720	KILLED IN ACTION
PRIVATE	J. LINHAM	15668	KILLED IN ACTION
PRIVATE	O. ROBERTS	40142	KILLED IN ACTION

RANK	NAME	SERVICE NO.	WOUND
PRIVATE	J. PHILLPOT	26578	DIED OF WOUNDS
PRIVATE	W. WINDRIDGE	36120	DIED OF WOUNDS

RANK	NAME	SERVICE NO.	WOUND
CAPTAIN	C. P. C. DANIELL		WOUNDED
LIEUTENANT	A. W. FISH		WOUNDED
LIEUTENANT	W. G. DANIEL		WOUNDED
LIEUTENANT	F. J. DALE		WOUNDED
LIEUTENANT	W. A. COWIE		WOUNDED SHELL SHOCK
LIEUTENANT	D. T. WILLIAMS		WOUNDED
LIEUTENANT	V. H. PIERCY		WOUNDED
2ND LIEUTENANT	W. MACAULAY		WOUNDED
2ND LIEUTENANT	O. L. JONES		WOUNDED
2ND LIEUTENANT	W. C. WELLS		WOUNDED
COY SERGEANT-MAJOR	E. ROBERTS	15313	WOUNDED REPORTED MISSING
SERGEANT	GRIFFITHS	14662	WOUNDED
SERGEANT	N. EDWARDS	15643	WOUNDED
SERGEANT	D. J. LEWIS	5732	WOUNDED
SERGEANT	J. HOLL	16027	WOUNDED
SERGEANT	J. W. BRIDLE	15413	WOUNDED
CORPORAL	R. N. PHILLIPS	15405	WOUNDED
CORPORAL	P. DAVIES	15564	WOUNDED

RANK	NAME	SERVICE NO.	WOUND
CORPORAL	J. RICKETTS	19644	WOUNDED
CORPORAL	G. H. HUGHES	15504	WOUNDED
CORPORAL	J. JOHN	31578	WOUNDED
CORPORAL	D. LORD	16119	WOUNDED
CORPORAL	J. PHILLIPS	15690	WOUNDED
CORPORAL	A. PUNCHARD	15791	WOUNDED
CORPORAL	R. BATCHELOR	6225	WOUNDED
LANCE CORPORAL	JEFFERS	31499	WOUNDED
LANCE CORPORAL	W. J. TYSON	15409	WOUNDED
LANCE CORPORAL	J. TRIVETT	15291	WOUNDED
LANCE CORPORAL	H. JARVIS	33662	WOUNDED
LANCE CORPORAL	H. THOMAS	23172	WOUNDED
LANCE CORPORAL	F. BRIERLEY	15603	WOUNDED
LANCE CORPORAL	J. MORGAN	31306	WOUNDED
LANCE CORPORAL	W. C. WILLIAMS	15090	WOUNDED
LANCE CORPORAL	R. EVANS	40151	WOUNDED
LANCE CORPORAL	E. A. POLIN	15483	WOUNDED
LANCE CORPORAL	T. S. BREARLEY	15367	WOUNDED
LANCE CORPORAL	T. HULL	15684	WOUNDED
LANCE CORPORAL	A. HUCKVALE	36483	WOUNDED
PRIVATE	R. JONES	34229	WOUNDED
PRIVATE	J. AMES	15402	WOUNDED
PRIVATE	A. LINDSAY	34649	WOUNDED
PRIVATE	R. G. JONES	40463	WOUNDED
PRIVATE	G. QUINNEY	10347	WOUNDED
PRIVATE	J. H. DAVIES	15171	WOUNDED SHELL SHOCK
PRIVATE	R. EDWARDS	15138	WOUNDED
PRIVATE	R. POWER	33600	WOUNDED
PRIVATE	W. HAYWOOD	23438	WOUNDED
PRIVATE	S. SAUNDERS	34121	WOUNDED
PRIVATE	M. PHILLIPS	23306	WOUNDED
PRIVATE	W. A. JONES	15012	WOUNDED
PRIVATE	E. ROBERTS	25188	WOUNDED
PRIVATE	E. JONES	15537	WOUNDED
PRIVATE	W. T. JONES	29606	WOUNDED
PRIVATE	C. FEAR	23417	WOUNDED
PRIVATE	C. T. ROSSITER	15361	WOUNDED
PRIVATE	D. THOMAS	14988	WOUNDED
PRIVATE	R. PRITCHARD	14934	WOUNDED
PRIVATE	T. W. JONES	14984	WOUNDED
PRIVATE	A. E. JONES	5673	WOUNDED
PRIVATE	R. EVANS	36600	WOUNDED
PRIVATE	J. JONES	34696	WOUNDED
PRIVATE	P. JONES	15212	WOUNDED
PRIVATE	W. JONES	14825	WOUNDED

RANK	NAME	SERVICE NO.	WOUND
PRIVATE	J. PETERS	15351	WOUNDED
PRIVATE	M. JONES	40474	WOUNDED
PRIVATE	J. FRANCE	23302	WOUNDED
PRIVATE	T. ARNOLD	33640	WOUNDED
PRIVATE	J. BEDSON	23212	WOUNDED
PRIVATE	F. BRYDGES	13649	WOUNDED
PRIVATE	A. CAMPION	23310	WOUNDED
PRIVATE	T. CLAYTON	33677	WOUNDED
PRIVATE	F. DAY	33696	WOUNDED
PRIVATE	J. E. EVANS	40086	WOUNDED
PRIVATE	D. H. DAVIES	40370	WOUNDED
PRIVATE	D. E. EDWARDS	16149	WOUNDED
PRIVATE	D. WILE	34060	WOUNDED
PRIVATE	W. A. BLACKMAN	34797	WOUNDED
PRIVATE	DOBBLE	16454	WOUNDED
PRIVATE	F. J. DIXON	35056	WOUNDED
PRIVATE	G. EVANS	15146	WOUNDED
PRIVATE	H. LEWIS	25798	WOUNDED
PRIVATE	F. DAVIES	36689	WOUNDED
PRIVATE	W. DUNKLEY	13603	WOUNDED
PRIVATE	J. FOSTER	33715	WOUNDED
PRIAVTE	T. LEWIS	15666	WOUNDED
PRIVATE	H. MANSFIELD	34637	WOUNDED
PRIVATE	W. P. PARRY	46315	WOUNDED
PRIVATE	J. ROGERS	33824	WOUNDED
PRIVATE	C. SMITH	23427	WOUNDED
PRIVATE	A. S LLOYD	15096	WOUNDED
PRIVATE	R. HURDLEY	34096	WOUNDED
PRIVATE	H. JONES	37234	WOUNDED
PRIVATE	J. BEDDISON	36396	WOUNDED
PRIVATE	J. GARDNER	23463	WOUNDED
PRIVATE	F. GREEN	23423	WOUNDED
PRIAVTE	J. C. HOWARD	34786	WOUNDED
PRIVATE	J. D. JONES	16177	WOUNDED
PRIVATE	E. LIPTROTT	17310	WOUNDED
PRIVATE	P. O'NEILL	16279	WOUNDED
PRIVATE	T. OWEN	16295	WOUNDED
PRIVATE	R. BRODIE	15641	WOUNDED
PRIVATE	C. CRAWFORD	36237	WOUNDED

RANK	NAME	SERVICE NO.	WOUND
PRIVATE	A. CRUMP	31875	WOUNDED
PRIVATE	B. CHADWICK	36287	WOUNDED
PRIVATE	C. E. COPLEY	34721	WOUNDED
PRIAVTE	A. DANCE	36897	WOUNDED
PRIVATE	M. DOUBLER	4379	WOUNDED
PRIVATE	W. J. EVANS	15438	WOUNDED
PRIVATE	D. FREW	36662	WOUNDED
PRIVATE	G. GOODWIN	23245	WOUNDED
PRIVATE	W. GREEN	19126	WOUNDED
PRIVATE	H. HUGHES	15501	WOUNDED
PRIVATE	P. HUMPHREY	15503	WOUNDED
PRIVATE	A. C. JONES	25339	WOUNDED
PRIVATE	R. E. JONES	15488	WOUNDED
PRIAVTE	D. JONES	25385	WOUNDED
PRIVATE	D. JONES	15223	WOUNDED
PRIVATE	J. H. JONES	31817	WOUNDED
PRIVATE	W. JONES	15638	WOUNDED
PRIVATE	C. JOHNSON	31826	WOUNDED
PRIVATE	W. JACKMAN	36516	WOUNDED
PRIVATE	E. H. KITCHEN	23228	WOUNDED
PRIVATE	J. C. KEITH	34774	WOUNDED
PRIVATE	J. LLOYD	15514	WOUNDED
PRIVATE	R. PARRY	27235	WOUNDED
PRIAVTE	J. ROBERTS	15517	WOUNDED
PRIVATE	H. REES	15515	WOUNDED
PRIVATE	C. STREET	36530	WOUNDED
PRIVATE	R. THOMAS	36424	WOUNDED
PRIVATE	F. WILLIAMS	40362	WOUNDED
PRIVATE	J. ROBERTS	33387	WOUNDED
PRIVATE	P. RAYNOR	33819	WOUNDED
PRIVATE	W. DOMINEY	27219	WOUNDED
PRIVATE	T. W. WILLIAMS	37780	WOUNDED
PRIVATE	A. SUGARS	26576	WOUNDED
PRIAVTE	G. LAITY	15685	WOUNDED
PRIVATE	E. HOLLINSWORTH	15197	WOUNDED
CORPORAL	J. WRIGHT	15719	WOUNDED LATER REPORTED PRISONER OF WAR
PRIVATE	E. J. POWELL	33800	SHELL SHOCK
PRIVATE	T. W. LLOYD	15724	SHELL SHOCK
PRIVATE	G. SPENCER	23442	SHELL SHOCK
PRIVATE	J. GREENING	5608	SHELL SHOCK
SERGEANT	E. JACKSON	15785	MISSING REPORTED KILLED IN ACTION

RANK	NAME	SERVICE NO.	WOUND
PRIVATE	T. F. DAVIES		MISSING REPORTED KILLED IN ACTION
COY SERGEANT MAJOR	G. JONES	16051	MISSING
LANCE SERGEANT	J. SMITH	15278	MISSING
CORPORAL	M. WILLIAMS	14672	MISSING
LANCE CORPORAL	R. WILLIAMS	16297	MISSING
LANCE CORPORAL	W. JONES	23480	MISSING
LANCE CORPORAL	W. A. DEAN	33685	MISSING
LANCE CORPORAL	C. SHEPHARD	9741	MISSING
LANCE CORPORAL	J. H. ROSTANCE	36343	MISSING
PRIVATE	E. O. EDWARDS	12915	MISSING
PRIVATE	G. KENNEDY	14910	MISSING
PRIVATE	R. B. OWEN	5906	MISSING
PRIVATE	F. W. JONES	22180	MISSING
PRIVATE	B. WALTERS	36058	MISSING
PRIVATE	A. PLASTER	33799	MISSING
PRIVATE	F. MCDONNELL	34321	MISSING
PRIVATE	S. L. DURBIN	33682	MISSING
PRIVATE	J. RHODES	24299	MISSING
PRIVATE	R. JONES	10766	MISSING
PRIVATE	H. GOWER	34957	MISSING
PRIVATE	J. CARROLL	15383	MISSING
PRIVATE	R. WYNNE	4697	MISSING
PRIVATE	J. H. L. REES	21939	MISSING
PRIVATE	J. HILL	24810	MISSING
PRIVATE	C. WILLIAMS	14666	MISSING
PRIVATE	G. W. BIRCHALL	24779	MISSING
PRIVATE	D. EVANS	24407	MISSING
PRIVATE	O.H. HUGHES	40374	MISSING
PRIVATE	G. P. JONES	40413	MISSING
PRIVATE	T. C. JONES	36826	MISSING
PRIVATE	G. LEWIS	40366	MISSING
PRIVATE	I. J. MORRIS	23980	MISSING
PRIVATE	W. G. PIERCY	36976	MISSING
PRIVATE	J. REGAN	34104	MISSING
PRIVATE	C. THONGS	12285	MISSING
PRIVATE	T. BRINDLEY	31816	MISSING
PRIVATE	T. COLOHAN	8931	MISSING
PRIVATE	W. C. DEAN	26626	MISSING
PRIVATE	T. DERRY	13679	MISSING
PRIVATE	T. GREEN	23220	MISSING
PRIVATE	W. HUGHES	17251	MISSING
PRIVATE	C. MORGAN	33776	MISSING
PRIVATE	R. J. OWEN	40095	MISSING

RANK	NAME	SERVICE NO.	WOUND
PRIVATE	J. ROBERTS	40167	MISSING
PRIVATE	J. G. SHAW	24490	MISSING
PRIVATE	A. THOMAS	40174	MISSING
PRIVATE	E. T. WILLIAMS	18370	MISSING

'A' Coy was ordered to send one platoon to move in extended order East, with their 'Right Flank' being on South Street and to continue this movement, keeping at right angles to the outside edge of the wood. The purpose of this was to protect the 'Right Flank' and prolong the original Front-Line as the deployment of the three Coys had not reached the edge of the wood. The following casualties occurred during the occupation of the Breslam Trenches: -

RANK	NAME	SERVICE NO.	WOUND
PRIVATE	G. WILLIAMS	15198	WOUNDED
PRIVATE	L. ROBERTS	15366	WOUNDED
PRIVATE	H. CRAZE	34187	WOUNDED SHELL SHOCK

Private George Culpitt 35115 wrote in his Diary: -

"The day was devoted to rest and wash in a mine crater, and in the evening a voluntary thanksgiving service was held by the Welsh Minister and never have I attended such an impressive service. It was held in the open with occasional shell sfalling nearby and was indeed a real and sincere thanksgiving for our preservation from danger." - Private George Culpitt, 35115 10th (Service) Battalion Royal Welsh Fusiliers

Lieutenant J. H. L. Glasbrook joined the Battalion for duty.

JULY 22nd

'A' Company provided a 'Carrying Party' of 60 men to carry rations to the 1st Gordon Highlanders who were still in the Front-Line. 2nd Lieutenant E. Dixon joined the Battalion for duty.

JULY 23rd

A 'Working & Carrying Party' of 300 men of all ranks proceeded to Delville Wood and Langueval accompanied by the East Riding Battalion and 56th Coy Royal Engineers. The following casualties were received:-

RANK	NAME	SERVICE NO.	WOUND
2ND LIEUTENANT	J. THOMPSON		WOUNDED
LANCE CORPORAL	W. D. HOWARTH	15209	WOUNDED
PRIVATE	J. LEWIS	33560	WOUNDED
PRIVATE	D. R. JONES	37781	WOUNDED
PRIVATE	L. ROBERTS	15366	WOUNDED
PRIVATE	D. LLOYD	37456	WOUNDED
PRIVATE	T. KELLETT	33609	WOUNDED
PRIVATE	J. BAILEY	23184	WOUNDED
PRIVATE	T. A. PROSSER	31401	WOUNDED

JULY 24th

The Battalion remained in the Breslau Trenches, there was intense enemy shelling taking place along the Montauban Alley (North End) where the 8th Kings Own Royal Lancaster Regiment was sent to reinforce 9th Brigade in case of a German counter attack. Also the 1st Gordon Highlanders were heavily shelled in their positions in Delville Wood.

JULY 25th

The Battalion was relieved by the 17th Battalion Middlesex Regiment and marched to bivouacs at Bois-De-Tailles, two miles West of Bray. The Battalion were complimented on it's marching by the Divisional Commander.

JULY 26th

The day was spent resting, reorganising and bathing for the men in the afternoon.

JULY 27th

There was a conference held at 76th Brigade's Head Quarters for all Commanding Officers of the Battalion to discuss the actions of July 19th and 20th. A draft of 50 other ranks (O. R.) joined the Battalion for duty.

JULY 28th

There was an inspection of the Battalion by the Commanding Officer (C. O.). At 3.20pm in the afternoon, the Battalion marched to billets at Mericourt L'Abbe a distance of 12.1km (7 ½ miles).

JULY 30th

There was a 'Battalion Parade' held for the 'Presentation of Cards' to N. C. O.'s and men recommended for decorations. A draft of 53 other ranks (O. R.) joined the Battalion for duty.

JULY 31st

The day was spent training which included: -
- Bayonet Fighting
- Handling Arms under Company Arrangements
- Inspection of Rifles (carried out by the Armourer)

Troops bathed in the river Ancre in the very hot weather.

A telegram was received from Lieutenant-General Commanding Fourth Army, Sir Henry Rawlinson Bt. K.C.B K.c. V.O. – *"Please convey to all ranks of the 3rd Division my sincere thanks and admiration for their very gallant behaviour since they joined the Fourth Army. Their attack on the Longueval Ridge on the 14th July will go down to history as a feat of arms of which every Officer and man of the Division may well feel proud. Their defence of Longueval Village and Delville Wood, under very heavy and incessant bombardment, is yet another proof of their gallantry and determination."*

A draft of 97 other ranks (O. R.) joined the Battalion for duty.

AUGUST 1916

AUGUST 1st

Training continued for the Battalion and there was a lecture given to the men on **'Gas Shells'** by the Medical Officer. Weather was reported as 'very hot'.

AUGUST 2nd

There was an inspection by the Brigadier of 76th Brigade of all new drafts that had joined the Battalion in the last few days. The Brigadier mentioned the gallant conduct of the 10th Battalion in Delville Wood. The Battalion's band played in the village for the local residents. Permission was given for three Officers of the Battalion to be sent to Paris on a 72 hour pass.

AUGUST 3rd

Training continued for the Battalion which included:-
- Bayonet Fighting
- Handling Arms
- Gas Helmet Drill

Innoculations were held for any men who had not been innoculated within the last 12 months. A route march was held in the evening. The very hot weather continued.

AUGUST 4th
Training continued. 'A' Coy had 'Musketry Training' on the range.
The remaining Coys had 'Extended Order Drill'. A 'Bathing Parade' was held in the afternoon where Companies Coys would bathe or swim in the river, this was very much appreciaited by the troops due to the continuing hot weather.

AUGUST 5th
A 'Working Party' of 200 men from the Battalion, under Major F. A. Samuel joined other Battalions from the Brigade to carry out work digging support lines near Montauban.

AUGUST 6th
There was a lecture by General Officer Commanding (G. O. C.) on recent operations in which was mentioned the very difficult situation the 10th Battalion R. W. F. was placed in, in Delville Wood and again, he spoke of the fine discipline and courage shown by the men on that occasion.

AUGUST 7th
Brigadier General C. J. Deverell took over command of 3rd Division.

Brigadier General C. J. Deverell

AUGUST 8th, 9th & 10th

Training continued for the Battalion during these days. A 'Working Party' of 1 Officer and 30 other ranks (O. R.) were employed to build cages for German prisoners and an extended work order was carried out in Marett Wood. The men in the Battalion would have now known an attack was planned to be carried out in the next few days.

AUGUST 11th

The Battalion received orders to march to Sand Pits near Meaulte at 3pm, a distance of 8km (5 miles). The 'Working Party' from the Battalion, that left on August 5th rejoined the Battalion. Lieutenant M. Murray rejoined the Battalion for duty.

AUGUST 12th & 13th

The Battalion continued it's training for the impending attack.

AUGUST 14th

The Battalion paraded at Sand Pits at 6pm then marched to Talus-Bois, a temporary halt was made at Minden Post as the enemy was shelling Carnoy Valley. After this temporary halt, the Battalion continued, but the platoons were marching at 50 yard intervals causing a considerable congestion of troops and the Battalion did not arrive into Talus-Bois Trenches until very late in the evening.

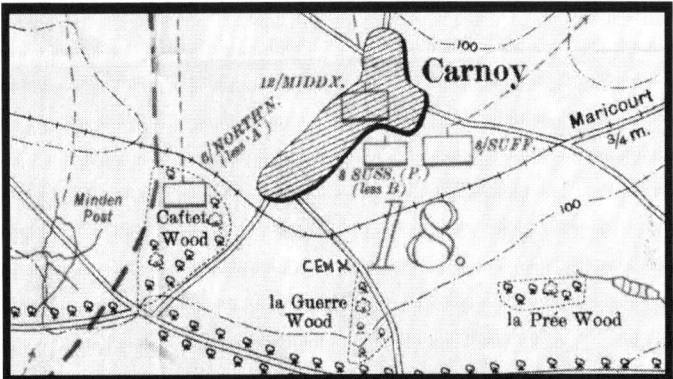

Minden Post Map & Photograph

AUGUST 15th

The Officer Commanding the Battalion and his Adjutant joined with the Commanding Officer of the 1st Gordon Highlanders at 76th Brigade Head Quarters to 'Reconnoiter' the trench areas where the Battalions would launch the attack. They were taken around the area by the Commanding Officers of the 8th Kings Own Royal Lancaster Regiment and the 2nd Suffolk Regiment and objectives were pointed out. The Commanding Officer of the Battalion also visited Colonel Duvallon Commanding Officer of the 53rd French Division who were going to be on the Battalions 418 Regiment's 'Right Flank' during the attack. 2nd Lieutenant A. O. Williams, 2nd Lieutenant Thomas and 2nd Lieutenant H. D. Evans, along with 43 other ranks (O.R.) joined the Battalion for duty.

AUGUST 16th

The Battalion moved into the Casement and Dublin Trenches at 8.30am. In the afternoon 'A' and 'D' Coys moved to Chimpanzee Trench with two consolidation sections of 'C' Coy. The Battalion received 3 killed and 4 wounded casualties whoes names are included in the casualty lists - 17th to 19th August.

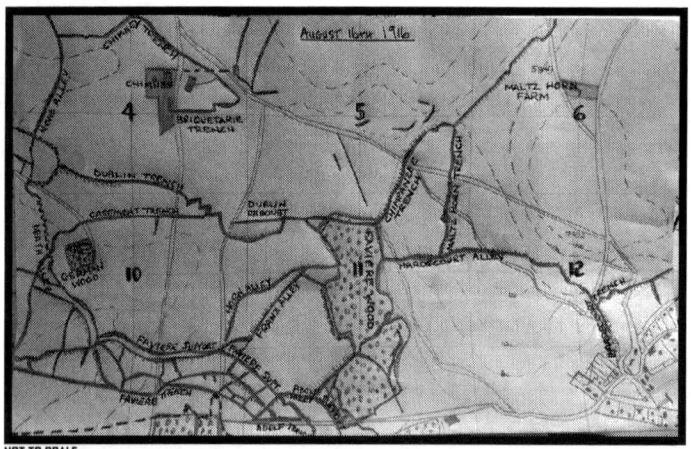

NOT TO SCALE

AUGUST 17th

In the morning, the Battalion spent time improving the dug outs in the trench area. In the afternoon instructions were given that two Companies of the Battalion, in conjunction with two Companies of the 9th Brigade, were to attack 'Lonely Trench'. Orders were given to Royal Field Artillery to heavily bombard Lonely Trench during the day. At 5pm, the attacking troops were issued with flares, smoke bombs, tools, wire cutters and white bands. At 8pm 'B' & 'C' Coys moved off accompanied by 'Specially Detailed Guides' and by the Brigade Major of 76th J. W. Skipwith R. E., the Commanding Officer and Adjutant of the 10th Battalion R. W. F., Long and James, moving at the rear of the two Companies but followed by a Head Quarters Coy and the Battalions Machine Gun Reserve (Lewis Guns). After proceeding some distance along the 'French Trench' after a delay because the 'French Guides' assigned to the Battalion were unsure of their bearings, they found that the Brigades artillery were 'Firing Short' and were landing among the Battalion. An order was issued to move back until the adjustments were made to the artillery bombardment. After a delay of half an hour, the two Battalion Coys got into the Front-Line and were in position for the attack at 9.30pm. At 9.50pm the order was given for the men to move forward to the tape (tape had been placed earlier by a 'Covering Party' of the 8th Kings Own lancaster Regiment.)

Guide tape was used to mark **'Jumping Off Points'** for assaults and attacks. A roll would be unravelled along the ground to define the width of an attack, generally aligning with the intended compass direction of the attack. They were also used as paths to guide troops forward to their **'Forming Up Line'**. On the 'Left Flank' of the Battalion were two Companies of 12th West Yorkshire Regiment. The Officer Commanding the West Yorkshire Regiment informed Colonel LLong that the planned attack had been postphoned until 10.30pm. This created major problems for the 10th Battalion R. W. F. as the men were all over the parapet and could not be withdrawn as it would be impossible to communicate with the artillery in time and the surprise effect on the German Front-Line would be lost if the time of the attack was altered. Colonel Llong advised the Officer Commanding the 12th West Yorkshire to get his men over the parapet at once as the attack would proceed at the allotted time of 10pm.

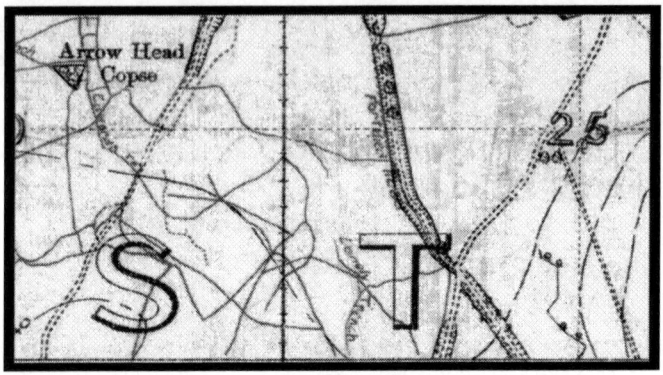

At 10pm the attacking Companies advanced out of their Front-Line Trenches. The Battalion received hostile machine gun fire almost immediately. Shortly after 11pm Colonel Llong received reports from 'C' Coy Commander on the 'Left Flank' that the Coy were held up 15 yards from the German trench by wire and German bombers. Colonel Llong ordered a platoon of the 8th Kings Own Royal Lancaster Regiment (K. O. R. L.) to reinforce. Colonel Llong ordered a 'Working Party' to dig a trench on the tap alignment and word was sent back to Head Quarters to send more men, as the first attack was held up. Colonel Llong received orders to organise a fresh attack.

AUGUST 18th

After speaking to the Officers Commanding the 12th West Yorks and the 2nd Suffolks, it was decided to launch a fresh attack at 4am. At 1.30am two Coys from the Battalion moved from Chimpanzee Trench to the Assembly Trench under the command of Major Samuel. At 5.52am it was reported that again, the attack had failed and the order was given to withdraw the remainder of the attacking troops.

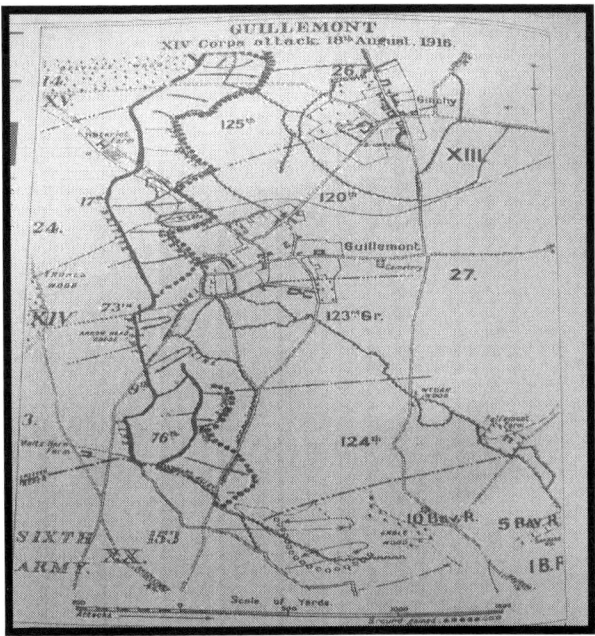

Throughout the morning of the 18th August, the Battalions Front-Line Trenches were heavily shelled by hostile 5-9 Howitzers, which continued into the early afternoon. At 2.45pm after artillery preparation and in conjunction with the 1st Battalion Gordon Highlanders, 'B' and 'C' Coys advanced on the 'Left Flank' with two Coys of the 1st Battalion Gordon Highlanders on the 'Right'. 'C' Coys suffered severe casualties from hostile machine gun fire as soon as they topped the parapet. The Officer Commanding the Supporting Coy of the Kings Shropshire Light Infantry realising the situation, ordered two of his platoons to join in the attack and support 'C' Coy. The Battalion, under horrendous hostile machine gun fire and enemy artillery fire, managed to take their objective and held the Southern portion of Lonely Trench and also some of the Battalion pushed on to take some objectives on the Guillemot-Hardecourt Road. During late afternoon and early evening heavy German artillery was landing accurately on the newly taken trenches and also on the Battalions original Front-Line Trenches. The Battalion Head Quarters was having to be continually moved because of this. The Adjutant (James) proceeded to the captured Lonely Trench and found the 1st Gordon Highlanders and the remnants of the 10th Battalion R. W. F. consolidating their positions.

AUGUST 19th

The General Officer Commanding, having reviewed the situation, issued orders to the 2nd Battalion Suffolk Regiment and to the 10th Battalion R. W. F. to withdraw their men forthwith, the Suffolks to Casement Trench and the 10th Battalion R. W. F. to Chimpanzee Trench. Due to enemy counter attacks and heavy artillery bombardments it was deemed impossible to hold on to the Southern section of Lonely Trench. The Battalion was withdrawn and relieved by the 7th Battalion Kings Shropshire Light Infantry. Before the relief was carried out 'Parties' were sent out to collect the wounded over the ground in which the attack was carried out. The Battalion later moved to the 'Transport Lines' above Minden Post.

The following list of casualties occurred during the periods of 16th – 19th August: -

RANK	NAME	SERVICE NO.	WOUND
2ND LIEUTENANT	J. E. EDWARDS		KILLED IN ACTION
2ND LIEUTENANT	E. DIXON		KILLED IN ACTION
2ND LIEUTENANT	L. WILLIAMS		KILLED IN ACTION
2ND LIEUTENANT	A. O. WILLIAMS		KILLED IN ACTION
COY SERGEANT MAJOR	J. CLARKE	15522	KILLED IN ACTION
SERGEANT	E. GRIFFITHS	16048	KILLED IN ACTION
CORPORAL	H. HUSSEY	24891	KILLED IN ACTION
CORPORAL	G. MURPHY	22800	KILLED IN ACTION

RANK	NAME	SERVICE NO.	WOUND
PRIVATE	J. R. BALLARD	15175	KILLED IN ACTION
PRIVATE	J. LEWIS	34175	KILLED IN ACTION
SERGEANT	W. S. JONES	15722	KILLED IN ACTION
SERGEANT	W. H. MOORE	17319	KILLED IN ACTION
LANCE CORPORAL	T. J. BUNNELL	15087	KILLED IN ACTION
LANCE CORPORAL	G. MOON	35405	KILLED IN ACTION
LANCE CORPORAL	G. ASHBY	27782	KILLED IN ACTION
PRIVATE	G. SANDERS	15015	KILLED IN ACTION
PRIVATE	C. THOMAS	23114	KILLED IN ACTION
PRIVATE	W. WILLIAMS	15058	KILLED IN ACTION
PRIVATE	P. WILLIAMS	13553	KILLED IN ACTION
PRIVATE	A. BUTTERTON	33219	KILLED IN ACTION
PRIVATE	J. HEALEY	33535	KILLED IN ACTION
PRIVATE	R. HUGHES	33348	KILLED IN ACTION
PRIVATE	J. ROBERTS	39178	KILLED IN ACTION
PRIVATE	T. FEARNS	23455	KILLED IN ACTION
PRIVATE	W. E. PHILLBRICK	23916	KILLED IN ACTION
PRIVATE	S. WILLCOCK	21495	KILLED IN ACTION
PRIVATE	J. ROLFE	22762	KILLED IN ACTION
PRIVATE	H. V. PETTITT	39779	KILLED IN ACTION
PRIVATE	M. WILLIAMS	15367	KILLED IN ACTION
PRIVATE	E. ATHERTON	32515	KILLED IN ACTION

RANK	NAME	SERVICE NO.	WOUND
PRIVATE	E. HEATH	23494	KILLED IN ACTION
PRIVATE	H. HUGHES	15464	KILLED IN ACTION
PRIVATE	T. HOLLAND	39331	KILLED IN ACTION
PRIVATE	T. JONES	15640	KILLED IN ACTION
PRIVATE	F. COOK	23465	KILLED IN ACTION
PRIVATE	R. HUGHES	24488	KILLED IN ACTION
PRIVATE	P. WILLIAMS	17603	KILLED IN ACTION
PRIVATE	H. MORRIS	15216	KILLED IN ACTION
PRIVATE	D. SIDES	26252	KILLED IN ACTION
LANCE CORPORAL	W. H. MANNING	16049	KILLED IN ACTION

RANK	NAME	SERVICE NO.	WOUND
CAPTAIN	C. A. R. FOLLITT		DIED OF WOUNDS
LIEUTENANT	S. F. BANCROFT		DIED OF WOUNDS REPORTED MISSING THEN KILLED
LANCE CORPORAL	M. HUGHES	8943	DIED OF WOUNDS
LANCE CORPORAL	R. W. HUGHES	21578	DIED OF WOUNDS
PRIVATE	J. H. JONES	14649	DIED OF WOUNDS
PRIVATE	J. JONES	15471	DIED OF WOUNDS
PRIVATE	J. DADE	15459	DIED OF WOUNDS
PRIVATE	B. OWEN	39135	DIED OF WOUNDS

RANK	NAME	SERVICE NO.	WOUND
LIEUTENANT	W. J. D. HALE		WOUNDED
2ND LIEUTENANT	W. D. EVANS		WOUNDED
2ND LIEUTENANT	A. B. BROTHERTON		WOUNDED
COY SERGEANT MAJOR	H. H. GRUNDY	15458	WOUNDED
COY SERGEANT MAJOR	W. H. HEWITT	11553	WOUNDED
COY SERGEANT MAJOR	W. ROWLEY	8780	WOUNDED
SERGEANT	R. B. CRABB	15482	WOUNDED
SERGEANT	W. AMBURY	38456	WOUNDED
SERGEANT	E. THOMAS	17709	WOUNDED
SERGEANT	L. THOMAS	29507	WOUNDED
SERGEANT	J. DAVIES	34314	WOUNDED
SERGEANT	D. M. MCSWEENY	15137	WOUNDED
SERGEANT	J. W. LLOYD	33764	WOUNDED
SERGEANT	W. H. WILCOCK	13461	WOUNDED
SERGEANT	J. W. PETTIFOR	15481	WOUNDED
SERGEANT	W. THOMAS	15544	WOUNDED
CORPORAL	F. W. SMITH	15547	WOUNDED
CORPORAL	L. JONES	23301	WOUNDED
LANCE CORPORAL	G. PHILLIPS	34387	WOUNDED

RANK	NAME	SERVICE NO.	WOUND
COY QR.-MR. SERGEANT	G. BOWEN	15180	WOUNDED
LANCE SERGEANT	F. WALKER	9534	WOUNDED
LANCE SERGEANT	P. MURPHY	16298	WOUNDED
LANCE SERGEANT	T. KEAY	15205	WOUNDED
CORPORAL	W. JONES	14981	WOUNDED
CORPORAL	S. ASTILL	9233	WOUNDED
CORPORAL	E. J. EDWARDS	15134	WOUNDED
CORPORAL	J. ROW;EY	15250	WOUNDED
CORPORAL	J. PHILLIPS	15690	WOUNDED
CORPORAL	M. PETERS	15109	WOUNDED
CORPORAL	H. DRISCOLL	15312	WOUNDED
CORPORAL	J. R. SIFLEET	15756	WOUNDED
CORPORAL	D. PHILLIPS	40214	WOUNDED
CORPORAL	A. T. JOHN	15450	WOUNDED
CORPORAL	R. O. HUGHES	34926	WOUNDED
LANCE CORPORAL	G. COLE	34058	WOUNDED
LANCE CORPORAL	J. R. OWEN	26617	WOUNDED
LANCE CORPORAL	K. EVANS	40017	WOUNDED
LANCE CORPORAL	T. COUPE	38879	WOUNDED
LANCE CORPORAL	J. LEWIS	31307	WOUNDED
LANCE CORPORAL	H. HARRIS	23728	WOUNDED
LANCE CORPORAL	W. CLIFFE	39955	WOUNDED
LANCE CORPORAL	S. L. LEWIS	20809	WOUNDED
LANCE CORPORAL	F. G. LATIMER	21677	WOUNDED
2ND LIEUTENANT	G. H. JENNINGS		WOUNDED
2ND LIEUTENANT	S. J. THOMAS		WOUNDED
2ND LIEUTENANT	F. A. LAWSON		WOUNDED
LANCE CORPORAL	W. WEBB	34897	WOUNDED
PRIVATE	E. BUMFORD	35020	WOUNDED
PRIVATE	E. DAVIES	39667	WOUNDED
PRIVATE	H. EVANS	13279	WOUNDED
PRIVATE	E. J. EDWARDS	15007	WOUNDED
PRIVATE	G. M. FOX	14960	WOUNDED
PRIVATE	C. M. FRYER	34093	WOUNDED
PRIVATE	J. GRIFFITHS	19953	WOUNDED
PRIVATE	E. HOWCROFT	33971	WOUNDED
PRIVATE	W. JONES	25419	WOUNDED
PRIVATE	W. R. MORGAN	15041	WOUNDED
PRIVATE	S. MCCARTHY	13731	WOUNDED
PRIVATE	C. MURPHY	35055	WOUNDED
PRIVATE	J. NAGLE	34228	WOUNDED

RANK	NAME	SERVICE NO.	WOUND
PRIVATE	S. ASHCROFT	33502	WOUNDED
PRIVATE	A. W. BOULTON	34801	WOUNDED
PRIVATE	E. L. BURFORD	34056	WOUNDED
PRIVATE	W. DAVIES	12985	WOUNDED
PRIVATE	W. OWENS	15136	WOUNDED
PRIVATE	S. J. SLATER	36581	WOUNDED
PRIVATE	J. E. THOMAS	36300	WOUNDED
PRIVATE	W. E. THOMAS	12043	WOUNDED
PRIVATE	W. J. BOXHALL	45782	WOUNDED
PRIVATE	W. DOUGHERTY	36523	WOUNDED
PRIVATE	A. EDWARDS	34084	WOUNDED
PRIVATE	B. MORRIS	5592	WOUNDED
PRIVATE	T. PARRY	21200	WOUNDED
PRIVATE	C. ARMSTRONG	33607	WOUNDED
LANCE CORPORAL	J. JONES	15256	WOUNDED
LANCE CORPORAL	H. BOWKER	15285	WOUNDED
LANCE CORPORAL	J. E. HUGHES	18323	WOUNDED
LANCE CORPORAL	W. J. CROSS	34075	WOUNDED
LANCE CORPORAL	R. EVANS	39082	WOUNDED
LANCE CORPORAL	E. EVANS	38522	WOUNDED
LANCE CORPORAL	B. DAVIES	38104	WOUNDED
LANCE CORPORAL	E. CONNAH	13646	WOUNDED
LANCE CORPORAL	R. W. CATHERALL	35497	WOUNDED
LANCE CORPORAL	A. G. CROW	22802	WOUNDED
LANCE CORPORAL	W. DAVIES	50051	WOUNDED
LANCE CORPORAL	D. DAVIES	38055	WOUNDED
LANCE CORPORAL	D. W. DAVIES	32588	WOUNDED
LANCE CORPORAL	E. EVANS	15289	WOUNDED
LANCE CORPORAL	E. EVANS	13971	WOUNDED
LANCE CORPORAL	M. R. EDMUNDS	16653	WOUNDED
LANCE CORPORAL	W. FERGUSON	34064	WOUNDED
LANCE CORPORAL	W. HENSHALL	15269	WOUNDED
LANCE CORPORAL	T. HUGHES	13810	WOUNDED
LANCE CORPORAL	W. HERBERT	40456	WOUNDED
LANCE CORPORAL	L. HUGHES	35436	WOUNDED
LANCE CORPORAL	J. HARDACRE	19660	WOUNDED
LANCE CORPORAL	E. J. F. HALL	20828	WOUNDED
LANCE CORPORAL	W. JONES	31914	WOUNDED
LANCE CORPORAL	C. KERSLEY	24352	WOUNDED
LANCE CORPORAL	T. LEWIS	33559	WOUNDED
LANCE CORPORAL	A. LEAKEY	26853	WOUNDED
LANCE CORPORAL	H. MELROSE	35341	WOUNDED
LANCE CORPORAL	W. T. OWEN	29580	WOUNDED
LANCE CORPORAL	C. PIFF	23450	WOUNDED
LANCE CORPORAL	A. PETRIE	15105	WOUNDED
LANCE CORPORAL	W. PRICE	34912	WOUNDED
LANCE CORPORAL	S. PHILLIPS	5466	WOUNDED
LANCE CORPORAL	H. REES	13431	WOUNDED
LANCE CORPORAL	J. H. ROBERTS	13692	WOUNDED
PRIVATE	W. SUTTON	30888	WOUNDED
PRIVATE	E. WILLIAMS	15884	WOUNDED
PRIVATE	D. WILLIAMS	29607	WOUNDED

RANK	NAME	SERVICE NO.	WOUND
PRIVATE	A. H. BALL	27335	WOUNDED
PRIVATE	W. BOWYER	38814	WOUNDED
PRIVATE	H. BENDORFFE	38161	WOUNDED
PRIVATE	F. BOOKER	8354	WOUNDED
PRIVATE	T. CARBERRY	33673	WOUNDED
PRIVATE	A. CLARKE	33113	WOUNDED
PRIVATE	D. DAVIES	39934	WOUNDED
PRIVATE	J. M. DAVIES	38513	WOUNDED
PRIVATE	W. J. DAVIES	23470	WOUNDED
PRIVATE	H. ELLISON	36234	WOUNDED
PRIVATE	E. HUGHES	15818	WOUNDED
PRIVATE	F. J. HARDING	14464	WOUNDED
PRIVATE	J. JOHN	15667	WOUNDED
PRIVATE	J. JONES	16316	WOUNDED
PRIVATE	G. F. JONES	4428	WOUNDED
PRIVATE	H. T. JONES	40180	WOUNDED
PRIVATE	F. LINES	15389	WOUNDED
PRIVATE	H. LANGSTAFF	31718	WOUNDED
PRIVATE	T. J. OWEN	15699	WOUNDED
PRIVATE	D. OWEN	29985	WOUNDED
PRIVATE	W. R. H. SLEIGH	27143	WOUNDED
PRIVATE	J. R. M. TURNER	27366	WOUNDED
PRIVATE	H. WALTERS	15764	WOUNDED
PRIVATE	T. NIXON	15056	WOUNDED
PRIVATE	T. CROMPTON	8455	WOUNDED
PRIVATE	T. POWNALL	35454	WOUNDED
PRIVATE	W. T. SMITH	22686	WOUNDED
PRIVATE	W. ARTHUR	43194	WOUNDED
PRIVATE	W. BAGSHALL	22231	WOUNDED
PRIVATE	H. H. BLACKBURN	39761	WOUNDED
PRIVATE	E. BIDMEAD	38052	WOUNDED
PRIVATE	H. DIXON	29060	WOUNDED
PRIVATE	B. DUNNING	38096	WOUNDED
PRIVATE	G. EGAN	19979	WOUNDED
PRIVATE	J. GIBSON	23215	WOUNDED
PRIVATE	A. GREEN	36315	WOUNDED
PRIVATE	W. GEORGE	50053	WOUNDED
PRIVATE	E. HUGHES	15485	WOUNDED
PRIVATE	J. JONES	50040	WOUNDED
PRIVATE	J. KENNEDY	4061	WOUNDED
PRIVATE	B. LLOYD	15597	WOUNDED
PRIVATE	W. MAGINN	28005	WOUNDED
PRIVATE	J. MORGAN	24359	WOUNDED
PRIVATE	J. NIXON	31782	WOUNDED
PRIVATE	A. PROBERT	18146	WOUNDED
PRIVATE	D. ROBERTS	37230	WOUNDED
PRIVATE	W. ROBERTS	43250	WOUNDED
PRIVATE	J. SYKES	24346	WOUNDED
PRIVATE	H. THOMAS	21069	WOUNDED
PRIVATE	J. S. WALKER	36519	WOUNDED
PRIVATE	W. WIEL	35130	WOUNDED
PRIVATE	G. SCAMMELL	22825	WOUNDED

RANK	NAME	SERVICE NO.	WOUND
PRIVATE	J. POLLARD	35455	WOUNDED
PRIVATE	J. HOWARTH	14992	WOUNDED
PRIVATE	F. H. GALDIS	35205	WOUNDED
PRIVATE	J. H. STARKEY	39298	WOUNDED

RANK	NAME	SERVICE NO.	WOUND
LANCE SERGEANT	T. BARTON	14914	WOUNDED SHELL SHOCK
PRIVATE	A. TURNER	36361	WOUNDED SHELL SHOCK
PRIVATE	G. JENNINGS	36451	WOUNDED SHELL SHOCK
PRIVATE	E. KERSHAW	31244	WOUNDED SHELL SHOCK
PRIVATE	D. R. JONES	40388	WOUNDED SHELL SHOCK
PRIVATE	W. HOCKING	31797	WOUNDED SHELL SHOCK
PRIVATE	T. E. GRIFFITHS	39081	WOUNDED SHELL SHOCK

RANK	NAME	SERVICE NO.	WOUND
SERGEANT	H. DOOLEY	14017	WOUNDED REPORTED MISSING
SERGEANT	A. SPROSTON	23059	WOUNDED REPORTED MISSING
PRIVATE	P. GALLAGHAM	23280	WOUNDED REPORTED MISSING
PRIVATE	N. SIEGAL	35358	WOUNDED REPORTED MISSING
PRIVATE	H. T. GREENWOOD	27184	WOUNDED REPORTED MISSING
LANCE CORPORAL	M. TOOHEY	5373	WOUNDED REPORTED MISSING
LANCE CORPORAL	H. W. COSTER	35042	WOUNDED REPORTED MISSING

RANK	NAME	SERVICE NO.	WOUND
SERGEANT	T. GEORGE	38089	REPORTED MISSING
LANCE SERGEANT	G. T. WICKLAND	15511	REPORTED MISSING
CORPORAL	R. J. SALTWELL	26780	REPORTED MISSING
LANCE CORPORAL	W. E. JONES	35371	REPORTED MISSING
LANCE CORPORAL	D. J. EVANS	37950	REPORTED MISSING
LANCE CORPORAL	B. H. BRETT	36890	REPORTED MISSING
PRIVATE	P. COSTELLO	14197	REPORTED MISSING
PRIVATE	A. DAVIES	18525	REPORTED MISSING
PRIVATE	S. T. DAVIES	15147	REPORTED MISSING
PRIVATE	W. J. JONES	15025	REPORTED MISSING
PRIVATE	B. W. LEWIS	16334	REPORTED MISSING
PRIVATE	W. ROBERTS	15073	REPORTED MISSING
PRIVATE	J. WILLIAMS	15143	REPORTED MISSING
PRIVATE	S. BONE	36940	REPORTED MISSING
PRIVATE	J. CLAYTON	19968	REPORTED MISSING
PRIVATE	W. DAVIES	20365	REPORTED MISSING

RANK	NAME	SERVICE NO.	WOUND
PRIVATE	T. DOWNING	36575	REPORTED MISSING
PRIVATE	W. EDWARDS	5376	REPORTED MISSING
PRIVATE	E. W. SMITH	35058	REPORTED MISSING
PRIVATE	H. P. WILLIAMS	21173	REPORTED MISSING
PRIVATE	W. J. DAVIES	40387	REPORTED MISSING
PRIVATE	W. BAXTER	27674	REPORTED MISSING
PRIVATE	H. BROUGHTON	12736	REPORTED MISSING
PRIVATE	J. BARLOW	38158	REPORTED MISSING
PRIVATE	W. CLEWES	38835	REPORTED MISSING
PRIVATE	E. W.DAVIES	35434	REPORTED MISSING
PRIVATE	W. DAVIES	38177	REPORTED MISSING
PRIVATE	G. DOWDLE	38180	REPORTED MISSING
PRIVATE	H. ELLIS	26285	REPORTED MISSING
PRIVATE	J. M. EDWARDS	38057	REPORTED MISSING
PRIVATE	H. GARNER	12940	REPORTED MISSING
PRIVATE	G. GITTENS	50003	REPORTED MISSING
PRIVATE	J. H. GREEN	19701	REPORTED MISSING
PRIVATE	J. D. HUNT	4919	REPORTED MISSING
PRIVATE	D. T. JONES	37503	REPORTED MISSING
PRIVATE	R. JONES	44580	REPORTED MISSING
PRIVATE	F. LOCKE	21561	REPORTED MISSING
PRIVATE	J. LEASE	36036	REPORTED MISSING
PRIVATE	E. MURPHY	43220	REPORTED MISSING
PRIVATE	J. P. MORRIS	37288	REPORTED MISSING
PRIVATE	H. J. NICHOLS	17567	REPORTED MISSING
PRIVATE	I. J. ROBERTS	26100	REPORTED MISSING
PRIVATE	E. O. ROBERTS	25802	REPORTED MISSING
PRIVATE	H. W. SMITH	26856	REPORTED MISSING
PRIVATE	J. L. WILLIAMS	14972	REPORTED MISSING
PRIVATE	D. E. WHYBRA	35496	REPORTED MISSING
PRIVATE	J. WILLIAMS	24288	REPORTED MISSING
PRIVATE	H. AINSWORTH	39775	REPORTED MISSING
PRIVATE	C. ALBON	35391	REPORTED MISSING
PRIVATE	T. ALDERMAN	38813	REPORTED MISSING
PRIVATE	I. ANTHONY	12897	REPORTED MISSING
PRIVATE	W. BUNNELL	38162	REPORTED MISSING
PRIVATE	C. BLUNT	36480	REPORTED MISSING
PRIVATE	S. BELLIS	18360	REPORTED MISSING
PRIVATE	A. BROOKS	35185	REPORTED MISSING
PRIVATE	J. DYER	31899	REPORTED MISSING
PRIVATE	H. G. DAVIES	40571	REPORTED MISSING
PRIVATE	E. EDWARDS	36977	REPORTED MISSING
PRIVATE	D. EVANS	37321	REPORTED MISSING
PRIVATE	D. GWILLIAM	35771	REPORTED MISSING
PRIVATE	W. GYSSER	22022	REPORTED MISSING
PRIVATE	A. HILL	39765	REPORTED MISSING
PRIVATE	H. JONES	37234	REPORTED MISSING
PRIVATE	W. L. JONES	19034	REPORTED MISSING
PRIVATE	D. OWENS	39274	REPORTED MISSING
PRIVATE	T. KENNEDY	12417	REPORTED MISSING
PRIVATE	J. OWENS	4856	REPORTED MISSING

RANK	NAME	SERVICE NO.	WOUND
PRIVATE	L. JONES	16829	REPORTED MISSING
PRIVATE	J. ROWLANDS	36825	REPORTED MISSING
PRIVATE	I. ROBERTS	15517	REPORTED MISSING
PRIVATE	H. SELLINGS	43285	REPORTED MISSING
PRIVATE	J. SCHOLE	39261	REPORTED MISSING
PRIVATE	G. J. TIMMS	37254	REPORTED MISSING
PRIVATE	W. VERNON	39277	REPORTED MISSING
PRIVATE	G. WILLIAMS	39782	REPORTED MISSING
PRIVATE	J. W. COX	36426	REPORTED MISSING
PRIVATE	T. HEENEY	33139	REPORTED MISSING
PRIVATE	R. HUGHES	39326	REPORTED MISSING
PRIVATE	R. T. JONES	39659	REPORTED MISSING
PRIVATE	W. LEVERS	39954	REPORTED MISSING
PRIVATE	F. LEES	29988	REPORTED MISSING
PRIVATE	T. SMITH	15665	REPORTED MISSING
PRIVATE	C. W. BULLEN	34820	REPORTED MISSING
PRIVATE	W. H. BRANCH	18351	REPORTED MISSING
PRIVATE	J. L. WILLIAMS	34847	REPORTED MISSING
PRIVATE	T. THOMPSON	24125	REPORTED MISSING

AUGUST 20th

The Battalion marched to Happy Valley.

AUGUST 21st

The Battalion in Brigade marched to Morlancourt. A draft of 1 Officer, Lieutenant H. J. K. Lewis and 133 other ranks (O. R.) joined the Battalion for duty.

AUGUST 23rd

At 6am the Battalion marched to Mericourt L'Abbe a distance of 7.4km

(4 ½ miles) where they were entrained. Arriving at Fienvillers-Candas Station, they marched to billets at Bois Bergues, arriving at 5. 50pm.

AUGUST 25th

The Battalion in Brigade marched to the Fortel area a distance of 20km (13 miles) and were billeted in Vacquerie De Boucq.

It was reported in the 76th Brigade's War Diary for this date, that: -

"Many Men From the 8th Kings Own Royal Lancaster Regiment & the 10th R. W. F. Fell Out".

This was probably due to the very hot weather on that day. It was noted in the diary that the **"Number of Stragglers = 77"**.

AUGUST 26th

The Battalion in Brigade marched to the Croix area and were billeted at Oeuf.

AUGUST 27th

The Battalion in Brigade marched to the Bergueneuse area, the starting point where Pierremont and Beauvais Road crosses the main St. Pol Headin Road. They were billeted at Fiefs. This was a long march, with the last 4km (2 ½ miles) uphill. The 3rd Division came under orders of the 1st Corps 1st Army and it was known that the 3rd Division would be entering the line at Loos on September 1st.

AUGUST 28th

The Battalion marched to billets at Sachin a distance of 4.5km (2.8 miles).

AUGUST 29th

The Battalion marched in Brigade to Bruay, a distance of 13.5km (8 ½ miles). The weather had changed dramatically and it rained all day with heavy thunderstorms.

AUGUST 30th

The Battalion had a very welcomed day of rest at their billets in Bruay. Baths were available to the men.

The following Officers joined the Battalion for duty with 25 other ranks (O. R.):-

- Captain W. S. Brocklehurst
- Captain E. H. Howard
- Captain W. F. Rudd
- Captain E. W. Bishop
- 2nd Lieutenant R. H. Williams
- 2nd Lieutenant A. F. Williams
- 2nd Lieutenant H. R. Davies
- 2nd Lieutenant F. H. Sewell
- 2nd Lieutenant C. G. N. Morgan
- 2nd Lieutenant D. Davies
- 2nd Lieutenant A. C. Daniel
- 2nd Lieutenant D. G. Quin
- 2nd Lieutenant G. Thomas
- 2nd Lieutenant L. E. Roberts
- 2nd Lieutenant P. Williams
- 2nd Lieutenant H. M. Jones
- 2nd Lieutenant H. G. Thomas

AUGUST 31st

The Battalion paraded at 1.50pm and then marched to Noeux Les Mines under command of Major Samuel. The Officers Commanding the Coys, Specialist Officers and N. C. O.'s visited the trenches in the Loos area and the following Officers rejoined the Battalion:-

- Lieutenant W. B. Morgan – 'B' Coy
- 2nd Lieutenant E. Vaughan-Jones – 'C' Coy

SEPTEMBER 1916

SEPTEMBER 1st

The Battalion marched to trenches in the Loos sector, relieving the 8th East Lancaster Regiment and went into support lines in the tenth avenue and village line under the command of Major F. A. Samuel with acting rank of Lieutenant Colonel, taking over from Lieutenant Colonel A. De L. Long who reported sick.

SEPTEMBER 2nd

A 'Working Party' of 170 other ranks (O. R.) repaired the trenches and wire.

SEPTEMBER 3rd

A 'Working Party' of 105 other ranks (O. R.) continued repairing the trenches which were in a very poor state.

SEPTEMBER 4th

A larger 'Working Party' of 244 other ranks (O. R.) continued the repair of the trenches and the wire immediately in front of the Front-Line Trenches. One casualty was reported as wounded **Private R. Hindley** service number 84096. The weather was reported as wet.

SEPTEMBER 5th

It continued to rain during the day which made the conditions for the 'Working Party' of 235 other ranks (O. R.) difficult.

SEPTEMBER 6th

A British aeroplane fell behind the Battalion lines at 5.15pm. The pilot and observer bodies could not be found as the plane burst into flames upon impact. The 8th Brigade on the 'Left' of the Battalion carried out trench mortar and artillery fire on the enemys Front-Line Trenches at 7.30pm. The enemys artillery retaliated at 7.40pm and caused the following casualties to the 121 other ranks (O. R.) Working Party:-

RANK	NAME	SERVICE NO.	WOUND
PRIVATE	J. JONES	8410	WOUNDED
PRIVATE	F. WILLIAMS	31933	WOUNDED
PRIVATE	J. DOYLE	43562	WOUNDED
PRIVATE	A. WEDGE	50036	WOUNDED
PRIVATE	J. MCDONAGH	15452	WOUNDED

There was also a 'Gas Alert Alarm' raised, but this proved to be a false alarm.

SEPTEMBER 7th

A 'Working Party' of 375 other ranks (O. R.) continued to work on the trenches and wire. Again, the Battalion were shelled by the enemy artillery at 8pm but this time, no casualties were reported.

SEPTEMBER 8th

The Battalion moved up into the Front-Line Trenches and took over the following sections from the 2nd Suffolk Regiment: -

- **'A' Coy in bays 44 to 46**
- **'B' Coy bay 47**
- **'C' Coy bays 48 & 49**
- **'D' Coy in reserve**

The Battalion also sent a 'Working Party' of 31 other ranks (O. R.) to help the Royal Engineers. 'A', 'B' & 'C' Coy worked on building up parapets, 'D' Coy repaired the trenches.

The following Officers joined the Battalion for duty: -

- 2nd Lieutenant A. E. Capel
- 2nd Lieutenant H. Pritchard
- 2nd Lieutenant C. W. Wilmore
- 2nd Lieutenant M Watcyn-Williams
- 2nd Lieutenant A. I. Hughes
- 2nd Lieutenant J. G. Williams

2nd Lieutenant Morgan Watcyn-Williams, after the War, went on to serve the Church and wrote about his life and about his time serving with the 10th Battalion R. W. F. in the Great War, in his book **"From Khaki to Cloth."**

"On September 8th I was back in the line once more, this time, with the famous 10th Battalion of the Royal Welsh Fusiliers. They had been through ghastly battles at Guillemont and Delville Wood, where two men earned the 'Victoria Cross.' The Battalion was cock-a-hoop with pride at their success, but down underneath, I detected a great worry and weariness. Twice in a month, they had been 'Cut to Ribbons'." – 2nd Lieutenant Morgan Watcyn-Williams 10th (Service) Battalion Royal Welsh Fusiliers

SEPTEMBER 10th

There was combined bombardment by the Brigades Royal Field Artillery and Trench Mortar Battery on the enemys Front-Line which started at 5pm and lasted for 20 minutes. The enemy retaliated with their own trench mortars causing the following casualties to the Battalion: -

RANK	NAME	SERVICE NO.	WOUND
PRIVATE	M. HUGHES	15427	WOUNDED
PRIVATE	J. JONES	15488	WOUNDED
PRIVATE	E. WILKINSON	33057	WOUNDED DIED OF WOUNDS 14TH SEPTEMBER

SEPTEMBER 11th

The General Officer Commanding (G. O. C.) visited the Front-Line Trenches. Enemy trench mortars were again active and one casualty was wounded **Private W. J. Biggs**, service number 21968.

SEPTEMBER 12th

The Battalion were visited by the Assistant Director of Medical Services (A. D. M. S.) of 3rd Division and the General Officer Commanding (G. O. C.) of 1st Corps. Enemy trench mortars were again active and two casualties were reported: -

RANK	NAME	SERVICE NO.	WOUND
PRIVATE	G. WILSON	23266	KILLED
PRIVATE	S. WILLIAMS	14659	WOUNDED

A 'Gas Alarm' was sounded by the 1st Gordon Highlanders which proved to be in error due to the wind blowing in a Westerly direction away from the Battalion Front-Line.

SEPTEMBER 13th

The Battalion were visited in the Front-Line by the Brigade Major and Divisional General. Again, the Battalion suffered casualties from the enemy trench mortars: -

RANK	NAME	SERVICE NO.	WOUND
PRIVATE	T. VOST	39754	KILLED
PRIVATE	T. WILLIAMS	1706	WOUNDED
2ND LIEUTENANT	F. WILLIAMS		WOUNDED
SERGEANT	W. J. BRIDGE	15413	WOUNDED

SEPTEMBER 14th

The Battalion was visited by the General Officer Commanding (G. O. C.) 3rd Division and the Trench Mortary Battery Officer. A very quiet night in the trenches was reported.

SEPTEMBER 15th

'D' Coy supplied a 'Carrying Party' of 100 other ranks (O. R.) to carry 'Trench Mortar Ammunition' to the front. The Battalion received the following casualties: -

RANK	NAME	SERVICE NO.	WOUND
PRIVATE	J. M. WILLIAMS	1796	WOUNDED
PRIVATE	J. MOODY	1792	WOUNDED
PRIVATE	H. WAGSTAFFE	1628	WOUNDED

SEPTEMBER 16th

The Battalion was relieved in the trenches at 4pm by the 2nd Suffolk Regiment and marched into billets at Mazingarbe, arriving at 6.30pm. The Battalion received the following casualties before being relieved from the Front-Line: -

RANK	NAME	SERVICE NO.	WOUND
PRIVATE	B. LITTLE	15193	WOUNDED
PRIVATE	J. JONES	28419	WOUNDED
PRIVATE	R. H. ROBERTS	15526	WOUNDED

A draft of 7 other ranks (O. R.) joined the Battalion for duty.

SEPTEMBER 17th

The Battalion were at rest, baths were available for the men and a welcome change of clothing was available too.

SEPTEMBER 18th

The following 'Acting Appointments' were made to the Battalion: -

- **Captain A. J. S. James to Acting Second in Command**
- **Captain E. H. Howard to Acting Adjutant**

40 other ranks (O. R.) attended a Royal Engineering Wiring Class.

SEPTEMBER 19th

The Battalion spent the day training. A medical inspection was also carried out. The following Decorations were announced: -

- Sergeant J. Davies 34314 – Cross of Saint George 1st Class (Russian)
- Private A. Hill 15280 – Croix De Guerre (French)
- Company Sergeant-Major W. E. Hewitt 11553 – Distinguished Conduct Medal
- Sergeant W. T. Jones 15722 – Distinguished Conduct Medal
- Sergeant A. Punchard 15791 - Distinguished Conduct Medal
- Sergeant J. Mills 6614 – Military Medal
- Private D. Walters 15286 – Military Medal
- Private A. E. Roberts 15084 – Military Medal
- Private J. Roberts 31075 - Military Medal

SEPTEMBER 20th

The Battalion continued their training. 'A' & 'B' Coys – Bayonet Fighting, 'C' & 'D' Coys - Bombing. There was an inspection of the Battalion by the Commanding Officer (C. O.) Lieutenant Colonel F. A. Samuel. Some sport activities were allowed in the afternoon. A draft of 7 other ranks (O. R.) joined the Battalion which included Private George Culpitt, service number 35115, who returned to the Battalion after being ill in hospital with influenza.

SEPTEMBER 22nd

The Battalion were inspected by General Officer Commanding (G. O. C.) of 3rd Division and presented **'Ribbons & Cards'** for gallantry shown during the fighting at Delville Wood in July (see list September 19th).

See Chapter 9 for details on the various awards

Private George Culpitt 35115 wrote in his Diary: -

"We were inspected by the Divisional Commander during the morning, these inspections were always a nuisance as there was so much waiting about before anyone came along and then they just walked down the lines, said perhaps a few words to one or two men and then after taking a salute and march past, the job was finished. What lacked in colour was made up in impressivness and it was a very fine sight to see a Battalion or Brigade at review, although, it was always so very trying for the men." – Private George Culpitt, 35115 10th (Service) Battalion Royal Welsh Fusiliers

SEPTEMBER 23rd

The Battalion in Brigade marched into billets at Lozinghem a distance of 24.4km (15.1 miles).

Private George Culpitt 35115 wrote in his Diary: -

"The first day proved the worst for those Battalions which had just been relieved and it was a common sight to see a man stagger out of the ranks to collapse in a heap on the side of the road and fall asleep. It was really too much to expect of men who had been in the line for 12 days at a stretch." - Private George Culpitt, 35115 10th (Service) Battalion Royal Welsh Fusiliers

SEPTEMBER 24th

The Battalion marched into billets at Liettres a distance of 18.7km (11 ½ miles). The award of the following Decorations were announced: -

- 2nd Lieutenant L. P. Vernon – Military Cross
- Private E. Ouldcott 15335 - Distinguished Conduct Medal)
- Private J. R. Ballard 15175 – Military Medal
- Private A. W. Cox 24515 - Military Medal
- Lance Corporal J. M. Price – Military Medal

SEPTEMBER 25th & 26th

Training began in earnest and they practiced the 1st and 3rd stages of the planned attack. A lecture by the Commanding Officer (C. O.) was given to the Officers and N. C. O.'s on the forthcoming attack. 2nd Lieutenant F. H. Sewell was appointed 'Musketry Officer'. A draft of 87 other ranks (O. R.) joined the Battalion for duty.

SEPTEMBER 27th

Today was the 'Anniversary of Embarkment of the Battalion for France'. Training for the Battalion continued in the morning. A Brigade 'Ceremonial March Past' and presentation of 'Ribbons' and Battalion sports were held in the afternoon. A concert was held by 3rd Division in the evening.

SEPTEMBER 28th

The Battalion was on the training area practising the attack by Companies. 2nd Lieutenant A. C. Daniel appointed 'Sniping and Intelligence Officer'. Captain H. Hall Morgan joined the Battalion and was posted to

'C' Company. The award of the **'Victoria Cross'** was announced to Corporal J. Davies service number 34314 and Private A. Hill service number 15280.

See Chapter 9 for details on the various awards

SEPTEMBER 29th

Training continued for the Battalion. 'C' & 'D' Coys on range in the morning, 'A' & 'B' Coys on range in the afternoon, with 'C' & 'D' Coy having physical training. During bombing practice with live bombs the following casualties were incurred: -

RANK	NAME	SERVICE NO.	WOUND
LANCE SERGEANT	J. E. HUGHES	26595	DIED OF WOUNDS
LIEUTENANT	W. B. MORGAN		WOUNDED
PRIVATE	A. KIRK	57022	WOUNDED
PRIVATE	J. JONES	21281	WOUNDED
PRIVATE	G. HUGHES	23289	WOUNDED

Private George Culpitt 35115 wrote in his Diary: -

"We commenced to throw live mills grenades into a big hole about 25 yards from the barricade. At first, all went well, and I threw mine and returned to the rest of the classes who were taking cover from flying bits of shrapnel in a hollow. About 20 yards behind the sandbags, suddenly, while two men were in the act of throwing with the Officer and Sergeant supervising behind them, one of the bombs exploded prematurely with the result that the Officer, Sergeant and two men of the bombing post were wounded and also on of those lying back with us. For the first moments we were stunned by the unexpectedness of the catastrophe, but quickly, regaining our self control, set to work, to bandage the wounded. The one who suffered the worst was the one who had the bomb in his hand at the time, while the other three at the post had 5 or 6 pieces in different parts of their body. The fifth only had one piece in his cheek, but all the others were stretcher cases. We were told afterwards, that the Sergeant had died as a result of his injuries, for which we were all very sorry for as he was a very decent chap." - Private George Culpitt, 35115 10th (Service) Battalion Royal Welsh Fusiliers

SEPTEMBER 30th

There was a 'Brigade Ceremonial Parade' and 'March Past in Column'. The Battalion was under command of Captain A. J. S. James for the parade. There was also a Farewell Address by Brigadier General R. J. Kentish D. S. O.

OCTOBER 1916
OCTOBER 1st

The Following **'Farewell Order'** by Brigadier General R. S. Kentish D. S. O. on relinquishing Command of the 76th Brigade was published, it said: -

"I am issuing this special order to your Battalion, both to mark my keen sense of appreciaition of the magnificent gallantry displayed by your Battalion and also in order that you may use it as a record for all the time of your conduct as a Battalion in the great battle of the Somme during the period you were engaged. The period commenced on the 6th July, and terminated, as far as my command of the Brigade is concerned, on 20th August. Throughout the whole of that period, your Battalion showed the same courage, endurance, and devotion to duty that has ever been conspicuous in the history of the Royal Welsh Fusiliers. Your gallantry in Delville Wood on the 20th July will never be forgotten, and when history of the Somme battle comes to be written, and especially of the intense fighting around and in the wood, the part played by your Battalion on the night of the 20th and the early hours of the 21st, will provide a page in history, and which, as a record of staunchness and devotion to duty of a Battalion misled by Guides, and shot into by friend and foe, will possibly be unsurpassed in this War. Two Victoria Crosses, one gained by Corporal J. Davies and the other by Private A. Hill, on that night, will remain for ever a lasting proof of the magnificent conduct of your Battalion. More experienced troops might well have broken without incurring the adverse criticism of their superiors. You, a young Battalion of inexperienced soldiers, neither broke nor did you incur this adverse criticism; on appointed, charged forward to the attack, not once but twice and three times, and in so doing carried your duty and gained the praise of your Commanders. Again, during all the hard fighting in and around Maltz Horn Ridge from the 18th to 20th August, and especially of the night of the 17th and afternoon of the 18th, you gave some splendid examples of courage and devotion to duty that had always been traditional with you, and this in spite of your ranks being filled with newly joined drafts. Your casualties are themselves severe and lasting proof of the severity of the fighting in which you have been engaged. I personally deeply regret the loss of every single Officer and man of your Battalion, each of whom I had come to regard as a personal friend. You have however, consolation in knowing that you have emerged from the Somme fighting with the greatest credit, and that today you stand in the ranks of a Battalion that can lay claim to a great record, a record of which the old parent Battalion of the Royal Welsh Fusiliers and His Majesty the King, your Colonel in Chief, will ever be justly proud. I thank you for the support you have accorded me in all the severe fighting, and I trust that

your conduct may be held up in front of every Officer, N. C. O., and man, joining for the first time, your splendid Battalion." – R. J. Kentish, Brigadier General Commanding 76th Brigade

Brigadier C. L. Porter from 17th Division assumed command of the 76th Brigade Infantry. Captain A. J. S. James attended a conference of the 3rd Divisional Staff with Brigadier and Commanding Officers in the training area.

OCTOBER 3rd

Major F. A. Samuel who was in temporary command of the Battalion, reported sick and was taken to hospital. Captain A. J. S. James assumed temporary command of the Battalion in the training area. The Battalion, with the 76th Brigade carried out a 'Practice Attack' on the 1st and 2nd lines of trenches in preperation for the divisional attack planned. The Battalion were warned on an impending move Southwards.

OCTOBER 4th

Major Charles Beauman Hore from the 1st Battalion Royal Warwickshire Regiment assumed command of the Battalion with acting rank of Lieutenant Colonel.

OCTOBER 5th

The Battalion marched into billets at Fiefs a distance of 14km (8 ½ miles).

OCTOBER 6th

The Battalion rested at Fiefs.

OCTOBER 7th

The Battalion left at 2.30am and marched to St. Pol a distance of 20.4km (12 ½ miles) and entrained for Acheux. The following Officers joined the Battalion for duty: -

- 2nd Lieutenant W. H. Morris – posted to 'B' Coy
- 2nd Lieutenant H. L. Harries – posted to 'D' Coy

OCTOBER 8th

The Battalion marched to Bertrancourt and billeted at Camp X. which was just within range of the enemys guns and were occasionally shelled. It was reported that Major F. A. Samuel and Captain M. Murray were transported to England for further treatment.

OCTOBER 9th

The Battalion rested. Awards of the **'Military Medal'** to the following N. C. O.'s and men were announced and appeared in the London Gazette: -

- Sergeant P. Murphy 16298
- Sergeant D. M. McSweeney 15137
- Corporal M. Peters 15109
- Private J. Pritchard 15689
- Private W. Thomas 15424
- Private R. Wynne 4697
- Private L. Stembridge 27575
- Private N. Williams 15728
- Private G. W. Able 15589

OCTOBER 10th

A 'Working Party' of 4 Officers and 300 other ranks (O. R.) under the command of 2nd Lieutenant E. Vaughan-Jones spent the evening supplying and repairing the Front-Line Trenches and the Battalion suffered one wounded casualty, **Private R. Duckett** service number 57006.

OCTOBER 12th

A 'Working Party' of 30 and 158 other ranks (O. R.) continued to work and supply the Front-Line Trenches. A draft of 18 other ranks (O. R.) joined the Battalion for duty.

OCTOBER 14th

Three 'Working & Carrying Parties' consisting of:- 1 Officer and 36 other ranks (O. R.): 1 Officer and 50 other ranks (O. R.): 1 Officer and 60 other ranks (O. R.) continued their work on the Front-Line and Support Trenches. The Battalion suffered the following casualties: -

RANK	NAME	SERVICE NO.	WOUND
PRIVATE	E. J. WILCOX	54446	KILLED
PRIVATE	J. WINDSOR	34951	KILLED
LANCE CORPORAL	W. SUTTON	30888	WOUNDED
PRIVATE	J. JONES	50007	WOUNDED
PRIVATE	W. ACKLEY	39762	WOUNDED

The weather was reported as 'wet'.

OCTOBER 15th

Work continued under the command of 2nd Lieutenant H. L. Harries and 60 other ranks (O. R.). The remainder of the Battalion were on the training area.

OCTOBER 16th

Officers of the Battalion reconnoitred the trenches as instructed. One casualty was reported as **Private J. Williams**, service number 15017 who died of his wounds.

OCTOBER 17th

The Battalion marched to Louvencourt a distance of 6.5km (4 miles).

OCTOBER 19th

The Battalion marched to trenches in the Serre District and took over sections of the trenches in the 'Right Sub-Section' from the 13th Battalion the Kings (Liverpool) Regiment. One casualty was reported as wounded, **Private J. Roberts** service number 56790

OCTOBER 20th

The Brigade's artillery carried out a programme of destroying the enemies wire and was active for most of the day. The Battalion, working with the 8th Kings Own Royal Lancaster Regiment, sent out patrols to access the strength of the enemy lines in front of them. Both patrols reported that the enemy lines were strongly held. The General Officer Commanding (G. O. C.) the Brigade visited the Battalions trenches at night.

OCTOBER 21st

The Battalion were relieved in trenches by the 13th Battalion Yorks & Lancs Regiment who were recently attached to the 76th Brigade. Relief was not completed until 11.50pm that night. Once relieved, the Battalion marched back to billets at Bus Les Artois.

Private George Culpitt 35115 wrote in his Diary –

"On the way up we had to pass a very muddy and holey road with the result we got our feet soaked with mud and water and by the time we had reached our position we were fairly crippled. As there were no clean or dry socks to be had, we had to have wet feet the whole of the three days we remained in the trench. There was not a great deal of shelling but at times, he put a few over in our vicinity, too near to be pleasant." – Private George Culpitt 35115 10th (Service) Battalion Royal Welsh Fusiliers

A draft of 3 Officers with 11 other ranks (O. R.) joined the Battalion for duty: -

- **Captain B. M. Cutbush**
- **2nd Lieutenant T. Rea**
- **2nd Lieutenant H. D. Taylor**

OCTOBER 22nd

Major Geoffrey L. Compton-Smith of the 1st Battalion Royal Welsh Fusiliers joined the Battalion and assumed command with the acting rank of Lieutenant Colonel. The Battalion at this time were in the training area.

OCTOBER 23rd

The Battalion returned to the trenches and relieved the 13th Battalion Yorks & Lancs Regiment. The relief was completed by 2.30pm. There was heavy enemy artillery activity between 2pm and 5pm. Weather was poor with rain and mist. The following casualty was reported as – **2nd Lieutenant H. W. Rayner** who was wounded when he was serving with the Trench Mortar Battery.

OCTOBER 25th

The Battalion were relieved in the trenches by the 1st Battalion Royal Scots and returned to billets. Some of the Battalion Coys worked on repairing the road leading up to the Front-Line.

OCTOBER 26th

'Working Parties' continued working on repairing the roads. There was an inspection on the billets by the new Commanding Officer (C.O.) Lieutenant Colonel G. L. Compton-Smith.

OCTOBER 27th, 28th, 29th & 30th

'Working Parties' continued on working on repairing the roads as the rest of the Battalion continued on the training area. During this time Major C. B. Hore left the Battalion to join the 12th Battalion South Wales Borderers. A draft of 3 other ranks (O. R.) joined the Battalion for duty. Captain and Adjutant A. J. S. James was promoted to the rank of Temporary Major.

OCTOBER 31st

The Battalion attended a lecture entitled 'Care of Feet & Sanitation' given by the Battalions Medical Officer.

NOVEMBER 1916

2nd Lieutenant Morgan Watcyn-Williams wrote about the Battalion's new Commanding Officer: -

"Lieutenant G. L. Compton-Smith took command of our Battalion, he was a magnificent Officer, tall, strong and sensitive, inclined to be patient and not given to tolerating fools gladly, with that one weakness he was a rare ruler of men. He explained to us that while he expected orders to be obeyed instantly, he regarded our brains as at least the equal of his own. Unlike many regular Officers, he was always willing to learn from his juniors and believed thoroughly in pooling ideas. It fell to his immediate lot to supervise our attack on four lines of trenches and the village of Serre." - 2nd Lieutenant Morgan Watcyn-Williams 10th (Service) Battalion Royal Welsh Fusiliers November 1916

2nd Lieutenant Morgan Watcyn-Williams became very good friends with Compton-Smith and wrote fondly of him in his autobiography "From Khaki to Cloth."

NOVEMBER 1st TO 5th

The Battalion were in the training area preparing for the attack. At night 'Working & Carrying Parties' continued to repair and supply the Front-Line.

Private George Culpitt 35115 wrote in his Diary: -

"The weather during this period was bad. For one week we were on fatigue at night carrying 60lb trench mortars from the dump up various places near the line, doing sometimes, two or three journeys a night. This proved to be very hard work, for the trenches were some 2 – 3 feet deep in mud in some places, not a

great slog at ordinary times but weighted as we were with our load of 60lb. It was as much as I could do to finish the journey. Also it meant wet feet, not wet feet as a civilian knows them but sodden with mud and water, swollen so that once one's boots are off it is painful to put them back on again, boots filled with liquid mud which oozed through the lace holes at every step. By the time the week of fatigues were finished, everyone felt fairly knocked and the number of sick had increased owing to an outbreak of diarrhoea, brought on by the cold and wet. " - Private George Culpitt 35115 10th (Service) Battalion Royal Welsh Fusiliers

The Battalion were exhausted and this was before the impending attack had even began. The award of the 'Distinguished Service Order' (D. S. O.) to the late **Captain C. A. R. Follitt M. C.** (killed in August 1916) was announced.

NOVEMBER 6th
A draft of 47 other ranks (O. R.) joined the Battalion for duty and were posted to 'B' Coy.

NOVEMBER 7th, 8th & 9th
Training continued for the Battalion. On the 9th a draft of 3 other ranks (O. R.) joined the Battalion for duty. The weather was reported as 'Atrocious' as the rain was very heavy.

NOVEMBER 10th
The Battalion marched to the Front-Line Trenches but orders were received when en-route to return to billets.

NOVEMBER 11th
Training continued. A conference for Officers took place to go over the final details of the attack which was planned for the 13th November.

NOVEMBER 12th

'A' and 'C' Coys marched to the Front-Line Trenches in the early morning. 'B' and 'D' Coys marched to the trenches in the evening. The Battalion's orders were to attack and hold four lines of the enemy trenches in front of Serre.

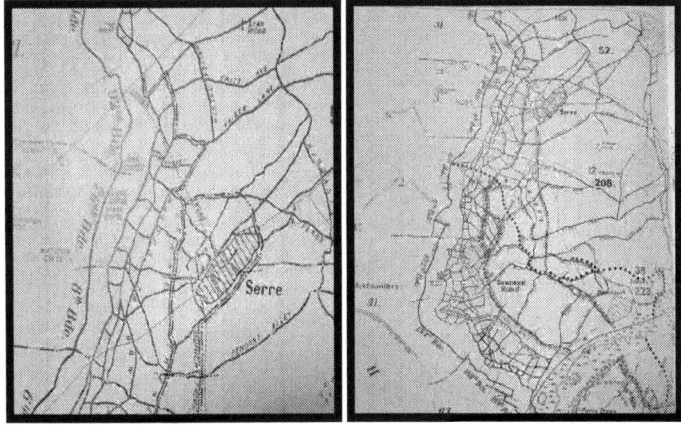

Serre Maps November 1916

NOVEMBER 13th - Battle of Ancre

The Battalion attacked the Serre Trenches at 5.45am in **'Eight Lines'** in the following order – 'B', 'D', 'C' and 'A' Coys. The two 'Leading Companies' deployed successfully in 'No Mans Land' and the two rear Companies in the front of 'Rob Roy Trench'. The left of the Leading Company was on Mark Copse. The right Company, in front of Matthew Copse with a frontage of 250 yards. Touch was obtained with the 2nd Battalion Suffolk Regiment on the Battalions 'Left Flank' and with the 1st Battalion Royal Scots Fusiliers on our 'Right Flank'. The 1st Battalion Gordon Highlanders were in Campion Trench to the rear of the 10th Battalion Royal Welsh Fusiliers with orders to attack Serre Village after the four German trench lines in front had been taken.

The Battalion started splendidly and at 6.38am a message was received at Brigade Head Quarters – *"Welsh Doing Well!"*

At 6.46am another message was received saying - ***"Welsh On Objective."*** At 7.50am a message received reported that the 2nd Battalion Suffolk Regiment and the 8th Battalion The Kings Own Royal Lancaster Regiment were on the 10th Battalion Royal Welsh Fusilier's 'Left Flank' and were held up in the German 1st and 2nd lines. The two Leading Companies of the 10th Battalion R. W. F. had reached their objective of the German fourth line trench and in their advance had taken numerous German prisoners but had lost touch with the Suffolk Regiment on their 'Left Flank' and the Royal Scots Fusiliers on the 'Right Flank' leaving the two Leading Companies in a perilous situation. The fourth German line was heavily defended and the Companies, because of the vulnerability on each side, had to use half of the Companies to form the 'Defensive Flanks' and reduced the impitus to go forward. The Germans attacked around the flanks and many Germans emerged from deep shelters in front to surround the two Companies and swamped Captain Rudd and the remaining survivors of 'B' Coy and Captain E. W. Bishop with 'D' Coy.

It was reported in the Battalion's War Diary that these two Coys ***"Just Disappeared From View."***

'C' Coy had advanced as far as the third German line and now tried to consolidate this position alongside the 1st Gordon Highlanders. Knee deep in mud, they managed to hold for an hour, but with both flanks exposed, they were forced to retire to their original position at Copse Trench. By nightfall, all survivors had been brought back to their original positions. During the night 2nd Lieutenant Pritchard managed to return to the Battalion after spending 18 hours in the German fourth line.
The attack on Serre had once again failed, as it had, on the 1st July.

2nd Lieutenant Morgan Watcyn-Williams wrote: –

"We went over the top at 5.45am behind a most terrific artillery bombardment, non the less, we ran into uncut wire, neither the Suffolks on our left, nor the Royal Scots Fusiliers on our right, succeeded in reaching their objective. Captain W. N. Davies, my Skipper, and Lieutenant Vaughan-Jones, were severely wounded and 2nd Lieutenant David Davies was killed, so I was left alone in my first attack cut off in a large shell hole between the second and third German lines. For two hours, ten men and I hung on to it's lip warding off three determined counter

attacks, and by that time, our number had dwindled to five. By midday, we managed to struggle back to our own Front-Line." – 2nd Lieutenant Morgan Watcyn-Williams 10th (Service) Battalion Royal Welsh Fusiliers

Lieutenant Colonel Geoffrey L. Compton-Smith wrote:-

"Zero hour came 5.45am, two men were moving near me, climbing through the torn wire, all along the line explosives in the air, explosions on the ground, sparks, drifting smoke, golden rain, red lights, green lights, white lights, and with a crash pandemonium descended and reigned over all. In the semi orange light the land was alive with bowed figures all moving forwards. I rushed from my mound, bumbling and scrambling, I overtook them, shaking hands with as many as I could and cheered them on their way, but they needed no cheering, it would have been much harder to discourage them. And the end of it was at 6.30pm that the Battalion was utterly wiped out, all the Officers, but two, killed or wounded. And many of the wounded drowned in the mud. Nothing was gained." – Lieutenant Colonel Geoffrey L. Compton-Smith Officer Commanding 10th (Service) Battalion Royal Welsh Fusiliers

Casualties for the Battalion during the action of 13th November were as follows: -

RANK	NAME	SERVICE NO.	WOUND
2ND LIEUTENANT	A. E. CAPELL		KILLED IN ACTION
2ND LIEUTENANT	P. WILLIAMS		KILLED IN ACTION
2ND LIEUTENANT	G. THOMAS		KILLED IN ACTION
2ND LIEUTENANT	R. H. WILLIAMS		KILLED IN ACTION
2ND LIEUTENANT	H. G. THOMAS		KILLED IN ACTION
2ND LIEUTENANT	H. M. JONES		KILLED IN ACTION
2ND LIEUTENANT	D. DAVIES		KILLED IN ACTION
2ND LIEUTENANT	H. L. HARRIES		KILLED IN ACTION
PRIVATE	D. EVANS	14961	KILLED IN ACTION

RANK	NAME	SERVICE NO.	WOUND
PRIVATE	W. G. PERKINS	23031	KILLED IN ACTION
PRIVATE	C. EVANS	56990	KILLED IN ACTION
PRIVATE	H. EARLY	35702	KILLED IN ACTION
PRIVATE	W. ABLE	13243	KILLED IN ACTION
PRIVATE	J. JONES	12636	KILLED IN ACTION
PRIVATE	J. CLUTTON	57076	KILLED IN ACTION

RANK	NAME	SERVICE NO.	WOUND
PRIVATE	F. EDWARDS	54440	KILLED IN ACTION
PRIVATE	J. E. PRITCHARD	5806	KILLED IN ACTION
PRIVATE	WILLIAMS	6284	KILLED IN ACTION
PRIVATE	J. H. LANE	15357	KILLED IN ACTION
PRIVATE	W. T. DAVIES	19254	KILLED IN ACTION
CORPORAL	T. R. KNOWLES	29651	KILLED IN ACTION
CORPORAL	C. MURPHY	8190	KILLED IN ACTION

RANK	NAME	SERVICE NO.	WOUND
CAPTAIN	W. F. RUDD		MISSING REPORTED KILLED

RANK	NAME	SERVICE NO.	WOUND
PRIVATE	J. CRABTREE	56992	DIED OF WOUNDS
PRIVATE	J. R. EDWARDS	27774	DIED OF WOUNDS
PRIVATE	W. HOARE	22532	DIED OF WOUNDS

RANK	NAME	SERVICE NO.	WOUND
CAPTAIN	W. N. DAVIES		WOUNDED
2ND LIEUTENANT	I. A. HUGHES		WOUNDED
2ND LIEUTENANT	E. VAUGHAN-JONES		WOUNDED
LANCE CORPORAL	E. THOMPSON	54432	WOUNDED
LANCE CORPORAL	H. V. MAJOR	35071	WOUNDED
LANCE CORPORAL	J. DAVIES	12715	WOUNDED
LANCE CORPORAL	R. BILLINGHURST	18142	WOUNDED
PRIVATE	C. FRYER	34093	WOUNDED
PRIVATE	H. WILLIS	33595	WOUNDED
PRIVATE	I. A. HUGHES	15260	WOUNDED
PRIVATE	T. LEWIS	15026	WOUNDED
PRIVATE	F. D. HAYES	57048	WOUNDED
PRIVATE	H. P. THOMAS	56760	WOUNDED
PRIVATE	A. W. CHILD	34812	WOUNDED
PRIVATE	H. FREEMAN	57035	WOUNDED
PRIVATE	D. E. THORPE	56761	WOUNDED
PRIVATE	R. H. WILLIAMS	54439	WOUNDED
PRIVATE	W. CLOUGH	36431	WOUNDED
PRIVATE	W. H. BAILEY	33506	WOUNDED
CORPORAL	R. ROBERTS	15165	WOUNDED
PRIVATE	E. MORRIS	10533	WOUNDED
PRIVATE	G. MARDEN	24430	WOUNDED
LANCE CORPORAL	J. HARVEY	34375	WOUNDED
PRIVATE	W. WEBB	10009	WOUNDED
PRIVATE	H. YONDS	23968	WOUNDED
PRIVATE	D. T. DENNIS	17312	WOUNDED
PRIVATE	W. H. JOHNSON	12381	WOUNDED
PRIVATE	J. N. JONES	57003	WOUNDED
SERGEANT	W. LEWIS	15261	WOUNDED
SERGEANT	J. MILLS	6414	WOUNDED
SERGEANT	R. CARR	14643	WOUNDED
LANCE SERGEANT	W. C. PRICE	15368	WOUNDED
CORPORAL	T. A. DUNNING	57014	WOUNDED
LANCE CORPORAL	W. KNOTT	15281	WOUNDED
PRIVATE	J. BUTLER	57064	WOUNDED
PRIVATE	N. DAVIES	54711	WOUNDED
PRIVATE	J. ELCOCK	17178	WOUNDED
PRIVATE	R. H. GEORGE	19830	WOUNDED
PRIVATE	J. HUGHES	11128	WOUNDED
PRIVATE	A. HARRIS	57018	WOUNDED
PRIVATE	F. JAMES	31562	WOUNDED
PRIVATE	E. W. JONES	54736	WOUNDED
PRIVATE	F. MARSH	33783	WOUNDED
PRIVATE	J. H. ROBERTS	13692	WOUNDED
PRIVATE	W. C. SHUFFLEBOTHAM	54430	WOUNDED
PRIVATE	H. THOMAS	54434	WOUNDED
PRIVATE	S. A. WELLS	15306	WOUNDED
PRIVATE	A. BLACKSHAW	57040	WOUNDED
PRIVATE	D. J. DAVIES	17460	WOUNDED
PRIVATE	L. B. DAVIES	56949	WOUNDED
PRIVATE	L. P. JONES	16301	WOUNDED
PRIVATE	N. MCLEOD	33777	WOUNDED

RANK	NAME	SERVICE NO.	WOUND
PRIVATE	D. OWEN	15741	WOUNDED
PRIVATE	C. RALPH	24680	WOUNDED
PRIVATE	C. WATFORD	33855	WOUNDED
SERGEANT	R. WHITE	15500	WOUNDED
SERGEANT	G. H. HUGHES	15504	WOUNDED
CORPORAL	H. HARRIS	23728	WOUNDED
LANCE CORPORAL	A. JONES	23067	WOUNDED
LANCE CORPORAL	S. BATES	36699	WOUNDED
PRIVATE	D. POWELL	57077	WOUNDED
PRIVATE	W. TROW	54435	WOUNDED
PRIVATE	R. A. WALTERS	23278	WOUNDED
SERGEANT	R. THOMAS	54814	WOUNDED
LANCE SERGEANT	W. WEBB	34897	WOUNDED
LANCE CORPORAL	A. JAYS	8717	WOUNDED
LANCE CORPORAL	G. DANIELS	54618	WOUNDED
LANCE CORPORAL	G. GALLAGHER	36189	WOUNDED
LANCE CORPORAL	J. BLUNDELL	8209	WOUNDED
PRIVATE	G. HUGHES	16120	WOUNDED
PRIVATE	R. HENSHAW	57019	WOUNDED
PRIVATE	M. JONES	31163	WOUNDED
PRIVATE	P. NEWTON	29987	WOUNDED
PRIVATE	P. RAYNER	33818	WOUNDED
PRIVATE	E. H. SEALEY	27648	WOUNDED

RANK	NAME	SERVICE NO.	WOUND
PRIVATE	W. DALE	22169	WOUNDED & MISSING
PRIVATE	J. W. LLOYD	54259	WOUNDED & MISSING
PRIVATE	WILLIAMS	59260	WOUNDED & MISSING
PRIVATE	E. WILLIAMS	15129	WOUNDED & MISSING
PRIVATE	W. JAMES	33554	WOUNDED & MISSING
PRIVATE	T. BROOKES	54700	WOUNDED & MISSING
PRIVATE	J. MCFARLANE	15346	WOUNDED & MISSING
CORPORAL	D. WALTERS	5192	WOUNDED & MISSING
PRIVATE	W. JAMES	33554	WOUNDED & MISSING
PRIVATE	J. N. JONES	57003	WOUNDED & MISSING
PRIVATE	A. AYERS	10783	WOUNDED & MISSING
PRIVATE	C. HATCH	18232	WOUNDED & MISSING
PRIVATE	W. H. JOHNSON	12381	WOUNDED & MISSING
PRIVATE	S. ROBERTS	34033	WOUNDED & MISSING
PRIVATE	S. DAVIES	15045	WOUNDED & MISSING
PRIVATE	W. ALEXANDER	5021	WOUNDED & MISSING
CORPORAL	H. O. ELLIS	40367	WOUNDED & MISSING
PRIVATE	S. BAILEY	15825	WOUNDED & MISSING
PRIVATE	R. H. JONES	54737	WOUNDED & MISSING
SERGEANT	W. J. BRIDLE	15413	WOUNDED & MISSING
CORPORAL	T. ROBERTS	36333	WOUNDED & MISSING
PRIVATE	R. L. PEARSON	5398	WOUNDED & MISSING
PRIVATE	D. S. EVANS	54397	WOUNDED & MISSING
PRIVATE	J. EVANS	29611	WOUNDED & MISSING
PRIVATE	A. E. MANSFIELD	34633	WOUNDED & MISSING

RANK	NAME	SERVICE NO.	WOUND
PRIVATE	R. JONES	39122	WOUNDED & SUBSEQUENTLY REPORTED PRISONER OF WAR
PRIVATE	J. MCCANN	56728	WOUNDED & SUBSEQUENTLY REPORTED PRISONER OF WAR
PRIVATE	A. HEROD	54401	WOUNDED & SUBSEQUENTLY REPORTED PRISONER OF WAR
LANCE CORPORAL	A. PEGG	56999	WOUNDED & SUBSEQUENTLY REPORTED PRISONER OF WAR
LANCE CORPORAL	A. J. F. WEBBER	26785	WOUNDED & SUBSEQUENTLY REPORTED PRISONER OF WAR
PRIVATE	J. W. B. JOHNSON	57079	WOUNDED & SUBSEQUENTLY REPORTED PRISONER OF WAR
PRIVATE	J. A. ROWLANDS	54438	WOUNDED & SUBSEQUENTLY REPORTED PRISONER OF WAR
PRIVATE	J. EVANS	54715	WOUNDED & SUBSEQUENTLY REPORTED PRISONER OF WAR
SERGEANT	W. THOMAS	15544	WOUNDED & SUBSEQUENTLY REPORTED PRISONER OF WAR
LANCE SERGEANT	D. M. HUGHES	38845	WOUNDED & SUBSEQUENTLY REPORTED PRISONER OF WAR
PRIVATE	J. W. DAVIES	23415	WOUNDED & SUBSEQUENTLY REPORTED PRISONER OF WAR
PRIVATE	A. MORT	57042	WOUNDED & SUBSEQUENTLY REPORTED PRISONER OF WAR

RANK	NAME	SERVICE NO.	WOUND
PRIVATE	T. WILLIAMS	54260	MISSING & SUBSEQUENTLY REPORTED KILLED
PRIVATE	W. PARRY	54427	MISSING & SUBSEQUENTLY REPORTED KILLED
CORPORAL	J. S. TRIVETT	15291	MISSING & SUBSEQUENTLY REPORTED KILLED

RANK	NAME	SERVICE NO.	WOUND
PRIVATE	H. F. HUNT	29656	MISSING & SUBSEQUENTLY DIED WHEN PRISONER OF WAR
PRIVATE	J. W. FORSTER	54399	MISSING & SUBSEQUENTLY DIED WHEN PRISONER OF WAR
PRIVATE	J. GREENWOOD	18695	MISSING & SUBSEQUENTLY DIED WHEN PRISONER OF WAR

RANK	NAME	SERVICE NO.	WOUND
LANCE CORPORAL	S. J. LOMAS	33950	MISSING & SUBSEQUENTLY PRISONER OF WAR
PRIVATE	A. CUMMINGS	54707	MISSING & SUBSEQUENTLY PRISONER OF WAR
PRIVATE	R. H. DAVIES	27024	MISSING & SUBSEQUENTLY PRISONER OF WAR
PRIVATE	R. E. GRIFFITHS	54721	MISSING & SUBSEQUENTLY PRISONER OF WAR
PRIVATE	J. P. HUGHES	54730	MISSING & SUBSEQUENTLY PRISONER OF WAR
PRIVATE	D. JONES	54739	MISSING & SUBSEQUENTLY PRISONER OF WAR
PRIVATE	W. S. LAUNCHBURY	20389	MISSING & SUBSEQUENTLY PRISONER OF WAR
PRIVATE	G. F. PATTISON	23584	MISSING & SUBSEQUENTLY PRISONER OF WAR
PRIVATE	G. W. WILLIAMS	56786	MISSING & SUBSEQUENTLY PRISONER OF WAR
CORPORAL	R. E. BATES	11386	MISSING & SUBSEQUENTLY PRISONER OF WAR
PRIVATE	A. BECKWITH	57083	MISSING & SUBSEQUENTLY PRISONER OF WAR
PRIVATE	E. CARTER	57059	MISSING & SUBSEQUENTLY PRISONER OF WAR

RANK	NAME	SERVICE NO.	WOUND
PRIVATE	R. I. DAVIES	18076	MISSING & SUBSEQUENTLY PRISONER OF WAR
PRIVATE	A. B. MORRELL	54421	MISSING & SUBSEQUENTLY PRISONER OF WAR
PRIVATE	J. E. MARSH	54417	MISSING & SUBSEQUENTLY PRISONER OF WAR
PRIVATE	W. J. PRITCHARD	15558	MISSING & SUBSEQUENTLY PRISONER OF WAR
PRIVATE	A. ROBERTS	57066	MISSING & SUBSEQUENTLY PRISONER OF WAR
PRIVATE	A. WEBSTER	23244	MISSING & SUBSEQUENTLY PRISONER OF WAR
PRIVATE	R. BIRKS	57064	MISSING & SUBSEQUENTLY PRISONER OF WAR
PRIVATE	E. DAVISON	13647	MISSING & SUBSEQUENTLY PRISONER OF WAR
PRIVATE	H. GOODWIN	57063	MISSING & SUBSEQUENTLY PRISONER OF WAR
PRIVATE	J. J. HODGKINSON	54403	MISSING & SUBSEQUENTLY PRISONER OF WAR
PRIVATE	R. A. JONES	57005	MISSING & SUBSEQUENTLY PRISONER OF WAR
PRIVATE	W. LEWIS	33338	MISSING & SUBSEQUENTLY PRISONER OF WAR
PRIVATE	R. MOODY	57078	MISSING & SUBSEQUENTLY PRISONER OF WAR
PRIVATE	T. ROBERTS	56773	MISSING & SUBSEQUENTLY PRISONER OF WAR
SERGEANT	F. T. POST	22209	MISSING & SUBSEQUENTLY PRISONER OF WAR
CORPORAL	L.V. W. ARCHER	57041	MISSING & SUBSEQUENTLY PRISONER OF WAR
PRIVATE	J. CRAVEN	17226	MISSING & SUBSEQUENTLY PRISONER OF WAR
PRIVATE	A. COCKROFT	54395	MISSING & SUBSEQUENTLY PRISONER OF WAR
PRIVATE	W. H. EVANS	33456	MISSING & SUBSEQUENTLY PRISONER OF WAR
PRIVATE	H. INGHAM	57080	MISSING & SUBSEQUENTLY PRISONER OF WAR
PRIVATE	A. INGHAM	57044	MISSING & SUBSEQUENTLY PRISONER OF WAR
PRIVATE	J. E. OWEN	15227	MISSING & SUBSEQUENTLY PRISONER OF WAR
PRIVATE	E. T. PROBERTS	54428	MISSING & SUBSEQUENTLY PRISONER OF WAR
PRIVATE	C. THOMPSON	56789	MISSING & SUBSEQUENTLY PRISONER OF WAR
PRIVATE	G. A. THOMPSON	35479	MISSING & SUBSEQUENTLY PRISONER OF WAR
CORPORAL	W. J. PARRY	36439	MISSING & SUBSEQUENTLY PRISONER OF WAR
LANCE CORPORAL	G. T. DAVIES	57052	MISSING & SUBSEQUENTLY PRISONER OF WAR
LANCE CORPORAL	S. KIMBERLIN	5333	MISSING & SUBSEQUENTLY PRISONER OF WAR
PRIVATE	F. DOWBIGGIN	54461	MISSING & SUBSEQUENTLY PRISONER OF WAR
PRIVATE	E. D. EVANS	57020	MISSING & SUBSEQUENTLY PRISONER OF WAR
PRIVATE	A. HUGHES	46088	MISSING & SUBSEQUENTLY PRISONER OF WAR
PRIVATE	G/ HIGHAM	48841	MISSING & SUBSEQUENTLY PRISONER OF WAR
PRIVATE	W. R. JONES	40865	MISSING & SUBSEQUENTLY PRISONER OF WAR
PRIVATE	H. C. MANNER	26796	MISSING & SUBSEQUENTLY PRISONER OF WAR
PRIVATE	W. E. SHAW	56788	MISSING & SUBSEQUENTLY PRISONER OF WAR
CORPORAL	E. FOX	28370	MISSING & SUBSEQUENTLY PRISONER OF WAR
PRIVATE	E. CHARLTON	54394	MISSING & SUBSEQUENTLY PRISONER OF WAR
PRIVATE	R. O. CAMBRIDGE	54396	MISSING & SUBSEQUENTLY PRISONER OF WAR
PRIVATE	E. EVANS	57051	MISSING & SUBSEQUENTLY PRISONER OF WAR
PRIVATE	G. HARRIS	54400	MISSING & SUBSEQUENTLY PRISONER OF WAR
PRIVATE	O. HUGHES	43672	MISSING & SUBSEQUENTLY PRISONER OF WAR

RANK	NAME	SERVICE NO.	WOUND
PRIVATE	W. R. JONES	56996	MISSING & SUBSEQUENTLY PRISONER OF WAR
PRIVATE	A. C. JONES	37657	MISSING & SUBSEQUENTLY PRISONER OF WAR
PRIVATE	J. S. RAYMOND	23045	MISSING & SUBSEQUENTLY PRISONER OF WAR
PRIVATE	R. W. EVANS	54712	MISSING & SUBSEQUENTLY PRISONER OF WAR
PRIVATE	E. WILLIAMS	15129	MISSING
PRIVATE	S. ROBERTS	34033	MISSING
PRIVATE	S. DAVIES	15045	MISSING
PRIVATE	W. ALEXANDER	5021	MISSING
LANCE CORPORAL	H. DAVIES	18770	MISSING
LANCE CORPORAL	R. LEWIS	19825	MISSING
LANCE CORPORAL	E. H. JONES	40096	MISSING
PRIVATE	W. ANDERSON	16917	MISSING
PRIVATE	F. ALLEN	54697	MISSING
PRIVATE	W. BAGSHALL	22231	MISSING
PRIVATE	H. BAILEY	54702	MISSING
PRIVATE	H. BARLOW	54705	MISSING
PRIVATE	A. BERRY	54703	MISSING
PRIVATE	A. BOOKER	54701	MISSING
PRIVATE	J. BROADHURST	54699	MISSING
PRIVATE	J. DONOVAN	10543	MISSING
PRIVATE	J. DERRICK	54710	MISSING
PRIVATE	I. T. EVANS	54717	MISSING
PRIVATE	A. FLEET	54719	MISSING
PRIVATE	E. T. FELL	54718	MISSING
PRIVATE	L. HARRIS	23487	MISSING
PRIVATE	D. W. HARRIS	54728	MISSING
PRIVATE	J. J. HILL	54725	MISSING
PRIVATE	E. R HUGHES	54726	MISSING
PRIVATE	W. T. HUGHES	54727	MISSING
PRIVATE	R. HUMPHREYS	54723	MISSING
PRIVATE	E. HILL	54731	MISSING
PRIVATE	W. H. JONES	54733	MISSING
PRIVATE	T. H. JONES	54732	MISSING
PRIVATE	F. H. MOUNTFORD	54422	MISSING
PRIVATE	R. ROBERTS	28541	MISSING
PRIVATE	J. STOKER	54695	MISSING
PRIVATE	L. THOMAS	14936	MISSING
PRIVATE	P. WAINWRIGHT	17701	MISSING
PRIVATE	A. ASH	38112	MISSING
CORPORAL	H. CORDIER	34303	MISSING
CORPORAL	W. JONES	11487	MISSING
PRIVATE	R. ASHBURG	24568	MISSING
PRIVATE	J. BOLDERSTON	57021	MISSING
PRIVATE	D. DONOVAN	22750	MISSING

RANK	NAME	SERVICE NO.	WOUND
PRIVATE	J. T. DEARDON	57068	MISSING
PRIVATE	A. ENDERSLY	26666	MISSING
PRIVATE	W. EDGE	57072	MISSING
PRIVATE	J. R. GILMORE	31280	MISSING
PRIVATE	J. GRIFFITHS	54441	MISSING
PRIVATE	E. HUGHES	15485	MISSING
PRIVATE	E. HUGHES	56994	MISSING
PRIVATE	J. E. HUGHES	54402	MISSING
PRIVATE	H. JONES	12005	MISSING
PRIVATE	E. MARSHALL	43255	MISSING
PRIVATE	D. MORRIS	54419	MISSING
PRIVATE	W. F. MORGAN	54416	MISSING
PRIVATE	P. WILLIAMS	50039	MISSING
PRIVATE	T. WILLIAMS	37929	MISSING
PRIVATE	T. FOULKES	25207	MISSING
PRIVATE	E. DITCHFIELD	54459	MISSING
PRIVATE	J. EVANS	29611	MISSING
PRIVATE	R. EVANS	54398	MISSING
PRIVATE	E. HOLLINGSWORTH	15197	MISSING
PRIVATE	J. JONES	54412	MISSING
PRIVATE	W. A. JONES	54409	MISSING
PRIVATE	C. JONES	18561	MISSING
PRIVATE	D. ROBERTS	56777	MISSING
PRIVATE	G. RICHARDS	56768	MISSING
PRIVATE	G. SWANCOTT	54431	MISSING
PRIVATE	A. E. TANNER	54433	MISSING
PRIVATE	V. L. WALLEY	54437	MISSING
PRIVATE	R. LEE	54413	MISSING
PRIVATE	J. MCHUGH	36233	MISSING
PRIVATE	W. J. OCONNOR	21859	MISSING
PRIVATE	S. W. ROBERTS	12015	MISSING
PRIVATE	T. J. WILLIAMS	54436	MISSING
CORPORAL	E. LALLIMONT	57055	MISSING
LANCE CORPORAL	W. F. NEWBOULD	57054	MISSING
PRIVATE	C. EVANS	36320	MISSING
PRIVATE	E. J. EVANS	15693	MISSING
PRIVATE	E. GRIFFITHS	39912	MISSING

RANK	NAME	SERVICE NO.	WOUND
PRIVATE	D. W. JONES	54411	MISSING
PRIVATE	A. JONES	54410	MISSING
PRIVATE	R. JONES	43668	MISSING
PRIVATE	G. LAMBERT	54414	MISSING
PRIVATE	H. ROBERTS	56781	MISSING
PRIVATE	G. SEAGER	35100	MISSING
PRIVATE	J. SPEED	36209	MISSING
PRIVATE	D. E. WILLIAMS	56767	MISSING

NOVEMBER 15th

The 76th Brigade listed their casualties for the attack on November 13th & 14th as 14 Officers killed, 15 Officers wounded, 13 Officers missing, 97 other ranks (O. R.) killed, 393 other ranks (O. R.) wounded and 370 other ranks (O. R.) missing.

The 10th (Service) Battalion Royal Welsh Fusiliers were relieved in the trenches by the 8th Battalion Kings Own Royal Lancaster Regiment and marched into billets in Courcelles. A draft of 9 other ranks (O. R.) joined the Battalion for duty.

Private George Culpitt 35115 wrote in his Diary: -

"We made our way back through the trenches to Courcelles passing on every hard evidence of the heavy reply that Fritz had made to our bombardment. Here we rested for the night in huts and the next day, had a roll call to see how many remained. The casualties were somewhere about 350 Officers and men, a costly days work with no result thus far, it was with great sorrow that I found my chum, 'Early', amoung the killed." - Private George Culpitt 35115 10th (Service) Battalion Royal Welsh Fusiliers

The friend Private George Culpitt mentioned above was **Private Harold Early**, service number 35072, killed in action on 13th November 1916. He is buried at Railway Hollow Cemetery, Hebuterve, France.

Private Harold Early

One of the many soldiers killed on 13th November 1916 was one, **Private William (Bill) Hoare**, service number 22532. He transferred to the 10th Battalion R. W. F. from the 15th Battalion R. W. F. in the Summer of 1916. Private Hoare wrote a letter to his Mother, dated 11th November, two days before the battle, thanking his parents for sending him a haul of goodies which included nuts! He ended the letter – *"Well Ma, have little to say so will close. Best love to all. Your loving Son Bill xxx"*

Two days later Bill was dead. He had suffered gunshot wounds to his face and chest and was evacuated to No. 4 Casualty Clearing Station (C.C.S) at Varennes, where he later died of his wounds, aged just 22 years old.

The family received the telegram dated 17th November 1916 from the War Office informing them of Bill's death.

The family also received a letter from Sister Bulman of No. 4 Casualty Clearing Station.

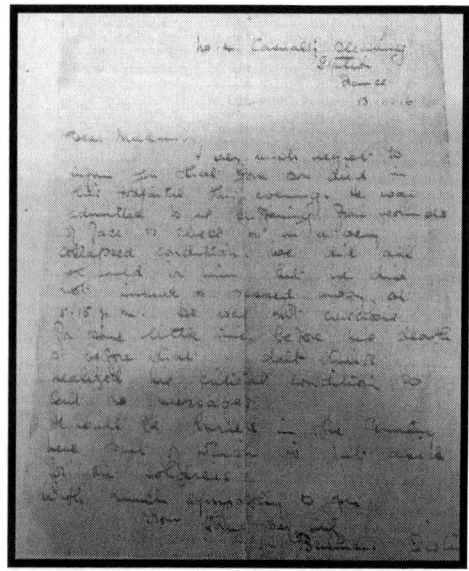

Transcribed on the next page

"Dear Madam, I very much regret to inform you that your son died in this hospital this evening. He was admitted to us suffering from wounds of face and chest and in a very collapsed condition. We did all we could for him but he did not improve and passed away at 5.15pm. He was not conscious for some time before his death and before that I don't think he realised his critical condition so sent no messages. He will be buried in the cemetery here, part of which is put aside for the soldiers. With much sympathy to you. From yours very truly. G. M. Bulman, Sister."

NOVEMBER 16th

The Battalion spent the day resting in billets.

NOVEMBER 17th

A Battalion made up of men from the 10th Battalion Royal Welsh Fusiliers and 2nd Battalion Suffolk Regiment marched back to the Serre Trenches and relieved the 1st Battalion Gordon Highlanders and held the Reserve Trenches. A patrol led by Lieutenant Pritchard succeded in bombing an 'Enemy Wiring Party' inflicting casualties on them. A draft of 25 other ranks (O. R.) joined the Battalion for duty.

NOVEMBER 19th

The Battalion was relieved at night in the Serre Trenches by the 12th Battalion West Yorkshire Regiment and marched into billets.

NOVEMBER 20th

A draft of 6 other ranks (O. R.) joined the Battalion for duty.

NOVEMBER 21st

Baths were available to the Battalion which I am sure were pretty welcome after what they had been through. There was also a 'Rifle Inspection' and the Medical Officer carried out a 'Feet Inspection'. A draft of 75 other ranks (O. R.) joined the Battalion for duty.

NOVEMBER 22nd

A 'Battalion Inspection' was held by the General Officer Commanding (G. O. C.) and also a 'Kit Inspection' was carried out.
The G. O. C. complimented the Battalion on the excellent spirit they had shown during the recent fighting.

NOVEMBER 23rd

Very wet weather was reported on this day. The Battalion sent a 'Working Party' of 200 other ranks (O. R.) to work on the roads leading to the Front-Line

NOVEMBER 24th

Training continued for the Battalion, which included 'Bombing & Bayonet Fighting' and 'Arms & Marching Drill'. A 'Working Party' of 300 other ranks continued working on the roads. A draft of 18 other ranks (O. R.) joined the Battalion for duty.

NOVEMBER 25th & 26th

'Working Parties' continued their work on the roads and clearing areas. On the 26th a draft of 48 other ranks (O. R.) joined the Battalion for duty, making a total of 181 other ranks (O. R.) having joined the Battalion in the last eleven days.

The Officer Commanding the 10th Battalion wrote: -

"I learned to love my men almost more than I would have thought it possible to love anything in this world. The more angular corners of human nature were rubbed down in the bond of common suffering and danger, there was no room for conceit, no room for petty bullying and selfishness. Their bearings and endurance were incredible, their self sacrifice and loyalty to each other and the Officers was wonderful, and as they died, others came and were ever as those that were gone.

**The older men, scoundrels of the deepest dye, some of them, and these were best of all, took it on themselves to protect the boys, and show them what was what, how to find fuel in barns, and cover up the place where the (light) beam was out with mud, to avoid detection, how to keep dry when it was wet, and warm when it was cold, how to look after their feet and how to recognise which Hun batteries were shelling certain points, and at certain times to avoid them accordingly." – Lieutenant Colonel Geoffrey L. Compton-Smith: Officer in Command 10th (Service) Battalion Royal Welsh Fusiliers

I would like to think my Taid Edwin, who was classed in this (****the older men)** group above, as he was already 37 years old and had been with the Battalion since it's formation and on the Western Front since it landed in October 1915.

NOVEMBER 27th

The Battalion marched to the Front-Line Trenches relieving the 4th Battalion Royal Fusiliers on the right sector. One casualty was wounded, **Private E. J. Wainwright**, service number 29787.

NOVEMBER 28th

The General Officer Commannding (G. O. C.) of the 76th Brigade inspected the line in the morning, spending lunch with the 10th Battalion R. W. F. Visibility was very good and the state of the wire defences in the front of the line could be checked quite easily. The Battalion received the following casualties on this day: -

RANK	NAME	SERVICE NO.	WOUND
PRIVATE	J. R. JAMES	35441	KILLED
PRIVATE	W. G. HETHINGTON	34040	KILLED
PRIVATE	S. HOWLEY	19711	KILLED

RANK	NAME	SERVICE NO.	WOUND
PRIVATE	W. G. NICHOLAS	29480	WOUNDED
PRIVATE	E. W. MILLARD	24039	WOUNDED
PRIVATE	W. MORGAN	54938	WOUNDED
PRIVATE	H. G. JONES	40463	WOUNDED
PRIVATE	C. H. HAYES	39136	WOUNDED
PRIVATE	F. THOMAS	54888	WOUNDED

NOVEMBER 29th

The Battalion were still in the Front-Line Trenches and received heavy enemy shelling during this time. The casualties were as follows:-

RANK	NAME	SERVICE NO.	WOUND
PRIVATE	J. H. ROBERTS	24906	KILLED
PRIVATE	T. WRITER	54982	DIED OF WOUND
PRIVATE	A. BOWEN	14757	WOUNDED
PRIVATE	G. WATKINS	54979	WOUNDED
PRIVATE	W. HOLGATE	54983	WOUNDED
PRIVATE	E. W. SANDERS	54883	WOUNDED
PRIVATE	T. COOPER	36578	WOUNDED
PRIVATE	J. G. JOHNSON	54992	WOUNDED
PRIVATE	C. H. WORTHING	54895	WOUNDED
PRIVATE	H. CHIDLEY	54910	WOUNDED

NOVEMBER 30th

The Battalion were still in the Front-Line Trenches and received heavy enemy shelling during this time. The casualties were as follows:-

RANK	NAME	SERVICE NO.	WOUND
PRIVATE	O. OWENS	31857	KILLED
LANCE CORPORAL	C. TUNE	21866	DIED OF WOUND
PRIVATE	J. HUNT	54987	WOUNDED
PRIVATE	W. G. RICHARDS	40090	WOUNDED
PRIVATE	A. PROBERT	54875	WOUNDED

DECEMBER 1916

DECEMBER 1st

The Battalion was relieved in the trenches by the 2nd Battalion Suffolk Regiment and marched into billets at Courcellers.

The award of the **Military Medal** to the late **Corporal H. Hussey, service number 24891** was announced.

Private George Culpitt 35115 wrote about these last few days in the Front-line:-

"During the four days that we held this position on the line, we got very little to eat and nothing to drink while the trench was in such a terrible state of mud and water owing to the snow and bombardments, that it was extremely difficult to get about. To our great joy, we were told that we were going to be relieved that night at 10pm, but although we were all ready before the time indicated, it was long after midnight before they turned up." - Private George Culpitt, 35115 10th (Service) Battalion Royal Welsh Fusiliers

DECEMBER 2nd

The Battalion were in billets at rest. 2nd Lieutenant J. O. Caldwell joined the Battalion for duty.

DECEMBER 3rd

'Church Parade' was held in the morning. 'Working Parties' continued through the afternoon and evening. A draft of 93 other ranks (O. R.) joined the Battalion for duty. One casualty was recorded as wounded, **Private D. Hughes,** service number 12540.

DECEMBER 4th

The Battalion were instructed on 'Wiring Defences'.

DECEMBER 5th

The Battalion marched into billets at Louvencourt. A 'Fatigue Party' was ordered to guard German prisoners.

DECEMBER 6th

A draft of 5 other ranks (O. R.) joined the Battalion for duty.

DECEMBER 7th, 8th, 9th, 10th, 11th & 12th

For the next six days the Battalion spent their time in 'Working Parties' or 'Training'. The weather was reported as 'very wet'.

Private George Culpitt 35115 wrote about these last days in his Diary: -

"There were usually nightly fatigues up the line for the R. E.'s. Some 25 men under a Corporal or Sergeant would report to the R. E.'s billets about 4 o'clock in the afternoon, and after a wait of perhaps half an hour, would start off to the Dump under the leadership of a Private in the R. E.'s. Here each man would be given perhaps a sheet of corrogated iron, a piece of winter work for the side of the trench, or large planks for dugouts etc., and with these, we would stagger and slip on the muddy ground. If we had a good chap in charge, we would go along the top (of the trench) and get there quickly, but if there happened to be a windy fellow leading and Fritz would drop a shell or two over, he would promptly drop into a nearby trench and carry on through some two or three feet of mud to finally arrive in a temper, wet through, to our destination." – Private George Culpitt, 35115 10th (Service) Battalion Royal Welsh Fusiliers

DECEMBER 13th

The Battalion marched to the Serre Trenches and relieved the 4th Battalion Royal Fusiliers.

DECEMBER 14th

The Battalion received the following casualties on this day, in the Front-Line Trenches in Serre:-

RANK	NAME	SERVICE NO.	WOUND
PRIVATE	A. ELLIS	26915	KILLED
PRIVATE	H. CHARLES	16216	WOUNDED
PRIVATE	F. L. DURHAM	54918	WOUNDED

DECEMBER 15th

Major George Daniel Trusler joined the Battalion for duty from the 4th Battalion Royal Welsh Fusilier Territorial Force.

2nd Lieutenant Morgan Watcyn-Williams, having survived the 'Battle of Ancre' in November 1916, was promoted to Captain to Command 'C' Coy and was mentioned in despatches for his actions in the battle.

He wrote:- *"Almost my first duty as Company Commander was to write some fifty letters to relatives of the fallen. They were a mixed fellowship, all bearing the mark of pain: some Fathers and Mothers, some Wives and Sisters, and a few Children who had lost their sole remaining Parent. Every letter seemed to draw away a drop of my own blood, and the more I wrote the more convinced I became, that nothing could ever justify the final folly and sin of War." – Captain Morgan Watcyn-Williams 10th (Service) Battalion Royal Welsh Fusiliers*

DECEMBER 16th

The Battalion were visited in the trenches by Corps Staff Officers.

DECEMBER 17th

The Battalion, less 1 Company, were relieved in the Front-Line Trenches by the 2nd Battalion Suffolk Regiment and marched into billets at Corcelles.

DECEMBER 18th & 19th

'Working Parties' continued to repair the trenches and roads. On the 19th, a draft of 5 other ranks (O. R.) joined the Battalion for duty.

DECEMBER 20th

'Working Parties' continued. The award of the **'Military Cross'** to the following Officers was announced: -

- **Captain, the Rev. D. C. Williams (Chaplain)**
- **2nd Lieutenant H. Pritchard**

DECEMBER 21st

The remaining Company in the Front-Line Trenches was relieved by the 4th Battalion Royal Fusiliers and marched to billets at Louvencourt and rejoined the rest of the Battalion.

DECEMBER 22nd

'Working Parties' continued. A draft of 4 Officers joined the Battalion for duty.

- 2nd Lieutenant J. M. Wardlaw
- 2nd Lieutenant J. W. Broxup
- 2nd Lieutenant S. C. Kirby
- 2nd Lieutenant E. Williams

Lieutenant E. Evans, Royal Army Medical Corps (R. A. M. C.) joined the Battalion to take over duties of the Medical Officer from Captain B. Grellier M.E.

DECEMBER 23rd & 24th

'Working Parties' continued for the Battalion. On the 24th, 2nd Lieutenant H. Curran joined the Battalion for duty.

DECEMBER 25th – CHRISTMAS DAY

Brigadier General Deverell

It was a very wet Christmas Day, with a 'Church Parade' in the morning (voluntary). The Battalion remained in billets.

There was a Battalion concert held in the evening attended by Brigadier General Deverell, who later dined with the Officers of the Battalion.

The following telegram was received from the Commander in Chief, Sir Douglas Haig:-

"I desire to convey to all ranks under my command, my hearty good wishes for Christmas and the New Year. It is indeed a privilege to command such Officers and such men, and I feel confident that the magnificent qualities they have already displayed in the face of the enemy will carry our arms to ultimate victory." - Sir Douglas Haig Commander in Chief B. E. F.

Private George Culpitt, 35115, wrote in his Diary: -

Christmas Day came and with it our allowance of Christmas Pudding or rather that which the newspapers had collected during the year. For dinner we had roast meat, nearly all fat and a small portion of potato followed by some of this pudding which was really very good. Of course, most of the chaps had parcels or money to procure such luxuries, as they desired from the BFF Canteen and so no one went without." - Private George Culpitt, 35115 10th (Service) Battalion Royal Welsh Fusiliers

DECEMBER 26th

'Working Parties' continued during the day and evening. Captain B. Grellier M. C. Royal Army Medical Corps left for duty at Base Hospital.

DECEMBER 27th & 28th

'Working Parties' continued. The rest of the Battalion were in billets.

DECEMBER 29th

The Battalion marched to trenches in front of Serre and relieved the 4th Battalion Royal Fusiliers in the right sub sector. 2nd Lieutenant G. A. Hall and 6 other ranks (O. R.) joined the Battalion for duty.

DECEMBER 30th & 31st

The remaining two days of 1916 passed without incident or casualties for the Battalion.

1916 had seen the Battalion take part in four major battles on the Western Front. They suffered tremendous casualties. What would 1917 hold for them?

Chapter 6
1917 - Through Mud & Bullets

JANUARY 1917

The Battalion were still in trenches at Serre at the beginning of the new year of 1917.

JANUARY 1st

The Battalion, less one Company, were relieved in the trenches by the 2nd Battalion Suffolk Regiment and marched into billets at Courcelles.

At the end of three days in the Front-Line, the Brigadier thought that the Battalion, after all they had been through in the last few months, and with the weather deteriorating day by day, would be best relieved, have rest for two days, then return to the Front-Line for the remaining two days of their **'Stretch'**. He had the best interest of the Battalion at heart but after the Battalion were relieved after three days, the next morning, there was a large increase in the number of soldiers reporting sick, over 250 soldiers in fact; 40 of which were marked as **'Attend'** as unfit to go to the trenches. The main ailments being **'Fever'** and **'Trench Foot'**. These ailments were due mainly to the standing water in the trenches and the continuing rainfall and cold weather that the soldiers had to endure. Private George Culpitt, service number 35115 was included in this list.

The Winter of 1916/1917

After the **'Final Battle of the Somme Campaign'** in November 1916 the following Winter was the most severe for over 40 years. Large scale operations ceased and both allies and central powers **'Dug in to await the arrival of Spring'**. Heavy autumn rains had turned the shell cratered battlefields into an impassable quagmire of mud. For eight weeks there was continious rain, sleet and snow. The soldiers serving on the Front-Line, although frequently rotated, suffered greatly. The trenches provided no protection from the bitter Winter. Abnormally low temperatures, especially at night, froze their clothes and blankets. There were **'Trench**

Collapses' caused by mud slides and still the poor **'Tommy'** had to contend with daily problems of the **'Body Lice'** and **'Swarm of Rats'** which continued to eat anything and everything. The situation improved marginally in mid January when four weeks of sub-zero temperatures and clearer skies froze the ground, bringing some respite from the muddy trenches.

JANUARY 2nd

2nd Lieutenant A. G. Williams joined the Battalion for duty. The Battalion were still in billets.

JANUARY 3rd

The Battalion, less one Company, joined the remaining Company who were left in the trenches on the 1st January and relieved the 2nd Battalion Suffolk Regiment.

JANUARY 4th

Lieutenant O. S. Hughes rejoined the Battalion for duty.

JANUARY 5th

The Battalion, less one Company, was relieved in the trenches by the 2nd Battalion Suffolk Regiment and marched into billets at Courcelles.

JANUARY 6th

The Battalions remaining Company in the Front-Line Trenches was relieved by a Company of the 17th Battalion Highland Infantry and rejoined the rest of the Battalion at Courcelles. The whole Battalion proceeded by **'Motor Lorries'** to Rubempre and went into billets there.

JANUARY 8th

Captain and Adjutant E. H. Howard assumed 'Acting Appointment' of Second in Command of the Battalion taking over from Major A. J. S. James M. C. who proceeded to England to join the 'Senior Officers School of Instruction'.

JANUARY 9th

The Battalion marched from Rubempre to Halloy Training Area, a distance of 19.3km (12 miles) into billets.

JANUARY 10th

A draft of 15 other ranks (O. R.) joined the Battalion for duty. The Battalion remained at rest.

JANUARY 11th

Lieutenant H. Beswick joined the Battalion for duty.

JANUARY 12th

The Battalion were at rest. A draft of 15 other ranks (O. R.) joined the Battalion for duty.

JANUARY 14th

'Kit Inspection' was held after 'Church Parade'. There was a lecture held for all Officers at Brigade Head Quarters.

JANUARY 15th

The Battalion commenced training after a few days much needed rest. A draft of 12 other ranks (O. R.) joined the Battalion for duty.

JANUARY 16th & 17th
The Battalion continued it's training.

JANUARY 18th
A draft of 66 other ranks (O. R.) joined the Battalion for duty. 2nd Lieutenant F. A. Lawson also rejoined the Battalion. Training continued.

JANUARY 19th
The weather was reported as 'Dry & Cold'. A draft of 16 other ranks (O. R.) joined the Battalion for duty. There was training for the Battalion in the morning with recreational training for the men in the afternoon.

JANUARY 20th
2nd Lieutenant H. D. Evans rejoined the Battalion for duty. The Battalion training was in the morning and in the afternoon there was a inter-platoon football competition.

"Each platoon of the sixteen in the Battalion were invited to enter a team for a knock-out competition in seven-a-side soccer. The game was extremely fast and kept us in excellent training. Ultimately, No. 1 platoon of 'A' Coy, captained by Sergeant-Major Bowen, won the honours and we celebrated the final with a concert and a feast, to which the Brigadier and his staff came." – Captain Morgan Watcyn-Williams 10th (Service) Battalion Royal Welsh Fusiliers

JANUARY 21st
'Church Parade' was held, followed by a 'Kit & Billets Inspection'.

JANUARY 22nd & 23rd
The Battalion, less one Company were training, the other Company was on the range. The following Officers joined the Battalion for duty with 6 other ranks (O. R.):-

- 2nd Lieutenant J. H. Parry
- 2nd Lieutenant W. E. Parry

JANUARY 24th TO 27th
The Battalion continued it's training, split between 'The Range', 'General Drill' and 'Bayonet Training'.

JANUARY 28th

The Battalion marched into billets at Amplier, a distance of 17.7km (11 miles). Roads were reported as very slippery with ice and the weather was cold and frosty.

JANUARY 29th

The Battalion marched into billets at Neuvillette a distance of 11.2 km (7 miles). A draft of 24 other ranks (O. R.) joined the Battalion for duty.

JANUARY 30th

The Battalion marched into billets at Haute Cote a distance of 12.8km (8 miles).

JANUARY 31st

The Battalion marched into billets at Bethonsart. The weather was reported as snowing and very cold.

Private George Culpitt, 35115, now recovered from his feet troubles wrote about the last few days of January:-

"The weather at this time was bitterly cold. We left the village and started on a four day march. I was again marked 'Attend because of feet' and should have been carried on a transport, but finding there was no room on the already overloaded wagons, had to walk. The whole Brigade shifted at the same time and the first days march covered 12 miles but by stint of resolution and exertion of will power, I managed to stick it and finally landed some two hours after the Battalion at the village where we were staying that night. The remaining three days march I managed to keep with the Company and therefore, when I went to have my leg dressed, after we had arrived and settled down, as I had walked all of the way, I was considered fit for duty and never troubled the Doctor again, although my feet were still paining at times." – Private George Culpitt, 35115 10th (Service) Battalion Royal Welsh Fusiliers

FEBRUARY 1917

Training had now begun in earnest for the next attack which would be known as **"The Battle of Arras."**

FEBRUARY 1st & 2nd
The Battalion had two days of rest after marching over 30 miles in the last four days.

FEBRUARY 3rd
The Battalion commenced their training for the upcoming attack. A lecture was given by Lieutenant Colonel G. L. Compton-Smith Commanding Officer to the Officers and N. C. O.'s.

FEBRUARY 4th TO 7th
Training for the Battalion continued with lectures given by the Commanding Officer (C. O.) to Officers and N. C. O.'s.

Lieutenant Colonel G. L. Compton-Smith wrote: -

"It was a commonplace idea among the Army of Instructors that initiative was lacking, knowledge was lacking, leadership was lacking, and so they must teach it more and more. The more they taught, the more disappointed they were, for the orgy of teaching and helping simply 'Taught Away' the individuality of the Junior Officers. The real backbone of the Army were rapidly being reduced to a state of the most pitiful incompetence. The C. O. is often sent to attend conferences here, there and everywhere, often miles away, quite regardless of his own arrangements and pressing work. He makes schemes for training which are all altered, he lectures his Officers and men, then other people come and lecture them and tell them the same thing. He takes them out of the field for days, then the Staff arrives in troops and criticises. I would love to say - 'If I don't know my job, kick me out. If I do know it, for Heavens sake, go away and let me do it!" - Lieutenant Colonel G. L. Compton-Smith Commanding Officer (C. O.) 10th (Service) Battalion Royal Welsh Fusiliers

FEBRUARY 8th
The Battalion marched into billets at Hauteville a distance of 14.4km (9 miles)

FEBRUARY 9th & 10th
The Battalion were training in the morning with recreational training in the afternoon. i.e. sports, etc.

FEBRUARY 11th
The Battalion less one Coy marched into billets in Arras a distance of

14.4km (9 miles). One Coy relieved 'A' Coy of the 9th Battalion Royal Fusiliers in the Support Trenches in front of Arras. Two Officers, Lieutenant W. J. D. Hale (rejoining) and 2nd Lieutenant T. E. Williams and 67 other ranks (O. R.) joined the Battalion for duty.

Private George Culpitt, 35115 wrote in his Diary: -

"A Company was to occupy the town defences which ran through to suburbs of Arras on the further side. We did not leave until nearly 2am the next morning (12th February) and were supposed to have reached our destination and take over the trenches before dawn as it was not safe to move large bodies of men by daylight. Unfortunetly, the Captain in charge lost his way and took us two miles out of our way before he discovered his mistake. It was therefore, about 7am and broad daylight when we finally arrived, dead tired at our destination and took over the trenches alloted to us" – Private George Culpitt, 35115 10th (Service) Battalion Royal Welsh Fusiliers

FEBRUARY 12th

The Battalion were in billets. One Coy in trenches. 'Working Parties' were organised. Major E. H. Howard Second in Command of the Battalion was attached to 76th Brigade Head Quarters. Captain H. Hall Morgan assumed Acting Appointment of Second in Command.

FEBRUARY 13th & 14th

'Working Parties' continued. One Coy in trenches. Weather was reported as 'Snowing'. The Battalion spent most of the day in billets which were cellars of houses in the centre of the town, as the Germans were continually bombarding the town with shells of every size, but not all of the Battalion were in cellars.

Lieutenant Colonel G. L. Compton-Smith wrote: -

"We are now billeted in a most sumptuous private house. I write this in a tapestried dining room in a comfortable armchair. I have a splendid bedroom with full length mirrors and hot and cold water laid on. The houses on either side are complete and hideous ruins. The Cathedral and Museum just across the way, mere heaps huge and shapeless of battered masonry, but our house, with the exception of a piece of shell through a picture on one of the bedroom walls, still stands intact. All day the bombs and bangs of guns and explosions blare and echo through the deserted streets but after nightfall, shops open and the place is

itself again, what's left of it." – Lieutenant Colonel G. L. Compton-Smith
Commanding Officer (C. O.) 10th (Service) Battalion Royal Welsh Fusiliers

FEBRUARY 15th

The Battalion less One Coy marched to the trenches and relieved 1st Battalion Gordon Highlanders taking over the St. Sauveur Defences.

FEBRUARY 17th

The Battalion who were still in the Front-Line Trenches received the following casualties:-

RANK	NAME	SERVICE NO.	WOUND
PRIVATE	W. SCHOFIELD	55133	KILLED
LANCE CORPORAL	E. MURPHY	55071	WOUNDED
PRIVATE	C. LOMAS	54950	WOUNDED

FEBRUARY 19th

The Battalion, less One Coy were relieved in the trenches by 1st Gordon Highlanders and marched into billets in Arras. A draft of two Officers, 2nd Lieutenant J. Thompson and 2nd Lieutenant C. W. Jones joined the Battalion for duty.

FEBRUARY 20th

The Battalion, less One Coy in billets and one Coy was in trenches. A draft of 40 other (O. R.) joined the Battalion for duty.

FEBRUARY 23rd

The Battalion Commanding Officer (C. O.) held a conference with the Officers. The Battalion, less One Coy, marched to the Front-Line Trenches and relieved the 1st Battalion Gordon Highlanders.

FEBRUARY 24th, 25th & 26th

The Battalion were in the Front-Line Trenches. On the 26th, 1 casualty was reported as wounded, **Lance Sergeant S. Powell**, service number 33895. Trenches were reported as very muddy due to the thaw.

FEBRUARY 27th

The Battalion suffered the following casualties:-

RANK	NAME	SERVICE NO.	WOUND
PRIVATE	E. STRODE	15178	DIED OF WOUNDS
PRIVATE	W. DAVIES	19897	WOUNDED
PRIVATE	S. LEWIS	55646	WOUNDED
PRIVATE	W. TURNER	54890	WOUNDED

FEBRUARY 28th

The enemy artillery and trench mortar were very accurate on this day causing the Battalion the following casualties:-

RANK	NAME	SERVICE NO.	WOUND
PRIVATE	T. SMITH	56035	KILLED
PRIVATE	R. SMALLMAN	55088	KILLED
PRIVATE	T. MEREDITH	55068	KILLED
PRIVATE	T. LEWIS	19801	KILLED
PRIVATE	G. THOMPSON	24125	KILLED
LANCE CORPORAL	S. STONE	33881	KILLED
PRIVATE	T. OWEN	37787	KILLED
PRIVATE	A. WILKINSON	43959	KILLED
PRIVATE	H. FORSTER	27024	KILLED
PRIVATE	G. TUDOR	43990	KILLED

RANK	NAME	SERVICE NO.	WOUND
PRIVATE	W. LANE	33870	WOUNDED
PRIVATE	F. THOMAS	54888	WOUNDED
PRIVATE	W. BUTTLE	56010	WOUNDED
PRIVATE	W. E. HOWELLS	54928	WOUNDED
PRIVATE	W. BENTLEY	44614	WOUNDED
PRIVATE	E. W. WAY	55091	WOUNDED
PRIVATE	H. MILLICHAMP	54860	WOUNDED
PRIVATE	E. J. F. HALL	20828	WOUNDED
PRIVATE	J. LLOYD	55569	WOUNDED
PRIVATE	G. J. CARTER	54914	WOUNDED

One of the soldiers killed on this day was **Private Thomas Oliver Owen** 37787. He was the Son of John and Alice Owen of Tal y Cafn Terrace, Eglwysfach, Denbighshire and worked as an Apprentice Gardner at Bodnant Garden near Colwyn Bay. **(shown below – still open today and ran by The National Trust)** He had two Brothers, David and John and a Sister Mary.

Prior to the War, Thomas enlisted at Conway on 11th December 1915 and was posted to the 10th (Service) Battalion Royal Welsh Fusiliers after the Battalion had moved out of the Somme area. He was 23 years old when he was killed on 28th February 1917 and he has no known grave. He is remembered on The Arras Memorial, Pas De Calais, Bay 6, France.

The Battalion were relieved by the 1st Battalion Gordon Highlanders and marched into billets at Hauteville.

MARCH 1917

MARCH 1st – St. David's Day (Dydd Dewi Sant)

The Battalion were in billets resting.

MARCH 2nd

The Battalion had a days holiday today which was usually taken on the 1st March, St. David's Day but the Battalion were too tired on the 1st due to their stint in the Front-Line Trenches. A concert and dinner was held. 2nd Lieutenant Edwin G. Williams joined the Battalion for duty.

MARCH 3rd, 4th & 5th

Training continued for the Battalion over the next few days. On the 5th of March, 2nd Lieutenant J. A. James joined the Battalion for duty.

MARCH 6th

The Battalion was inspected by General Sir Douglas Haig the Commander in Chief. He expressed *"His highest praise and entire satisfaction on the turn out of the 10th Battalion R. W. F."*

Private George Culpitt, 35115 wrote:-

"On the 6th March we were inspected by Sir Douglas Haig. The day before saw us busily engaged shining and polishing every article of equipment for this morrow. The morning of the 6th was spent in two parades for preliminary inspection by Company Officer and Colonel. We had taken up our position, the usual preliminations been got through we stood at ease to await the coming of the Field Marshall. His car, with the Union Jack at the front, having reached the edge of the field, he alighted and held a short conference with the Divisional General, after which, he walked along the ranks now standing to attention. The inspection over, he took the salute and we marched off the ground and back to billets." – Private George Culpitt, 35115 10th (Service) Battalion Royal Welsh Fusiliers

MARCH 7th TO 11th

Training continued and 'Working Parties' helped with ammunition carrying for the A. O. C. at a dump at Avesnes. Preparations were now in full swing for the impending attack.

Lieutenant Colonel G. L. Compton-Smith Commanding the 10th Battalion Royal Welsh Fusiliers went to witness a demonstration by the tanks of their methods of attack. Tanks were beginning to create interest within the British Army, the **'Mark 1'** had entered service in August 1916 as part of the Somme Offensive, but it was not until the Battle of Cambrai in November 1917 that the **'Mark IV'** was used onmasse.

Lieutenant Colonel G. L. Compton-Smith reported the next day:-

"They moved about a bit and eventually one of them fell into a ditch and couldn't get out. I travelled for a short distance on one of the tanks and was surprised to find how little the various bumps and jerks and climbing up banks and over trenches affected me. It was like being in a boat at sea." – Lieutenant Colonel G. L. Compton-Smith Commanding Officer Royal Welsh Fusiliers

MARCH 12th

The weather was reported as 'wet'. The Battalion continued training. 'Working Parties' continued but in the afternoon there was a rugby match between a team from the 10th Battalion Royal Welsh Fusiliers and the 8th Battalion Kings Own Royal Lancaster Regiment with the 10th Battalion R. W. F. winning 9-4.

MARCH 13th TO 14th

Training and 'Working Parties' continued for the Battalion.

MARCH 16th

The Battalion marched into billets at Berlencourt a distance of 12km (7 ½ miles).

Captain Morgan Watcyn Williams wrote: -

"We marched away to Berlencourt a village well behind the trenches. My billets was in a house attached to the school where a handful of children assembled for lessons. Running below the school was a trout stream from which Private Hugh Morris, service number 15427, provided delicious breakfasts, until the others tried to emulate him by resorting to bombing the fish. We had to place the stream out of bounds, but we left the odd poacher (Morris) continue to adorn his craft and show us what a master he was at 'Tickling Trout'!" – Captain Morgan.Watcyn Williams 10th (Service) Battalion Royal Welsh Fusiliers

MARCH 17th

Captain M. Murray rejoined the Battalion for duty. Training continued.

MARCH 18th

'Church Parade' was held. The Battalion was instructed to prepare to move in two hours notice. Lieutenant D. E. Davies joined the Battalion for duty.

MARCH 19th TO 21st

Training continued. Weather was poor with rain and snow reported. The Commanding Officer (C. O.) held a conference with all of the Officers.

MARCH 22nd TO 26th

Training continued. Weather still remained wet and cold. Brigadier General held a conference with the Commanding Officer (C. O.), Adjutant and Coy Commanders. 2nd Lieutenant A. P. Comyns and one other rank (O. R.) joined the Battalion for duty on the 25th.

MARCH 27th TO 31st

Training continued over the final days of March. The Battalion spending time on the 'Flagged Course'. A draft of 13 other ranks (O. R.) joined the Battalion for duty.

Captain Morgan Watcyn Williams wrote about these last few days of training:-

"We underwent intensive training for the 'Battle of Arras', the trenches and wood which we were to attack were reproduced for us from aeroplane photographs, so day in, day out, of strenious work, during March, we traversed it's length and breadth, scarcely a contingency was unforseen, and the final capture of the wood was a very pretty piece of drill. The men toilled at the rifle ranges, or at their bombing schools, while the Officers practised revolver shooting, and poured over maps and photographs, we were as fit as fiddles." - Captain Morgan Watcyn Williams 10th (Service) Battalion Royal Welsh Fusiliers

Priavte George Culpitt, 35115 wrote in his Diary:-

"Now we were getting near the end of March and we entered upon the final stages of our training on a large track of open country, which had been trenched to an exact representation of the piece of the enemy's line we were to take. Every day until the end of our training, we went once or twice every morning in full fighting kit over the ground until every man knew the exact position in the attack." - Private George Culpitt, 35115 10th (Service) Battalion Royal Welsh Fusiliers.

The following honours and awards were announced: -

Military Medal for Bravery in the Field – 19th February 1917 London Gazette

- Private M. Hughes Morris 15427
- Corporal H. Hussey 24891
- Sergeant R. White 15500

The undermentioned N. C. O. is awarded The **Russian Cross of St. George** 1st Class – 15th February 2017 London Gzette

- Sergeant J. Davies V.C. 34314

APRIL 1917

APRIL 1st, 2nd & 3rd

Training continued for the Battalion. Heavy snowfall was reported on the 2nd and 3rd April. The Battalion practised the attack on the training ground as Brigade.

APRIL 4th

The Battalion marched into billets at Wanquetin a distance of 14.4km (9 miles).

Priavte George Culpitt, 35115 wrote in his Diary:-

"Falling in at 4.30pm we marched through Avesnes and Hautsville to Wanquetin we were now on the line of march for the 'Big Battle' and everyone was in high spirits and as a result of the training that everyone had undergone, were all as fit as we had ever been." - Private George Culpitt, 35115 10th (Service) Battalion Royal Welsh Fusiliers

APRIL 5th

The Battalion received orders to get ready to move up to the trenches, but this order was later cancelled. Major A. J. S. James rejoined the Battalion and resumed his appointment as Second in Command of the Battalion.

Lieutenant Colonel G. L. Compton-Smith wrote: -

"Spent all morning and most of the afternoon looking over my operation orders. At tea time had a visit from Lieutenant General Sir James Wolfe Murray K. C. B. and Lieutenant Colonel A. De. L. Long who formally commanded this Battalion. At 6pm move to trenches was cancelled for 24 hours. Can hear but little of the bombardment, wind the wrong way. Went for a walk in the evening. A glorious evening. Played bridge after dinner. Major James returned today after a three month course in England. Rather uncomfortable during the night as all surplus kit has been dumped." - Lieutenant Colonel G. L. Compton-Smith Commanding Officer 10th (Service) Battalion Royal Welsh Fusiliers

Captain Morgan Watcyn Williams also wrote about the upcoming battle: -

"On April 5th I had a pow-wow with Brigadier General Porter, a fine leader, Lieutenant Colonel Compton-Smith and Captain Don Quin our Adjutant and they decided that I should be in charge of 'Forward Operations' with 'A' Company and 'C' Company leading the way to Devil's Wood."

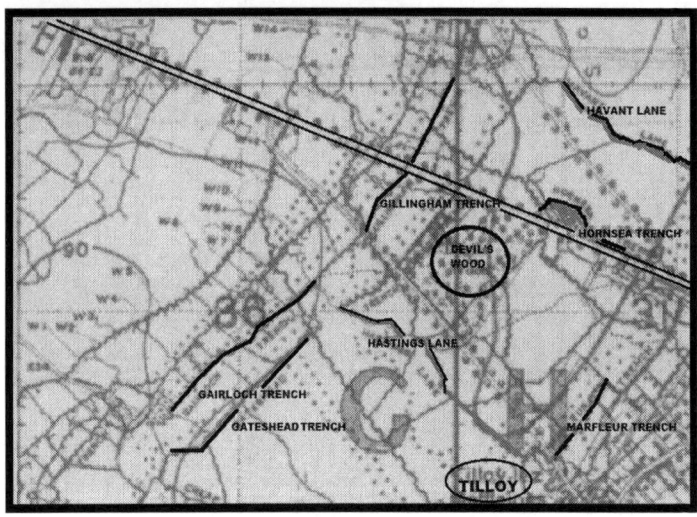

"In the evening I strolled through the dusk into an orchard, where my men were camping, suddenly my thoughts were interupted by a harsh strong voice saying 'The only good boche is a dead one'. The speaker stood by a brazier, talking to a group of his fellows, and as the flames shot up I could see the hate in his eyes. I knew Jones' story. He was the sole survivor of three brothers, who had joined the Army. 'You remember Bill' he continued, ' cheerier kid never left Wales, and the Devils watched him shrieking on the wire at Ypres until he died and Bert was blown to hell at Loos. I'll get even with the swines yet'. With a smothered curse, which was half a sob, he turned abruptly away. Hurrying off into the darkness with his sorrow. I slipped away quietly, and sauntering to my Quarters found myself on the old eternal treadmill, to butcher prisoners was to break faith, but was killing anyone more justifiable?" - *Captain Morgan Watcyn Williams 10th (Service) Battalion Royal Welsh Fusiliers*

The question of doing the right thing would have crossed many a soldiers mind during the heat of battle.

APRIL 6th

The Battalion vacated it's billets at Wanquetin and at 7pm marched for Arras. The evening was wet and cold. The Battalion arrived at Arras about 10pm and billeted in cellars in the Rue Ronville, close to the railway station.

APRIL 7th & 8th

The next two days the Battalion rested. The Officers spent time reconnoiting their assembly positions and observing wire cutting progress in the neighbourhood of Tilloy and Devil's Wood. At 7pm the Coys left by tunnel to go up to the Assembley Trench. At 11pm Lieutenant Colonel G. L. Compton-Smith Commanding Officer (C. O.) went around the Companies to wish them 'Good Luck' for the impending attack.

The photograph below was probably taken in the ruined city of Arras before the battle on the 8th April. The photograph shows Lieutenant G. L. Compton-Smith (without cap) in the centre, with two other Officers eitherside, who are probably Major A. J. S. James and Captain E. H. Howard and the entire Battalion's Sergeants' Mess.

At midnight, a final conference was held at Battalion Head Quarters. Zero hour was set for 5.30am the next morning of the 9th April.

APRIL 9th - The Battle of Arras (1st Battle of the Scarpe)

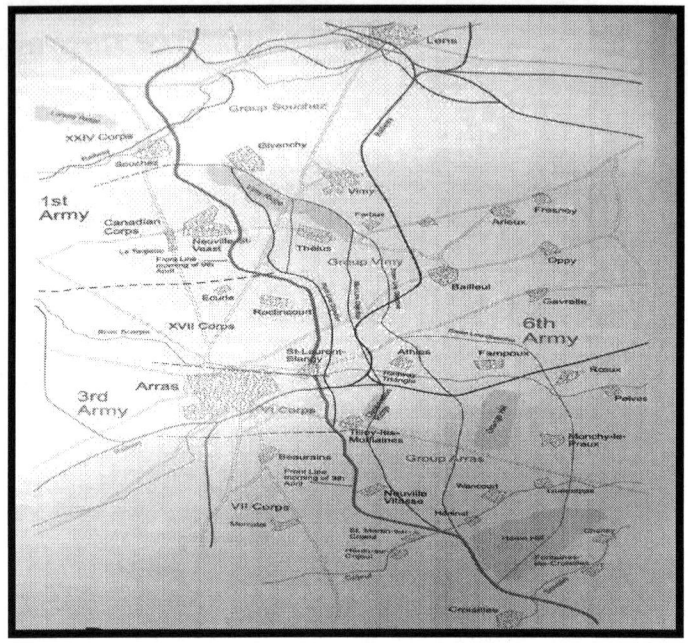

The preliminary bombardment of the enemy trenches in front of the Battalion had began on the 4th April and by the evening of the battle, the German Front-Line Trenches ceased to exist and their **'Barbed Wire Defences'** had been blown to pieces. The assault at 5.30am was preceeded by a hurricane bombardment lasting five minutes. The Battalion went **'Over the Top'** at 5.30am following behind a creeping artillery barrage and the 1st Battalion Gordon Highlanders, both Battalions made very good progress, so much so, the first hostile shelling which began at about 5.38am on our Front-Line fell well behind them, causing little damage, although a shell burst amongst a platoon of 'D' Coy causing some casualties. **Lieutenant E. Evans**, the Medical Officer (R. A. M. C.) was killed by a shell whilst tending to the wounded. The 1st Battalion Gordon Highlanders captured their objective 'Glasgow Trench', the German's fourth line at 5.50am whilst the 10th Battalion Royal Welsh Fusiliers took Devil's Wood which was taken at 6.40am.

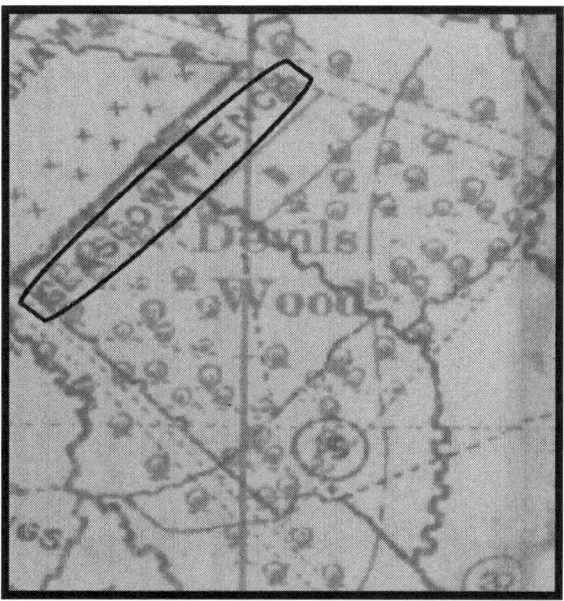

1st Battalion Gordon Highlanders take Glasgow Trench

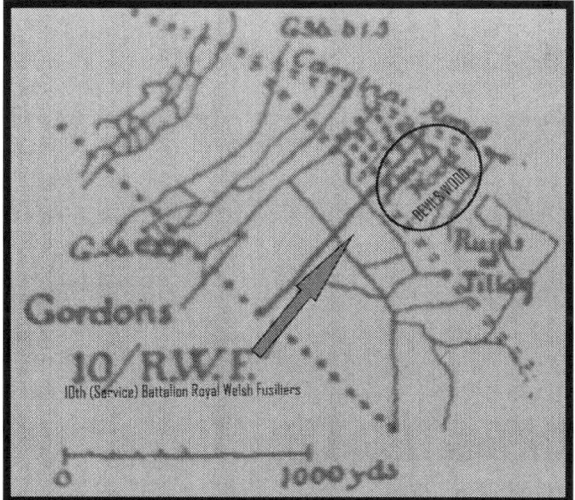

10th (Service) Battalion R. W. F. take Devil's Wood

Captain Morgan Watcyn Williams wrote:-

"We swept through Devil's Wood without a hitch. Our casualties were very light, two men killed and twenty three wounded. Out of a vast dugout, underneath a ruined house in the wood, prisoners poured, and down the steps we found two machine guns ready for action. Had we allowed time for them to be mounted? They would have spelled disaster for the Battalion. But we captured them and their crews without loss. One poor fellow in a green uniform, obviously a hopeless case, who begged of me to put him out of his misery, our Doctor Lieutenant Edward Evans R. A. M. C., had been killed by a shell and even had I possessed a pellet of morphia, I could see that the man was in no condition to swallow it. Was I to kill a prisoner on his own request? I felt I ought to, wrong though the feeling may have been, and I knew that I couldn't, his wounds were beyond description and in a moment or two, kindly death solved his problem and mine."

Captain Morgan Watcyn Williams was spared that decision to take a life of a prisoner, but the ordeal was not over.

"A few minutes later, Jones came down the trench, pushing before him a very small German. 'What shall I do with this Sir?' he asked grimly. The question was jerked out, the harshness of the voice, trying in vain to conceal the humour that danced in his eyes. I told him he'd better feed it, so without more ado, he stood the little prisoner on the first step and plied him with biscuits and bully beef. All the time Jones stood over him shouting 'Now tell us your blasted submarines are starving us.' We gave the boy, for that is what he really was, a cigarette and sent him down to the Corps cage. A long silence ensued, broken by my question. 'Well Jones, what about killing prisoners now?' He looked straight at me, his face, set and white, but his eyes laughing still. 'Not in cold blood Sir, I couldn't do it in cold blood, besides he was a kid.' So the temptation passed and the poison gas which descended upon his soul lifted forever." - Captain Morgan Watcyn Williams 10th (Service) Battalion Royal Welsh Fusiliers

Private George Culpitt, 35115 wrote about the first day of the attack:-

"Four minutes to go!!! The platoon Officer comes along just to see that all is well. Three minutes, two minutes, one minute, then the earth seems to rock under feet, the air is filled with noise of flying shells as every gun on the British side opens out. It is deafening, but we take no notice. 'Over you go', and we scale the parapet and steadily cross the open ground to our First Line Trench from which the 1st Gordons have already gone. Across the trench by bridges and on to 'No Mans Land. In front is the German 1st line trench, myriads of light rise and fall. Red, green, orange colours. Golden rain. All appaers to his artillery to

concentrate on us. Looking again at the enemy trench we see great spouts of flame and earth as shell after shell falls accurately in or nearby the trench. Nothing on earth can live in such as this. A glance to the left towards Vimy and there the scene is the same. The whole of the ridge one mass of flame and rising earth. Around us, almost deadened in the terrible din, Fritz's shells are exploding as he vainly endeavours to stay our advance. Now and then a man falls dead or wounded but we take no notice but our casualties are slight, for the terrible bombardment is too much for the enemy machine gunners who are either killed or cowering down a deep dugout. We reach the first line, now almost battered out of recognition and here we see a mopping up party of the Jacks clearing the dugout and sending the prisoners back to our lines. Now on again to the second and third lines which have been taken without much resistance, and here for a short space we halt. Everything has gone well so far and now we are waiting for our barrage which is playing on the wood to lift before we do our part and take the wood. On the right edge of the wood can be seen a few of the enemy and shots are exchanged. We now move on again to the center of the wood.

Our shells are now falling with clockwork regularity on the German 4th line which runs along the far side of the wood and which is our objective. A ten minute wait close under our own barrage and we move forward again to our objective. No resistance meets us for the Hun has long since left in an endeavour to seek safety further back. A few dead lie in the trench but no living enemy is there to meet us and we occupy the position, and commence to consolidate in anticipation of a counter-attack. We have achieved our mission without resistance and at comparitively slight cost to ourselves. So far all goes well and we shall never forget Easter Monday. We now have time to breath fully and take stock of our position which is a good one: in front, nearly 1000 yards away, lies the village of Tillery on which or barrage is now concentrated, and a little nearer in front of the village is an enemy trench deserted as far as we can see." - Private George Culpitt, 35115 10th (Service) Battalion Royal Welsh Fusiliers

Lieutenant Colonel G. L. Compton Smith wrote: -

"The wood was badly broken up and difficult to move through. The Hun was putting shrapnel through it from the North-West. We got along with considerable difficulty and half way through, I was hit by a shrapnel bullet in the arm. I eventually reached our Front-Line post and found them all in position and very cheery." - Lieutenant Colonel G. L. Compton-Smith Commanding Officer 10th (Service) Battalion Royal Welsh Fusiliers

At 7.15am the enemys artillery began shelling Devil's Wood and this continued for the rest of the day. At 11.16am, it was reported that the 10th Battalion Royal Welsh Fusiliers had now taken over the defence of the whole of the captured system within the 3rd Division boundries. The attack of the 3rd Division was temporarily held up in front of it's objective.

Private George Culpitt, 35115 wrote:-

"On our front there has been no hitch and as far as we can gather everything has gone well and all along the line. Two hours pass uneventfully and now behind us we can see the advanced line of the 8th Brigade coming to carry on from where we left off, to take Tillery village and some ground behind. Our machine guns suddenly start on the right and we hastily turn our attention in this direction. Through a gap in the enemy trench we can see the Boche hatless, without equipment or rifle, running for his life, but not many of them get away for they run into our barrage or are caught by our machine gun fire. By this time the advanced line of the 8th Brigade has mearly reached our trench and after a short halt to get into line they go forward across 1000 yards of open country to the village. We are now spectators of the battle which is taking place in front of us, and which we watch eagerly. They reappear at intervals among the piles of bricks and stone which were once houses. Again our attention is drawn to the right for here a sharp scrap is taking place. It transpires that here is a sort of Brigade HQ and here we capture an entire German staff. A short time elapses and now the scene has changed as we see the Germans coming back, but without arms for they are prisoners, 20 or 30 in a batch in charge of one or two British Tommies. Some mere lads, some old men, a few well set up, well built chaps and here and there a haughty Officer walking with his nose in the air. Once more the noise of battle lessens for a time, the advance has stayed according to programme. By 10am the Germans have been driven back over a mile and are almost out of range of our light guns, which are now busy limbering up and moving forward to take up a position in the open. Soon on the right and left we see our batteries gallop into action, swing round, unlimber and after a few sighting shots, once more proceed to harrass the retreating enemy." - Private George Culpitt, 35115 10th (Service) Battalion Royal Welsh Fusiliers

The Battalion were told to rest as much as possible, while the 1st Gordon Highlanders and the 8th Kings Own Royal Lancasters moved forward to attack. The attack failed and a fresh attack was ordered for the morning. During the night there was a heavy snow storm which made the conditions even worse.

APRIL 10th

Orders were received at midday that the Battalion should be prepared to move forward at an hours notice. The Battalion were ordered to advance and take up a position already occupied by the 111th Brigade at Guemappe. About 4.30pm the Battalion received orders to **'Stand Fast'** until further orders. Monchay had not been taken. Orders were given that they should be ready later to move up at dawn. It was a miserable wet evening.

Captain Morgan Watcyn Williams wrote:-

"Late in the afternoon on the 10th of April Lieutenant Colonel Compton-Smith sent for his Company Commanders and explained that we were to attack the village of Guemappe the next morning. A Heavy 'Creeping Barrage' would support us and with the Kings Own and the Suffolk to lead the way through the few trenches that were left, all would be well. He was gay and confident in his manner, but I detected a good deal of anxiety in his eyes, it seemed to me that he knew in his bones that it was doomed to be a rotten show." - Captain Morgan Watcyn Williams 10th (Service) Battalion Royal Welsh Fusiliers

APRIL 11th

At 2.45am the Battalion moved forward to Feuchy Chappelle ready for the attack on Guemappe. There was a considerable amount of hostile shelling during the forming up in the assembly positions causing the Battalion casualties. The allied artillery barrage was inadequate to deal with the situation, hence the heavy enemy artillery and machine gun fire continued to cause problems for the Battalion. Zero hour was at 7am. The Battalion was to be in support of the 2nd Suffolk Battalion and the 8th Kings Own Royal Lancaster Regiment. By 7.30am the attack was held up on it's left by heavy machine gun fire from Les Fosses Farm and it's right on the ridge overlooking Guemappe. The situation remained like this for most of the day. At 2.30pm the 1st Battalion the Gordon Highlanders who were in reserve, launched an attack to try and break through, although supported by a considerable reinforced and improved artillery barrage, the attack also failed. Casualties were reported as heavy. The Battalion and the Brigades were relieved at midnight on the line it held by the 12th Battalion West Yorks.

Captain Morgan Watcyn Williams wrote:-

"We were now walking into a hell of a machine gun fire, heavier even than at Serre and the air was alive with the ping-ping and zip-zip of bullets. By 7.30am there were no troops in front of us, for the Kings Own and Suffolks were smashed by the appauling fire. All I could do was to reform the land and occupy shell holes. The casualties were terrible and any attempt to get them away was almost suicidal, for all that the stretcher-bearers stuck to their jobs magnificently." – Captain Morgan Watcyn Williams 10th (Service) Battalion Royal Welsh Fusiliers

The War Diary noted that it would be impossible to praise too highly the behaviour of the men during this exceedingly trying day. The night was bitterly cold and the men had been practically without sleep for three days. Casualties for the Battalion during the First Battle of the Scarpe April 8th to 11th were as follows:-

RANK	NAME	SERVICE NO.	WOUND
SERGEANT	H. WATSON	15433	KILLED IN ACTION
SERGEANT	S. EVANS	40849	KILLED IN ACTION
CORPORAL	G. H. PROSSER	15729	KILLED IN ACTION
LANCE CORPORAL	A. HUMPHREYS	57017	KILLED IN ACTION
LANCE CORPORAL	A. CROSS	56011	KILLED IN ACTION
CORPORAL	S. A. PARKER	55074	KILLED IN ACTION
PRIVATE	V. ASHES	555553	KILLED IN ACTION
PRIVATE	W. LEWIS	14230	KILLED IN ACTION
PRIVATE	T. JENNINGS	12522	KILLED IN ACTION
PRIVATE	A. W. CORNWALL	34987	KILLED IN ACTION
PRIVATE	W. C. DUNKLEY	13603	KILLED IN ACTION
PRIVATE	J. DEAN	54841	KILLED IN ACTION
PRIVATE	H. MCCANDISH	37205	KILLED IN ACTION
PRIVATE	J. BRADSHAW	54902	KILLED IN ACTION
PRIVATE	E. M. RYAN	25905	KILLED IN ACTION

RANK	NAME	SERVICE NO.	WOUND
PRIVATE	M. WILLIAMS	40161	KILLED IN ACTION
PRIVATE	W. F. MARTIN	54861	KILLED IN ACTION
PRIVATE	S. PRITCHARD	55647	KILLED IN ACTION
LANCE CORPORAL	E. J. BROWN	54903	KILLED IN ACTION
PRIVATE	F. FROST	56047	KILLED IN ACTION
PRIVATE	T. S. JONES	44130	KILLED IN ACTION
RANK	W. LEWIS	40947	KILLED IN ACTION
PRIVATE	T. J. ROBERTS	39154	KILLED IN ACTION
PRIVATE	D. JONES	20698	KILLED IN ACTION
PRIVATE	A. L. E. WILLEY	55565	KILLED IN ACTION
PRIVATE	C. F. BLUNT	36480	KILLED IN ACTION
PRIVATE	J. DYER	16647	KILLED IN ACTION
PRIVATE	W. R. PEARMAN	56030	KILLED IN ACTION
PRIVATE	F. ARTHEY	56044	KILLED IN ACTION
PRIVATE	E. LLOYD	39066	KILLED IN ACTION
PRIVATE	P. RAYNOR	36819	KILLED IN ACTION
LIEUTENANT	E. EVANS	R.A.M.C.	KILLED IN ACTION
2ND LIEUTENANT	E. WILLIAMS		KILLED IN ACTION

RANK	NAME	SERVICE NO.	WOUND
2ND LIEUTENANT	J. C. E. DAVIES		DIED OF WOUNDS
PRIVATE	J. JENKINS	1111	DIED OF WOUNDS
PRIVATE	M. LYNCH	9442	DIED OF WOUNDS

RANK	NAME	SERVICE NO.	WOUND
PRIVATE	S. JONES	44292	DIED OF WOUNDS
PRIVATE	M. MALONEY	36145	DIED OF WOUNDS
PRIVATE	E. EDWARDS	54922	DIED OF WOUNDS
2ND LIEUTENANT	J. W. BROXUP		DIED OF WOUNDS
SERGEANT	R. N. PHILLIPS	15045	DIED OF WOUNDS
PRIVATE	J. BUTTERFIELD	55040	DIED OF WOUNDS
PRIVATE	E. T. ROBERTS	15824	DIED OF WOUNDS
PRIVATE	R. R. WILLIAMS	44208	DIED OF WOUNDS

RANK	NAME	SERVICE NO.	WOUND
CAPTAIN	W. S. BROCKLEHURST		WOUNDED
2ND LIEUTENANT	T. REA		WOUNDED
2ND LIEUTENANT	J. THOMPSON		WOUNDED
2ND LIEUTENANT	H. D. TAYLOR		WOUNDED
2ND LIEUTENANT	T. E. WILLIAMS		WOUNDED
COY SERGEANT MAJOR	G. BOWEN	15181	WOUNDED
SERGEANT	D. REES	15159	WOUNDED
LANCE SERGEANT	J. AMES	15402	WOUNDED
LANCE SERGEANT	T. P. L. GRIFFITHS	34502	WOUNDED
LANCE SERGEANT	S. P. PARRY	14915	WOUNDED
CORPORAL	P. MURPHY	16298	WOUNDED
CORPORAL	A. SMART	6522	WOUNDED
CORPORAL	W. WEBB	10009	WOUNDED
LANCE CORPORAL	G. CHADD	17704	WOUNDED
LANCE CORPORAL	G. DAVIES	9222	WOUNDED
LANCE CORPORAL	E. T. JAMES	17068	WOUNDED
PRIVATE	C. B. ARNOLD	22040	WOUNDED
PRIVATE	H. BARLOW	55568	WOUNDED
PRIVATE	E. J. BORTON	54907	WOUNDED
PRIVATE	C. A. BAILEY	15166	WOUNDED
PRIVATE	E. A. F. CHIVERS	57046	WOUNDED
PRIVATE	W. R. DAVIES	15133	WOUNDED
LIEUTENANT COLONEL	G. L. COMPTON SMITH		WOUNDED
2ND LIEUTENANT	C. W. JONES		WOUNDED
2ND LIEUTENANT	J. M. WARDLE		WOUNDED
2ND LIEUTENANT	J. A. JAMES		WOUNDED
PRIVATE	A. DAVIES	13582	WOUNDED
PRIVATE	S. EDWARDS	5492	WOUNDED
PRIVATE	F. FITZPATRICK	57009	WOUNDED
PRIVATE	D. FLETCHER	36520	WOUNDED
PRIVATE	B. FORD	22110	WOUNDED
PRIVATE	D. GENT	56012	WOUNDED
PRIVATE	T. HARRISON	36912	WOUNDED
PRIVATE	L. HILL	2186	WOUNDED
PRIVATE	E. JOHNSON	44387	WOUNDED
PRIVATE	A. E. JELLICOE	12367	WOUNDED
PRIVATE	J. JONES	22079	WOUNDED
PRIVATE	S. LIGHTFOOT	55650	WOUNDED
PRIVATE	F. H. JONES	40383	WOUNDED
PRIVATE	W. D. MORGAN	34177	WOUNDED
PRIVATE	W. O'GRADY	54959	WOUNDED
PRIVATE	B. PRICE	34361	WOUNDED

RANK	NAME	SERVICE NO.	WOUND
PRIVATE	S. T. ROWLANDS	34920	WOUNDED
PRIVATE	F. RICHARDS	34142	WOUNDED
PRIVATE	E. REES	15048	WOUNDED
PRIVATE	H. SCOTT	55648	WOUNDED
PRIVATE	H. TAYLOR	56009	WOUNDED
PRIVATE	T. LEWIS	33559	WOUNDED
PRIVATE	T. OWENS	20989	WOUNDED
SERGEANT	J. JONES	15256	WOUNDED
SERGEANT	J. W. LITTLECHILD	56001	WOUNDED
LANCE CORPORAL	G. H. REDMOND	54876	WOUNDED
LANCE CORPORAL	R. JENKINS	33994	WOUNDED
LANCE CORPORAL	W. H. JOHN	18150	WOUNDED
PRIVATE	J. W. E. CONLEY	54911	WOUNDED
PRIVATE	W. CARMAN	55042	WOUNDED
PRIVATE	J. COPELAND	33694	WOUNDED
PRIVATE	W. DAVIES	31181	WOUNDED
PRIVATE	W. J. DAVIES	55643	WOUNDED
PRIVATE	D. EVANS	57086	WOUNDED
PRIVATE	H. EDWARDS	56049	WOUNDED
PRIVATE	J. FURY	41786	WOUNDED
PRIVATE	W. HILLIER	33745	WOUNDED
PRIVATE	W. K. JONES	54740	WOUNDED
PRIVATE	J. H. JONES	44249	WOUNDED
PRIVATE	D. W. JONES	43989	WOUNDED
PRIVATE	W. J. LEWIS	19287	WOUNDED
PRIVATE	E. LLOYD	26088	WOUNDED
PRIVATE	W. H. LAWLESS	27434	WOUNDED
PRIVATE	A. MOSS	54863	WOUNDED
PRIVATE	R. OWENS	36536	WOUNDED
PRIVATE	E. Y. PRICE	54866	WOUNDED
PRIVATE	W. L. PRICE	55075	WOUNDED
PRIVATE	A. ROSS	54877	WOUNDED
PRIVATE	A. ROBERTS	44225	WOUNDED
PRIVATE	H. J. SKINNER	55997	WOUNDED
PRIVATE	A. TUNLEY	54887	WOUNDED
PRIVATE	A. THOMAS	54884	WOUNDED
PRIVATE	W. J. VOWLES	54891	WOUNDED
PRIVATE	J. R. WRIGHT	44355	WOUNDED
LANCE CORPORAL	D. ROGERS	24945	WOUNDED
PRIVATE	J. R. EVANS	55716	WOUNDED
PRIVATE	J. HUGHES	11128	WOUNDED
COY SERGEANT MAJOR	C. H. TAYLOR	7990	WOUNDED
SERGEANT	S. BOLVER	57053	WOUNDED
SERGEANT	F. ABERCROMBY	57032	WOUNDED
SERGEANT	J. E. BOOTH	21083	WOUNDED
SERGEANT	J. JONES	9495	WOUNDED
CORPORAL	P. F. WITTEN	22770	WOUNDED
CORPORAL	H. SMITH	15585	WOUNDED
LANCE CORPORAL	J. CURLEY	35833	WOUNDED
LANCE CORPORAL	L. W. LEWIS	55655	WOUNDED
LANCE CORPORAL	H. D. HALL	54931	WOUNDED
PRIVATE	W. BARNFIELD	55658	WOUNDED

RANK	NAME	SERVICE NO.	WOUND
PRIVATE	A. WHITE	56031	WOUNDED
PRIVATE	G. BISHOP	9354	WOUNDED
PRIVATE	W. L. BATCUP	29603	WOUNDED
PRIVATE	M. SMITH	54972	WOUNDED
PRIVATE	J. HUGHES	25613	WOUNDED
PRIVATE	T. H. BAKER	6022	WOUNDED
PRIVATE	H. SMITH	54880	WOUNDED
PRIVATE	J. F. WILLIAMS	40371	WOUNDED
PRIVATE	W. JONES	44036	WOUNDED
PRIVATE	W. BEDDOWES	56904	WOUNDED
PRIVATE	W. MAGINN	28005	WOUNDED
PRIVATE	D. COLERIDGE	17556	WOUNDED
PRIVATE	R. WILLIAMS	39126	WOUNDED
LANCE CORPORAL	J. CHESTER	11054	WOUNDED
PRIVATE	J. W. THOMAS	20238	WOUNDED
PRIVATE	G. LEWIS	23980	WOUNDED
PRIVATE	E. LEECH	23682	WOUNDED
PRIVATE	C. SMITH	13318	WOUNDED
PRIVATE	E. WILKINSON	33057	WOUNDED
PRIVATE	A. MILNER	10932	WOUNDED
PRIVATE	T. RICHARDSON	24599	WOUNDED
PRIVATE	H. CHIDLEY	54910	WOUNDED
PRIVATE	J. MORRIS	55069	WOUNDED
COY QUARTER MASTER	W. E. PHILLIPS	15546	WOUNDED
SERGEANT	D. HUGHES	25394	WOUNDED
SERGEANT	R. E. BRADBURY	56000	WOUNDED
SERGEANT	A. BARRY	23500	WOUNDED
SERGEANT	T. TEDSTONE	55654	WOUNDED
LANCE SERGEANT	S. A. POWELL	36887	WOUNDED
CORPORAL	S. WOODHOUSE	54894	WOUNDED
LANCE CORPORAL	G. SPENCER	23442	WOUNDED
LANCE CORPORAL	T. CUFFE	4643	WOUNDED
LANCE CORPORAL	H. WILLIAMS	265754	WOUNDED
PRIVATE	T. CHICK	38857	WOUNDED
PRIVATE	G. COLE	34058	WOUNDED
PRIVATE	S. S. DEBONNAIRE	56019	WOUNDED
PRIVATE	H. W. EVANS	15678	WOUNDED
PRIVATE	W. EDGAR	26613	WOUNDED
PRIVATE	J. GRUPMAN	55047	WOUNDED
PRIVATE	H. JONES	37398	WOUNDED
PRIVATE	L. JACKSON	54993	WOUNDED
PRIVATE	J. G. JOHNSON	54992	WOUNDED
PRIVATE	J. MORRIS	23326	WOUNDED
PRIVATE	W. J. PICKERS	54962	WOUNDED
PRIVATE	S. SCOGING	54882	WOUNDED
PRIVATE	J. H. STEVENSON	54972	WOUNDED
PRIVATE	J. THORLEY	54977	WOUNDED
PRIVATE	E. C. VAUGHAN	53111	WOUNDED
PRIVATE	A. WARD	54893	WOUNDED
PRIVATE	G. WOODHOUSE	54982	WOUNDED
PRIVATE	G. ROBERTS	55554	WOUNDED
PRIVATE	J. JENNINGS	54935	WOUNDED

RANK	NAME	SERVICE NO.	WOUND
PRIVATE	J. MORGAN	55662	WOUNDED
PRIVATE	T. ROGERS	10515	WOUNDED
PRIVATE	W. EDMUNDS	36399	WOUNDED
PRIVATE	J. EDWARDS	13576	WOUNDED
PRIVATE	G. EADE	56048	WOUNDED
PRIVATE	L. H. HILL	54991	WOUNDED
PRIVATE	T. HUME	33871	WOUNDED
PRIVATE	A. JONES	56993	WOUNDED
PRIVATE	E. T LUDLOW	15698	WOUNDED
PRIVATE	A. PRANDLE	23435	WOUNDED
PRIVATE	P. PREECE	55076	WOUNDED
PRIVATE	E. ROWLANDS	40963	WOUNDED
PRIVATE	J. H. STARKEY	39298	WOUNDED
PRIVATE	J. THOMPSON	55663	WOUNDED
PRIVATE	D. WILLIAMS	16314	WOUNDED
PRIVATE	T. WHITTLE	55069	WOUNDED
PRIVATE	W. C. THOMAS	44193	WOUNDED
PRIVATE	F. R. DYKE	56021	WOUNDED
PRIVATE	J. JONES	34353	WOUNDED
PRIVATE	O. RICHARDS	33880	WOUNDED
PRIVATE	A. MORRIS	55552	WOUNDED

RANK	NAME	SERVICE NO.	WOUND
PRIVATE	G. C. CATLING	55555	MISSING
PRIVATE	J. REID	54968	MISSING
PRIVATE	R. JONES	54734	MISSING
PRIVATE	J. CLAYTON	26392	MISSING

2nd Lieutenant **John Charles Edmunds Davies** was born in 1894 the Son of Alderman Walter Davies J. P. and Agnes Davies of London House, Lampeter. He was commissioned in the Royal Welsh Fusiliers on the 26th July 1915, prior to being sent to France on the 11th March 1916 to join the 10th Battalion. While on leave in October 1916 he married Olive Gwynedd Davies of Priory Street, Camarthen.

Edmunds Davies was wounded at Devil Wood on the 9th April 1917 and died of his wounds three days later.

APRIL 14th

The Battalion was relieved and marched into billets at Arras. Lieutenant F. W. Harrowell Royal Army Medical Corps (R. A. M. C.) assumed medical charge of the Battalion replacing Lieutenant E. Evans (R. A. M. C.) who was killed in action.

APRIL 15th, 16th & 17th

The Battalion began training near Daineville and on the 17th and a draft of 12 other ranks (O. R.) joined the Battalion for duty.

APRIL 18th

The Battalion were training in the morning and then in the afternoon the General Officer Commanding (G. O. C.) General Deverell inspected the Battalion. A draft of 68 other ranks (O. R.) joined the Battalion for duty.

APRIL 19th

The Battalion continued it's training. Lieutenant Colonel G. L. Compton-Smith Commanding Officer (C. O.) held a meeting with the Officers. 2nd Lieutenant C. W. Rowlands joined the Battalion for duty.

APRIL 20th & 21st

The Battalion continued it's training. 2nd Lieutenant C. W. Wilmore rejoined the Battalion for duty. 34 other ranks (O. R.) also joined the Battalion for duty.

APRIL 23rd

The Battalion marched out of Arras and occupied trenches at the Bois Des Bocufs. 2nd Lieutenant J. G. Williams was appointed Regimental Quartermaster, with honorary rank of Lieutenant. Lieutenant and Quartermaster E. H. Chapman was transferred to the Army Pay Corps.

APRIL 24th

The Battalion moved forward at 4.30am from the Support Trenches into what was known as 'The Brown Line Trenches' which were situated 2500 yards West of Monchy and was the old German third line system.

Private George Culpitt 35115 wrote in his Diary:-

"Now we were in a system of trenches know as the Brown Line and we're to go up and relieve a Battalion that was going 'Over' that afternoon.
Relieving is always a nerve trying job, for if it were spotted, it meant the enemy would be sure to turn his guns upon us, and here with only a shallow trench for protection, the chances of detection was trebled." – Private George Culpitt 35115 10th (Service) Battalion Royal Welsh Fusiliers

At 10.30pm the Battalion relieved the Royal Inniskilling Fusiliers in the Monchy Trenches. The Battalion received the following casualties:-

RANK	NAME	SERVICE NO.	WOUND
PRIVATE	J. HARRIS	14526	KILLED
PRIVATE	W. CHALLIS	56006	WOUNDED
PRIVATE	W. J. BYRNE	46162	WOUNDED
PRIVATE	P. THOMPSON	13526	WOUNDED
SERGEANT	H. HARTLEY	15149	WOUNDED

APRIL 25th

On completion of the relief, work was once again commenced in consolidating the line, which in places, was nothing more than shell holes with gaps occuring at various points. It was important to try and link up these gaps in the line. The enemy shelled the Battalions positions throughout the day.

Private George Culpitt 35115 wrote in his Diary:-

"Fritz was not long in replying. We came in for a large amount of heavy stuff which he threw over for a barrage. Shell after shell burst with stunning force around us, for a time things looked very black. No. 1 platoon, which was on the extreme left of the line, were having an even worse time than us, for the trenches got shallower as they extended to the left, while the artillery fire in that quarter grew worse." - Private George Culpitt 35115 10th (Service) Battalion Royal Welsh Fusiliers

The Battalion received the following casualties: -

RANK	NAME	SERVICE NO.	WOUND
2nd LIEUTENANT	H. CURRAN		KILLED IN ACTION

RANK	NAME	SERVICE NO.	WOUND
SERGEANT	J. HOLLIS	57030	WOUNDED
PRIVATE	W. J. BROWN	40960	WOUNDED
PRIVATE	W. CROMPTON	62881	WOUNDED
PRIVATE	D. OWEN	43797	WOUNDED
PRIVATE	D. H. JONES	55560	WOUNDED
LANCE CORPORAL	E. THOMPSON	54432	WOUNDED
LANCE CORPORAL	D. T. TREHEARNE	13146	WOUNDED
PRIVATE	W. HEIGHWAY	44270	WOUNDED
PRIVATE	T. H. MATHEWS	54862	WOUNDED
PRIVATE	B. SODEN	200334	WOUNDED

APRIL 26th

The Battalion were still holding the line but with the constant enemy shelling received the following casualties:-

RANK	NAME	SERVICE NO.	WOUND
LANCE CORPORAL	J. HARDACRE	19660	WOUNDED
LANCE CORPORAL	H. G. THOMAS	34946	WOUNDED
PRIVATE	C. J. MARKHAM	44278	WOUNDED
PRIVATE	A. J. WYRE	55090	WOUNDED
PRIVATE	J. HUGHES	241546	WOUNDED
PRIVATE	J. WILKINSON	65257	WOUNDED
PRIVATE	C. MURPHY	35055	WOUNDED
PRIVATE	J. JONES	21279	WOUNDED
PRIVATE	G. ATKINSON	39533	WOUNDED
PRIVATE	W. HUGHES	45117	WOUNDED

APRIL 27th

The constant heavy shelling from the enemy continued and an SOS was received on the Battalions left. The enemy attacked in numbers and came within 100 yards of the allies Front-Line, but the attack was beaten off by the 8th Battalion Kings Own Royal Lancaster Regiment and the 1st Battalion Gordon Highlanders with support from Machine Gun Company (M. G. C.) and the 10th Battalion Royal Welsh Fusiliers. The Battalion received the following casualties:-

RANK	NAME	SERVICE NO.	WOUND
PRIVATE	B. LEWIS	23233	KILLED
PRIVATE	E. ROWLANDS	40179	KILLED

RANK	NAME	SERVICE NO.	WOUND
PRIVATE	J. BENJAMIN	15028	KILLED
PRIVATE	W. R. GOULD	235023	KILLED
PRIVATE	F. A. GITSON	56312	KILLED
PRIVATE	G. M. POWELL	235443	KILLED
PRIVATE	T. PARBUTT	23279	KILLED
PRIVATE	W. GROOM	10199	KILLED
PRIVATE	R. S. LONSDALE	35324	KILLED
PRIVATE	R.T. WRIGHT	56033	KILLED
PRIVATE	J. OSBOURNE	14193	KILLED
PRIVATE	W. BENNETT	56005	KILLED

RANK	NAME	SERVICE NO.	WOUND
CORPORAL	P. GREENRIDGE	33299	WOUNDED
CORPORAL	G. THOMAS	55672	WOUNDED
LANCE CORPORAL	T. O. EDWARDS	29573	WOUNDED
PRIVATE	P. LEWIS	55065	WOUNDED
PRIVATE	P. CLIFFORD	63948	WOUNDED
PRIVATE	C. HEMMING	235103	WOUNDED
PRIVATE	T. WELLS	45055	WOUNDED
PRIVATE	G. LINHAM	56013	WOUNDED
PRIVATE	D. HUGHES	54729	WOUNDED
PRIVATE	W. JONES	200129	WOUNDED
PRIVATE	T. LENNON	15292	WOUNDED
PRIVATE	H. THOMAS	32581	WOUNDED
CORPORAL	J. CONDON	11290	WOUNDED
LANCE CORPORAL	W. J. TYSON	15409	WOUNDED
LANCE CORPORAL	F. COWAN	16369	WOUNDED
PRIVATE	H. THOMAS	25887	WOUNDED
PRIVATE	E. V ROBERTS	65772	WOUNDED
PRIVATE	W. MAINWAIRING	15038	WOUNDED
PRIVATE	E. CONDLIFFE	24265	WOUNDED
PRIVATE	W. L. DAVIES	201282	WOUNDED
PRIVATE	W. C. COWEN	235033	WOUNDED
PRIVATE	A. V. ROBERTS	56775	WOUNDED
PRIVATE	W. JONES	200290	WOUNDED
PRIVATE	A. H. EELES	54921	WOUNDED
PRIVATE	A. PEARCE	55656	WOUNDED
PRIVATE	G. R. EVANS	15793	WOUNDED
PRIVATE	T. W. BLAKE	56295	WOUNDED
PRIVATE	J. HINDS	54926	WOUNDED
PRIVATE	W. R. WRIGHT	27068	WOUNDED
PRIVATE	W. PHEYSEY	54960	WOUNDED
PRIVATE	R. H. JONES	17873	WOUNDED

APRIL 28th

As a result of the previous days attack the Battalion relieved the 8th Battalion Kings Own Royal Lancaster Regiment in the Front-Line. Orders were received informing them that the Battalion would remain in the Front-Line for another four days. The Battalion received the following casualties:-

RANK	NAME	SERVICE NO.	WOUND
CAPTAIN	W. J. O. HALE		KILLED IN ACTION

RANK	NAME	SERVICE NO.	WOUND
SERGEANT	W. MILES	17630	WOUNDED
SERGEANT	A. SMITH	34007	WOUNDED
PRIVATE	G. HAIGH	55644	WOUNDED
PRIVATE	S. WILLIAMS	14659	WOUNDED
PRIVATE	R. CLEMENTS	26704	WOUNDED
PRIVATE	R. JONES	4400	WOUNDED
PRIVATE	J. ROBERTS	14660	WOUNDED
LANCE CORPORAL	J. PREECE	48866	WOUNDED
PRIVATE	W. T. GRAHAM	267068	WOUNDED
PRIVATE	O. JONES	44349	WOUNDED
PRIVATE	T. HOWARD	55053	WOUNDED
PRIVATE	W. TUCKLEY	56763	WOUNDED
PRIVATE	W. STONEBRIDGE	55675	WOUNDED

APRIL 29th

No rations had arrived in the night so the Battalion had to go hungry all day as rations are impossible to move during the day.

Thant night Private George Culpitt 35115 wrote:-

"I was picked with nine others for what was the most risky of jobs on the front, like this - that of patrol. About 10pm we started out going to the left and made our way to where the Kings Own held a portion of the line, and where a new trench was being dug. From here we struck out towards the enemys lines going from shell hole to shell hole in pairs, for his snipers and machine gunners were busy and watchful and at the slightest movement, shots came in our direction. We had not been out very long when we encountered one of the enemy. He approached us unknowingly from the rear and must have thought we were Germans for he spoke to us in his native tongue. But on perceiving his mistake, he turned and ran for it, my chum was quicker than I, for before I could get my rifle to my shoulder, his rifle rang out and the Hun dropped, mortally wounded. After this nothing occurred worth mentioning and we finally returned to our own lines as dawn was breaking and were lucky in getting in just before our guns opened out in a ten minute bombardment of the enemys lines to see that the range was correct." - Private George Culpitt 35115 10th (Service) Battalion Royal Welsh Fusiliers

The Battalion received the following casualties: -

RANK	NAME	SERVICE NO.	WOUND
PRIVATE	W. R. EVANS	235034	KILLED IN ACTION
PRIVATE	J. WILKINSON	40725	KILLED IN ACTION
PRIVATE	C. J. BEHRENS	52237	KILLED IN ACTION
PRIVATE	C. NEWTON	57092	KILLED IN ACTION

RANK	NAME	SERVICE NO.	WOUND
CORPORAL	A. F. WARREN	22741	WOUNDED
PRIVATE	A. D. LATHWELL	34799	WOUNDED
PRIVATE	A. BAINBRIDGE	43166	WOUNDED
PRIVATE	J. T. ROBERTS	291215	WOUNDED

APRIL 30th

The Battalion still held the line. They were still under enemy artillery fire and rifle grenades. The Battalion received the following casualties:-

RANK	NAME	SERVICE NO.	WOUND
PRIVATE	D. DAVIES	44639	KILLED IN ACTION
PRIVATE	J. EVANS	54920	KILLED IN ACTION
PRIVATE	W. SHEPHERD	27046	KILLED IN ACTION
PRIVATE	J. WRIGHT	23155	KILLED IN ACTION
PRIVATE	J. W. HAYHURST	26690	KILLED IN ACTION

RANK	NAME	SERVICE NO.	WOUND
PRIVATE	R. HUGHES	11524	WOUNDED
LANCE CORPORAL	C. W. JONES	18316	WOUNDED
PRIVATE	T. LAND	20822	WOUNDED
PRIVATE	H. V. PIPER	56024	WOUNDED
PRIVATE	J. BASSETT	15020	WOUNDED BY GAS
PRIVATE	D. JONES	25385	WOUNDED
PRIVATE	A. D. NEWHAM	22225	WOUNDED

The Battalion received notification of the award of the **Military Medal** to the following:-

- **Sergeant H. Hartley 15149**
- **Private J. Bassett 15020**
- **Private H. Parry 36978**
- **Lance Sergeant J. Ames 15402**
- **Sergeant D. Hughes 25394**
- **Private D. Hughes 15081**

MAY 1917

MAY 1st

The Battalion continued to hold the line. The Battalion received the following casualties: -

RANK	NAME	SERVICE NO.	WOUND
SERGEANT	J. PARRY	56997	KILLED IN ACTION

RANK	NAME	SERVICE NO.	WOUND
2ND LIEUTENANT	EDWIN G. WILLIAMS		DIED OD WOUNDS

RANK	NAME	SERVICE NO.	WOUND
PRIVATE	D. T. REYNOLDS	25767	WOUNDED
PRIVATE	G. H. HANLEY	24911	WOUNDED
SERGEANT	W. WEBB	34897	WOUNDED
PRIVATE	J. H. DAVIES	62641	WOUNDED
2ND LIEUTENANT	A. G. WILLIAMS		WOUNDED

MAY 2nd

The Battalion were finally relieved in the Front-Line Trenches by the 4th Battalion Royal Fusiliers at 2am and returned to the old German trenches at Tilloy.

April had been a terrible month for the Battalion having suffered heavy casualties in the attack on the 9th, 10th and 11th of April. They suffered further casualties holding the Front-Line for over eight days. The men were exhausted, cold and hungry.

MAY 3rd

2 Coys of the Battalion, a strength of five Officers and 160 other ranks (O. R.) under the command of Major A. J. S. James M. C. proceeded under heavy enemy barrage of gas shells and high explosives (H. E.) to move up and hold the Monchy Defences, the Coys reached their objective but under very difficult circumstances. The remainder of the Battalion, under Colonel G. L. Compton-Smith Commanding Officer (C. O.) moved into trenches East of Bois Des Boeufs, having being relieved from the Front-Line only one day before (2nd May). Many of the men would have thought they would have a period of rest, with a chance to recover, but this was not to be.

Private George Culpitt 35115 wrote in his Diary:-

"In the afternoon rumours started going around that we were to go up again that night, but it seemed hardly creditable for the whole Brigade was very badly damaged and not fit to return, but nevertheless, as time passed 'Limbers' began to arrive with bombs, ammunition, picks, shovels, flares etc. to replenish each man's stock and it became evident that we were indeed going up again. This announcement fairly put everyone in the dumps. About 11.15pm, we moved off, a sorry spectacle indeed, worn out, unwashed or shaved for eight days and few in numbers. We travelled slowly up the road in the direction on Monchy and for some distance all went well, gradually we drew nearer and found that gas shells were also falling around us, we therefore, received orders to put on our gas helmets and this we did, continuing to march in this fashion. This made our progress very slow, for we could not see very far in our helmets and the road was dotted with shell holes. We were getting along as quickly as possible when all of a sudden I heard a whizz and received a terrific blow in the left side of the face, smashing my gas helmet and sending me flying into a hole, where I stayed until I recovered my wits and felt my face to see how much of it was left. Upon examination, however, I found that I had a cut above my lip, my left eye entirely closed up and in addition to several cuts and bruises, the left side of my face had already commenced to swell." – Private George Culpitt 35115 10th (Service) Battalion Royal Welsh Fusiliers

Private George Culpitt's injuries and the Battalion's casualties for the 3rd of May were as follows:-

RANK	NAME	SERVICE NO.	WOUND
2ND LIEUTENANT	F. A. LAWSON		WOUNDED BY GAS
PRIVATE	W. J. HARVEY	235035	WOUNDED
PRIVATE	R. THOMAS	202536	WOUNDED
PRIVATE	R. OWENS	40003	WOUNDED
PRIVATE	T. W. ROBERTS	54966	WOUNDED
PRIVATE	T. CHARLES	235045	WOUNDED
PRIVATE	P. S. TUCKER	5290	WOUNDED
PRIVATE	R. LUCAS	55063	WOUNDED
PRIVATE	W. JONES	235049	WOUNDED
LANCE CORPORAL	B. HODGKINSON	56989	WOUNDED
PRIVATE	J. EVANS	56007	WOUNDED
PRIVATE	H. C. ELLIS	48879	WOUNDED
PRIVATE	J. JONES	54445	WOUNDED
PRIVATE	H. ROWLANDS	54970	WOUNDED
PRIVATE	W. JONES	15226	WOUNDED
PRIVATE	*G. J. CULPITT*	*35115*	*WOUNDED*

Private George John Culpitt

George was born on the 22nd April 1887 in Noel Street, Islington, London, the first Son of Rachael and George Thomas Culpitt. He attended Ecclesbourne Road School.

George joined up at the age of 17 in December 1915, joining the 10th (Service) Battalion Royal Welsh Fusiliers with a Welsh friend, who joined at the same time.

George was wounded twice during the Great War, the injuries he received on the 3rd May 1917 proved quite severe and he was sent home to England for treatment and recuperation, spending nine weeks in hospital at Shrewsbury, before returning to France, serving this time, with the 13th Battalion Royal Welsh Fusiliers to the end of the War. He ended the War as an Anti Aircraft Gunner attached to his Battalion Head Quarters. George was demobbed in 1919 and returned to his job as a clerk for Palmyra Manufacturing Company Ltd in Newington. In 1921, George and his Father set up their own business 'G. T. Culpitt & Sons Ltd' a Wholesale & Export Artificial Florist. The business remained in the family for another 78 years and employed over 300 people and had an annual turnover of 7 million at it's peak. George married Charlotte King in 1922 and had two Sons Peter and David. George died in April 1962 aged 75 years, after a heart attack. His Wife lived for a further 27 years keeping the photograph below on her bedside table until she died.

MAY 5th

The Battalion based in the trenches at Bois Des Boeufs moved to trenches at Tilloy. At 11pm the detachment of the Battalion under the command of Major A. J. S. James were relieved in the trenches at Monchy by the 2nd Battalion Suffolk Regiment and rejoined the rest of the Battalion at Tilloy. One casualty was recorded as Missing – **Private T. Davies** service number 45030. The 76th Head Quarters wrote in the Brigades War Diary - *"The fighting strength of the Brigade after the battle of the Scarpe were holding the line."*

BRIGADE	OFFICERS	OTHER RANKS
8th Kings Own Royal Lancaster Regiment	16	417
2nd Battalion Suffolk Regiment	15	558
10th Battalion Royal Welsh Fusiliers	16	375
1st Battalion Gordon Highlanders	16	431
Machine Gun Corps	8	137
TOTAL	**71**	**1918**

The Battalion remained in the trenches at Tilloy until the 10th of May.

MAY 10th

On the night of the 10th May the Battalion moved back in the trenches at Monchy relieving the 13th Battalion Kings Liverpool Regiment. The Battalion was holding the center with the 8th Kings Own Royal Lancaster Regiment on their left and the 1st Battalion Gordon Highlanders on their right. One casualty was reported as Killed – **Private W. Wroe** service number 56783.

Two platoons of 'D' Coy and two platoons 'A' Coy were attached to the 1st Battalion Gordon Highlanders for relief duties and reported at the Battalions Head Quarters at 9.30pm in the 'Brown Line' Trench, once the relief was completed, the four platoons rejoined the Battalion in the line.

MAY 11th

The Battalion were still holding the line. One casualty was reported as Killed – **Private H. Davies** service number 29121.

MAY 12th

An attack by the 8th Kings Own Royal Lancaster Regiment on Devil's Trench in conjunction with 36th Brigade on their left was carried out. The Regiment suffered severe casualties and the attack failed. The 10th Battalion R. W. F. remained in the Front-Line Trench and suffered one wounded casualty – **Private J. Jackson** service number 55055.

MAY 13th & 14th

The Battalion remained in the Front-Line Trenches at Monchy but received the following casualties on the 13th of May:-

RANK	NAME	SERVICE NO.	WOUND
LANCE SERGEANT	R. JONES	12979	KILLED
PRIVATE	C. MASKERY	23553	KILLED

Casualties on the 14th of May:-

RANK	NAME	SERVICE NO.	WOUND
PRIVATE	G. J. LINHAM	235027	KILLED
LANCE CORPORAL	G. H. JONES	39311	KILLED
PRIVATE	J. MARSHALL	235028	KILLED
PRIVATE	J. H. JONES	54732	KILLED

RANK	NAME	SERVICE NO.	WOUND
PRIVATE	T. JONES	53746	MISSING

RANK	NAME	SERVICE NO.	WOUND
CAPTAIN	H. PRITCHARD		WOUNDED
2ND LIEUTENANT	A. P. COMYNS		WOUNDED
PRIVATE	E. KALE	28220	WOUNDED
PRIVATE	C. A. BROWNE	267089	WOUNDED
PRIVATE	W. DRURY	20246	WOUNDED
PRIVATE	W. JONES	12886	WOUNDED
PRIVATE	H. LEWIS	55059	WOUNDED
PRIVATE	H. WALSHAW	57098	WOUNDED
2ND LIEUTENANT	C. W. JONES		WOUNDED
PRIVATE	J. KERFOOT	37148	WOUNDED
PRIVATE	E. A. CHEW	201348	WOUNDED
PRIVATE	G. DUGGAN	54915	WOUNDED
PRIVATE	D. S. EVANS	235048	WOUNDED
PRIVATE	T. O. JONES	40160	WOUNDED
PRIVATE	F. W. CHANDLER	290590	WOUNDED

MAY 15th

In the early morning the Battalion was relieved in the Front-Line Trenches by 1 ½ Coys of the Kings Own Scottish Borderers and ½ Coy of the Royal Inniskilling Fusiliers and moved back to the old German third line at Tilloy where they received a hot meal (the first for quite a while). At 7.30am the Battalion marched to Arras Station where they were loaded into motor lorries and transported to billets at Duisans a distance of 7.6km (4 ½ miles).

MAY 16th

Weather was reported as 'fine'. The Battalion had a 'Kit Inspection' and the men were to have baths, which were very welcome.

MAY 17th

The Battalion marched into billets at Lattre St. Quentin a distance of 11.7km (7 ½ miles).

MAY 18th

The Battalion marched into billets at Berlencourt a distance of 11.7 km (7 ½ miles). Captain E. H. Howard rejoined the Battalion and resumed his position as Adjutant.

MAY 19th, 20th, 21st & 22nd

The following days were spent resting, cleaning and reorganising the Companies. Orders were received that platoons were to have a minimum strength of 28 men per platoon. Training began again on the 21st. On the 22nd there was a conference for all Officers at Battalion Head Quarters.

MAY 23rd, 24th & 25th

Training continued for the Battalion. Attack practice and a lecture by Major H. M. Hutchinson D. S. O. for all Subalterns on **'Messages and Reports'**.

MAY 26th

The following Officers joined the Battalion for duty:-

- **2nd Lieutenant J. H. Jones**
- **2nd Lieutenant W. A. Richards**
- **2nd Lieutenant G. A. Hall (rejoined after being wounded)**

MAY 27th

A draft of 10 other ranks (O. R.) joined the Battalion for duty. The Battalion continued with the training programme.

MAY 28th

Training continued with One Coy on the range and the rest at attack training. In the afternoon an inter-platoon football match was held.

MAY 29th

2nd Lieutenant D. L. Jenkins joined the Battalion for duty. The Battalion trained in the morning and in the afternoon there was the Battalion football final between 'A' Coy and the Quarter Master Stores. 'A' Coy won by six goals to nil. In the evening a concert was held.

MAY 31st

The following awards were announced:-

- Lieutenant G. L. Compton Smith – Distinguished Service Medal (D. S. O.)
- Lieutenant G. L. Compton Smith – Legion D' Honneur (Chevalier)
- Captain M. Watcyn Williams – Military Cross (M. C.)
- Sergeant H. Hartley 15149 – Distinguished Conduct Medal (D. C. M.)
- Sergeant H. Hartley 15149 – Military Medal (M. M.)
- Private J. E. Parry 36978 – Military Medal (M. M.)
- Sergeant J. Ames 15042 – Military Medal (M. M.)
- Private J. Bassett 15020 – Military Medal (M. M.)
- Sergeant D. Hughes 25394 – Military Medal (M. M.)
- Private D. Hughes 15081 – Military Medal (M. M.)
- Corporal S. Edge 57047 – Military Medal (M. M.)
- Private F. Jenks 54408 – Military Medal (M. M.)
- Private D. P. Parry 54961 – Military Medal (M. M.)

An additional **'Bar' for Military Medal** (M. M.) for **Private D. Watters 15286**

Lieutenant Colonel G. L. Comptom-Smith wrote to his Wife: -

"I have been awarded the D. S. O. for gallantry in the field and that is something, as they are very sticky about decorations in this Division. I have also been created an Officer of the Legion D' Honneur, the best medal really that is possible to get next to the V. C." – Lieutenant Colonel G. L. Compton-Smith Commanding Officer (C. O.) 10th (Service) Battalion Royal Welsh Fusiliers

Captain Morgan Watcyn Williams also wrote about the award of his Military Cross:-

"A few days after I got back he (Compton-Smith) told me that he had been awarded the D. S. O. and the Legion D' Honneur and that I was to get the Military Cross (M. C.) to pretend that I got no satisfaction out of it would be rank hypocrisy but Smith was fed up because he had recommended me for something better and for a French Order as well. Scores of them went to Staff, while my pals were over looked and forgotton, referring to the former. The Colonel remarked, 'If I had my way I'd hang 'em with their own ribbons!' I mention these things because they illustrate a principle which operates everywhere. Men in the trenches can never hope to receive the rewards off the Staff because the Staff decides who is to be rewarded. The rest of us, if we are all wise, will learn with ignatius 'to fight and not to heed for any reward save that knowing that we do the will.'" – Captain Morgan Watcyn Williams 10th (Service) Battalion Royal Welsh Fusiliers

JUNE 1917

JUNE 1st

A draft of 160 other ranks (O. R.) joined the Battalion for duty. The following Officers also joined the Battalion:-

- 2nd Lieutenant - Ll. Jones
- 2nd Lieutenant – F. A. Stringer
- 2nd Lieutenant – H. L. Williams
- 2nd Lieutenant – R. A. Thomas

Weather was reported as 'fine'.

JUNE 2nd

The Battalion marched to Ambrines and from Ambrines they were transported by motor lorries to billets in the Cavalry Barracks in Arras. The general Officer Commanding, Brigade Major and two Battalion

Commanders went to select the site for practice attack on 'No Mans Land' East of Arras, preparing the proposed attack on Hook and Long Trenches East of Monchy.

JUNE 4th

Captain J. H. Addie joined the Battalion for duty. The Battalion continued training.

JUNE 5th

The Battalion moved into billets at St. Sacrament Hostel Rue D' Amiens just off Grand Place Arras due to the constant heavy shelling of their previous billets which provided a lack of sufficient cellar accommodation. In the evening a 'Working Party' of the Battalion worked at the practice area digging trenches.

FROM JUNE 6th TO JUNE 12th

The Battalion continued with their training routine, preparing for the impending attack. During the night of the 12th the Battalion moved up to the trenches under heavy hostile enemy shelling and took over the 'Brown Line Trenches' from the 8th Battalion East Yorks Regiment. One Coy of the Battalion attached to 1st Gordon Highlanders relieved the 1st Battalion Royal Scots Fusiliers (R. S. F.) in the left sector trenches. The Battalion received the following casualties:-

RANK	NAME	SERVICE NO.	WOUND
PRIVATE	J. BREWER	56041	KILLED

RANK	NAME	SERVICE NO.	WOUND
PRIVATE	C. PRITCHARD	44247	WOUNDED
PRIVATE	J. MOULT	55070	WOUNDED
PRIVATE	E. OWEN	60343	WOUNDED
PRIVATE	W. H. SCHOFIELD	60294	WOUNDED
PRIVATE	W. ANDERSON	44614	WOUNDED
PRIVATE	G. S. GARNETT	60352	WOUNDED
PRIVATE	D. FRAIN	60338	WOUNDED
PRIVATE	R. MARSHLAND	60344	WOUNDED
PRIVATE	N. SLATER	60315	WOUNDED
PRIVATE	W. WILLIAMS	43934	WOUNDED
PRIVATE	F. H. WHITE	56046	WOUNDED

JUNE 14th

All attacking troops including the 10th Battalion Royal Welsh Fusiliers were in assembly positions by 2am. At 7.20am the attack on Hook and Long Trenches commenced with the 2nd Suffolks and One Coy of the 10th Battalion Royal Welsh Fusiliers on the right and 1st Battalion Gordon Highlanders with One Coy of the 10th Battalion Royal Welsh Fusiliers on the left. The attack started well with the first wave arriving in Hook Trench as intended before the opening barrage and thus taking the enemy by surprise. The barrage opened exactly 1 ½ minutes after zero hour as planned. The attack was entirely successful. Prisoners were taken in this action.

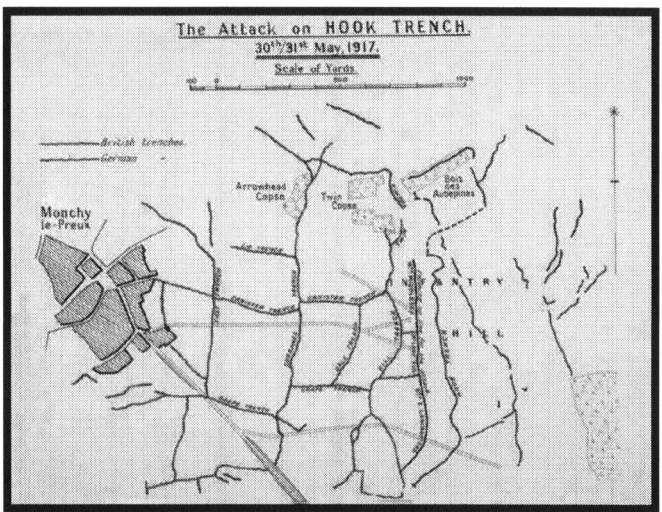

The Battalion received the following casualties:-

RANK	NAME	SERVICE NO.	WOUND
PRIVATE	H. E. EDMUNDS	54462	KILLED
PRIVATE	W. STANT	56766	KILLED
PRIVATE	A. V. HEWITT	60340	KILLED
PRIVATE	R. H. T. ARTIS	60224	KILLED
PRIVATE	W. E. DAVIES	49028	KILLED
PRIVATE	C. J. MARKHAM	44278	KILLED
PRIVATE	E. TURRELL	55985	KILLED
PRIVATE	R. D. JONES	60322	KILLED
PRIVATE	S. J. SLATER	36581	KILLED
PRIVATE	C. HIGGINS	55952	KILLED

RANK	NAME	SERVICE NO.	WOUND
CAPTAIN	H. HALL MORGAN		WOUNDED
LANCE SERGEANT	A. EDWARDS	34084	WOUNDED
LANCE CORPORAL	E. J. ELCOCK	17178	WOUNDED
LANCE CORPORAL	F. REEVES	241717	WOUNDED
LANCE CORPORAL	J. BIRMINGHAM	60904	WOUNDED
LANCE CORPORAL	J. R. JONES	15714	WOUNDED
PRIVATE	A. CHAPMAN	60308	WOUNDED
PRIVATE	W. HIMBURY	235024	WOUNDED
PRIVATE	R. T. JONES	25630	WOUNDED
PRIVATE	R. H. JOHNSON	60310	WOUNDED
PRIVATE	A. SIDEBOTTOM	55081	WOUNDED
PRIVATE	A. SPARKES	15148	WOUNDED
PRIVATE	A. SMITH	60402	WOUNDED
PRIVATE	H. S. HARE	60375	WOUNDED
PRIVATE	A. BAGULEY	60306	WOUNDED
PRIVATE	J. REED	60317	WOUNDED
PRIVATE	J. LAW	16113	WOUNDED
PRIVATE	D. WILLIAMS	60305	WOUNDED
PRIVATE	J. T. CLARKE	56203	WOUNDED
PRIVATE	H. GREENHALGH	55046	WOUNDED
PRIVATE	C. LOMAS	54956	WOUNDED
PRIVATE	T. HADDOCK	53468	WOUNDED
PRIVATE	R. W. JONES	60323	WOUNDED
PRIVATE	S. SHUKER	60419	WOUNDED
PRIVATE	J. H. NETHERWOOD	60131	WOUNDED
PRIVATE	F. WILLIAMS	39138	WOUNDED
PRIVATE	W. HUMPHREYS	60905	WOUNDED
PRIVATE	J. BROOKS	60357	WOUNDED
PRIVATE	J. JONES	266708	WOUNDED
PRIVATE	T. HILLIARD	56038	WOUNDED
PRIVATE	C. TAYLOR	54889	WOUNDED
PRIVATE	J. E. LADD	235040	WOUNDED
PRIVATE	W. B. LEWIS	235041	WOUNDED
PRIVATE	F. J. WARING	60420	WOUNDED
PRIVATE	T. H. BROCKBANK	19493	WOUNDED
PRIVATE	W. H. DAVIES	201347	WOUNDED
PRIVATE	A. GRUFMAN	55087	WOUNDED
PRIVATE	D. A. PRANDLE	23435	WOUNDED
PRIVATE	T. VALENTINE	60413	WOUNDED

RANK	NAME	SERVICE NO.	WOUND
PRIVATE	C. HEMMING	235013	MISSING
PRIVATE	W. JONES	235647	MISSING

JUNE 15th

At 2.15am the enemy made a strong counter attack against the position taken by the Battalion on the 14th. The attack was repulsed and heavy casualties were inflicted on the enemy. With support from the artillery, all positions were retained with the exception of one advance post.

The Battalion received the following casualties: -

RANK	NAME	SERVICE NO.	WOUND
PRIVATE	A. OATES	36462	KILLED

RANK	NAME	SERVICE NO.	WOUND
LANCE CORPORAL	G. GRIFFITHS	54924	WOUNDED
LANCE CORPORAL	L. BOWDEN	5599	WOUNDED
PRIVATE	F. ANSON	22060	WOUNDED
PRIVATE	G. CHAMBERS	15400	WOUNDED
PRIVATE	R. EDWARDS	60209	WOUNDED
PRIVATE	R. JEFFERSON	60211	WOUNDED
PRIVATE	W. F. OWEN	60328	WOUNDED
PRIVATE	E. PIERCE	60216	WOUNDED
PRIVATE	J. A. KELLY	41645	WOUNDED
PRIVATE	R. HUTCHINSON	54986	WOUNDED
PRIVATE	R. H. JONES	17873	WOUNDED
PRIVATE	T. RICHARDSON	24599	WOUNDED

Lieutenant Colonel G. L. Compton-Smith wrote to his Wife: -

"It has been a most unpleasant but highly successful trench snatching show on a small front. We came in for most of the shelling, our casualties I fear, have been severe. We may be relieved tonight or maybe not, but if we are, I think we shall never have been out of shell fire since April 1st or 2nd, nearly three months, most of the time, in the vicinity of this infernal village (Monchy)." - Lieutenant Colonel G. L. Compton-Smith Commanding Officer (C. O.) 10th (Service) Battalion Royal Welsh Fusiliers

JUNE 16th

There was very heavy hostile enemy shelling especially on the Shrapnel Trench, where the Battalions Head Quarters were established. The Battalion received the following casualties:-

RANK	NAME	SERVICE NO.	WOUND
PRIVATE	F. BAILEY	60196	KILLED
PRIVATE	W. ROBERTS	20914	KILLED
PRIVATE	T. G. CHAPLAIN	60354	KILLED
PRIVATE	J. W. GIBBS	60386	KILLED
PRIVATE	E. MORRIS	57050	KILLED
PRIVATE	L. THOMAS	49816	KILLED

RANK	NAME	SERVICE NO.	WOUND
PRIVATE	J. MCINTEE	32548	KILLED
PRIVATE	E. BUTTLE	56010	KILLED
PRIVATE	S. G. CHANNON	60358	KILLED
PRIVATE	A. HILLS	60367	KILLED
PRIVATE	W. MESSENGER	48903	KILLED
PRIVATE	H. TRIPPIER	60409	KILLED

RANK	NAME	SERVICE NO.	WOUND
2ND LIEUTENANT	L. E. ROBERTS		WOUNDED
PRIVATE	R. EDWARDS	57004	WOUNDED
PRIVATE	P. HUGHES	60747	WOUNDED
PRIVATE	F. W. WASDELL	60408	WOUNDED
PRIVATE	A. H. COCKAYNE	66209	WOUNDED
PRIVATE	W. STEWART	60403	WOUNDED
LANCE SERGEANT	W. J. MILWARD	54420	WOUNDED
LANCE CORPORAL	F. COGAN	235020	WOUNDED
PRIVATE	G. A. LEWIS	34826	WOUNDED
PRIVATE	G. S. PITMAN	60390	WOUNDED
PRIVATE	T. M. WEBBER	60291	WOUNDED

RANK	NAME	SERVICE NO.	WOUND
PRIVATE	J. O'DONNELL	60389	MISSING

JUNE 17th

Two Coys of the Battalion were placed under orders of the Commanding Officer (C. O.) of the 1st Gordon Highlanders with orders to retake the advanced post that was lost to the enemy during their counter attack on June 15th. This attack was unsuccesful. The Battalion suffered the following casualties:-

RANK	NAME	SERVICE NO.	WOUND
SERGEANT	T. G. WILSON	56002	KILLED
LANCE CORPORAL	G. WRIGHT	15086	KILLED

RANK	NAME	SERVICE NO.	WOUND
PRIVATE	H. PETTINGER	6418	KILLED
PRIVATE	W. J. LLOYD	23542	KILLED
PRIVATE	W. DACKOMBE	56016	KILLED
PRIVATE	F. BWYE	12365	KILLED
PRIVATE	J. C. ARDERN	54696	KILLED
PRIVATE	J. WRIGHT	60377	KILLED

RANK	NAME	SERVICE NO.	WOUND
SERGEANT	J. T. JONES	14647	WOUNDED
PRIVATE	E. BURNE	60356	WOUNDED
PRIVATE	T. KELLY	57031	WOUNDED
PRIVATE	G. BARKER	240167	WOUNDED
PRIVATE	A. LLOYD	55062	WOUNDED
PRIVATE	W. SPENCER	10436	WOUNDED
PRIVATE	W. R. BRTOHERTON	60201	WOUNDED
PRIVATE	E. BEYNON	60298	WOUNDED
CORPORAL	J. DAVIES	15521	WOUNDED
LANCE CORPORAL	H. YONDS	23968	WOUNDED
PRIVATE	J. JONES	20279	WOUNDED
PRIVATE	P. J. ROBERTS	15164	WOUNDED
PRIVATE	G. V. LLOYD	55669	WOUNDED
PRIVATE	R. M. ROBERTS	45129	WOUNDED
PRIVATE	E. BURNS	60337	WOUNDED
PRIVATE	L. CLARKE	60309	WOUNDED

JUNE 18th

The Battalion in the trenches were again heavily shelled and a counter attack by the enemy was again repulsed. The Battalion suffered the following casualties:-

RANK	NAME	SERVICE NO.	WOUND
LIEUTENANT	L. P. VERNON M. C.		KILLED
CORPORAL	H. JONES	39944	KILLED
PRIVATE	J. E. SIMISTER	267074	KILLED

RANK	NAME	SERVICE NO.	WOUND
LIEUTENANT	D. E. DAVIES		KILLED
PRIVATE	T. CLARKE	60299	KILLED
PRIVATE	W. J. ROBERTS	56762	KILLED

RANK	NAME	SERVICE NO.	WOUND
CAPTAIN	D. S. HUGHES		WOUNDED
SERGEANT	R. WILLIAMS	11097	WOUNDED
CORPORAL	J. FERRIS	13529	WOUNDED
PRIVATE	J. BRADLEY	56297	WOUNDED
2ND LIEUTENANT	LL. JONES		WOUNDED
PRIVATE	H. M. BATSTONE	56296	WOUNDED
PRIVATE	F. C. CORNWALL	56034	WOUNDED
PRIVATE	F. J. WILLIAMSON	56770	WOUNDED
PRIVATE	W. D. LEWIS	6353	WOUNDED
LANCE SERGEANT	F. JERVIS	33602	WOUNDED
LANCE CORPORAL	A. BUTLER	13814	WOUNDED
PRIVATE	T. HUME	33871	WOUNDED
PRIVATE	E. JOHN	235036	WOUNDED
PRIVATE	F. EVANS	60906	WOUNDED
PRIVATE	T. GRIFFITHS	44280	WOUNDED
PRIVATE	W. HOLLERAN	63632	WOUNDED
PRIVATE	J. W. MASSEY	64015	WOUNDED
PRIVATE	T. ROBERTS	54967	WOUNDED
PRIVATE	J. W. WARDLE	60320	WOUNDED
PRIVATE	H. T. JONES	40180	WOUNDED
PRIVATE	E. GILL	60300	WOUNDED
PRIVATE	G. H. PRITCHARD	44287	WOUNDED
PRIVATE	J. WHITE	55088	WOUNDED GAS
PRIVATE	J. STANFIELD	60318	WOUNDED GAS
PRIVATE	J. BRADSHAW	266867	WOUNDED
PRIVATE	A. THOMPSON	60319	WOUNDED
PRIVATE	W. KING	60198	WOUNDED
PRIVATE	H. ROBERTS	40954	WOUNDED
PRIVATE	H. HEWITT	60679	WOUNDED
PRIVATE	D. T. DENNIS	173102	WOUNDED GAS
PRIVATE	T. J. STEER	60317	WOUNDED GAS

RANK	NAME	SERVICE NO.	WOUND
PRIVATE	W. H. GRICE	60353	MISSING

Lieutenant David Ethelston Davies

David Ethelston Davies was born on 11th April 1894 to Reverend John Davies and Edith Annie Davies of Llanwrst. He was educated at St. John's School Leatherhead and Ystrad Meurig and was to study Theology at

Lampeter College in preparation to enter the Ministry when War broke out. He was commissioned into the Royal Welsh Fusiliers on 3rd June 1916. He trained at Kinmel Park North Wales before joining the 10th Battalion on the Somme. He was killed on the 18th June 1917 aged 23. David Ethelston's Sister Harriet (known as Nellie) died following the sad news of her Brother's death. At the time of his death she was suffereing from TB and the close bond she had with her Brother left her heart broken. They say she died of a broken heart. He is buried at the Feuchy Chapel British Cemetery, Wancourt and remembered on a 'stained glass window' in Llanarmon Church.

DAVIES, DAVID ETHELSTON, Lieut., 12th (Service) Battn. The Royal Welsh Fusiliers, eldest s. of the Rev. John Davies, Rector of Llangybi and Llanarmon, co. Carnarvon, by his wife, Edith Annie, dau. of William Ethelston; b. Llanrwst, 11 April, 1894; educ. St. John's School, Leatherhead, and Ystrad Meurig, and was about to proceed to one of the universities with a view to taking Holy Orders, but on the outbreak of the European war volunteered for foreign service; was gazetted 2nd Lieut. Royal Welsh Fusiliers 3 June, 1915, and promoted Lieut. 11 April, 1916; trained at Kinmel Park, where he was Brigade Signalling Instructor; served with the Expeditionary Force in France from Aug. 1916, and was killed in action at Infantry Hill 18 June, 1917. His Colonel wrote: "That the attacks failed was entirely due to the magnificent bravery of Lieut. D. E. Davies, and others like him, who stuck to their posts imbuing their men with their own splendid spirit until they fell on the ground they defended so well. . . . As an officer he was fearless, cool and resolute in the highest degree, and as a man he was universally popular and beloved by both officers and men. I have no hesitation in saying he was one of the best platoon commanders I ever had." Unm.

David Ethelston Davies.

Newspaper article about David Ethelston Davies

Stained Glass Window in Llanarmon Church

Headstone in Feuchy Chapel British Cemetery

This poem was written by Rev. John Davies following the death of his Son in the Great War & the death of his Daughter Nellie. It was originally published in Yr Haul (The Sun) a Welsh Church monthly paper.

The news came by wire: just as lightning it fled on
And wounded me sore and deep down on that day.
The flash of the light made thus clear to my reason
My boy as of old, so reserved and so gay.
***

His life it arose – every period recounted,
Such vivid impressions I's like to relate,
I saw a golden haired lad, how well guarded,
As walking together he reached man's estate.
***

His face by his bashfulness rendered so beauteous,
The blush as the sunshine o'er spreading lustrous,
Looked out of the blackness so bright and so clear.
***

My eyes they grew dim and, lo, he also withdrew,
Receded from sight in the mists of the vale,
My spirit from longing did groan just then anew
My heart, badly wounded, had left me so pale.
***

My dearest of lads say how went thou managing
When fording that deep flowing river so drear?
Did someone come forward to help in assuaging
By drying the tear and lessening the fear?
***

When there in the midst of the terrible laments
Thy head from its wounds bent so lowly and meek
Thy lips did they utter the names of they parents
And did just a tear for them sallow they cheek?
***

Oh! Came there an appeal from Heaven to assist,
To bring thee in safety to creak and to shore?
Upheld thee to stand on being called to resist
And strengthened to do just the same as of yore?
***

I'd like if some day that the angel would tell me
Who snatched in his flagon the tear thou didst yield,
And also to see just the tear that did travel,
And read just the message that it thus concealed.
***

On one bed of pain there was one closely watching,
Her thought and her prayer to thyself were e'er tied.
For three solid years she was ever rememb'ring
And anxious for thee thus away from her side.
***

The news as it flashed – she received the suggestion
Though loved by so many, of thee she did dream.
With smiles on her face, she made haste on her mission
And girded her loins for to cross the wide stream.
***

A week althogether did death's tender finger
Just keep you entirely apart each from each.
Compassion it showed when the two hearts did linger
And longing like rust corrupted the breach.
***

Oh blessed Sabbath day, ye both together
And we away back in the shades of the vale.
Our bitter cup turns into joy to remember
And sing of them both in our home in the dale.
***

What deep mysticism! Who etenity derives
Of fruits of the tree he has sought and does love?
The bitter turns sweet and the earth draws supplies
In spite of its sorse from Heaven above.
***

Our longing is great: we'd give all that we possess
To have you come back once again face to face.
You both here together we'd made haste to caress
And hold you so warmly in loving embrace.
***

Inside the porch, one whose mystery ne'er ceases,
Expecting in hope that the door will rebound,
And hear all the murmers of twilight's soft breezes
That carry their burden of heavenly sound.
***

I marvel how little I knew of my children!
What sacrifice lay so concealed in their breasts!
Twas death that revealed that such treasures lay hidden;
At times such a thought to my heart brings such rest.
***

He fell, my dear boy, whilst he fought, says the comment.
For days, that the gains might not go es a flood.
His spirit unyielding, brought fame to his regiment
And purchased the conquest by shedding his blood.
***

He fell while still young, very young, with a glory
That filled a whole lifetime of honourable strife.
He fell to a far fuller life by his story –
A death that made pure the sum total of life.
***

In Feuchy Cahppelle, on the crossroads to Cambria
From Arras, the cross just denoting the grave.
How restfully there where such horrors they portray
In folds that are splendid with honour so brave.
***

Oh! Ethelston, Ethelston, there will I journey,
When granted – a flower so sadly in hand,
From Nellie's own grave in the dear old home land.
***

Thy cross of thy regiment will I make a crown and
A wreath out of mother's own roses be made.
The grass off thy grave will I bereave there a garland
To place on a grave of our Nelli, fair maid.
***

The wreaths like a rainbow in clouds will bring so tight
Both graves each to each in knot of such calm.
And on it I'll gaze, tho' my heart's grief's sad fight –
A bow so resplendent in the grasp of its palm.
***

Farewell, my dear lad, the farewell from my sad heart.
The shadow o'er spreads and the night will repose.
The sun in the west does now slowly depart,
The lids of my eyes with such longing do close.

Translated from Welsh by Rev. D. C. Williams M. C.

Lieutenant Leonard Patrick Vernon M. C.

Leonard Patrick Vernon was born on 23rd September 1894 to Captain William Henry and Elizabeth Vernon in Wrexham. He was educated at Grove Park School and was a Bank Clerk before joining the Manchester University Officer Training Corps (O. T. C.) in 1913. At the outbreak of the War he enlisted in the 20th (Public Schools) Battalion Royal Fusiliers. He was commissioned in the Royal Welsh Fusiliers, (his Father's Regiment) on 14th August 1915 and in March 1916 was posted to the 10th (Service) Battalion R. W. F. Vernon was awarded the Military Cross for gallantry on the Somme in August 1916. He was killed on the 19th June 1917 whilst holding an advanced outpost. He was 22 years old. He is buried at Feuchy Chapel British Cemetery, Wancourt.

Feuchy Chapel Cemetery Wancourt

British Army, De Ruvigny's Roll of Honour 1914-1918

JUNE 19th

Heavy enemy shell fire continued throughout the day. The Battalion received the following casualties:-

RANK	NAME	SERVICE NO.	WOUND
PRIVATE	W. EPWORTH	63213	MISSING

RANK	NAME	SERVICE NO.	WOUND
2ND LIEUTENANT	F. A. STRINGER		WOUNDED
SERGEANT	A. W. CARPENTER	27619	WOUNDED

JUNE 20th

In the early hours of the morning the Battalion was relieved in the Monchy Trenches by the 8th Battalion Royal Fusiliers and marched to billets in the Cavalry Barracks in Arras. At noon the Battalion was transported in buses to Halloy (near Doullens) and went into billets. Lieutenant J. R. Williams joined the Battalion for duty.

Lieutenant Colonel G. L. Compton-Smith wrote a letter to his Wife dated 17th June:-

"We are still here in the trenches being shelled and shelled. I am feeling very depressed. If only they would take us out after we had completed what everyone admits is a strikingly successful operation – but no! if only all Divisions in the Army had half the fighting we have to do – but again, no! we are one of six or seven selected for every possible battle. I was talking to General Ford the other day, my old Colonel, he is now with the 38th Division, since July 3rd 1916 they have not been in a single battle. We have been at Delville Wood, Guillemont, Serre, Arras, Guemappe, Monchy and now again Monchy. Our casualties in three days from shelling alone has been nearly 200. My Head Quarters are in a dugout in what was once a trench – now merely a wide sunbaked ditch of loose earth in a waste of parched shell holes in front of hideous ruins of the village. Rotting corpses line the bottom of the ditch and thousands of great green flies infest everything. The smell of death is literally sick whenever one moves. Many of the men have been buried by shells and some are half mad and shaking in every limb. I have had this sort of thing now with hardly a rest for two months. We are all about finished." - Lieutenant Colonel G. L. Compton-Smith Commanding Officer (C. O.) 10th (Service) Battalion Royal Welsh Fusiliers

It was plain to see from the above letter that Lieutenant Colonel G. L. Compton-Smith was suffereing from the early signs of **'Shell Shock'**.

JUNE 21st, 22nd & 23rd

The Battalion rested for the next few days.

Captain Morgan Watcyn Williams wrote in his memoirs 'From Khaki to Cloth' of his return to the Battalion after his leave in England where he had received the Military Cross from the King, George V, at Buckingham Palace:-

"When I reached my unit the ranks of Officers were thinner than ever. Lieutenant Vernon M. C. who had been in charge of the Signallers for over a year was dead and Captain Hall Morgan and 2nd Lieutenant L. E. Roberts had gone down the line wounded. Once again, I had a new Company Mess and the thing which made me marvel was the quality of the men who joined us. It is a terrible thing to feel old at twenty five, but I did then, we were shouldering responsibilities which would stagger and frighten the modern middle class critics of youth with their eternal patriotism. I like the definition 'Patriotism is giving your life for my country.'" - *Captain Morgan Watcyn Williams 10th (Service) Battalion Royal Welsh Fusiliers*

JUNE 24th

The Battalion held a Memorial Service in memory of all the men that had fell in the recent fighting.

Captain Morgan Watcyn Williams wrote:-

"On the 24th June we held a Memorial Service to those who had fallen and I spent the rest of the day reading Donald Hankey's 'A Stand in Arms' which Harry Curran's Father had sent to me. That clean gay spirit was the only Son his parents had, and in a letter which accompanied the book, a letter full of pride and resignation, I saw between the lines, all the heartbreak of the world." - *Captain Morgan Watcyn Williams 10th (Service) Battalion Royal Welsh Fusiliers*

2nd Lieutenant Henry (Harry) Curran was the Son of Henry E. Curran, of 70 Rice Lane, Wallasey, Cheshire. He was born in Liverpool in 1892 and was killed in action on the 25th April 1917 aged 25. He is buried in Feuchy Chapel British Cemetery, Wancourt.

JUNE 25th

The Battalion commenced training which consisted of:-
- Physical Drill
- Musketry Drill and Wiring
- Close Order Drill
- One Coy was on The Range

Lectures were given to Officers and N. C. O.'s by the Commanding Officer (C. O.) G. L. Compton-Smith.

JUNE 26th, 27th & 28th

The Battalion continued training. On the 27th, Major A. J. S. James M. C. was temporarily attached to the 2nd Battalion Suffolk Regiment.

JUNE 29th

The award of the **'Military Medal'** was presented to the following soldiers by the General Officer Commanding (G. O. C.) IVth Corps Lieutenant General Sir Charles Louis Woollcombe K. C. B. :-

- Sergeant H. Mountford 23410
- Sergeant A. P. Carter 235021
- Lance Corporal H. V. Major 35071
- Lance Corporal J. A. Leeder 54953

JUNE 30th

The Battalion continued training which included an early morning run. Later in the day there was the final of the Battalions boxing competition.

JULY 1917

JULY 1st

The Battalion marched to Doullens where they entrained for Achiet Le Grand. Once they had arrived the Battalion marched into camp in the Bihucourt area a distance of 1.9km (1/2 mile).

JULY 3rd

The Battalion moved into Brigade reserve area at Velu Wood.

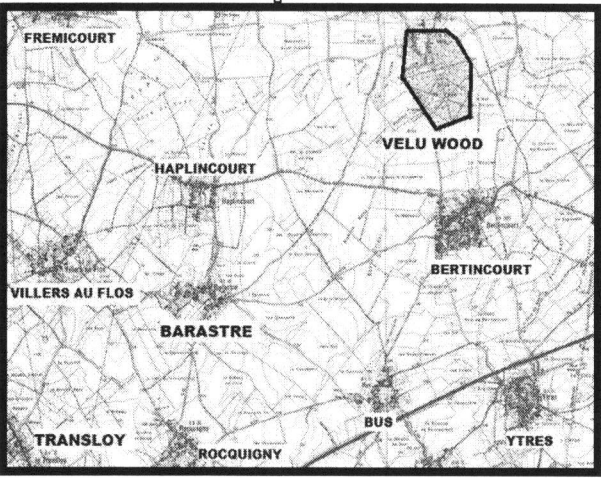

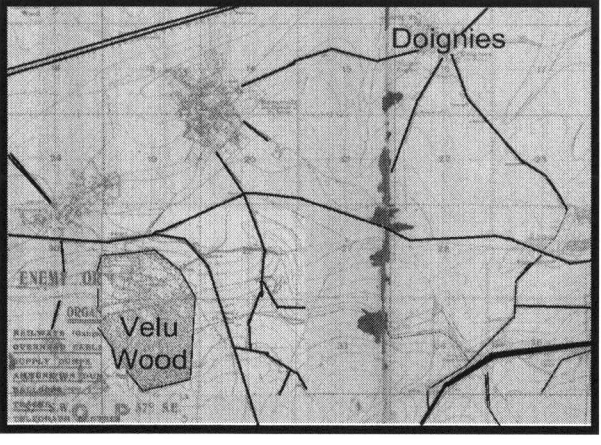

JULY 4th & 5th
The Battalion continued training in the 'Training Area' in Velu Wood.

JULY 6th
A draft of 62 other ranks (O. R.) and the following Officers joined the Battalion for duty:-
- **2nd Lieutenant C. H. Elphick**
- **2nd Lieutenant R. T. Owen**
- **2nd Lieutenant D. C. Hunter**

In the afternoon inter-Battalion boxing matches were held between the Battalion and the 8th Own Royal Lancaster Regiment, followed by a Battalion concert.

JULY 7th
The Battalion were inspected by the Commanding Officer (C. O.) of IV Corps Lieutenant General Sir C. L. Woollcombe K. C. B. Major A. J. S. James M. C. rejoined the Battalion from the 2nd Suffolk Regiment and resumed his appointment of Second in Command.

There was a Battalion 'Cross Country Run' held. The following results were:-
- **'D' Coy – 153 points**
- **'B' Coy – 121 points**
- **'C' Coy – 96 points**
- **'A' Coy – 90 points**

JULY 8th & 9th
The Battalion continued it's training. On the 9th, 2nd Lieutenant T. M. Davies and 10 other ranks (O. R.) joined the Battalion for duty.

JULY 10th
The Battalion moved into the center subsection of the trenches in the Louerval area relieveing the 8th Battalion the East Yorks Regiment.

JULY 11th, 12th, 13th & 14th
The Battalion held the Front-Line Trenches. The sector was reported as 'Quiet' with the occasional shelling by the enemy. The distance between

the enemy's Front-Line was between 1000 yards from the left sector and 2000 yards from the right sector.

JULY 15th

The Battalion carried out a successful bombing raid on the advance enemy post and the Battalion occupied the post.

Trench Bombing Raids

The ever evolving nature of **'Trench Warfare'** led to the new patterns of fighting. The area of 'No Mans Land' was key ground, especially at night. Patrols were sent out to gather information about enemys defences. The purpose of trench bombing raids was to gain temporary entry into the enemys Front-Line Trench or Advance Post and to destroy fortifications and weapons, for example; a machine gun post that would cause major casualties in an upcoming attack. Also, the purpose of trench bombing raids was to gain intelligence by the capture of maps and documents and to find out which Regiment is 'Holding' that particular part of the trench. Are they elite troops or just normal infantry troops? When returning with prisoners. Whichever troops they were, could be invaluable; to interrogate them to find out as much information as they could and to find out what the morale is like.

Trench bombing raids were lightly equipped for fast, unimpeeded movement. The 'Raiding Parties' were armed with deadly, sometimes homemade weapons, bayonets, entrenchment tools, trench knives, clubs, hatchets, pick handles, brass knuckles, clubs and mills bombs.

Trench Knife

Mills Bomb

Knuckle Duster

Trench Club

Trench Raiding Party - the day after a Trench Bombing Raid

Typical raids were carried out by small teams of men who would black up their faces with burnt cork before proceeding to no mans land. Standard practice was to creep slowly up on the sentries guarding a small sector of the enemy Front-Line Trench or Post and then kill them as quietly and as quickly as possible and when the section of the trench was secured, they would complete their objectives as quickly as they could. They did not want to be in the trench any longer than a few minutes, the longer they spent in them, the greater the risk of being discovered. Bombs would then be thrown into dugouts where the enemy troops were sleeping before they left the enemy trench. Danger was still not over. Returning to their own trenches could instigate friendly fire incidents, therefore, it was standard proceedure to notify sentries along our own line when a raid was taking place. A password system was used, so returning raiders could identify themselves when challenged in the dark. The Battalion received one wounded casualty, **Captain C. G. Morgan M. C.**

2nd Lieutenant D. F. Davies and a draft of 16 other ranks (O. R.) joined the Battalion for duty.

Captain Morgan Watcyn Williams wrote in his memoirs from 'Khaki to Cloth':-

"During July 1917 the Battalion took over a section of the line in front of Louveral and opposite Pronville, slightly to our right and quite a mile away from us lay Bourlon Wood, into which we often watched small parties of Germans disappearing on fatigue. The advance posts we held had never been linked up with each other, so our first duty was to dig the connecting trenches which would make a continious line. The work of course had to be done at night with 'Covering Parties' out ahead of us as protection against sudden attack. The Colonel (Compton-Smith) stood with me watching its progress and said 'I want a belt of wire at least ten yards across, wire and more wire, that's the stuff.' A chuckle from the trench below us was followed by the droll comment, 'Damn. I believe the old man's got shares in the wire factory!' Conditions were comparatively quiet, a little shelling, with the occasional bursts of machine gun fire after dark, disturbed us slightly, but on the whole we had a restful tour. One of my best colleagues, Captain CGN Morgan, who received the Military Cross with Bar, for brilliant work at Arras and Infantry Hill, was wounded on July 15th returning safely to Breaconshire, his going left us lonelier than ever." - Captain Morgan Watcyn Williams 10th (Service) Battalion Royal Welsh Fusiliers

JULY 16th

The Battalion were still holding the line and received one casualty due to enemy shelling – **Private H. Mayo** 266976 was wounded.

JULY 17th

A party of the enemy about 100 strong attacked the advanced post. The enemy were driven off by rifle and Lewis gun fire and bombs. The post remained intact, although the post also received a heavy barrage from the enemy. The Battalion suffered the following casualties:-

RANK	NAME	SERVICE NO.	WOUND
PRIVATE	C. DAVIES	21353	KILLED

RANK	NAME	SERVICE NO.	WOUND
PRIVATE	A. RANGE	33815	WOUNDED
PRIVATE	R. AIKEN	54897	WOUNDED
PRIVATE	B. W. JONES	29318	WOUNDED
PRIVATE	B. PEACHEY	56032	WOUNDED

JULY 18th

The 76th Brigade were issued with new orders and the 10th (Service) Battalion R. W. F. were moved to a new section of the trench covering the Front-Line on the North-West side of Louveral Wood. The Battalion were holding the Right Sector Trenches no. 26 to 30 and the 1st Battalion Gordon Highlanders were holding the Left Sector Trenches no. 31 to 37.

JULY 19th, 20th, 21st, 22nd & 23rd

The Battalion were still holding the line and suffered the following casualties:-

20th & 21st July

RANK	NAME	SERVICE NO.	WOUND
PRIVATE	A. E. MICHAEL		WOUNDED

RANK	NAME	SERVICE NO.	WOUND
LANCE CORPORAL	J. HALL	20828	WOUNDED
PRIVATE	W. SERGEANT	55557	WOUNDED

JULY 24th

The Battalion were relieved in the trenches by the 8th Battalion the Kings Own Royal Lancaster Regiment at night and marched into camp at Fremicourt having served fourteen days on the Front-Line. The men were exhausted. The following officers joined the Battalion for duty:-

- 2nd Lieutenant E. Swainson
- 2nd Lieutenant R. P. Batty
- 2nd Lieutenant T. S. Jones
- 2nd Lieutenant F. Cross
- 2nd Lieutenant R. G. Smith-Owen
- 2nd Lieutenant R. V. Jones

JULY 25th, 26th, 27th, 28th & 29th

The Battalion spent the last few days of July by training, baths and Church Parade.

JULY 30th
The Battalion trained in the morning. Sports were held in the afternoon and a concert for the troops was held in the evening.

JULY 31st
The Battalion spent the morning tidying and improving the camp. In the afternoon a cricket match was held.

The following decorations were awarded:-

- **Captain C. G. N. Morgan – Bar to Military Cross (M. C.)**
- **Captain O. S. Hughes – Military Cross (M. C.)**
- **Private M. Hughes 15427 – Distinguished Conduct Medal (D. C. M.)**

Lieutenant Colonel G. L. Comptom-Smith was appointed to Temporary Forward Observation Officer for the Brigade and Major A. J. S. James assumed Temporary Command of the Battalion.

Captain Morgan Watcyn Williams wrote:-

"The intervals we spent out of the line, Major Philips of the Montgomery Yeomanry and Lieutenant A. P. Comyns M. C. organised a few cricket matches, both of them were delightful bats and made a stand of a centuary against the Corps to which we belonged. We are strange people, no one but British Officers would have dreamed of bringing out cricket gear on the off chance of an odd game or two, but the effect on all was refreshing in the extreme." - Captain Morgan Watcyn Williams 10th (Service) Battalion Royal Welsh Fusiliers

It was so important to take the mind off the horrors of War, even for just a little while.

AUGUST 1917

AUGUST 1st
The Battalion marched to the trenches and relieved the 8th Battalion Kings Own Royal Lancaster Regiment in the right sector of the Louverval Trenches. The following Officers joined the Battalion for duty:-

- **Lieutenant B. M. Alexander**
- **Lieutenant T. A. Evans**
- **Lieutenant R. K. Holmes**
- **2nd Lieutenant S. A. H. Granville**

AUGUST 3rd

The enemy of about 20 men attempted a trench raid on Trench no. 25, held by the 10th Battalion R. W. F. They were beaten off by rifle and Lewis gun fire.

AUGUST 4th

The Battalion held the line. Lieutenant D. G. Isaacs and a draft of 13 other ranks (O. R.) joined the Battalion for duty. Lieutenant A. W. Fish also rejoined the Battalion after being previously wounded.

AUGUST 5th

The enemy again attempted a trench raid on Trench no. 25, held by the 10th Battalion R. W. F. The attack again, was beaten off but the Battalion suffered the following casualties:-

RANK	NAME	SERVICE NO.	WOUND
PRIVATE	R. J. ASHBURY	60355	KILLED
PRIVATE	P.H. SMITH	28306	KILLED

RANK	NAME	SERVICE NO.	WOUND
PRIVATE	G. CHESTER	11054	WOUNDED
PRIVATE	F. WILKINSON	33057	WOUNDED
PRIVATE	J. RICHARDS	201073	WOUNDED
PRIVATE	T. DAY	60366	WOUNDED
PRIVATE	J. WILLIS	60297	WOUNDED

AUGUST 7th & 8th

The Battalions were in the Front-Line Trenches. Patrols were sent out, but met with no enemy. One casualty was recorded as wounded – **Private J. J. Mitchell** service number 20215.

AUGUST 9th

The Battalion less 'A' Coy were relieved in the Front-Line Trenches by the 8th Battalion the Kings Own Royal Lancaster Regiment and marched into camp at Fremicourt.

AUGUST 10th

The Battalion were at rest in camp. 'A' Coy remained in the Front-Line Trenches.

AUGUST 11th

The Battalion less 'A' Coy, who were in the Front-Line Trenches, began training. 2nd Lieutenant H. R. Davies and a draft of 10 other ranks (O. R.) joined the Battalion for duty. Captain H. Pritchard M. C. also rejoined the Battalion after recovering from his wounds he received on the 14th May 1917.

AUGUST 13th

Training continued for the Battalion. 'A' Coy remained in the Front-Line Trenches. 2nd Lieutenant J. D. Jones and a draft of 4 other ranks (O. R.) joined the Battalion for duty. A Battalion concert was held in the evening.

AUGUST 14th

'C' Coy relieved 'A' Coy in the Front-Line Trenches. 'A' Coy rejoined the Battalion at Fremicourt. One casualty was recorded as wounded – **Sergeant D. Griffiths** service number 15005.

AUGUST 15th

'B' Coy and 'D' Coy continued training. 'A' Coy were at rest and having baths. Major F. A. Philips (Montgomery Yeomanry) joined the Battalion for duty. At night 'B' Coy relieved 'C' Coy in the Front-Line Trenches.

AUGUST 16th

'A', 'C' and 'D' Coys continued training. 'B' Coy were in the Front-Line Trenches.

AUGUST 17th

During the day 'A' and 'D' Coys were at rest. 'C' Coy continued training whilst 'B' Coy remained in the Front-Line Trenches. At night 'A' and 'D' Coys relieved two Companies of the 8th Battalion the Kings Own Royal Lancaster Regiment in the Front-Line Trenches. 'C' Coy remained in camp.

AUGUST 18th

'C' Coy and the Battalion's Head Quarters joined the remainder of the Battalion in the Front-Line Trenches.

AUGUST 19th, 20th & 21st

The Battalion remained in the Front-Line Trenches and suffered one wounded casualty – **Private H. Hinks** service number 54927.

AUGUST 22nd

The Battalion remained in the Front-Line Trenches and suffered the following casualties: -

RANK	NAME	SERVICE NO.	WOUND
PRIVATE	L. PHILLIPS	36846	WOUNDED
PRIVATE	P. H. SMITH	44557	WOUNDED

A draft of 10 other ranks (O. R.) joined the Battalion for duty.

AUGUST 23rd

'C' Coy made a raid on the enemy trenches in the early morning of the 23rd. The 'Raiding Party' left the Front-Line and proceeded forward to a position of about 150 yards in front of the German wire, a distance of about 650 yards from their own Front-Line. As the 'Bangalore Torpedo Parties' advance from their positions to the wire itself, a 'Vary Light' was sent up, which fell amongst the patrol. They were instantly observed by the enemy and several trench mortar bombs were fired by the enemy, falling about 100 yards in front of their wire. At the same time, heavy machine gun fire was opened up on the 'Raiding Party' from the left and the right. The Bangalore Torpedoes were fired and by this time the enemy were fully on alert and began leaving their parapet, and therefore, the 'Raiding Party' was unable to advance and returned to their own trenches. Two casualties were wounded: -

RANK	NAME	SERVICE NO.	WOUND
LANCE CORPORAL	J. EDWARDS		WOUNDED
PRIVATE	J. T. CLARKE	56023	WOUNDED

This was the report from the raid in the 76th Brigades War Diary but Captain Morgan Watcyn Williams saw the raid differently and he wrote:-

"My suggestion was to capture this sap head swiftly and silently by a small group of hand-picked men, as the object of the raid was to take prisoners for identification purposes. My platoon commanders and Lieutenant Colonel Compton-Smith agreed with the plan but it was tabooed by the Divisional General, substituting it for a most elaborate raid, with a diversion barrage on the left, Bangalore Torpedoes to cut the wire and sixty men to do the job. I had told both and the Brigade that I thought it ridiculous, but as they had little choice in the matter as did I, we set out on our task. We divided into three 'Parties', our faces and buttons blackened, but between the row we ourselves made and the noise created by the torpedoes and the barrage, the whole of the German Front-Line awoke to startled life, eight or nine machine guns kept sweeping no mans land and when J. R. Williams and Owen got into the sap head it was empty. Half our men had never been over the top before, not even on a 'Wiring Party' and I spent hours collecting them together. It was a pretty dud show." - Captain Morgan Watcyn Williams - 'C' Coy - 10th (Service) Battalion Royal Welsh Fusiliers

AUGUST 25th

The Battalion less 'C' Coy were relieved in the trenches by the 8th the Kings Own Royal Lancaster Regiment and marched into camp at Fremicourt. 'C' Coy, for the next two nights attempted 'Trench Raids' but without success.

AUGUST 26th, 27th & 28th

A draft of 136 other ranks (O. R.) joined the Battalion for duty on the 26th. The Battalion continued training whilst 'C' Coy remained in the trenches.

Captain Morgan Watcyn Williams, who was still in the Front-Line Trench with 'C' Coy wrote:-

"In the long run we fell back on my original simple plan, now made a hundredfold more difficult by the regular disturbance of the enemy with all the attempted raids. Three nights in succession J. R. Williams and Owen got as far as the enemy wire and on the last occasion, would have taken a prisoner, but for the over-eagerness of some of the men." - Captain Morgan Watcyn Williams – 'C' Coy – 10th (Service) Battalion Royal Welsh Fusiliers

AUGUST 29th

'D' Coy relieved 'C' Coy in the Front-Line Trenches and rejoined the Battalion in camp at Fremicourt.

AUGUST 30th

A draft of 61 other ranks (O. R.) joined the Battalion for duty. 'A' and 'B' Coys were training. 'C' Coy were resting and bathing. 'D' Coy were still in the Front-Line Trenches.

AUGUST 31st

The Battalion continued training. 'D' Coy were still in the trenches. They reported one casualty – **2nd Lieutenant J. H. Parry** as wounded. Sadly J. H. Parry succumbed to his wounds on the 5th September aged 26.

2nd Lieutenant J. H. Parry

James Hywel Parry was the Son of Reverend John Hywel Parry BSc. (Hons). He was born in Llansarnlet, Swansea, Glamorgan. He was wounded on 31st August and died of his wounds on 5th September 1917. He is buried at Grevillers British Cemetery, France – VII. B. 17. On his grave there is also marked - 'In memory of Lieutenant Thomas Ellis Parry'. This is James's older Brother who was killed in action on 23rd October 1916 whilst serving with the 2nd Battalion Lancashire Fusiliers aged 29. He, like his Brother, has no known grave. Thomas Ellis Parry is remembered on the Thiepval Memorial, Somme.

SEPTEMBER 1917

SEPTEMBER 1st

The Battalion continued training. 'D' Coy remained in the Front-Line Trenches. The Battalion's cricket team played a team from IV Corps Head Quarters. The results were:-

- **10th Battalion – 142 for 2**
- **IV Corps – 114 for 7**

A victory for the Battalion!

SEPTEMBER 2nd

The Battalion less 'D' Coy relieved the 8th Battalion the Kings Own Royal Lancaster Regiment in the right sector. 'D' Coy also remained in the Front-Line Trenches.

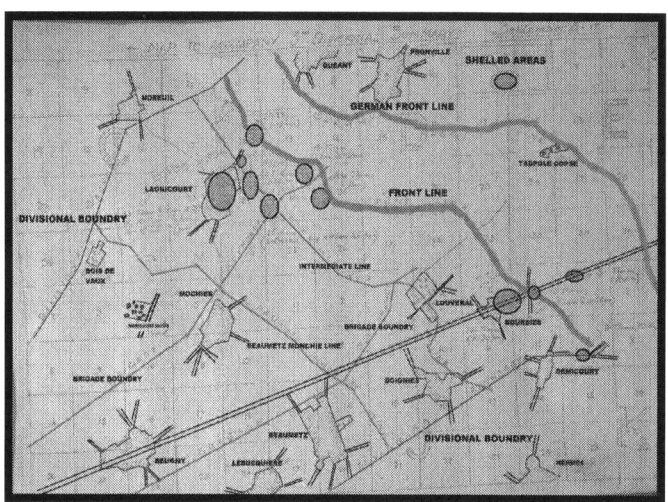

SEPTEMBER 3rd, 4th & 5th

The Battalion remained in the Front-Line Trenches. On the 4th of September the Battalion suffered one wounded casualty – **Private G. Peters** service number 240982.

SEPTEMBER 6th

The Battalion was relieved in the Front-Line Trenches by the 1st Battalion London Regiment and marched into camp at Barastre. One wounded casualty was reported – **Private C. Roberts** service number 61050.

SEPTEMBER 11th, 12th, 13th, 14th & 15th

The Battalion continued training which included practice on a flagged area. A conference of Officers was held afterwards. By now, the men of the Battalion would have realised that an imminent attack will be taking place soon, but when?

SEPTEMBER 16th

On this day transport of motor omnibuses was laid on to take all the men, who took part in the battle of Delville Wood on July 20th 1916, back to the scene of the battle and to pay their respects to the men killed on that day.

SEPTEMBER 17th

The Battalion marched to Bapaume West Station and entrained.

SEPTEMBER 18th

The Battalion detrained at Godersvelde and after dinner, which was provided in a field close by, marched into camp at Watoy, a distance of 10.5km (6 ½ miles). The Battalion were to take part in the Third Battle of Ypres, battle of Polygone Wood and Zonnerbek.

SEPTEMBER 19th

The Battalion commenced training in preparation for the attack and were instructed to prepare to move with an hours notice from midnight.

SEPTEMBER 20th

The Battalion continued training.

SEPTEMBER 21st

Major A. J. S. James and 2nd Lieutenant E. Swainson and 27 other ranks (O. R.) proceeded to trenches to take over assembly positions for the 76th Brigade.

SEPTEMBER 23rd

The Battalion marched into camp at Branhoek, a distance of 14.2 km (8 ½ miles).

Captain Morgan Watcyn Williams wrote:-

"For a couple of days we rested at Brandhoek where a fleet of Gothas (German Bombers) on a night raid attacked our camp, but, as most of the bombs fell in an adjoining field, our only casualties were a mule and one or two horses." - Captain Morgan Watcyn Williams 10th (Service) Battalion Royal Welsh Fusiliers

SEPTEMBER 25th

The Battalion entrained at Brandhoek and arrived at Ypres Asylum Railway Station. The train was bombed on route to the station. The Battalion was met by 2nd Lieutenant E. Swainson and the Guides. The Guides had been trained by Major A. J. S. James to learn the route to the assembly positions ready for the attack. The Battalion was led in columns of platoons at 100 yard intervals to Brigade Head Quarters in a former enemy concrete redoubt just behind the assembly positions. At this point the Battalion were met by 2nd Lieutenant J. T. Owen who had led them to the taped positions for the attack. The rear Coy suffered casualties from the German shelling.

Captain Morgan Watcyn Williams wrote:-

"There were no trenches on the assembly ground, nothing but shell holes, half filled with water. Our places were indicated by tape pegged to the earth. To reach them in the dark was no easy task, but 2nd Lieutenant Owen did a splendid night's work at very great personal risk, in guiding us to our stations. Enroute, we had to cross a small rise which the German's were shelling unmercifully. I noticed that bursts of fire were separated by regular intervals, which we used to rush the men over the ridge, platoon by platoon. Even then we did not escape scatheless and the rear of the Company suffered considerably." - Captain Morgan Watcyn Williams 10th (Service) Battalion Royal Welsh Fusiliers

By midnight the Battalion was in position ready for the attack. Captain Morgan Watcyn Williams, having reached his position with his Coy, wrapped himself in his macintosh, laid out in the open and fell asleep until 3am. On waking, Lieutenant Colonel G. L. Compton-Smith was standing over him and remarked – *"I am not rich Watcyn, but I'd cheerfully give a hundred pounds to be able to do what you've just done, you lucky devil!"*

SEPTEMBER 26th

Lieutenant Colonel G. L. Compton-Smith and Captain M. W. Williams went around the positions together to wish the men good luck.

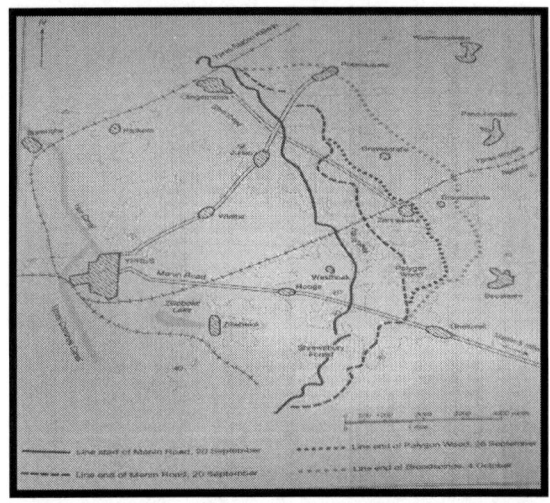

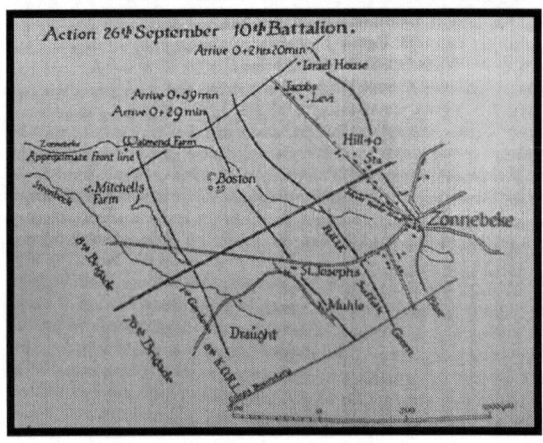

The allied bombardment commenced at 3.40am (Battle of Polygon Wood). The enemy artillery retaliated half an hour later inflicting severe casualties. At zero hour the advance commenced in heavy ground mist. The Brigade orders were for the 8th Battalion The Kings Own Royal Lancaster Regiment on the right with the 1st Gordon Highlanders to take and consolidate the first objective, the Green Line, with the 2nd Suffolk Regiment on the right and the 10th Battalion Royal Welsh Fusiliers on the left was to pass through the leading line (Green Line) and take Zonnebeke (Blue Line). The leading troops lost direction to a certain extent, bearing to their left to avoid the Steenbeke which was normally a narrow, insignificant rivulet but it had been blocked by the destruction of the culverts and the pounding of it banks by shell fire made it more a morass in some places 50 feet wide.

After crossing the Steenbeke, the advance continued towards the first objective. The Gordon Highlanders took St. Joseph's Institute, a deadly pill box full of machine gun menace: The first objective (Green Line) was taken. The 10th Battalion R. W. F. passed through the Green Line and pushed on to their objective Zonnebeke (Blue Line) including the Church. The ruins of an old hut caused the Battalion some trouble, but having initially being held up, managed to out flank the position and the Garrison occupying, surrendered.

After crossing Zonnebeke, with some difficulty, normally a small stream like the Steenbeke, this was too a morass, the Battalion came under heavy machine gun fire from the direction of the railway station. The right Battalion Coy succeeded in reaching the Church and was was entered by Captain A. W. Fish and 14 other ranks (O. R.), closely followed by a few men of the Suffolk Regiment.

The left Coy were still held up at a point 200 yards away from the station, with it's left flank on the railway embankment. Shortly afterwards, the Battalion managed to obtain contact with the Royal Scots Fusiliers on the other side of the embankment but there was a gap between the right half and the left half of the Battalion. This area was a swamp and was covered by a party of the 1st Battalion Gordon Highlanders.

At 2.30pm the first enemy counter attack was launched, but this was easily repulsed by Lewis gun fire, rifle fire and artillery, which was very accurate.

The main enemy counter attack took place at 6.35pm and a large number of Germans succeeded in getting through the artillery barrage and reached a point 100 yards in front of the Battalions left Company. They were held up by resolute steady Lewis guns and rifle fire which inflicted heavy casualties on the enemy troops. The counter attack on the extreme left of the Battalion met with better success. The 3rd Australian Division, on the North side of the railway had been forced back, but owing to the excellent work by the 1st Battalion Gordon Highlanders, they were able to restore the position later in the evening. About this time, Lieutenant Colonel G. L. Compton-Smith reported as a casualty suffering from severe shell shock. Major A. J. S. James was sent for and assumed command of the Battalion.

The position in the Front-Line at this time was very grave with the left flank being exposed and the majority of the men were down to their last clip of ammunition. 2nd Lieutenant D. C. Hunter and 2nd Lieutenant Elwyn G. Williams immediately organised parties to collect the ammunition from the dead and wounded and a party of the 1st Battalion Gordon Highlanders in the rear positions, immediately responded to the call for ammunition and Lewis gun magazines. Rum and more ammunition was sent up during the night. Had the Germans known how bad the situation was for the Battalion, another attack would have seen them take back ground they had lost, but luckily, the attack never came during this days action.

Men of the 10th Battalion R. W. F. moving forward at Zonnebeke 26th September 1917

Captain Morgan Watcyn Williams was severely wounded and he wrote:-

"As I was pushing forward through the maze of water-logged shell holes a shell burst right in my path, with a flash of orange flame, Parry's (William's Batman) prophecy had come true, and hit for the first time, we were hit together. I went down like a shot rabbit and suddenly, found that everything was a total blank, except the terrible din and the feel of blood running down my cheek. I groped about shouting Parry's name, I was blind. I heard Parry say, I've got it too Sir, but not so bad. A piece of shell casing had torn into his side. I asked him could he see and walk, to which he replied, I'm only bleeding a bit. Parry cleaned Williams' wounds and poured water onto a bandage and cleaned his eyes. Parry I can see!"
- Captain Morgan Watcyn Williams 10th (Service) Battalion Royal Welsh Fusiliers

Captain Morgan Watcyn Williams and Parry managed to get to a dressing station where both were treated. Within 24 hours Captain Morgan Watcyn Williams was on the operating table where they removed shrapnel from his left eye and head.

SEPTEMBER 27th

At 6.30pm another hostile counter attack was launched, but it failed to seriously threaten the Battalions Front-Line as protective artillery barrage again was effective and Lewis gun fire and rifle fire caused considerable losses on the enemy side. During the afternoon of the 27th a party of 8 German machine gunners with guns attempted to get into position near the Battalions right post at Zonnebeke Church. Corporal Thomas of 'A' Coy commanding the post, allowed them to approach within 30 yards before opening fire, killing seven and wounding the eighth. The Corporal then ran out and brought in the wounded German and the machine gun.

10th Battalion R. W. F. working at Zonnebeke

SEPTEMBER 28th

The Battalion were still holding the Front-Line Trenches. At 6.15pm the British artillery opened an intense barrage after the enemy were seen crossing the Battalions right front and the Battalion were able to inflict heavy casualties on the enemy.

SEPTEMBER 29th

The artillery activity on both sides greatly decreased. The Battalion were relieved by 'A' Coy 33rd Battalion Australian Infantry but this was carried out with great difficulty owing to the bright moonlight. The relief was observed by the enemy, who brought on a considerable amount of machine gun fire on the Battalion. Eventually the relief was completed and the weary Battalion marched back via Ypres to a camp near Ypres Asylum.

SEPTEMBER 30th

The Battalion was transported by motor omnibuses to Winnezeele and went into camp. The following casualties occurred during the operations of the 25th – 30th September:-

RANK	NAME	SERVICE NO.	WOUND
LIEUTENANT	D. L. JENKINS		KILLED IN ACTION
2ND LIEUTENANT	T. S. JONES	56023	KILLED IN ACTION
2ND LIEUTENANT	C. W. ROWLANDS		KILLED IN ACTION
SERGEANT	W. ROWLANDS	8780	KILLED IN ACTION
SERGEANT	H. S. WHITTINGHAM	54448	KILLED IN ACTION
SERGEANT	D. R. GRIFFITHS	15005	KILLED IN ACTION

RANK	NAME	SERVICE NO.	KILLED IN ACTION
SERGEANT	F. A. BROWN	27272	KILLED IN ACTION
SERGEANT	P. PLEVIN	43878	KILLED IN ACTION
SERGEANT	F. S. COOPER	60442	KILLED IN ACTION
SERGEANT	O. ELLIS	61233	KILLED IN ACTION
SERGEANT	J. BOOTH	63520	KILLED IN ACTION
SERGEANT	J. DUNN	14781	KILLED IN ACTION
SERGEANT	E. LUXFORD	60292	KILLED IN ACTION
SERGEANT	H. HAWKINS	56690	KILLED IN ACTION
SERGEANT	J. BROWN	60431	KILLED IN ACTION
SERGEANT	P. ACKERS	51438	KILLED IN ACTION
SERGEANT	J. LAMB	60482	KILLED IN ACTION
SERGEANT	P. A. ROBERTS	54964	KILLED IN ACTION
SERGEANT	J. W. GRIFFITHS	60991	KILLED IN ACTION
SERGEANT	T. ROBERTS	54967	KILLED IN ACTION
SERGEANT	E. BAILEY	60477	KILLED IN ACTION
SERGEANT	H. JONES	265653	KILLED IN ACTION
LANCE CORPORAL	W. HOWARTH	33224	KILLED IN ACTION
LANCE CORPORAL	W. DUNNICLIFFE	56018	KILLED IN ACTION
LANCE CORPORAL	W. BROWN	23570	KILLED IN ACTION
LANCE CORPORAL	A. GOULD	17364	KILLED IN ACTION
PRIVATE	R. J. BROWN	60516	KILLED IN ACTION
PRIVATE	A. B. COLBERT	34584	KILLED IN ACTION
PRIVATE	W. HARRY	60423	KILLED IN ACTION
PRIVATE	E. K. THOMAS	29236	KILLED IN ACTION
PRIVATE	J. DUNN	54919	KILLED IN ACTION
PRIVATE	J. R. THOMAS	33875	KILLED IN ACTION
PRIVATE	J. BALL	28589	KILLED IN ACTION
PRIVATE	O. GRIFFITHS	21419	KILLED IN ACTION
PRIVATE	A. HEARNE	23296	KILLED IN ACTION
PRIVATE	L. PIERCY	44032	KILLED IN ACTION
PRIVATE	A. HARNBLETT	54944	KILLED IN ACTION
PRIVATE	E. W. BAXTER	61260	KILLED IN ACTION
PRIVATE	W. REYNOLDS	201255	KILLED IN ACTION
PRIVATE	S. WILLIAMS	44137	KILLED IN ACTION

RANK	NAME	SERVICE NO.	WOUND
PRIVATE	L. JACKSON	54993	KILLED IN ACTION
PRIVATE	E. CHAMBERLAIN	60428	KILLED IN ACTION

RANK	NAME	SERVICE NO.	WOUND
PRIVATE	G. H. FLETCHER	60466	DIED OF WOUNDS
PRIVATE	C. TAYLOR	33843	DIED OF WOUNDS
PRIVATE	J. O'DONNELL	60389	DIED OF WOUNDS
PRIVATE	W. O'GRADY	34135	DIED OF WOUNDS
PRIVATE	J. W. EVANS	19388	DIED OF WOUNDS
PRIVATE	J. HUGHES	72892	DIED OF WOUNDS
LANCE CORPORAL	F. E. DICKENSON	60228	DIED OF WOUNDS

RANK	NAME	SERVICE NO.	WOUND
CAPTAIN	M. WATCYN WILLIAMS		WOUNDED
LIEUTENANT	ISAACS		WOUNDED
2ND LIEUTENANT	T. M. DAVIES		WOUNDED
2ND LIEUTENANT	ELWYN G. WILLIAMS		WOUNDED
CAPTAIN	F. H. SEWELL		WOUNDED
2ND LIEUTENANT	S. A. H. GRANVILLE		WOUNDED
2ND LIEUTENANT	R. V. JONES		WOUNDED
2ND LIEUTENANT	A. P. COMYNS		WOUNDED
2ND LIEUTENANT	D. C. HUNTER		WOUNDED
PRIVATE	D. R. JONES	61118	WOUNDED
PRIVATE	W. JONES	61228	WOUNDED
PRIVATE	H. MILLS	60432	WOUNDED
PRIVATE	R. T. ROBERTS	40968	WOUNDED
PRIVATE	F. SHACKLETON	60402	WOUNDED
PRIVATE	T. TINDAL	28717	WOUNDED
PRIVATE	E. J. WILLIAMS	34045	WOUNDED
SERGEANT	A. P. CARTER	235021	WOUNDED
SERGEANT	J. HOLLIS	57030	WOUNDED
CORPORAL	F. JARVIS	33602	WOUNDED
PRIVATE	C. HEMMING	235013	WOUNDED
PRIVATE	J. HASSELL	59328	WOUNDED
PRIVATE	H. DACKOMBE	60160	WOUNDED
PRIVATE	R. T. JONES	63882	WOUNDED
PRIVATE	H. SUTTON	235727	WOUNDED
LANCE SERGEANT	R. L. FRANCIS	54721	WOUNDED
LANCE CORPORAL	J. WILLIAMS	21722	WOUNDED
PRIVATE	A. BUTTER	13814	WOUNDED
PRIVATE	R. QUARTERMAIN	70144	WOUNDED
PRIVATE	H. WILLIAMS	235724	WOUNDED
LANCE CORPORAL	H. SALVAGE	204354	WOUNDED
LANCE CORPORAL	W. SATTERLEY	22680	WOUNDED
PRIVATE	W. BULLOCK	34047	WOUNDED
PRIVATE	E. CONDLIFFE	24265	WOUNDED
PRIVATE	E. DAVIES	39667	WOUNDED

RANK	NAME	SERVICE NO.	WOUND
PRIVATE	R. EDWARDS	57004	WOUNDED
PRIVATE	T. FOTHERGILL	60369	WOUNDED
PRIVATE	M. HUGHES	15427	WOUNDED
PRIVATE	R. S. HUNTS	60458	WOUNDED
PRIVATE	E. JONES	15140	WOUNDED
PRIVATE	R. E. A. BOYLE	60225	WOUNDED
PRIVATE	E. W. BREWER	44205	WOUNDED
PRIVATE	J. BOLGER	292855	WOUNDED
PRIVATE	T. DURHAM	54198	WOUNDED
PRIVATE	J. T. EVANS	54717	WOUNDED
PRIVATE	F. J. FIDLER	63778	WOUNDED
PRIVATE	A. HALL	54930	WOUNDED
PRIVATE	G. JONES	14656	WOUNDED
PRIVATE	T. KENYON	33297	WOUNDED
PRIVATE	E. LLOYD	26088	WOUNDED
PRIVATE	J. HYNDEMAN	93882	WOUNDED
PRIVATE	H. RIPLEY	60400	WOUNDED
SERGEANT	W. DAVIES	15922	WOUNDED
CORPORAL	V. D. CARTER	33997	WOUNDED
LANCE CORPORAL	D. W. JONES	43969	WOUNDED
LANCE CORPORAL	H. ALTREE	51331	WOUNDED
CORPORAL	J. H. SLOMAN	70153	WOUNDED
PRIVATE	D. JONES	61224	WOUNDED
PRIVATE	G. R. LEONARD	235036	WOUNDED
PRIVATE	H. PERIN	60222	WOUNDED
PRIVATE	C. PIFF	23450	WOUNDED
PRIVATE	W. ROBERTS	14996	WOUNDED
PRIVATE	D. ROBERTS	20051	WOUNDED
PRIVATE	A. F. J. SMITH	60470	WOUNDED
PRIVATE	J. STEVENS	54351	WOUNDED
PRIVATE	P. WATTS	202431	WOUNDED
PRIVATE	W. R. WILLIAMS	60187	WOUNDED
PRIVATE	E. T. WILLIAMS	29093	WOUNDED
PRIVATE	F. CHARLTON	15328	WOUNDED
PRIVATE	E. GRIFFITHS	54444	WOUNDED
PRIVATE	H. ROLFE	54602	WOUNDED
PRIVATE	F. TABOIN	53556	WOUNDED
PRIVATE	E. R. WILLIAMS	44344	WOUNDED
PRIVATE	J. H. WILLIAMS	60452	WOUNDED
CORPORAL	H. V. MAJOR	35071	WOUNDED
PRIVATE	C. PREECE	55076	WOUNDED
LANCE CORPORAL	H. CORDINGLEY	60502	WOUNDED
LANCE CORPORAL	H. J. CURTIS	235029	WOUNDED
LANCE CORPORAL	V. A. BODGER	27614	WOUNDED
PRIVATE	W. BRADLEY	235017	WOUNDED
PRIVATE	E. DAWSON	60484	WOUNDED
PRIVATE	V. A. EYNON	15052	WOUNDED

RANK	NAME	SERVICE NO.	WOUND
PRIVATE	D. E. EVANS	44268	WOUNDED
PRIVATE	C. M. FRYER	34093	WOUNDED
PRIVATE	R. PUGH	15455	WOUNDED
PRIVATE	R. SAXTON	31966	WOUNDED
PRIVATE	W. T. ELLIS	54945	WOUNDED
PRIVATE	S. BLYTHIN	49027	WOUNDED
PRIVATE	E. JAMES	54407	WOUNDED
SERGEANT	C. SAUNDERS	15406	WOUNDED
LANCE CORPORAL	F. BIRCH	36057	WOUNDED
PRIVATE	J. MANTLE	15524	WOUNDED
PRIVATE	W. JONES	39145	WOUNDED
PRIVATE	R. B. SCUTT	60427	WOUNDED
PRIVATE	T. LAND	20822	WOUNDED
PRIVATE	H. PAYNE	233723	WOUNDED
PRIVATE	J. E. DERRY	39982	WOUNDED
PRIVATE	D. J. BEYNON	15337	WOUNDED
PRIVATE	J. E. BULLEY	60333	WOUNDED
PRIVATE	W. BARLOW	62875	WOUNDED
PRIVATE	T. BRADFORD	70142	WOUNDED
PRIVATE	R. H. DAVIES	60472	WOUNDED
PRIVATE	J. EDMUNDSON	43068	WOUNDED
PRIVATE	W. HUGHES	21707	WOUNDED
PRIVATE	A. J. KESARD	202354	WOUNDED
PRIVATE	H. H. JONES	201134	WOUNDED
PRIVATE	J. H. KELLY	41645	WOUNDED
PRIVATE	T. MASON	51547	WOUNDED
PRIVATE	J. FITZMORRIS	33717	WOUNDED
PRIVATE	J. HUGHES	61253	WOUNDED
CORPORAL	J. LAW	16313	WOUNDED
SERGEANT	R. MORGAN	13793	WOUNDED
PRIVATE	W. J. PICKERS	54962	WOUNDED
PRIVATE	R. ROWLANDS	60528	WOUNDED
PRIVATE	J. T. BELL	39126	WOUNDED
PRIVATE	A. H. COCKAYNE	66209	WOUNDED
PRIVATE	A. G. CUTTING	44811	WOUNDED
PRIVATE	E. DURNLEY	54706	WOUNDED
PRIVATE	B. POSTELL	28798	WOUNDED
PRIVATE	A. ROSS	54877	WOUNDED
PRIVATE	F. REES	70188	WOUNDED
PRIVATE	J. SYMONDS	56919	WOUNDED
PRIVATE	A. VAUGHAN	19012	WOUNDED
PRIVATE	W. H. WILLIAMS	53841	WOUNDED
PRIVATE	T. WILLIS	60297	WOUNDED
LANCE CORPORAL	E. GREENHALGH	24187	WOUNDED
PRIVATE	C. FRICKE	56043	WOUNDED
PRIVATE	W. G. DAVIES	70181	WOUNDED
PRIVATE	T. J. ELKIN	26640	WOUNDED
PRIVATE	W. FISHWICK	70145	WOUNDED
PRIVATE	J. T. GEORGE	61258	WOUNDED
PRIVATE	G. SHIRES	60504	WOUNDED
PRIVATE	J. SANDIFORD	54789	WOUNDED
PRIVATE	H. THOMPSON	60319	WOUNDED

RANK	NAME	SERVICE NO.	WOUND
LANCE CORPORAL	T. J. STEER	60317	WOUNDED
PRIVATE	G. B. OWENS	39036	WOUNDED
PRIVATE	E. J. WILLIAMS	44041	WOUNDED
PRIVATE	J. PAGE	68392	WOUNDED
PRIVATE	W. R. WHEELER	560372	WOUNDED
PRIVATE	W. R. PRITCHARD	55077	WOUNDED
PRIVATE	J. WILLIAMS	240916	WOUNDED
PRIVATE	J. ROBERTS	60971	WOUNDED
PRIVATE	W. H. ROWLANDS	54875	WOUNDED
SERGEANT	P. HUGHES	15492	WOUNDED
LANCE CORPORAL	F. C. JOHNSON	46323	WOUNDED
PRIVATE	F. RICHMOND	57106	WOUNDED
LANCE CORPORAL	E. T. MOORE	57091	WOUNDED
LANCE CORPORAL	J. H. WATKINS	23238	WOUNDED
PRIVATE	F. BOUSALL	60195	WOUNDED
PRIVATE	J. A. TEEDER	54953	WOUNDED
PRIVATE	T. SLATER	60315	WOUNDED
PRIVATE	J. W. REED	31233	WOUNDED
PRIVATE	J. THOMPSON	60410	WOUNDED
PRIVATE	T. WHITE	55088	WOUNDED
PRIVATE	T. J. ILES	60500	WOUNDED
PRIVATE	R. STEVENS	54936	WOUNDED
PRIVATE	H. CHASE	60370	WOUNDED
PRIVATE	F. HEPPERSLEY	17946	WOUNDED
LANCE CORPORAL	W. GUISBERG	24478	WOUNDED
LANCE CORPORAL	J. E. RUSSON	33821	WOUNDED
PRIVATE	W. RANDLE	44104	WOUNDED
PRIVATE	G. ATKINSON	39533	WOUNDED
PRIVATE	R. WATKINS	33852	WOUNDED
PRIVATE	J. FOY	60464	WOUNDED
PRIVATE	T. RICHARDSON	24599	WOUNDED
PRIVATE	T. REEDER	56025	WOUNDED
PRIVATE	G. MORGAN	235050	WOUNDED
COY SERGEANT MAJOR	H. GREEN	15420	WOUNDED
PRIVATE	W. HART	33739	WOUNDED
SERGEANT	A. JAYS	8717	WOUNDED
PRIVATE	R. L. FOULKES	61230	WOUNDED
PRIVATE	G. HUGHES	16120	WOUNDED
PRIVATE	W. HEIGHWAY	44370	WOUNDED
PRIVATE	P. LAMB	62865	WOUNDED
PRIVATE	J. O'GRADY	60441	WOUNDED
PRIVATE	J. WILLIAMS	54943	WOUNDED
PRIVATE	C. H. BROOKS	34081	WOUNDED
LANCE CORPORAL	R. JONES	20761	WOUNDED
PRIVATE	T. MINTON	55067	WOUNDED
PRIVATE	W. JONES	235079	WOUNDED
PRIVATE	R. STEVENS	54976	WOUNDED
PRIVATE	R. JONES	54945	WOUNDED
PRIVATE	J. H. BARRELL	60476	WOUNDED
PRIVATE	J. F. HILL	33542	WOUNDED
LANCE CORPORAL	F. JACKSON	59390	WOUNDED
PRIVATE	W. PARRY	60481	WOUNDED

RANK	NAME	SERVICE NO.	WOUND
PRIVATE	J. BROOKS	60357	WOUNDED
LANCE CORPORAL	T. CUFFE	4643	WOUNDED
LANCE CORPORAL	J. F. CURRY	60444	WOUNDED
PRIVATE	M. O. DAVIES	60335	WOUNDED
PRIVATE	P. DOWLING	34917	WOUNDED
PRIVATE	W. E. DAVIES	54916	WOUNDED
PRIVATE	R. C. EVANS	24834	WOUNDED
PRIVATE	C. H. RENSHAW	60337	WOUNDED
PRIVATE	F. GREEN	23423	WOUNDED
PRIVATE	H. J. SHARPE	42091	WOUNDED
PRIVATE	W. SKINNER	22274	WOUNDED
PRIVATE	R. WILLIAMS	16179	WOUNDED
PRIVATE	J. H. CHARLES	61250	WOUNDED
PRIVATE	J. KYNASTON	54415	WOUNDED
PRIVATE	B. H. VAUGHAN	53111	WOUNDED
PRIVATE	P. AFFERION	31074	WOUNDED
PRIVATE	W. KIMBER	33588	WOUNDED
PRIVATE	A. VAYGHAN	49012	WOUNDED
SERGEANT	H. BRAMWELL	15688	WOUNDED
PRIVATE	A. PETERS	34909	WOUNDED

RANK	NAME	SERVICE NO.	WOUND
SERGEANT	M. WHITEHEAD	33905	MISSING
PRIVATE	E. W. HALL	70137	MISSING
PRIVATE	R. THOMAS	55467	MISSING
PRIVATE	R. WILLIAMS	49861	MISSING
PRIVATE	T. EVANS	315677	MISSING
PRIVATE	T. JONES	70149	MISSING
PRIVATE	A. LATHAM	60341	MISSING
PRIVATE	G. MUMFORD	60315	MISSING
PRIVATE	H. MANLEY	70160	MISSING
PRIVATE	W. SUTTON	54881	MISSING
PRIVATE	T. GATOCICAS	70171	MISSING
PRIVATE	D. HURLEY	33741	MISSING
LANCE CORPORAL	J. HILL	53548	MISSING
PRIVATE	W. B. KIRKHAM	60324	MISSING
PRIVATE	J. ATKINSON	33058	MISSING
PRIVATE	W. DANIELS	23965	MISSING
PRIVATE	J. HUGHES	43689	MISSING
PRIVATE	J. BLOUNT	69415	MISSING
PRIVATE	H. SETCHFIELD	70186	MISSING
PRIVATE	J. H. WILDE	200759	MISSING
PRIVATE	J. WILLIAMS	68476	MISSING
PRIVATE	W. E. HOWELLS	54928	MISSING
PRIVATE	E. H. KELLY	70143	MISSING
PRIVATE	T. LINLEY	60381	MISSING
PRIVATE	R. MATTHEWS	60385	MISSING
PRIVATE	J. MINLAND	41823	MISSING

RANK	NAME	SERVICE NO.	WOUND
PRIVATE	J. WILLIAMS	66291	MISSING ALSO WOUNDED
PRIVATE	H. BREAKWELL	60434	MISSING
PRIVATE	W. HEWITT	70191	MISSING
PRIVATE	J. COUNSELL	70170	MISSING
PRIVATE	R. J. JONES	44080	MISSING
PRIVATE	W. PARISH	55019	MISSING
PRIVATE	J. DAVIES	34335	MISSING
PRIVATE	W. T. ROBERTS	54546	MISSING
PRIVATE	E. WRIGHT	63739	MISSING

Lieutenant Colonel G. L. Compton-Smith never returned to the 10th (Service) Battalion Royal Welsh Fusiliers after suffereing severe shell shock. A great many soldiers suffered from shell shock at this time, although there was little understanding of its cause or its effects.

Robert Graves the Author of **"Goodbye To All That"** talks about his own experiences in this book:-

"Between three weeks and four months an Officer is at his best unless he happened to have any particular bad shock or a sequence of bad shocks, then he began to decline in usefullness as neurasthenia developed in him. At six months he was still more or less all right, but by nine or ten months, unless he had a few weeks rest on a technical course or in hospital, he began to be a drag on the other members of the Company. Officers had a less laborious but more nervous time than the men. There were proportionately twice as many neurasthenic cases among Officers as among men." - Robert Graves 2nd Battalion Royal Welsh Fusiliers

Lieutenant Colonel G. L. Compton-Smith returned to England straight after the battle at Polygon Wood. The relief at being away from the trenches and seeing his Wife again must have been overwhelming, although, deep sleep continued to elude him for well over a year, soon after his discharge from hospital he received news of his appointment as an Officer Trainer at Aldershot. Prior to his appointment, he received his D. S. O. from the King at Buckingham Palace.

Lieutenant Colonel Geoffrey Lee Compton-Smith D. S. O.

The portrait that his Wife's Sister, Kitty Lloyd painted

Geoffrey Lee Compton-Smith was born in 1889 in South Kensington, London. After finishing school, Geoffrey wanted to be an artist, but his Father insisted he joined the Army.

He studied at the Royal Military College at Sandhurst taking over command of the 10th (Service) Battalion Royal Welsh Fusiliers in November 1916, where he remained in command until the battle of Polygon Wood 26th September 1917 where he suffered severe shell shock. He married Gladys Mary Lloyd in 1916.

The farm is now deserted and in ruins

Geoffrey continued to serve in the Army after the War and was sent to serve in Ireland during the Independence Conflict as an Intelligence Officer. He was kidnapped and held hostage on the small farm of Jack & Mary Moynihan and after interrogation by the I. R. A. was murdered on the 30th April 1921. He was only 32 years old. Geoffrey, knowing he was going to be executed, wrote final letters to his Wife, his Regiment, to Major General Sir Peter Strickland at Head Quarters and his Father.

His letter to his Wife said:-

"My own darling little Wife. I am to be shot in an hours time, dearest, your Hubby will die with your name on his lips, your face before his eyes and he will die like an Englishman and a soldier. I cannot tell you Sweetheart, how much it is to me to leave you alone – nor how little to me personally to die – I have no fear, only the utmost, greatest and tenderest love to you and my sweet little Anne. I leave my cigarette case to the Regiment, my miniature medals to my Father – whom I have implored to befriend you in everything – and my watch to the Officer who is executing me because I believe him to be a gentleman and to mark the fact that I

bear no malice for carrying out what he sincerely believes to be his duty. Goodbye, my darling, my own. Choose from among my things some objects which you would practically keep in memory of me, and I believe that my spirit will be in it to love and comfort you. Tender, tender farewells and kisses, your own, Geof."

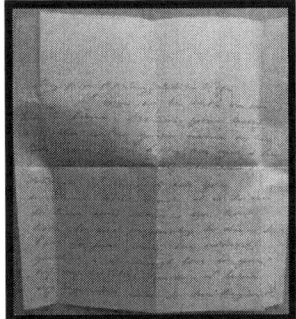 

Geof' last letter to his Wife & his wallet which she chose to keep his memory alive

His letter to the Regiment said:-

"Dear Royal Welsh Fusiliers – I am to be shot in an hours time. I should want you fellows to know that sentence has been passed on me and that I intend to die like a Welsh Fusilier with a laugh and forgiveness for those that are carrying out the deed. I should like my death to lessen rather than increase the bitterness which exists between England and Ireland. I have been treated with great kindness and during my short captivity have learned to regard Sinn Feiners rather as mistaken idealists than a murder gang. Will someone deal with my kit, selling the flying henry and the old yacht for anything that can be realised for them and forwarding the proceeds to my Wife at Hartford House, Winchfield, Hants. My cigarette case I leave to the Mess. I carried it with the Regiment throughout the War and I shall die with it in my pocket. God Bless you all comrades. G. L. C-S."

 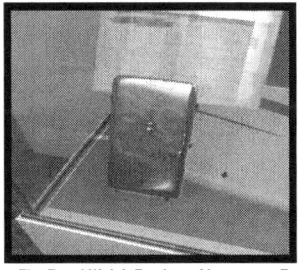

The cigarette case is on display at The Royal Welsh Fusiliers Museum at Caernarfon Castle along with the picture of his portrait his Wife's Sister Kitty Lloyd painted (shown on a previous page) and his last letters

His letter to the General said:-

"Dear General. As a result of my disobeying your orders and wandering about alone I have been captured by Sinn Feiners and am to be shot in a few minutes time. May I ask you to make it known, that it is my last wish that there should be no reprisals on my behalf. I am sure the feeling is bitter enough already without adding fuel to the fire. I believe these fellows are idealists who are doing what they earnestly believe is to be right. For our part let us try to forgive, which is more salutary and far more difficult than to revenge ourselves. Your sincerely. G. L. Compton-Smith."

His letter to his father did not survive.

OCTOBER 1917

OCTOBER 1st, 2nd & 3rd

The Battalion were at rest camp. On 3rd October the following Officers joined the Battalion for duty: -

- **Lieutenant G. W. Guttridge**
- **2nd Lieutenant W. T. Phillips**
- **2nd Lieutenant W. R. Rees**
- **2nd Lieutenant F. M. Arnold**
- **2nd Lieutenant M. Jones**
- **2nd Lieutenant J. T. Jones**
- **2nd Lieutenant D. E. Lawrence**

OCTOBER 4th

The Battalion marched to Arques a distance of 24.6km (15 miles) and went into billets.

OCTOBER 5th

The Battalion marched to Wizerns a distance of 6.7km (4 miles) and entrained, travelling overnight.

OCTOBER 6th

The Battalion detrained at Bapume and marched to Barastre a distance of 8.4km (just over 5 miles) and arrived at camp at 5pm. Captain A. E. Humphreys-Owen joined the Battalion for duty and was posted to 'D' Coy. 2nd Lieutenant C. H. Elphick was appointed Intelligence Officer and 2nd Lieutenant S. C. Kirkby was appointed Lewis Gun Officer.

OCTOBER 8th

The Battalion were addressed by General Officer Commanding (G. O. C.) of 76th Brigade. The Battalion also started training again. The following postings were carried out:-

- Lieutenant G. W. Guttridge to 'C' Coy
- 2nd Lieutenant W. T. Phillips to 'B' Coy
- 2nd Lieutenant W. R. Rees to 'B' Coy
- 2nd Lieutenant F. M. Arnold to 'D' Coy
- 2nd Lieutenant J. T. Jones to 'D' Coy
- 2nd Lieutenant D. E. Lawrence to 'C' Coy

OCTOBER 9th

The Battalion continued training. The following appointments were made:-

- Captain F. H. Sewell appointed to Second in Command of 'B' Coy
- Captain W. A. Richards attached to Brigade Staff – Intelligence Officer
- Captain J. R. Williams appointed Acting Adjutant
- 2nd Lieutenant J. T. Jones appointed Battalion Bombing Officer
- 2nd Lieutenant H. R. Davies appointed Temporary Command of 'C' Coy

OCTOBER 10th

The Battalion continued training. Captain R. A. Adamson and Lieutenant A. Nevitt M. C. rejoined the Battalion for duty after recovering from wounds.

OCTOBER 11th

The Battalion were transported by motor omnibuses to Mory and into camp.

OCTOBER 12th

The Battalion continued training. The following appointments were made:-

- Major A. J. S. James M. C. to be Acting Lieutenant Colonel
- Captain J. H. Addie to be Acting Major & Second in Command
- Lieutenant A. W. Fish to be Acting Captain

OCTOBER 13th TO 18th

For these days the Battalion continued training. On the 15th October two Officers and two N. C. O.'s went to reconnoitre the trenches that the Battalion were due to occupy.

Captain Arthur Erskine Owen Humphreys-Owen had joined the Battalion on the 6th October and during his time with the Battalion he kept a journel/correspondance book dating from 13th October to 9th November 1917. The journal is kept at the National Library of Wales at Aberyswyth.

In his first entry dated 13th October he wrote:-

"Fine day, Companies Parade and Inspection by C.O. in the morning, Pritchard has gone off to the C. C. S. they have not cured the wound in his head. I am taking over his Company. The Platoon Commanders are Gutteridge, Arnold, Jones the Bombing Officer and Hunter (away on leave). In the afternoon I go over to Olivers and get a bath there, then have tea with 'C' Mess of division details. Met a decent fellow there; Redmond, who has constructed an old ruined house into a very cosy place, and is planning an Officers Club. Canteen and mens club across the street on to Belagnies and dine at the club there with the C. O. and other Officers and play Bridge, lose 22 francs. Captain Adamson is going to take charge of 'D' Coy for the first tour of the trenches as he knows the system." - Captain Arthur Erskine Owen Humphreys-Owen 10th (Service) Battalion Royal Welsh Fusiliers

OCTOBER 19th

The Battalion entrained at Mory Abbey. Detrained at Ecoust and marched to the trenches where they relieved the 8th Battalion the Kings Own Royal Lancaster Regiment in the Bullecourt sector. Relief was complete by 11.40pm.

OCTOBER 20th & 21st

The Battalion were in the Front-Line Trenches, they suffered 1 casualty, other rank (O. R.) who was killed (but their name is not listed in the diary). A draft of three other ranks (O. R.) joined the Battalion for duty.

OCTOBER 22nd & 23rd

The following Officers joined the Battalion for duty:-

- 2nd Lieutenant R. E. Seel posted to 'D' Coy
- 2nd Lieutenant A. T. Worthington posted to 'A' Coy

Lieutenant W. B. Morgan rejoined the Battalion after recovering from his wounds and was appointed Acting Signalling Officer. Two Officers and 4 other ranks (O. R.) left the trenches to explore German dugouts.

On the 22nd October, Captain Arthur Erskine Owen Humphreys-Owen wrote: -

"1. Objective – German dugout in no mans land, 30 yards outside parapet of February Post.
2. Party consisting of two Officers and four other ranks thoroughly searched this dugout at 8pm October 22nd.
3. Four entrances led down about 30 feet deep to a long gallery about 100 yards long. Eight compartments facing the staircase opened off gallery and one on the other side.
4. The dugout appears to have been constructed to hold a complete unit of 200 infantry if necessary.
5. The whole dugout was littered with corpses and appears to have been taken by surprise and gassed. No man had his equipment on.
6. The patrol thoroughly searched the corpses and rubbish which littered the whole place but nothing of value in the way of documents could be found. Newspapers etc. that were found are enclosed. Also shoulder badges of greytcoats." - Captain Arthur Erskine Owen Humphreys-Owen 10th (Service) Battalion Royal Welsh Fusiliers

The description of the German dugout shows the vast scale of the defences the Battalion were facing. The reason for removing shoulder badges was to identify the Regiments the Battalion were facing.

OCTOBER 24th

A draft of 5 other ranks (O. R.) joined the Battalion for duty. The Battalion remained in the Front-Line Trenches. A patrol of four men under 2nd Lieutenant Elphick left the trench to explore Sunken Road to try and discover if there were anymore enemy dugouts. The entrance to two more dugouts were discovered and were blown in. Patrol returned at 11.20pm.

OCTOBER 25th & 26th

The Battalion were still in the Front-Line Trenches. The Battalion suffered the following casualties:-

RANK	NAME	SERVICE NO.	WOUND
PRIVATE	W. LEWIS	23980	WOUNDED
PRIVATE	J. HUGHES	65591	WOUNDED
PRIVATE	S. JONES	135537	WOUNDED

Captain Arthur Erskine Owen Humphreys-Owen wrote: -

"Lieutenant Arnold reported to me this morning that Sergeant Baverstock, who was the senior N. C. O. with the Wiring Party, last night (25th) remained in the trench and did not come out to the Wiring Party. Lieutenant Arnold states that as the party were running out into no mans land, he ordered two men to remain behind and assist in handing out the material and to follow when all material was out. Sergeant Baverstock heard this order and remained behind himself with another Private. The whole time the party were working, he alleges he understood what the meaning of Lieutenant Arnold's order. I do not wish to bring a serious charge against this N. C. O. as there is no evidence for this, but I consider him, under the circumstances, quite unfit to retain his rank." - Captain Arthur Erskine Owen Humphreys-Owen 10th (Service) Battalion Royal Welsh Fusiliers

If Captain Humphreys-Owen had proceeded with the charge, a Court Martial would have been held, with the charge of **'Disobeying an Order'** or even worse **'Cowardice in the face of the Enemy'**, which if found guilty, would have meant **'Death by Firing Squad'**. Senior N. C. O.'s would always accompany the Officer into no mans land on these types of 'Wiring Parties'.

OCTOBER 27th

The Battalion were relieved in the trenches by the 8th Battalion Kings Own Royal Lancashire Regiment and marched back to camp at Mory.

Captain the Reverend D. C. Williams M. C. (shown on the left) was transferred for duty at Kinmel Park Camp, North Wales.

Captain the Reverend D. Picton Evans took over the role as Battalion Chaplain.

OCTOBER 28th

A special farewell service was held by Captain Reverend D. C. Williams M. C. Captain C. J. F. Dent joined the Battalion for duty.

OCTOBER 29th, 30th & 31st

The Battalion were at rest and having baths and a general clean up for the next few days before training commenced on 31st October. Lieutenant J. G. Macaulay (R. A. M. C.) assumed medical charge of the Battalion. Captain Morgan Watcyn Williams returned to the Battalion in early October, but collapsed and returned to hospital and was later sent back to England. This was the end of Captain Williams' War. He spent months in hospital before being discharged as medically unfit for duty.

Captain Morgan Watcyn Williams

Morgan Watcyn Williams was born in 1891 to Father Watcyn W. Williams, a Presbyterian Minister, and Mother Annie M. Williams in Barry. He attended the University College of South Wales & Monmouthshire where he studied Philosophy. He married Janie Morgan in July 1919.

He wrote three books:-

1. Creative Fellowship – An Outline of the History of Calvinistic Methodism in Wales
2. The Beatitudes in the Modern World
3. From Khaki to Cloth – his autobiography.

He joined the Army in 1914 as a Private at the outbreak of War and after training at Kinmel Camp in North Wales with the Royal Welsh Fusiliers he transferred to the 10th (Service) Battalion Royal Welsh Fusiliers on 8th September 1916. He died in October 1938 aged 46.

The Western Mail, dated Saturday 22nd October 1938 wrote:-

Watcyn Williams Was a White Knight - "The passing of Morgan Watcyn Williams has cast a shadow over the Free Church life in Wales. He carved for himself a peculiar niche and that, in spite of terrific odds, was one of the Ministers who had passed through the last War, and instead of losing his ideals, as so many did, he found his soul. He got a firmer grip upon God, he developed a general love for his fellows and he discovered that henceforth, he must serve God by helping him to save men and save them in their entirety. He came out of the War realising the fruility of the whole business and he gave himself unstintingly to the proclamation of the Gospel of Peace. Watcyn Williams lived by the power of an endless life, and his soul goes marching on."

Full article from the Western Mail, dated Saturday 22nd October 1938

NOVEMBER 1917

NOVEMBER 1st

2nd Lieutenant J. R. Williams was appointed Acting Captain. The awards of the following decorations for Operations at Zonnebeke in September were announced:-

- Sergeant J. Edge 3924 – Military Medal

- Lance Corporal R. Jones 20761 - Military Medal
- Private W. H. Holden 18534 - Military Medal
- Private H. E. Ellis 48879 - Military Medal
- Private H. S. Evans 203336 - Military Medal
- Private F. Parsons 24406 - Military Medal
- Private H. Bailiff 16022 - Military Medal
- Sergeant J. Hollis 57030 - Military Medal
- Private A. Dutton 60451 - Military Medal
- Lance Sergeant J. Harvey 4120 - Military Medal
- Corporal J. H. Sloman 70158 - Military Medal
- Private W. Smith 23565 - Military Medal
- Corporal W. Skinner 34150 - Military Medal
- Corporal O. Jones 40940 - Military Medal
- Private M. Hughes D. C. M. M. M. 15427 – Bar to the Military Medal

NOVEMBER 2nd & 3rd

The Battalion remained in camp training.

NOVEMBER 4th

The Battalion marched to the Bullecourt sector and relieved the 8th Battalion the Kings Own Royal Lancaster Regiment in the Front-Line Trenches.

NOVEMBER 5th

The Battalion were still in the Front-Line Trenches and suffered the following casualties including **Lieutenant H. W. Raynor** who died of wounds (gas) and was attached to the 76th Trench Mortar Battery:-

Lieutenant Hubert William Raynor who was wounded by gas

RANK	NAME	SERVICE NO.	WOUND
PRIVATE	A. G. JONES	135503	WOUNDED (GAS)
PRIVATE	F. CALDER	135603	WOUNDED (GAS)
PRIVATE	W. H. GILLEARD	135631	WOUNDED (GAS)
PRIVATE	W. H. HALL	60503	WOUNDED (GAS)
PRIVATE	R. P. JONES	54847	WOUNDED (GAS)
PRIVATE	A. COLLEY	60376	WOUNDED (GAS)
PRIVATE	H. ANSCOMBE	60438	WOUNDED (GAS)

Captain Arthur Erskine Owen Humphreys-Owen wrote: -

"To Mess President – The Officers Mess would like some eggs, cheese, tinned fruit, sauce, mustard, no whisky is needed but more lime juice is. Other Officers Messes in the line get real tinned butter, which is excellent; make a note of it, also apples. Charcoal for fuel is needed, also candles." - Captain Arthur Erskine Owen Humphreys-Owen 10th (Service) Battalion Royal Welsh Fusiliers

How the other half lived! The poor **'Tommy'** had to put up with **'Trench Food'** which comprised of the following (if they were lucky!):-

MACONOCHIE – A thin watery broth containing sliced turnips and carrots, with fatty meat in gravy. Most soldiers despised it. It was named after the Company in Aberdeen who produced it.

BULLY BEEF – a tinned corned beef. On the Front-Line, where conditions were appauling, daily rations comprised of 90% of tinned meat.

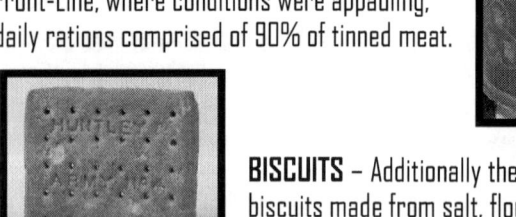

BISCUITS – Additionally the men received biscuits made from salt, flour and water and were compared to dog biscuits by the troops.

These biscuits were made under contract by Huntley & Palmers, which in 1914, was the worlds largest biscuit manufacturer. The very hard biscuit could crack teeth unless they were first soaked in tea or water.

PLUM & APPLE JAM – Produced by Thomas Tickler from Grimsby, who had a Government contract to supply tins of plum & apple jam to the troops.

<u>Oh It's a Lovely War</u>

Oh, Oh, Oh, it's a lovely War
What do we want with eggs and ham?
When we've got plum and apple jam.
Form Fours! Right turn!
How shall we spend the money we earned?
Oh, oh, oh, it's a lovely War

CONDENSED MILK – Condensed milk is cows milk from which 60% of the water has been removed then sugar added to make a thicker mixture. This was better for the soldiers at the front as it lasted longer than normal milk and it was easier to transport than fresh milk.

WATER – There was considerable pressure on water supplies to the Front-Line. The Army had to share resources with the civilian population. Much damage was inflicted on rivers, streams, reservoirs, lakes, ponds and wells, thus making water scarce. The water was usually transported to the Front-Line on water carts in petrol cans. The water was treated with chloride of lime, cleaning the water, but still not getting rid of the taste of petrol. Most of the time the water was used for tea, sometimes when the water was in really short supply, many of the troops at the front resorted to boiling filthy water from the bottom of the trench, or a shell hole. Drinking polluted water could lead to diarrhea and outbreaks of dysentry which there was many during the conflict.

BREAD – The bread ration for the Front-Line Trenches at the start of the War was 1lb or 18oz a day, just over half a 2lb loaf. Bread was another morale booster to the Front-Line soldiers. Bread and jam was a real treat, but sadly, due to supply problems of fresh bread, this treat was very rare. Occasionally the soldiers could buy bread from local residents in nearby towns and villages behind the Front-Line.

A roadside bread dump

BACON – The daily ration of bacon was 4oz (about 2 or 3 rashers). 'Tommy' was usually very happy when his rashers of bacon were frying at dawn, this of course, was not always possible due to either the location of the soldier i.e. the Front-Line and the supply of the bacon, which, as the size of the Army on the Front-Line increased, so did the problem of the supply.

Soldier frying bacon in the reserve trench

TEA RATION – Tea had to be hot, strong and heavily sweetened with condensed milk and sugar. If the 'Tommies' could not get their tea from the cooks in the transport lines, then 'Tommies' had to brew or 'Drum-up' some of their own using 'Tommy Cookers' which was basically a chunk of solidified fuel on a stand. Bryant & May's Kampite came in a container resembling a large box of matches. There were six fuel blocks with wicks and a stand. When not in use, 'Tommy' could just stick it in his pocket. The advantage of a 'Tommy Cooker' was smokeless. Smoke was a giveaway for snipers and enemy artillery.

'Tommies' having their cups of tea

ARMY RUM – 2.5 fluid ounces (about 70ml) per soldier, twice weekly for soldiers serving behind the Front-Lines or resting. Daily rations for those in the Front-Line Trenches. S. R. D. (Supply Reserve Depot) was better known to the soldiers as: -

S = Seldom
R = Reaches
D = Destination

Trench Food

NOVEMBER 6th & 7th

The Battalion was still in the Front-Line Trenches and suffered the following casualties:-

RANK	NAME	SERVICE NO.	WOUND
PRIVATE	J. THOMPSON	55663	WOUNDED
PRIVATE	J. OAKLEY		WOUNDED
PRIVATE	F. JARMAN	135025	WOUNDED

NOVEMBER 8th

The Battalion were relieved in the trenches by the 8th Battalion the Kings Own Royal Lancaster Regiment and marched back to camp at Mory.

NOVEMBER 9th

The Battalion were at rest in camp. A draft of 84 other ranks (O. R.) joined the Battalion for duty.

NOVEMBER 10th & 11th

The Battalion continued with their training. Lieutenant F. A. Lawson, who had rejoined the Battalion on the 11th, was attached to the 76th Trench Mortar Battery for duty.

NOVEMBER 14th

The Battalion continued training. 2nd Lieutenant J. R. Williams was promoted to Lieutenant. A draft of 6 other ranks (O. R.) joined the Battalion for duty.

NOVEMBER 16th

The Battalion marched to the Bullecourt sector and relieved the 8th Battalion the Kings Own Royal Lancaster Regiment and took over the Front-Line Trenches and the relief was complete by 10.30pm.

NOVEMBER 17th, 18th & 19th

The Battalion remained in the Front-Line Trenches until relieved by the 12th Battalion West Yorkshire Regiment and marched into camp at Favreuil.

NOVEMBER 20th

The Battalion were at rest in camp. Lieutenant E. T. Llewellyn was posted to 'C' Coy and 7 other ranks (O. R.) joined the Battalion for duty. Orders were received for the Battalion to be ready to move at 1 ½ hours notice.

NOVEMBER 21st

The General Officer Commanding (G. O. C.) and Brigade Major (B. M.) visited the Battalion and the 2nd Battalion Suffolk Regiment to observe the training.

NOVEMBER 22nd

The Battalion continued training. A draft of 80 other ranks (O. R.) joined the Battalion for duty.

NOVEMBER 23rd, 24th & 25th

The Battalion continued training. It was reported as 'wet'.

NOVEMBER 26th

The Battalion marched to the Bullecourt sector and relieved the 12th Battalion West Yorkshire Regiment and 1 ½ Coys of the 4th Battalion Royal Fusiliers in the Front-Line Trenches. The Battalion suffered the following casualties: -

RANK	NAME	SERVICE NO.	WOUND
SERGEANT	J. ROWLANDS	70152	KILLED
PRIVATE	T. LEES	23798	KILLED

RANK	NAME	SERVICE NO.	WOUND
PRIVATE	H. CULLIS	205087	WOUNDED

NOVEMBER 27th & 28th

The Battalion remained in the Front-Line Trenches. On the 27th at midnight the Battalion sent out three patrols of their front and discovered one hidden enemy trench, a fortified enemy post containing eight to ten men and the shell holes in front of the Battalions Front-Line were all unoccupied. A draft of 3 other ranks (O. R.) joined the Battalion for duty on the 28th.

NOVEMBER 29th

The enemy subjected the Front-Line to severe shelling which commenced at 6am and continued for an hour and a half. The Battalion received direct hits on their sector and suffered the following casualties:-

RANK	NAME	SERVICE NO.	WOUND
LANCE CORPORAL	O. E. JONES	70152	KILLED
PRIVATE	J. A. PARKER	42650	KILLED
PRIVATE	J. PRITCHARD	10290	KILLED

RANK	NAME	SERVICE NO.	WOUND
CORPORAL	E. J. ELCOCK	17178	WOUNDED
PRIVATE	A. A. FLAGG	34769	WOUNDED
PRIVATE	H. STEVENS	15279	WOUNDED
PRIVATE	H. CLARKE	238066	WOUNDED
PRIVATE	F. AUSTIN	55909	WOUNDED
PRIVATE	J. PENDLEBURY	54871	WOUNDED
PRIVATE	M. POWELL	19286	WOUNDED
PRIVATE	H. EVANS	70141	WOUNDED
PRIVATE	J. HODGSON	70499	WOUNDED
PRIVATE	H. JONES	61152	WOUNDED

NOVEMBER 30th

The Battalion were relieved in the Front-Line Trenches by the 8th Battalion the Kings Own Royal Lancaster Regiment and marched back to camp at Mory. 'D' Company remained in the Front-Line. The Battalion suffered the following casualties:-

RANK	NAME	SERVICE NO.	WOUND
SERGEANT	T. WILLIAMS	56756	WOUNDED
PRIVATE	S. WOODHOUSE	54892	WOUNDED
PRIVATE	R. JONES	25589	WOUNDED
PRIVATE	R. PHILLIPS	75825	WOUNDED

The award of the following decorations for operations at Zonnebeke on the 26th September were announced:-

- **Lieutenant/Captain A. W. Fish – Military Cross (M. C.)**
- **2nd Lieutenant D. C. Hunter – Military Cross (M. C.)**

Captain Arthur Erskine Owen Humphreys-Owen

Captain Arthur Erskine Owen Humphreys-Owen was born on 16th June 1876 at Berriew in Montgomeryshire in the year in which his Father Arthur Charles Humphreys inherited the Glansevern Mansion and Estates, taking the Arms and additional Surname of Owen.

Arthur was educated at Harrow, Trinity College Cambridge and in Germany from 1898 to 1904. He worked in the Diplomatic Service but resigned when he inherited the Glansevern and Llanrul Estates. In 1908 he became High Sherif of his county.

Arthur married Isabel Rosalind Sassoon, the Daughter of Sir Edward Sassoon in 1907. They had two children, a Son and a Daughter.

Arthur was commissioned into the Army a month after the War broke out in 1914 as 2nd Lieutenant, promoted to Captain on the 28th September 1916, having spent time in the 6th (Service) Battalion the Dorset Regiment, before joining the 10th (Service) Battalion Royal Welsh Fusiliers on the 6th October 1917. Arthur was aged 41 at this time. In 1918 Arthur became Second in Command of the 14th (Service) Battalion Royal Welsh Fusiliers until he was wounded in action on 23rd August 1918.

After the War, Arthur was a Barrister at Law but he had separated from his Wife, his estate was insolvent and he was last known to be in a club in London playing for considerable stakes. He left the club one night in 1929 before disappearing, never to be seen again. Newspaper reports eleven years later presumed his death after efforts to find him failed.

DEATH PRESUMED ELEVEN YEARS AFTER DISAPPEARANCE

Nearly eleven years ago, Mr. Arthur Erskine Owen Humphreys-Owen, late of Berriew (Montgomeryshire), left his London club, telling the steward that he was "going on the water for a few days." The steward thought he meant he was going yachting. From that time he disappeared.

In the Probate Court yesterday, Mr. Justice Hodson granted leave to presume that death occurred on or after July 16, 1928.

Counsel said that Mr. Humphreys-Owen, who was separated from his wife, had been playing in clubs for considerable stakes. He was pressed for money and his estate was still insolvent. Efforts to trace him had failed.

The Birmingham Post – Thursday June 29th 1939

> **THE MANCHESTER EVENING NEWS, WEDNESDAY, JUNE 28, 1939**
>
> ## 'I'm Going On the Water,' Said a Man Never Seen Again
>
> NEARLY eleven years ago Mr. Arthur Erskine Owen Humphreys-Owen, late of Berriew, Montgomeryshire, left his London club, telling the steward that he was "going on the water for a few days." The steward thought he meant he was going yachting.
>
> From that time he disappeared. In the Probate Court to-day Mr. Justice Hodson granted leave to presume that death occurred on or after July 16, 1928.
>
> Counsel said that Mr. Humphreys-Owen, who was separated from his wife, had been playing in clubs for considerable stakes.
>
> He was pressed for money, and his estate was still insolvent. Efforts to trace him had failed.

Manchester Evening News Wednesday 28th June 1939

DECEMBER 1917

DECEMBER 1st

'D' Coy remained in the Front-Line Trenches but were relieved by 'A' Coy at night and returned to join the remaining Battalion at rest camp in Mory.

DECEMBER 2nd & 3rd

'A' Coy remained in the Front-Line Trenches and suffered the following casualties:-

RANK	NAME	SERVICE NO.	WOUND
2ND LIEUTENANT	A. T. WORTHINGTON		WOUNDED
PRIVATE	J. DAWSON	202089	WOUNDED

DECEMBER 4th

The Battalion less 'A' Coy who remained in the trenches, marched to the Bullecourt sector and relieved the 8th Battalion the Kings Own Royal Lancaster Regiment in the Front-Line Trenches in the right subsector. Relief was complete by 8.15pm.

DECEMBER 5th & 6th

The Battalion remained in the Front-Line Trenches. On the 6th, the Battalion suffered the following casualties:-

RANK	NAME	SERVICE NO.	WOUND
PRIVATE	E. WORMAN	22441	WOUNDED (GAS)
PRIVATE	J. JONES	35725	WOUNDED

DECEMBER 7th, 8th & 9th

The Battalion remained in the Front-Line Trenches. Patrols were carried out every night and the area was reported as 'quiet'.

DECEMBER 9th & 10th

The Battalion were relieved in the trenches by the 8th Battalion the Kings Own Royal Lancaster Regiment and marched into camp at Mory. Hostile enemy aircraft bombed the rear trenches/back area during the night of the 9th and 10th. The Battalion suffered the following casualties: -

RANK	NAME	SERVICE NO.	WOUND
PRIVATE	J. REED	60314	WOUNDED
PRIVATE	J. WOOD	70529	WOUNDED
PRIVATE	W. FULLER	201815	WOUNDED
PRIVATE	J. THOMAS	69138	WOUNDED
PRIVATE	L. JACKLIN	70584	WOUNDED
PRIVATE	J. PRATT	238099	WOUNDED
PRIVATE	H. JONES	205107	WOUNDED

DECEMBER 11th

'C' Coy marched to the Bullecourt Trenches in support of the 8th Battalion the Kings Own Royal Lancaster Regiment. This was due to the hostile artillery being more active than usual and patrols had reported sounds of wiring and shouting in the front of the Front-Line Trenches.

A draft of 3 other ranks (O. R.) joined the Battalion for duty. Lieutenant T. A. Evans was transferred to the 19th Battalion Royal Welsh Fusiliers.

DECEMBER 12th

A heavy enemy barrage was put down on the Front-Line Trenches and was most severe from 6.15am to 7.30am and then from 3pm to 3.40pm. This barrage included gas shells. The enemy attacked the apex at 3pm. The 1st Gordon Highlanders and the Royal Engineers moved to their 'Alarm Posts'. The 10th (Service) Battalion Royal Welsh Fusiliers, less 'C' Coy, whom were already in the line, moved back into the trenches from their camp at Mory and went into the second line as support. The attack was repulsed by heavy machine gun and rifle fire.

DECEMBER 13th

At 9am the Battalion left the Front-Line Trenches and returned to camp at Mory Abbey. 'C' Coy remained in the Front-Line Trenches. One casualty was killed today – **Private N. Powell** service number 19286.

DECEMBER 14th, 15th & 16th

The Battalion less 'C' Coy, who had remained in the Front-Line Trenches, were at rest, although the Battalion were at **'Stand To'** from 6.30am to 8am every morning incase the enemy launched another attack on the line. Training commenced again on the 15th December.

DECEMBER 17th

The Battalion less 'C' Coy marched into the trenches and relieved the 8th Battalion the Kings Own Royal Lancaster Regiment. In the right section of Bullecourt sector it was snowing quite heavily during the day and with a hard frost at night. The relief was completed by 8.30pm. One casualty was reported as accidentally wounded – **Lance Corporal S. Cowell** service number 55779.

DECEMBER 18th, 19th & 20th

The Battalion were in the Front-Line Trenches. On the 19th a patrol under the command of 2nd Lieutenant R. T. Owen left the Front-Line Trenches to reconnoitre **'No mans Land'**. They found the German Front-Line to be thinly held. 2nd Lieutenant Owen managed to penetrate two belts of wire and got within a challenging distance of the enemy sentry. Casualties wounded were : -

RANK	NAME	SERVICE NO.	WOUND
PRIVATE	J. COOK	235019	WOUNDED
SERGEANT	C. O'NEILL	135270	WOUNDED
PRIVATE	R. OWENS	135010	WOUNDED

A draft of 6 other ranks (O. R.) joined the Battalion for duty on the 20th.

DECEMBER 22nd

The Battalion were still in the Front-Line Trenches. One casualty was reported as **Private F. Garnett** service number 70492. Captain R. A. Adamson was appointed Acting Second in Command as Major J. H. F. Addie reported sick.

DECEMBER 23rd

The Battalion less 'B' Coy were relieved in the Front-Line Trenches by the 8th Battalion the Kings Own Royal Lancaster Regiment and marched back into reserve at Ecoust. 'B' Coy remaining in the Front-Line Trenches. The following casualties were reported: -

RANK	NAME	SERVICE NO.	WOUND
PRIVATE	J. LIMERICK	74955	WOUNDED
PRIVATE	W. PRITCHARD	42488	WOUNDED (ACCIDENTILY)

DECEMBER 24th, 25th & 26th

The Battalion remained in reserve at Ecoust whilst 'B' Coy remained in the Front-Line Trenches. It snowed off and on over these days and it was bitterly cold. Not a happy time for the Battalion over the festive period.

DECEMBER 27th

The Battalion was relieved in reserve by the 13th Battalion Yorkshire Regiment and marched back to camp at Mory. 2nd Lieutenant J. Overton and 2nd Lieutenant J. W. Ellis were posted to 'B' Coy along with 50 other ranks (O. R.) and joined the Battalion for duty.

DECEMBER 29th
The Battalion marched into camp in the Blairville area.
DECEMBER 30th & 31st
The Battalion attended Church Parade and commenced training. Lieutenant F. J. Cutler (R. A. M. C.) assumed medical charge of the Battalion.

1917 had come to an end.

The Battalion had suffered tremendous casualties during the year.

The conditions had been atrocious.

The Battalion had lost very good Officers and many experienced men. The whole Battalion had changed since those long-off days of September 1915 when they landed in France full of hope, vigor and determination to see it through to the end.

Morale was low, men were weary and tired of it all, wondering when it would all be over.

Chapter 6
1918 - DISBANDMENT

JANUARY 1918

JANUARY 1st

The Battalion were given a day off to rest at the camp in Blairville. Captain R. A. Adamson was appointed as Second in Command of the Battalion.

JANUARY 2nd

The Battalion began training. 2nd Lieutenant D. C. Hunter M. C. reported sick and went to hospital. A draft of 30 other ranks (O. R.) joined the Battalion for duty.

JANUARY 3rd & 4th

The Battalion continued training. 2nd Lieutenant C. D. Alltree joined the Battalion for duty and was posted to 'D' Coy. 2nd Lieutenant J. M. Wardlaw rejoined the Battalion for duty and was posted to 'B' Coy. The weather was reported as 'very cold but dry'.

JANUARY 5th

The Battalion continued training. 2nd Lieutenant D. E. Lawrence reported sick to hospital.

JANUARY 6th

The Battalion continued training. Captain A. W. Fish M. C. reported sick to hospital and Captain R. A. Adamson Second in Command was granted the rank of Acting Major.

JANUARY 7th, 8th & 9th

The Battalion continued it's training in terrible conditions, heavy snow and a hard frost at night was reported.

JANUARY 11th

Major J. H. F. Addie was invalided to England suffereing from severe Asthma.

JANUARY 12th

The Battalion was inspected by the General Officer Commanding (G. O. C.) VI Corps Sir James Haldane K. C. B. G. C. MG D. S. O. A draft of 4 other ranks (O. R.) joined the Battalion for duty.

JANUARY 13th & 14th

The Battalion continued training. Captain A. W. Fish M. C. was invalided to England. Captain C. J. F. Dent reported sick to hospital.

JANUARY 15th

The Battalion continued it's training. The following Officers joined the Battalion for duty:-

- 2nd Lieutenant W. T. Jones
- 2nd Lieutenant J. Huxley
- 2nd Lieutenant G. H. Webb

JANUARY 16th TO 20th

For the next few days the Battalion continued training. During training, the Battalion tested **'Ground Flares'** with the help of the Royal Flying Corps (R. F. C.) and a new 'Trench Mortar Scheme' was practiced.

JANUARY 21st

The Battalion continued training. A draft of 11 other ranks (O. R.) joined the Battalion for duty.

JANUARY 22nd

The Battalion continued training. A draft of 3 other ranks (O. R.) joined the Battalion for duty.

JANUARY 24th

The Battalion marched to Wailly Rifle Range to witness a demonstration given by the 1st Battalion Gordon Highlanders.

JANUARY 27th

The Battalion marched into camp at Carlisle Lines Baeu-Rains.

JANUARY 28th & 29th

The Battalion continued training and on the 28th a draft of 4 other ranks (O. R.) joined the Battalion for duty.

JANUARY 30th

The Officers and N. C. O.'s attended a lecture by the Divisional Gas Officer. The lecture was then repeated to the rest of the Battalion. At night the Battalion marched into trenches and relieved the 1st Battalion Gordon Highlanders in the left subsection of the Wancourt sector. Guemappe Trench relief was completed by 10am.

JANUARY 31st

The Battalion were in the Front-Line Trenches. The award of the following Decorations were announced: -

- Captain A. Nevitt M. C. - The Albert Medal
- Acting Regimental Sergeant Major W. Webb D. C. M. 5796 - The Military Cross (M. C.)
- Sergeant F. Gibbs 15724 - Distinguished Conduct Medal (D. C. M.)
- Captain F. A. Sewell - Croix-De-Guerre Belgium
- Corporal E. W. Hughes 55058 - Croix-De-Guerre Belgium
- Lance Corporal D. Watters M. M. 15286 - Croix-De-Guerre Belgium
- Private J. Marchant 13861 - Croix-De-Guerre Belgium
- Private T. Profit 15092 - Croix-De-Guerre Belgium
- Sergeant Major R. G. Roberts 15386 - Mentioned in Despatches
- Sergeant A. Hancox 46466 - Mentioned in Despatches

FEBRUARY 1918

FEBRUARY 1st

The Battalion were relieved in the Guemappe Trenches by the 1st Gordon Highlanders and marched back to the Carlisle Lines Beau-Rains. Relief was completed by 6.30pm.

FEBRUARY 2nd

The pending disbandment of the 10th (Service) Battalion Royal Welsh Fusiliers was notified.

The Manpower Crisis of 1918

Prime Minister Lloyd George

In early October 1917 the British Prime Minister Lloyd George asked Commander in Chief, Sir Douglas Haig to consider taking over some of the French Front-Line due to the frailties of the French Army. Haig was opposed to this and submitted a report stating the 62 Divisions now in France should be brought up to full strength and that the line should not be extended.

The Army in France was already significantly short of its full strength, 70 to 80,000 men short in the Infantry alone and during the later battle of 1917 at Arras, Messines and Ypres, replacement drafts were not keeping up with the losses. In November 1917, Haig advised the War Office that unless more troops were forthcoming, he would have to break up 15 of his Divisions to bring the remaining formations back up to strength, the Cabinet Committee on Manpower disagreed and proposed an alternative idea, reducing every Brigade from four Battalions to three Battalions. The Military members of the Army Council protested against this idea, but to no avail and the order was passed. Haig also reluctantly agreed to extending the British Front-Line from 95 miles to 123 miles, an increase of 30%. The British Line was increased and protected by fewer men. According to the records on the 1st January 1918 over 600,000 Officers and men were trained and ready for service in Britain, but Lloyd George was unwilling to release them for the Western Front. During all the political bickering that was going on, Germany's strength on the Western Front was growing and growing due to the collapse of the Russians on the Eastern Front. A Spring offensive by the Germans was planned and the British and French Forces were depleated and weak.

The Disbandment of the 10th (Service) Battalion Royal Welsh Fusiliers was a consequence of this decision by the Army Council on the 8th February 1918. The "Fighting 10th" left the 76th Infantry Brigade and marched to Bailleulval, accompanied, for the first part of the march, by the Pipers of the 1st Battalion Gordon Highlanders playing Royal Welsh Airs.

The Battalion received the following farewell messages: -

> From General Officer Commanding 76th Brigade :
> "Lieut.-Colonel Hunt, acting in Command, feels certain he is voicing General Porter's wishes in conveying his thanks to the Battalion for their splendid work in the past, for their loyalty and esprit de corps, and for their gallantry on all occasions. For General Porter, he wishes the Officers, Non-commissioned Officers, and men, 'God-speed, and Farewell.'"

> From Lieut.-Colonel J. L. Likeman, D.S.O., Commanding 2nd battalion Suffolk Regiment :
> "I am expressing the feelings of the whole battalion, when I say that it is with the greatest regret that we regard the approaching break-up of the 10th battalion, and the termination of our close friendship. For two years the battalions have fought side by side, and have striven in friendly rivalship in the cricket and football fields.
> In these and many other ways we have learnt to appreciate the Royal Welch Fusiliers. We wish you all the best of luck in the battalions to which you will be going, and we trust that you will find there as warm a welcome (if that is possible) as awaits you at any time you may return to the 76th Brigade or the neighbourhood of this battalion."

> From the Officer Commanding (Major G. E. Malcolm) 1st Gordon Highlanders:
>
> "The Commanding Officer, Officers, and men wish to express their great regret at bidding you farewell. We have played against you, and fought alongside you, and have always found you the best of friends. May you have the best of luck wherever you may be, we will never forget you."

> From Officer Commanding (Lieut.-Colonel R. S. Hunt, D.S.O.) 8th battalion The King's Own (Royal Lancaster Regiment):
>
> "All ranks of the battalion under my command wish to convey to the Officers, Non-Commissioned Officers, and men, of the 10th battalion Royal Welch Fusiliers, their feeling of very great regret at losing the battalion from the Brigade. On its withdrawal, we of The King's Own, recognise how much the loss means, in comradeship and in mutual trust. We have relieved each other often in the trenches, we have attacked together, and we have beaten off German attacks, shoulder to shoulder.
>
> In bidding you 'Good-bye,' we feel a very real regret and the bursting of a tie that bound us all together in the 76th Brigade, but we wish you, all ranks, the best possible of luck in the future, and assure you that the past will not be forgotten."

Just before disbandment eight Officers and 150 other ranks (O. R.) were transferred to the 9th Battalion Royal Welsh Fusiliers (19th Division). The remainder of the Battalion, together, with the 19th Battalion Royal Welsh Fusiliers formed the 8th Entrenching Battalion, (one of the 25 created) and came under the command of VI Corps. Soon after the launching of the German offensive in March 1918, 15 Officers and a large proportion of the other ranks (O. R.) were transferred to the Royal Naval Division. The 10th (Service) Battalion Royal Welsh Fusiliers was solely raised for fighting purposes under the greatest national crisis.

The words 'Loyalty' and 'Devotion to Duty', 'Courage', 'Comradeship', 'Esprit De Corps' all have been spontaneously expressed by those who were on official or friendly contact with all ranks of the Battalion. The Battalion was fortunate in the beginning with a nucleus of retired Officers and non-commissioned Officers of the Regular Army, many of whom had served in the 1st or 2nd Royal Welsh Fusiliers and from whom pride in the traditions of the Regiment, were easily learned and absorbed by the 10th Battalion and the wisdom of which was so clearly foreseen in the proclamation incorporating the so-called Kitchener's Armies Battalions in the old historic Regiments of the Regular Army. The 'Call to Arms' during August and September 1914 resulted in a rush to serve and men from all backgrounds and ages joined the new Battalions. The 10th Battalion had the great fortune of being incorporated into the 3rd Division, famous as a first class fighting Division and composed of some of the crack Regiments of the Army, and very soon after the Battalions arrival on the Western Front, it proved it's mettle and after a time, became known as the 'Fighting 10'. The Battalion landed in France on 27th September 1915 and was disbanded on the 2nd February 1918, a period of two and a third years. During this time the Battalion spent 214 days actually in the Front-Line Trenches, sometimes within 30 yards of a vigilant and active enemy, and similar periods in so-called rest camps or billets, all within marching distance of the Front-Line and also not forgetting, within range of hostile enemy shellfire. The remaining time was passed in strenuous training at Brigade or at the Divisional Training Areas preparatory to battle action. The Battalion casualties, during this period were severe. Of the Officers serving with the Battalion, 51 were killed in action or died of wounds, 63 were wounded once, 6 were wounded twice and 1 became a Prisoner of War. Of the other ranks (O. R.), over 750 were killed in action or died of wounds, or were reported missing. Over 1500 were wounded, including some more than once and 70 became Prisoners of War. The Battalions 1st contact with the enemy was in the Hooge Trenches, Railway Wood. The Battalion was then prominent in the actions of The Bluff, St. Eloi in March 1916 and then moved further South to take part in the operations in the Somme area, where it fought in the Battles of Bazentine Ridge, Delville

Wood (including the attacks on Lonely Trench) and Ancre.
During 1917, the Battalion fought in the battles of Arras including the First, Second and Third Battle of Scarpe and also Arleux. These actions included the heavy fighting around Monchy Le Preux and the capture of Infantry Hill, situated about half a mile East of Monchy Le Preux.
In September 1917 the Battalion took part in the Third battle of Ypres which included the Battle of Polygon Wood and the capture of Zonnebeke. The Battalion also undertook the usual routine of 'Week In-Week Out' of manning the trenches, which entailed heavy works, exposure to enemy fire and a never ending drain of casualties.

For a full list of the Battle Honours for the Battalion and a list of the Individual Honours and Decorations awarded to the Battalion, please go to **Chapter 9** in the book.

My Taid Edwin Roberts was transferred to the 8th Entrenching Battalion on the disbandment of the 10th (Service) Battalion Royal Welsh Fusiliers, later joining the 63rd Royal Naval Division.

He had served with the 10th (Service) Battalion Royal Welsh Fusiliers since September 1914 and was wounded once in October 1915 and later wounded again when attached to the 'Hood Battalion' 63rd Royal Naval Division (R. N. D.)

List of Battalions disbanded in the reorganisation of the Army in 1918 are shown below:-

Bn	Regiment	Nation	type		Bn	Regiment	Nation	type
16th Bn	Northumberland Fusiliers	English	New Army		22th Bn	Northumberland Fusiliers	English	New Army
20th Bn	Northumberland Fusiliers	English	New Army		4th Bn	Bedfordshire Regiment	English	New Army
21st Bn	Northumberland Fusiliers	English	New Army		10th Bn	The South Wales Borderers	Welsh	New Army
26th Bn	Northumberland Fusiliers	English	New Army		11th Bn	The South Wales Borderers	Welsh	New Army
2/5th Bn	Royal Warwickshire Regt	English	TF		12th Bn	The South Wales Borderers	Welsh	New Army
11th Bn	Royal Warwickshire Regt	English	New Army		9th Bn	Duke of Wellington's Regiments (West Riding)	English	New Army
8th Bn	The Royal Fusiliers (City of London Regt)	English	New Army		11th Bn	The Border Regt	English	New Army
12th Bn	The Royal Fusiliers (City of London Regt)	English	New Army		12th Bn	Royal Sussex Regiment	English	New Army
22nd Bn	The Royal Fusiliers (City of London Regt)	English	New Army		8th Bn	South Staffordshire Regt	English	New Army
2/6th Bn	The King's (Liverpool Regt)	English	TF		2/5th Bn	South Lancashire Regiment	English	TF
2/8th Bn	The King's (Liverpool Regt)	English	TF		7th Bn	South Lancashire Regiment	English	New Army
2/9th Bn	The King's (Liverpool Regt)	English	TF		8th Bn	South Lancashire Regiment	English	New Army
20th Bn	The King's (Liverpool Regt)	English	New Army		10th Bn	The Welsh Regiment	Welsh	New Army
8th Bn	The Norfolk Regiment	English	New Army		14th Bn	The Welsh Regiment	Welsh	New Army
2/4th Bn	The Lincolnshire Regiment	English	TF		17th Bn	The Welsh Regiment	Welsh	New Army
2/5th Bn	The Lincolnshire Regiment	English	TF		10th Bn	Oxfordshire & Buckinghamshire Light Infantry	English	New Army
8th Bn	The Suffolk Regiment	English	New Army		13th Bn	The Essex Regiment	English	New Army
9th Bn	The Suffolk Regiment	English	New Army		2/7th Bn	Sherwood Foresters	English	TF
12th Bn	West Yorkshire Regiment	English	New Army		2/8th Bn	Sherwood Foresters	English	TF
16th Bn	West Yorkshire Regiment	English	New Army		17th Bn	Sherwood Foresters	English	New Army
8th Bn	East Yorkshire Regiment	English	New Army		7th Bn	Loyal North Lancashire Regiment	English	New Army
12th Bn	East Yorkshire Regiment	English	New Army		8th Bn	Loyal North Lancashire Regiment	English	New Army
13th Bn	East Yorkshire Regiment	English	New Army		9th Bn	Loyal North Lancashire Regiment	English	New Army
2/5th Bn	Leicestershire Regiment	English	TF		10th Bn	Loyal North Lancashire Regiment	English	New Army
9th Bn	Leicestershire Regiment	English	New Army		10th Bn	Berkshire Regiment	English	New Army
6th Bn	The Royal Irish Regiment	Irish	New Army		2/4th Bn	Queen's Own Royal (West Kent)	English	TF
7th Bn	Yorkshire Regiment	English	New Army		2/5th Bn	King's Own Yorkshire Light Infantry	English	TF
10th Bn	Yorkshire Regiment	English	New Army		2/4th Bn	King's Own Yorkshire Light Infantry	English	TF
2/8th Bn	Lancashire Fusiliers	English	TF		8th Bn	King's Own Yorkshire Light Infantry	English	New Army
3/5th Bn	Lancashire Fusiliers	English	TF		10th Bn	King's Own Yorkshire Light Infantry	English	New Army
20th Bn	Lancashire Fusiliers	English	New Army		5th Bn	King's Shropshire Light Infantry	English	New Army
13th Bn	The Cheshire Regiment	English	New Army		3/10th Bn	Middlesex Regiment	English	TF
15th Bn	The Cheshire Regiment	English	New Army		11th Bn	Middlesex Regiment	English	New Army
14th Bn	Gloucestershire Regt	English	New Army		12th Bn	Middlesex Regiment	English	New Army
2/7th Bn	Worcestershire Regt	English	TF		16th Bn	Middlesex Regiment	English	New Army
2/4th Bn	East Lancashire Regiment	English	TF		17th Bn	Middlesex Regiment	English	New Army
7th Bn	East Lancashire Regiment	English	New Army		10th Bn	KRRC	English	New Army
8th Bn	East Lancashire Regiment	English	New Army		2/9th Bn	Manchester Regiment	English	TF
7th Bn	East Surrey Regiment	English	New Army		2/9th Bn	Manchester Regiment	English	TF
6th Bn	Duke of Cornwall's Light Infantry	English	New Army		2/10th Bn	Manchester Regiment	English	TF
2/5th Bn	Duke of Wellington's Regiments (West Riding)	English	TF		18th Bn	Manchester Regiment	English	New Army
2/6th Bn	Duke of Wellington's Regiments (West Riding)	English	TF		19th Bn	Manchester Regiment	English	New Army
2/5th Bn	South Staffordshire Regt	English	TF		23rd Bn	Manchester Regiment	English	New Army
2/6th Bn	South Staffordshire Regt	English	TF		2/6th Bn	North Staffordshire Regiment	English	TF
10th Bn	Royal Welsh Fusiliers	Welsh	New Army		2/5th Bn	York & Lancaster Regiment	English	TF
15th Bn	Royal Welsh Fusiliers	Welsh	New Army		12th Bn	York & Lancaster Regiment	English	New Army
19th Bn	Royal Welsh Fusiliers	Welsh	New Army		13th Bn	York & Lancaster Regiment	English	New Army
2/6th Bn	The London Regiment	English	TF		14th Bn	York & Lancaster Regiment	English	New Army
2/7th Bn	The London Regiment	English	TF		13th Bn	Durham Light Infantry	English	New Army
2/8th Bn	The London Regiment	English	TF		14th Bn	Durham Light Infantry	English	New Army
2/9th Bn	The London Regiment	English	TF		7th Bn	Highland Light Infantry	Scottish	New Army
2/12th Bn	The London Regiment	English	TF		2th Bn	Royal Irish Rifles	Irish	New Army
					10th Bn	Royal Irish Rifles	Irish	New Army
					11th Bn	Royal Irish Rifles	Irish	New Army
					14th Bn	Royal Irish Rifles	Irish	New Army
					7th Bn	Royal Irish Fusiliers	Irish	New Army
					7th Bn	Leinster Regiment	Irish	New Army
					8th Bn	Royal Dublin Fusiliers	Irish	New Army
					10th Bn	Royal Dublin Fusiliers	Irish	New Army
					10th Bn	Rifle Brigade	English	New Army
					2/13th Bn	The London Regiment	English	TF
					2/14th Bn	The London Regiment	English	TF
					2/15th Bn	The London Regiment	English	TF

*Please note this is not a full list, but what I could source at the time and kindly provided by Gareth Davies and his late friend Martin Gillcot. Gareth is a member of the Great War Group (G. W. G.)

Chapter 8
8th Entrenching Battalion &
63rd Royal Naval Division (R. N. D.)

MARCH 1918 – 8th Entrenching Battalion

The 8th Entrenching Battalion was formed by VI Corps from the surplus of the 10th and 19th (Service) Battalions of the Royal Welsh Fusiliers and the 24th/27th Northumberland Fusiliers at Bailleuival on the 15th/16th February 1918. By March 1st 1918 the Battalion had moved to Durham Lines Camp for 'Fatigue Work' on the Corps Defence Line.

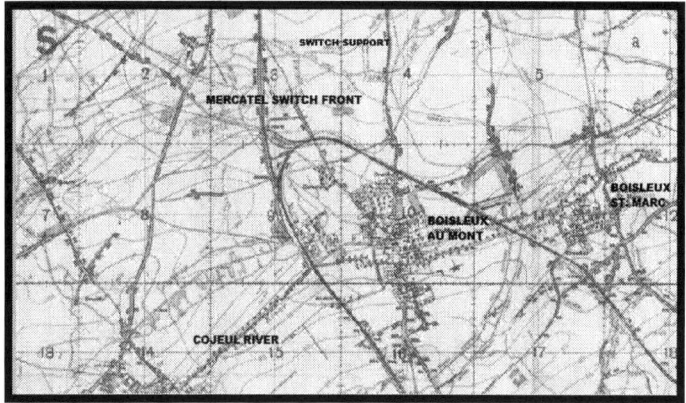

MARCH 1st

The Battalion were working on the Corps Defence Line, the following Officers reported for duty with the Battalion:-
- Captain A. E. O. Humphreys-Owen
- Lieutenant S. A. H. Granville
- Lieutenant G. W. Milner
- 2nd Lieutenant G. C. Manston

MARCH 2nd & 3rd

The Battalion continued work on the Corps Defence Line. Honorable Lieutenant & Quarter Master G. W. Wilnes was transferred.

MARCH 4th

The Battalion were working on the Corps Defence Line and 'A' & 'C' Coys were bathing.

MARCH 5th, 6th & 7th

The Battalion continued working on the Corps Defence Line.

MARCH 8th

Lieutenant Colonel A. J. S. James M. C. left the Battalion and joined the 8th Battalion Kings Own Royal Lancaster Regiment.

MARCH 9th, 10th & 11th

The Battalion continued to work on the Corps Defence Line.

MARCH 12th

The Battalion continued to work on the Corps Defence Line. 10 other ranks (O. R.) were transferred to the 3rd Battalion Machine Gun Corps and 5 other ranks (O. R.) were transferred to the 40th Battalion Machine Gun Corps. This was the start of a busy period of troops leaving the Battalion for other Regiments.

MARCH 13th

2 other ranks (O. R.) transferred to R. E. Signals.

MARCH 14th

2nd Lieutenant D. Vaughan joined the Battalion for duty.

MARCH 15th

The Battalion continued working on the Corps Defence Line. 15 other ranks (O. R.) transferred to the 3rd Battalion Machine Gun Corps.

MARCH 16th

Lieutenant J. G. Williams reported to the Battalion for duty. The Commanding Officer (C. O.) interviews all N. C. O.'s of the Battalion.

MARCH 18th

Lieutenant D. D. Phillips joined the Battalion for duty. 38 N. C. O.'s were posted from the Battalion to the 1/4th, 9th, 13th and 16th Battalions of the Royal Welsh Fusiliers

MARCH 19th & 20th

The Battalions were on **'Fatigue Duty'**. Lieutenant H. C. Kelly was admitted to hospital.

MARCH 21st

The German Spring Offensive was launched.

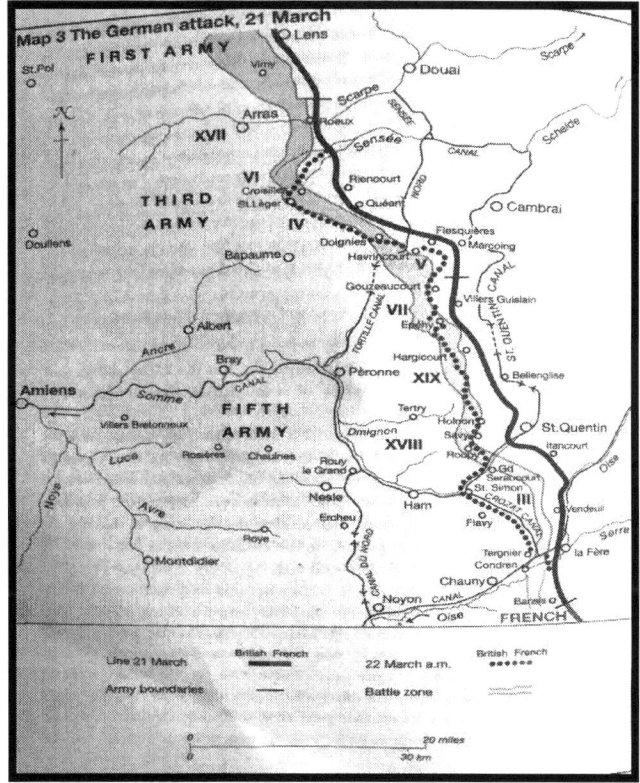

The Battalion was instructed to prepare to move.

MARCH 22nd

The Battalion moved by train to Authie only arriving at midnight due to the train being bombed by enemy aircraft.

MARCH 23rd & 24th

The Battalion started training. 35 other ranks (O. R.) left to join the 12th/13th Battalion Northumberland Fusiliers.

MARCH 27th

The Battalion were ordered to **'Stand To'** and **'Dig In'** outside of the villiage of Authie.

MARCH 29th

Captain W. B. Morgan and Captain J. W. Wardian left the Battalion for duty with the 9th Battalion Royal Welsh Fusiliers.

MARCH 30th & 31st

The Battalion entrained at Mondicourt at 5.30pm and detrained at Vignacourt at 7.30am on the 31st and marched into billets and rested for the remainder of the day.

The 8th Entrenching Battalion War Diary ends on the 31st March 1918.

APRIL 1918 – Hood Battalion 63rd Royal Naval Division

APRIL 6th

On April 6th 1918 according to the Diary of the Hood Battalion 63rd Royal Naval Division, 320 other ranks (O. R.) and the following Officers joined the Battalion for duty from the 8th Entrenching Battalion:-

- 2nd Lieutenant W. Russell Rees
- 2nd Lieutenant M. Jones
- 2nd Lieutenant D. D. Jones
- 2nd Lieutenant H. Pritchard
- 2nd Lieutenant W. H. Hooper

My Taid Edwin, was among the 320 other ranks (O. R.) that had been posted to the Hood Battalion.

The Battalion then proceeded by route march to Divisional Reserve at Englebelmer in the evening and the Battalion were billeted in cellars. The 'Advance Parties' proceeded to the Front-Line to take over from the 4th Bedfordshire Regiment.

APRIL 7th

'C' Coy the Hood Battalion were holding a long Front-Line in the 188th Infantry Brigade area and were stretched to the limit. 'B' Coy were in the support lines, 'A' Coy were in reserve cellars and shelters and 'D' Coy were attached to the Anson Battalion on the right sector. Enemy shelling was heavy and during this time casualties were reported as:-

- 2nd **Lieutenant H. Pritchard was killed**.
- **1 other rank (O. R.) was killed**
- **1 other rank (O. R.) was wounded.**

The War Diary of the Hood Battalion 63rd Division unfortunately does not list the casualties by name unless they were an Officer.

APRIL 9th

'A' Company of the 2nd Royal Marine Battalion relieved part of the Front-Line on the right held by 'C' Coy. 'A' Coy relieved 'C' Coy in the Front-Line positions. 'D' Coy moved into reserve. 'B' Coy moved into the support line and 'C' Coy moved into the cellars and shelters. 'Working Parties' were employed at night digging Front-Line systems and Communication Trenches and 'Wiring Parties' were also sent out to improve defences. Casualties were reported as:-

- **1 other rank (O. R.) was killed**
- **3 other ranks (O. R.) were wounded**

APRIL 10th

Wiring continued on the Front-Line and Communication Trenches. The Front-Line received spadmodic shell fire during the day. Casualties were reported as:-

- **3 other ranks (O. R.) were wounded**

APRIL 11th

'C' Coy relieved 'B' Coy in the Support Trench. 'B' Coy moved into cellars and shelters. The Front-Line and Support Trench were heavily shelled during the day. One Lewis gun post was completely wiped out during more enemy shelling at night. Casualties were reported as:-

- **7 other ranks (O. R.) wounded**
- **1 other rank (O. R.) missing** (blown to pieces – as reported in the War Diary for this day)

APRIL 12th

The day was reported as quiet except for aircraft activity. It was reported in the War Diary that one British aeroplane was seen to bring down a German aeroplane but then was chased by five German aeroplanes and brought down in flames. Another German aeroplane was brought down by Lewis gun fire and burst into flames. Casualties were reported as:-

- **1 other rank (O. R.) wounded**

APRIL 13th

The Battalion were relieved by Hawke Battalion and after digging on the Front-Line proceeded to cellars and shelters at Englebelmer, with 'C' Coy remaining in the trench in front of the village. Casualties were reported as:-

- **1 other rank (O. R.) killed**
- **5 other ranks (O. R.) wounded**

APRIL 14th

The Battalion remained in billets during the day. They were relieved by the 10th West Yorkshire Regiment in the evening and proceeded to Forceville by Coys. On arrival at Forceville, a distance of 6.8km (4 miles), they were billeted in houses and barns etc. Casualties were reported as:-

- **1 Officer wounded**

APRIL 15th & 16th

The Battalion left Forceville in the morning and marched to Toutencourt Wood a distance of 9.5km (just under 6 miles) where the whole Brigade were camped. Temporary Lieutenant J. C. Hilton M. C. joined the Battalion and resumed his duties as Adjutant. Rev. H. W. Chambers C. F. (Church of England) also joined as Chaplain.

Rev. H. W. Chamber

APRIL 18th

The Battalion carried out a practice occupation of the Vadencourt and Hedauville Lines in conjunction with other Battalions of the Brigade and the 63rd Divisional Machine Gun Battalion. The Battalion were in reserve but were called upon to reinforce the Front-Line.

APRIL 20th

The Battalion were employed to dig trenches on the Warloy-Hedauville Line. This took up most of the day.

APRIL 21st

Church Parade was held in the morning. During the afternoon the Battalion bathed at Toutencourt baths. The following Officers joined the Battalion for duty:-

- **Surgeon C. E. Leake R. N.**
- **Lieutenant & Quarter Master C. E. Jupp**

Surgeon C. E. Leake R. N.

APRIL 22nd

Training for the Battalion continued throughout the day. The following Officers joined the Battalion for duty: -

- Lieutenant H. T. Ely
- Sub Lieutenant T. I. C. Robson
- Sub Lieutenant C. P. Brown
- Sub Lieutenant W. L. Willison
- Sub Lieutenant W. Barbour
- Sub Lieutenant P. W. Dann
- Sub Lieutenant E. W. Holbert
- Sub Lieutenant F. M. Kirkhouse
- Sub Lieutenant F. J. Hill

- **Sub Lieutenant H. W. Hollingsworth**
- **Sub Lieutenant A. C. Currie**
- **Sub Lieutenant F. J. Willy**
- **Sub Lieutenant P. W. Weeks**
- **Sub Lieutenant J. W. Kerr**
- **Sub Lieutenant T. Dryden**

These Officers were brought in to replace the Battalion losses during March and early April during the German Offensive.

APRIL 24th

Two Coys were employed working on the Hedauville-Forceville Line. The Commander of the Battalion less Q. M. Stores, transport and 2nd Echelon moved to Bois Creftal by route march where they encamped with the other Battalions of the Brigade.

APRIL 26th

A 'Working Party' continued to work on the Hedauville-Forceville Line. The Commander of the Battalion was supervising the remaining Battalion's training schedule.

APRIL 27th

The Battalion continued training. Sub Lieutenant C. P. P. Dieterle joined the Battalion for duty.

APRIL 28th & 29th

The Battalion continued training.

APRIL 30th

The Battalion carried out a practice occupation of the Hedauville-Forceville Line in conjunction with the other Battalions of the Brigade. The Battalion was in reserve after practice was over. The Battalion then continued to work on the line.

MAY 1918

MAY 1st, 2nd & 3rd

The Battalion continued training. Sub Lieutenant A. S. Skipper and Sub Lieutenant J. W. E Dolman reported sick to hospital. Sub Lieutenant C. P. P. Dieterle transferred to Hawke Battalion.

MAY 5th, 6th & 7th

Training continued for the Battalion. Sub Lieutenant S. G. Luxton was sent on a Lewis Gun Course at Le Touquette.

MAY 8th

The Battalion moved off at 10.15am and relieved the 7th Battalion Lincolnshire Regiment.

MAY 9th

The Battalion in reserve, with 'B' Coy in road, provided a 'Working Party' of 3 Officers and 85 other ranks (O. R.) at night to work on the 'Purple Line'. Battle surplus of 107 other ranks (O. R.) moved off at 7.30am to Division Wing at Cramont.

MAY 10th

The Battalion supplied a 'Working Party' of 2 Officers and 100 other ranks (O. R.) from 'C' and 'D' Coys to bury cable lines during the day. At night 'B' Coy provided a party of 3 Officers and 85 other ranks (O. R.) to work on the 'Purple Line'. Reinforcements of 90 other ranks (O. R.) and the following Officers joined the Battalion for duty from Division Wing:-

- 2nd Lieutenant W. R. Rees – Royal Welsh Fusiliers
- 2nd Lieutenant D. J. Jones – Royal Welsh Fusiliers
- 2nd Lieutenant J. W. Ellis – Royal Welsh Fusiliers
- 2nd Lieutenant A. H. H. James – Royal Welsh Fusiliers

MAY 11th

The Battalion supplied a 'Working Party' of 6 Officers and 350 other ranks (O. R.) from 'A', 'C' and 'D' Coys to bury cable lines during the day. At night 'B' Coy provided a 'Working Party' of 3 Officers and 80 other ranks (O. R.) to work on the line.

Preparing to bury cables

MAY 12th

The Battalion supplied a 'Working Party' of 6 Officers and 350 other ranks (O. R.) to bury cable lines during the day. At night 'B' Coy provided a 'Working Party' of 3 Officers and 75 other ranks (O. R.) to work on the 'Purple Line'.

MAY 13th

The Battalion supplied a 'Working Party' of 6 Officers and 350 other ranks (O. R.) to continue to bury the miles and miles of communication cable that the Royal Engineers are laying during the day. At night 'B' Coy provided a 'Working Party' of 3 Officers and 75 other ranks (O. R.) to continue to work on the 'Purple Line'. Sub Lieutenant C. P. Brown proceeded to the UK on special Leave.

MAY 14th

The Battalion were relieved in the trenches by Drake Battalion and proceeded to the support line forward of Englebelmer and relieved the Hawke Battalion. 'D' Coy moved forward to the railway enbankment at Mesnil in support of the Hawke Battalion. Sub Lieutenant F. H. Kirkhouse proceeded to the UK on special leave.

MAY 15th

The Battalion were in support lines. A 'Working Party' of 10 Officers and 185 other ranks (O. R.) worked on widening and deepening the trenches forward of the support line. The Battalion suffered the following casualties:-

- 1 other rank (O. R.) killed
- 9 other ranks (O. R.) wounded

MAY 16th

The Battalion were in support lines. A 'Working Party' of 5 Officers and 209 other ranks (O. R.) continued working on the trenches forward of the support line at night.

MAY 17th & 18th

The Battalion were in support lines. A 'Working Party' of 6 Officers and 215 other ranks (O. R.) continued working on widening and deepening the trenches forward of the support line. The Battalion suffered the following casualties:-

- 3 other ranks (O. R.) wounded

MAY 19th

The Battalion were still in the support lines. A 'Working Party' of 6 Officers and 210 other ranks (O. R.) continued working on the trenches forward of the support line. The Battalion suffered the following casualties:-

- 3 other ranks (O. R.) wounded

MAY 20th

The Battalion were relieved by Drake Battalion and proceeded to the Front-Line and relieved the Hawke Battalion. 'C' Coy occupied the right front line with 'D' Coy occupying the left front. 'A' Coy were in support and 'B' Coy in reserve. Casualties were reported as:-

- **1 other rank (O. R.) wounded**

MAY 21st

The Battalion continued to hold the Front-Line. Lieutenant & Q. M. C. F. Wright R. M. reported for duty. Casualties were reported as:-

- **2 other ranks (O. R.) wounded**

MAY 22nd

The Battalion continued to hold the Front-Line. 20 other ranks (O. R.) and 4 Signallers joined the Battalion for duty from Divisional Wing. Casualties were reported as:-

- **1 other rank (O. R.) killed**
- **2 other ranks (O. R.) wounded**

MAY 23rd

The Battalion continued to hold the Front-Line. 'Working Parties' were digging and wiring at night. 10 other ranks (O. R.) joined the Battalion for duty. Casualties were reported as:-

- **5 other ranks (O. R.) wounded**

MAY 24th

A raid was planned for the night of the 24th and 25th of May. The 63rd Royal Naval Division (R. N. D.) working with the 12th Division on the left were to take prisoners and obtain papers and maps; and as a secondary task, as much damage as possible should be done to any enemy dugouts and shelters discovered during the raid. The Hoods 'A' Coy enjoyed complete success on the raid capturing two prisoners, but 'D' Coy came across some stiff opposition and suffered casualties. 'B' Coy, coming to the aid of 'D' Coy suffered a similar fate. The enemy posts found during the raid were ingeniously concealed and were sited only on the reverse slopes. Each post was covered by an overhanging tree surrounded by rusty old wire entangled in the grass, with a camouflaged path leading to a shelter dug in the bank. One was covered by two inch iron girders in a cone shape. The Battalion suffered a number of casualties during the raid. Lieutenant & Quarter Master G. T. Monk proceeded to Rouen for duty. Sub Lieutenant J. E. Webber R. N. V. R. joined the Battalion for duty.

MAY 25th

The Battalion's Front-Line positions were heavily shelled during the day and night. The Battalion were relieved by Drake Battalion in the Front-Line, but the Battalion had suffered the following casualties:-

- Sub Lieutenant E. W. L. R. Hulbert killed
- 5 other ranks (O. R.) killed
- 1 other rank (O. R.) died of wounds
- 2nd Lieutenant J. W. Ellis missing
- 2nd Lieutenant R. W. Dann missing
- Sub Lieutenant R. L. Stephenson missing
- 3 other ranks (O. R.) missing
- Sub Lieutenant P. W. Weekes wounded
- 2nd Lieutenant D. J. Jones wounded
- Lieutenant W. Wellwood wounded
- 71 other ranks (O. R.) wounded

Sub Lieutenant E. W. L. R. Hulbert

Sub Lieutenant R. L. Stephenson

MAY 26th

The Battalion were in Divisional reserve with 'A' Coy just forward of the reserve position. Sub Lieutenant E. G. C. Unwin reported to hospital sick.

MAY 27th

The Battalion were in Divisional reserve. The Battalion supplied a 'Working Party' of 3 Officers and 150 other ranks (O. R.) to bury communication cables. 'A' Coy supplied a 'Working Party' of 1 Officer and 71 other ranks (O. R.) to continue widening the trenches on the 'Purple Line' and 20 other ranks (O. R.) to carry out wiring work.

MAY 28th

The Battalion supplied a 'Working Party' of 3 Officers and 150 other ranks (O. R.) to bury communication cables. 'A' Coy supplied a 'Working Party' of 1 Officer and 55 other ranks (O. R.) to continue working on the 'Purple Line Trenches' and 1 Officer and 101 other ranks (O. R.) to carry out wiring duties. Owing to the enemy shelling, 'A' Coy's position was moved to the right sector. Training was carried out during the day for Lewis Gunners and Bombers. The following Officers reported to the Battalion for duty:-

- **Captain H. A. Christy Welsh Regiment**
- **Sub Lieutenant G. H. Munday R. N. V. R.**
- **Sub Lieutenant S. G. Luxton R. N. V. R.**

MAY 29th

The Battalion supplied a 'Working Party' of 3 Officers and 150 other ranks (O. R.) to bury communication cables. 'A' Coy supplied a 'Working Party' of 1 Officer and 30 other ranks (O. R.) to continue widening the 'Purple Line Trenches' and 31 other ranks (O. R.) to carry out wiring duties. Training continued for the Lewis Gun and Bombing Teams. The Battalion suffered the following casualties: -

- **3 other ranks (O. R.) gassed**
- **3 other ranks (O. R.) wounded**

Temporary Lieutenant Commander W. Arblaster proceeded to the UK on special leave. Lieutenant G. Maudsley reported for duty with the Battalion.

MAY 30th

The Battalion supplied a 'Working Party' of 3 Officers and 200 other ranks (O. R.) to bury communication cables. 'A' Coy supplied a 'Working Party' of 1 Officer and 78 other ranks (O. R.) to continue widening the 'Purple Line Trenches'. Training continued for the Lewis Gun and Bombing Teams. Sub Lieutenant E. T. C. Robinson reported sick to hospital.

MAY 31st

The Battalion moved forward and relieved the Hawke Battalion in the support lines. 'A' Coy moved forward to be in front of the support lines.

The following list of awards were announced for the actions on the 24th and 25th May 1918, to the following:-

- Able Seaman Ernest John Cook – Military Medal (M. M.)
- Able Seaman Albert John Perkins – Military Medal (M. M.)
- Able Seaman John Campbell – Military Medal (M. M.)
- Able Seaman Henry Mitchell – Military Medal (M. M.)
- Able Seaman Frederick Morris – Military Medal (M. M.)
- Leading Seaman James Galbraith – Military Medal (M. M.)
- Private Albert Edward Reece – Military Medal (M. M.)
- Chief Petty Officer William Blogg – Distinguished Conduct Medal (D. C. M.)
- Sub Lieutenant Thomas Irvine Carlyle Robinson – Military Cross (M. C.)

JUNE 1918

JUNE 1st

'B', 'C' and 'D' Coys in shelters. 'A' Coy forward in railway bank. The Battalion **'Stand To'** from 2am to 3am. At 3.25am the 35th Division on the Battalion's right carried out an attack, the objective being to capture and consolidate the South West corner of Aveluy Wood. The 63rd Divisional Artillery and 63rd Machine Gun Battalions carried out a feint bombardment in conjunction with the attack on the Battalion's right. The operation drew very little hostile enemy fire on the Battalion's support line. The Battalion suffered the following casualties: -

- 6 other ranks (O. R.) wounded (all from 'C' Coy)

The Battalions artillery continued to be active during the day.
'Working Parties' at night were organised. 2 Officers and 100 other ranks

(O. R.) from 'C' Coy were employed to dig and improve the trenches near Mesnil. 2 Officers and 85 other ranks (O. R.) from 'D' Coy were employed to wire the new reserve line near Mesnil Chateau. Casualties reported were:-
- **1 other rank (O. R.) wounded**
- **2 other ranks (O. R.) sick (trench fever)**

Sub Lieutenant T. L. Morton R. N. V. R. joined the Battalion for duty along with 25 other ranks (O. R.).

Trench Fever

Epidemic Typhus has always been the bane of Armies both in the field and barracks. 'Lice', which affected the body and head was rife in the trenches. It is estimated that up to 97% of Officers and men who served in the trenches were infected with lice. It was the cause of much discomfort to the troops who found it almost impossible to get rid of. Shaving their heads and moustaches off would largely control the head lice but the body lice, that hid in the folds, creases and pleats of their uniforms and that thrived in warm conditions which was provided by body heat and clothing which spread from person to person due to the close proximity of the soldiers who were huddled together to preserve a degree of warmth, were more difficult to eliminate. The prevalence of body lice did not cause an outbreak of Typhus (a disease known to be carried by lice) on the Western Front, however, body lice did cause another disease in the trenches that became known as 'Trench Fever'. This was closely related to Typhus and was transmitted by scratching the skin that then forced the infected faeces of the lice into the lesions made by the lice bites. The infected soldier did not show any signs or symptoms, anything from 1 week up to a month, but would suffer with a severe headache and develop debilitating muscle pains characteristically of the shins. At the time, there was no effective treatment for **'Trench Fever'** other than bedrest. As many as 80% of soldiers with the disease remaind unfit for duty for up to three months. Throughout the duration of the War, 800,000 cases of 'Trench Fever' were recorded in the British Army.

The Military Authorities tried numerous measures to try and control this disease and the prevention of it. Hot baths, clean laundry and frequent changes of clothing were tried but conditions in the Front-Line made this task very difficult. Soldiers themselves used to take matters into their own hands and a favourite way of killing the lice was to use a lighter or candle and run the flame along the seams and collars of their uniforms, as this would kill the lice and their eggs that had been laid. Lice reproduce with remarkable speed, each female could produce as many as a dozen eggs per day, which would hatch within a month. The fact that the soldiers would only be offered a full bath only two or three times a month merely exacerbated the issue.

Trench Fever in the Trenches

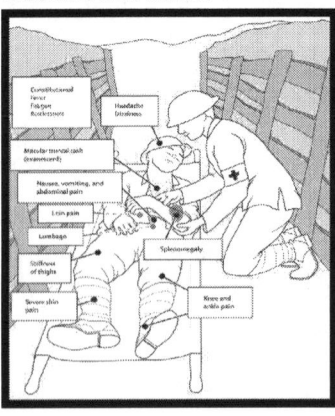

JUNE 2nd

At 1.50am the enemy artillery commenced a steady bombardment on the Battalions area using 'Blue Cross & Green Cross Gas Shells'.

- Blue Cross shells contained **Diphenyichloroarsine** which irritated the nasal passage and eyes.
- Green Cross shells contained **Chlorine** which attacks the lungs causing coughing and vomiting.

The majority of the shells fell on the Battalion's lines. The shelling lasted for over an hour but it was deemed neccessary for the men to keep their gas masks on until 3.30am. Luckily the Battalion suffered no casualties during the bombardment.

At 4.30am the Battalion was again shelled by the enemy using 'Blue Cross and Green Cross Gas Shells' and 'High Explosive Shells'. The bombardment lasted for half an hour. Casualties were reported as :-

- **1 other rank (O. R.) wounded**

Some of the men suffered discomfort to the eyes and nose but nothing serious. The Battalion sent out a 'Working Party' consisting of 10 Officers and 170 other ranks (O. R.) to the Mesnil area to continue work on the trench system. Casualties reported were:-

- **1 other rank (O. R.) wounded**
- **2 other ranks (O. R.) sick**

JUNE 3rd

The morning of 3rd June was quiet but in the afternoon at approximately 1.50pm the Battalion came under enemy artillery fire and the bombardment continued until 4.30pm. The Battalion calculated that they had received between 500 and 600 shells during that time. Casualties were reported as : -

- **2 other ranks (O. R.) killed**
- **6 other ranks (O. R.) wounded**

Once the shelling had stopped 'Working Parties' were sent out. 'B' Coy had 2 Officers and 70 other ranks (O. R.), 'C' Coy had 2 Officers and 100 other ranks and 'D' Coy had 1 Officer and 20 other ranks (O. R.) to work on digging near the reserve line near Mesnil, wiring the ridge around Mesnil Chateau and repairing two of the posts damaged in the artillery bombardment. The Battalion suffered the following casualties: -

- 2 other ranks (O. R.) killed
- 9 other ranks (O. R.) wounded
- 1 other rank (O. R.) sick

JUNE 4th

At 2.25am the enemy put down a heavy mortar and shell barrage to the left front of the Battalion which lasted about 45 minutes. During **'Stand To'** between 2.30am and 3.30am the Battalion received a gas attack which was carried by the wind. Gas helmets were worn until the gas had cleared. Company Commanders of the 10th Battalion South Wales Borderers arrived in the morning to see the positions they were to take over from the Battalion. All men in the Battalion had their feet washed and coated with **'Picric Acid'** which was used to treat **'Trench Foot'**. The Battalion was relieved in the trenches by the 10th Battalion South Wales Borderers. Casualties reported were: -

- 1 other (O. R.) rank wounded
- 6 other (O. R.) ranks sick

Trench Foot

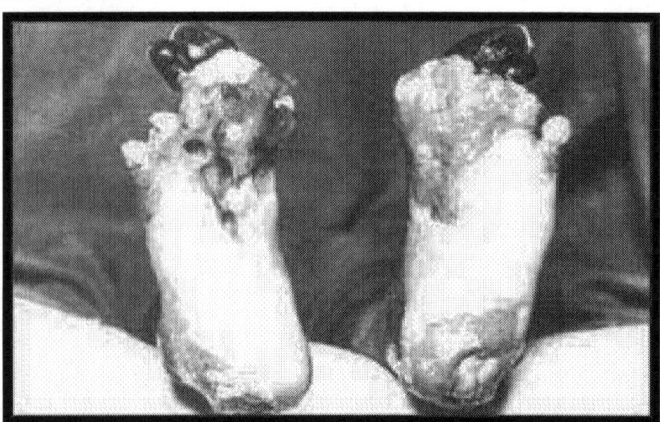

Once the trench lines were established in late 1914 and the first Winter of the War took hold, it quickly became apparent that the hastily dug out trenches were subject to flooding and were turning into quagmires of mud and water. The immobility of the soldiers in the trenches meant that they were forced to spend long hours, sometimes days, with their feet exposed to the wet and cold. Unfortunately, the British Army boot was made of leather and were not effectively waterproof. With no chance of drying out your feet or boots, or changes of socks, the circulation of blood to the feet became restricted and the affected feet became very painful. If these conditions continued, the skin on the foot would begin to breakdown. The feet became swollen, blisters formed and then eventually they became numb from nerve damage. Overtime the skin would become infected by fungus and if the situation wasn't resolved quickly by drying out the skin and circulation re-established, gangrene could ensue and in the worst cases, amputation became necessary. In 1914/1915 over 20,000 cases of 'Trench Foot' were recorded. To combat this later in the War, soldiers had frequent 'Foot Inspections' by the Medical Officer.

Trench Foot in the Trenches

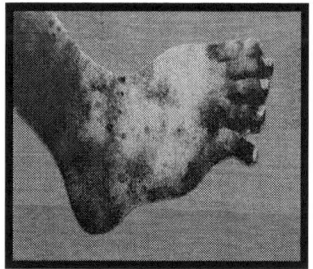

JUNE 5th

The Battalion marched to Rubempre a distance of 6.5km (4 miles) arriving at 9.25am and settled into billets. Hot baths and a change of uniforms were provided and the soldiers enjoyed a short time at rest. Sub Lieutenant Hall arrived for duty and was placed in charge of the Signallers. The following man was awarded the Military Medal (M. M.) for his actions of the 24th and 25th May:-

- **Leading Seaman J. G. Cowie CZ2047 – Military Medal (M. M.)**

Casualties were reported as:-

- **1 other rank (O. R.) reported sick**

Cigarettes and Pipes

Cigarettes, pipes and tobacco were an integral and essential part of Army life during the First World War. At the start of the War in 1914 smoking a pipe was more popular than a cigarette (fag), however, as the War progressed, the cigarette grew in popularity due to it's sheer practicality. If you consider the preperation required to smoke a pipe, pre rolled cigarettes were small and handy and easy to light in damp and muddy trench conditions. With advances in the manufacturing of cigarettes, mass production increased with the growing demands of the millions of men in uniform. Each Serviceman was provided with two oz's of tobacco per day but this allowance did not meet everyone's requirements, and cigarettes soon became a form of **'Trench Currency'**. These could be swapped for cake or souvenirs etc. Parcels from home usually contained tobacco to boost the Servicemans morale. There were many times during the War that there was a shortage of cigarettes caused by ever changing Front-Line positions and the supply chain trying to evolve and keep up with demand, especially in 1914. The favourite brand was 'Woodbines' but other names appeared on the market as 'White Cloud', 'Ruby Queen' and 'Red Hussar'. Many Tommies saved money by using ration tobacco and rizla cigarette papers to role their own. The other advantage of smoking cigarettes was that they masked the smell of death and decay and they kept the more nervous men calm. The soldiers were encouraged to smoke so that it would distract them from what they were facing everyday. Cigarettes were given to wounded and dying soldiers.

Cigarettes, Pipes and Tobacco in the Trenches

JUNE 6th

The Battalion were at rest in billets. Sub Lieutenant Kirkhouse and 125 other ranks (O. R.) joined the Battalion for duty. Casualties reported were: -

- **4 other ranks (O. R.) reported sick**

JUNE 7th

The Battalion commenced training. All rifles and Lewis guns were inspected by the Divisional Commander and were found to be in a satisfactory condition. A 'Working Party' of 80 other ranks (O. R.) worked on transport lines and building bomb protection walls. Casualties reported were: -

- **6 other ranks (O. R.) reported sick (trench fever)**

JUNE 8th

The Battalion continued training. Lewis Gunners were practicing on the firing range. A 'Working Party' of 80 other ranks (O. R.) continued to work on the transport lines. 80 other ranks (O. R.) with 2 Limbers (a two-wheeled cart designed to support the trail of an artillery piece) were at the town Mayors disposal for work. Casualties reported were:-

- **6 other ranks (O. R.) reported sick**

JUNE 9th

There was no training for the Battalion today. After Church Parade the Battalion was inspected by the Brigadier General. A 'Working Party' of 1 Officer and 60 other ranks (O. R.) worked on the Brigade ranges. Casualties reported were:-

- **3 other ranks (O. R.) reported sick**

JUNE 10th

The Battalion continued training. 'A' Coy practiced as the platoon in attack position training was observed by the Divisional General and the Brigadier General. Major James R. A. F. gave a lecture to the Officers and

N. C. O.'s of the Brigade on the benefits of cooperation between the Infantry and Aircraft. Casualties reported were:-

- **2 other ranks (O. R.) reported sick**

The men in sick camp now amounted to a total of 1 Officer and 39 other ranks (O. R.) all suffering from 'Trench Fever'.

JUNE 11th

The Battalion continued training. 1 Officer and 20 other ranks (O. R.) attended a 'Bayonet Fighting Course' in the afternoon. 2 other ranks (O. R.) joined the Battalion for duty. Orders were received informing the Battalion that the 63rd Royal Naval Division (R. N. D.) had been placed on General Head Quarter reserve (G. H. Q.) and must be prepared to move at 1 hours notice from 6am to 10am daily and at 3 hours notice for the remainder of the day. Casualties reported were:-

- **2 other ranks (O. R.) reported sick**

The following men were awarded the D. C. M. in the King's Birthday Honours:-

- **Able Seaman T. Coombe R. N. V. R. T2-3755 – Distinguished Service Medal**
- **Petty Officer H. S. Swallow R. N. V. R. KP-365 - Distinguished Service Medal**

JUNE 13th

The Battalion was inspected by the Brigadier General. 'Lewis Gun Training' was carried out in the afternoon. A Brigade football competition was also held with the Hood Battalion beating the Drake Battalion 4-1. Casualties reported were: -

- **4 Officers & 101 other ranks (O. R.) reported sick in the morning with fevers**

JUNE 14th

The Battalion trained in the morning and in the afternoon a 'Sports Day' was held for the 189th Brigade. The Hood Battalion had 8 first prizes, 6 second prizes and 1 third prize. The Brigadier General presented the prizes. An order was received from the Divisional Head Quarters informing the Battalion that the 12th Division will relieve the 35th Division in the Aveluy sector on the 16th, 17th and 18th of June. From the commencement of the relief, the 63rd Royal Naval Division (R. N. D.) will be transferred to the XXII Corps and the 35th Division will replace the 63rd R. N. D. in the G. H. Q. reserve. The 63rd R. N. D. will remain in their present locations and will be prepared in case of a hostile attack on the V Corps front to act as right supporting Division. Casualties reported were:-

- 4 Officers & 101 other ranks (O. R.) reported sick

JUNE 15th

The Battalion continued training. 'C' Coy were on the rifle range in the morning with 'D' Coy on the rifle range in the afternoon. 2 Limbers and a 'Working Party' of 20 other ranks (O. R.) were supplied to the town Mayor for 'Sanitary Duties'. In the Brigade football competition the Hood Battalion beat the Hawke Battalion 3-0 to win the cup. Sub Lieutenant C. P. Brown and 29 other ranks (O. R.) joined the Battalion for duty.

Two men from the Battalion, *Able Seaman High Grade G. Ratcliffe and Able Seaman H. Staniland* were tried by Field General Court Martial (F. G. C. M.) for deserting His Majesty's Service. Lieutenant Commander S. H. Fish M. C. R. N. V. R. was the President of the court.

Lieutenant Commander S. H. Fish M.C. R.N.V.R.

Able Seaman High Grade **George Ratcliffe** was born 11th March 1892. He was 5'2" tall with ginger hair and lived in Doncaster. George, a former Miner joined up on the 16th April 1915 joining the 3rd Battalion Royal Naval Depot.

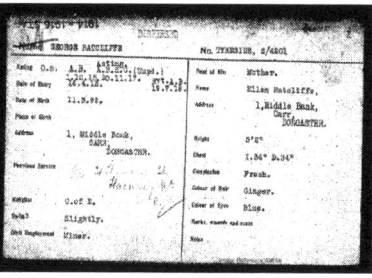

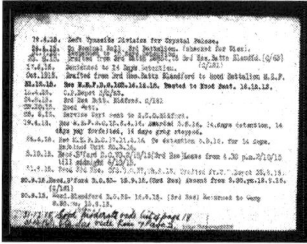

It was not long before George was in trouble. On the 17th June 1915 he was sentenced to 14 days detention then a month later on 31st July 1915 he was sentenced to 10 days detention. In August 1915 he was transferred to the 3rd Reserve Battalion Blandford and in October of the same year transferred to the Hood Battalion 63rd Royal Naval Division (R. N. D.). George's behaviour did not improve.

On the 5th March 1916 he was given 14 days detention, 14 days pay forfeited and 14 days grog (rum ration) stopped. George served on the Western Front with the Hood Battalion and he had two spells in hospital suffering from Pyrrohoea, a disease of the teeth and gums.

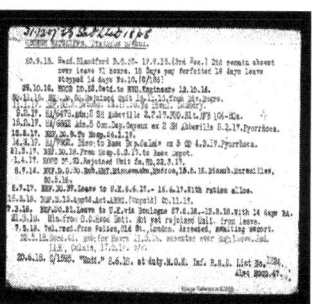

Georges troubles continued when he was granted leave to the UK on the 7th March 1918 for 14 days because he never returned and was arrested on the 7th May 1918 and held at a Police Station in Old Street London awaiting escort. George was charged with **'Desertion on Active Service'**. This was a very serious charge which could mean being sentenced to death. George was found **'Guilty'** and was sentenced to 5 years in prison by Field General Court Martial (F. G. C. M.).

This sentence was later commuted to 1 year hard labour and confirmed by Brigadier General H. De Pree 189th Infantry Brigade on the 15th July 1918. **(Photograph on the left)**

George was sent to No. 3 Military Prison in Le Havre to serve his sentence. On the 13th April 1919 George was returned to the UK and demobbed from the Navy and was not eligible for War Gratuity. George died in 1948 aged 56.

Able Seaman **Herbert Staniland** Was born in Sheffield on 13th November 1895 although, when he joined up on 8th September 1914, his date of birth was stated as 13th November 1894. He was 5'3 ½" tall and had fair hair. He joined the Hawke Battalion.

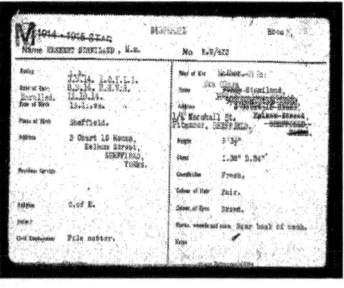

Herbert spent some time in hospital in Malta whilst serving with his Battalion as part of the Mediterranian Expeditionary Force suffering from Dysentry. He transferred to the Drake Battalion in August 1916.

Herbert was declared a deserter in November 1916 when he never returned from leave. He was sentenced to 35 days detention. On the 2nd January 1917 Herbert was transferred to the Howe Battalion serving on the Western Front. Herbert was admitted to hospital on 24th April 1917 suffering from **'Shell Shock'**. He rejoined his unit only a few days later. On the 5th March 1918 after the reorganisation of the Battalions on the Western Front, Herbert joined the 7th Entrenching Battalion, later being transferred to the Hood Battalion in April 1918. Herbert was charged with **'Desertion on Active Service'** when he failed to return from leave, remaining absent for just over a month. Herbert was found **'Not Guilty'** of desertion but **'Guilty of Absence Without Leave'** and was sentenced to 90 Field punishment No. 1 which was reduced to 30 days with a loss of 36 days pay, by Brigadier General H. De Pree.

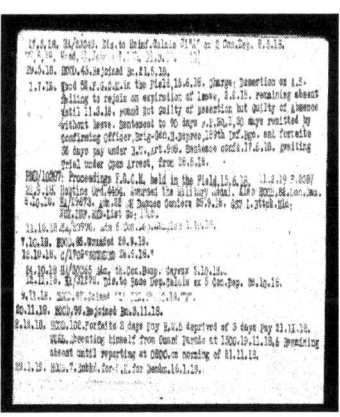
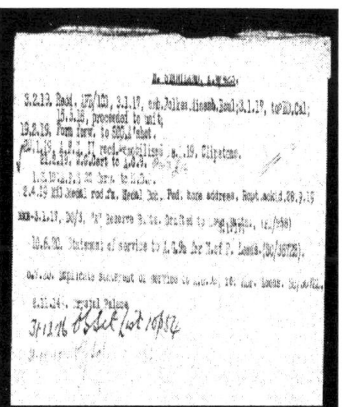

Field Punishment was introduced into the British Army in 1881 following the abolition of flogging. Field Punishment No. 1 nicknamed **'Crucifixion'** by the soldiers entailed labour duties and attachments to a fixed object, such as a post or wheel for two hours a day. Soldiers viewed Field Punishment No. 1 as particularly degrading, rendered immobile by their restraints, soldiers could not move or scratch against irritants such as fleas or lice.

Herbert returned to duty after serving his sentence and was awarded the Military Medal for his actions on the 21st August 1918. Herbert was wounded just seven days later. Herbert was demobbed on 16th January 1919 and returned home to his Wife Clara whom he had married in 1916. Herbert died in 1961 aged 65.

JUNE 16th

A conference was held at Brigade Head Quarters for all of the Battalion Commanders by the Corps Commander of XXII. Lieutenant and Quarter Master C. F. Wright was sent on a three day cooking course. Enemy aircraft carried out a bombing raid on Harrisart at night and caused several casualties to the men and animals of the 63rd Division. Casualties reported as: -

- **7 other ranks (O. R.) reported sick**

JUNE 17th

A Battalion training scheme was carried out. Three Coys practiced fighting a rear guard action, 'B' Coy acted as the enemy. The Battalion received four more Lewis guns making 36 in total, making it eight per Coy and four for anti aircraft duty which are attached to Battalion Head Quarters. Sub Lieutenant Kerr was appointed Battalion Education Officer. 300 other ranks (O. R.) attended a concert in the village in the evening. Casualties reported were:-

- **2 other ranks (O. R.) reported sick**

JUNE 18th

The Battalion continued it's training which included 'Bayonet Fighting' and 'Field Firing Practice'. A lecture was given to all Officers on the best usage of a Lewis gun. A 'Working Party' of 100 other ranks (O. R.) were working on bomb protection defences for the horses of the Division at the transport lines. 70 other (O. R.) ranks joined the Battalion for duty. Casualties reported were:-

- **2nd Lieutenant M. Jones reported sick**
- **4 other ranks (O. R.) reported sick**

JUNE 19th

An armoured car, which had seen action on the French held front about a week ago, visited the different Battalions of the Brigade. Two untrained Lewis Gun Teams spent time in the afternoon receiving instructions in the use of the equipment. Casualties reported were:-

- **2 other ranks wounded (O. R.) accidentally at Lewis Gun Instruction**
- **7 other ranks (O. R.) reported sick**

JUNE 20th

Training continued for the Battalion. One other rank (O. R.) arrived for duty with the Battalion. Casualties reported were:-

- **11 other ranks (O. R.) reported sick**

JUNE 21st

The Commanding Officer and the Company Commanders visited the new sector of the Front-Line which the Battalion is taking over on the night of the 23rd – 24th from 50th Infantry Brigade. The sector is between Hamel and Auchonvillers. The Corps Commander General Sir C. Shute inspected all the Brigade transport.

General Sir C. Shute

5 other ranks (O. R.) joined the Battalion for duty. The Battalion's Sergeant Major Kirkbride was awarded the Meritorious Service Medal. Casualties reported were: -

- **16 other ranks (O. R.) reported sick**

JUNE 22nd

The Battalion paraded at 10am. 'Advance Parties' left at 11am and proceeded by lorry to Acheux and then onto the Front-Line in the Mailly Mailet sector. The rest of the Battalion had baths and clean clothes. Casualties were reported as: -

- **45 other ranks (O. R.) reported sick**

JUNE 23rd

The Battalion marched to Herissart by road then across country to Acheux via Lealvillers arriving at 10.30am. The Battalion were followed by the Drake and Hawke Battalions. The whole Brigade rested in Acheux Wood for the rest of the day. At 9pm the Hood Battalion left Acheux Wood via a cross country track to the Front-Line (Mailly Mailet sector) and relieved the 10th Battalion West Yorkshire Regiment 17th Division.
The Battalions 'A', 'C' and 'D' Coys held the Front-Line Trenches with 'B' Coy in support. The Drake Battalion were also in support with the Hawke

Battalion in reserve. The 7th Battalion Royal Fusiliers were to the left of the Battalion (190th Infantry Brigade) Auchonvillers sector. 48 other ranks (O. R.) left for Divisional reception camp as battle surplus personnel. Sub Lieutenant T. A. Moon and 7 other ranks (O. R.) proceeded to the 3rd Army rest camp for four days rest. Lieutenant G. R. Bassett left for the UK for 14 days leave. Casualties reported were:-

- **Lieutenant G. Mansley reported sick**
- **9 other ranks (O. R.) reported sick**

JUNE 24th

The night of the 23rd was quiet on the Front-Line except for a few gas shells. The Commanding Officer (C. O.) and the Brigadier went around all of the Battalion's Front-Lines early in the morning of the 24th. The enemy artillery was quiet throughout the day. The 2nd Battalion Royal Welsh Fusiliers were holding the right sector next to the Hood Battalion. The Battalion worked on improving the trenches during the day and night, improving the firsteps and the draining system in the trench. Six other ranks (O. R.) returned from Army rest camp. Casualties reported were: -

- **4 other ranks (O. R.) reported sick**

JUNE 25th

The Divisional General visited part of the Battalion's Front-Line in the early morning. At 1.40pm the enemy launched a heavy bombardment with trench mortars and 4.2's on the Battalion sector lasting for half an hour. 'A' Coy worked on improving the trenches whilst 'B', 'C' and 'D' Coys worked on wiring posts. Sub Lieutenant A. Brackenridge returned from a course and reported for duty. Casualties were: -

- **2 other ranks (O. R.) reported wounded**
- **5 other ranks (O. R.) reported sick**

JUNE 26th

The enemy artillery was quiet for most of the day except for several short bursts. In the afternoon on Eaton and Reading Trenches work continued to improve the trenches. The 1st/28th London Regiment (Artist Rifles) relieved the 7th Battalion Royal Fusiliers on the Battalions left. Casualties were reported as: -

- 1 other rank (O. R.) wounded
- 10 other ranks (O. R.) reported sick

JUNE 27th

The enemy artillery was quiet for most of the day again, except for several short bursts aimed at the Battalion's Trench Mortar position (T. M.). Sub Lieutenant Kirkhouse left to attend a 'Gas Course' and was replaced by Sub Lieutenant A. Brackenridge in the Front-Line. Casualties reported were: -

- 1 other rank (O. R.) killed
- 3 other ranks (O. R.) wounded
- 2 Officers reported sick – Sub Lieutenant C. P. Brown & A. H. H. James
- 21 other ranks (O. R.) reported sick, all with symptoms of influenza

JUNE 28th

The Battalion continued to occupy the Front-Line Trenches. It was reported that aeroplanes from both sides were very active over the Front-Line. Two British planes were brought down over enemy lines by very heavy hostile anti aircraft fire. The 1st/28th London Regiment (Artist Rifles) were relieved on the Battalion's left sector by the 4th Battalion the Bedfordshire Regiment. The Drake Coy Commanders came up to the Front-Line to look around the sector prior to taking over from the Hood Battalion. Lieutenant Gibson left to attend a 'Lewis Gun Course' at Third Army Head Quarters. The Battalion received the following casualties: -

- 2 other ranks (O. R.) killed
- 2 other ranks (O. R.) wounded
- 9 other ranks (O. R.) reported sick

JUNE 29th

At 2.15am a special Coy of the Royal Engineers (R. E.) projected 1000 drums of gas onto the enemy Front-Lines near and on 'Y Ravine'.

In conjunction with this the Divisional artillery and Corps heavy artillery carried out a gas bombardment of the area in front of the Battalion's line. The enemy retaliated with a light barrage on the Battalion's Front-Line. An enemy patrol later in the evening threw stick bombs into the Battalion's Front-Line wounding two men. The Commanding Officer (C. O.) went to Brigade Head Quarters to act as Brigadier, covering the temporary absence of General De Pree. 'Advance Parties' from each Coy proceeded to the 'Purple Line (reserve) Trench' to take over from Hawke Battalion. Drake Battalion's 'Advanced Party' came up the line to take over from the Hood Battalion. Casualties reported were: -

- 1 other rank (O. R.) killed
- 5 other ranks (O. R.) wounded
- 12 other ranks (O. R.) reported sick

JUNE 30th

The Battalion were relieved in the Front-Line Trenches by the Drake Battalion. The Battalion proceeded to the reserve line (Purple Line) East of Mailly Maillet. Each Coy were given a particular area to defend in case of an enemy attack. 'A' and 'D' Coys supplied 'Working Parties' to the Front-Line system in the evening. Casualties reported were: -

- 6 other ranks (O. R.) reported sick

A total of 328 Officers and other ranks (O. R.) from the Battalion reported sick during the month of June 1918. First thought to be **'Trench Fever'**, but later was found to be **'Influenza'**. Even though it was quite common to have a common cold or flu during the War, a much more deadly virus popularly known as **'Spanish Flu'** started rearing it's ugly head in March 1918, with the main pandemic gathering pace from August 1918. The disease continued into 1919 and finally came to an end, almost as abruptly as it started, in 1920. Both sides of the conflict were equally effected. The numbers of people worldwide who caught the flu is unknown but between 50 to 100 million deaths worldwide from the virus were reported during that time.

The deadly virus seemed to have been more prevalent in the young fit and healthy members of the community rather than the old and weak. It was a most virulent outbreak and often resulted in massive haemorrhaging in the lungs, resulting in the victims literally drowning in their own blood.

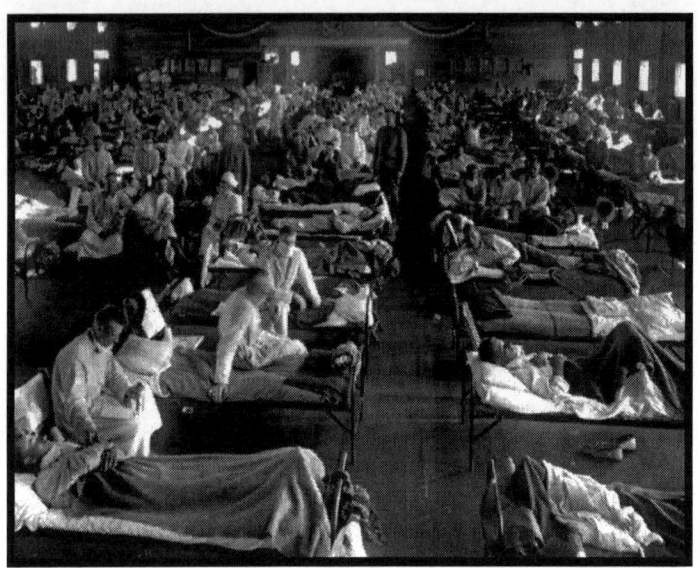

JULY 1918

JULY 1st

The Battalion were in reserve. 'B' Coy bathed at Acheux in the morning and 'A' Coy bathed in the afternoon. 'Working Parties' consisting of two Coys continued to work in the forward area. Casualties reported were: -

- **3 other ranks (O. R.) reported sick**

JULY 2nd

A 'Working Party' of two N. C. O.'s and 30 other ranks (O. R.) reported to Brigade Head Quarters for work in the morning and continued until 4pm.

1 ½ Coys continued digging trenches in the Front-Line areas and two platoons were used to carry wiring materials up to the Front-Line. Sub Lieutenant J. W. Kerr was temporarily attached to 189th Brigade Head Quarters as 'Intelligence Offier'. Casualties reported were: -

- **11 other ranks (O. R.) reported sick**

JULY 3rd

The Battalion were still in reserve. The Commanding Officer (C. O.) reported to Brigade Head Quarters to act as Brigadier. Lieutenant H. T. Ely proceeded to Le Touquat for a Lewis Gun Course. 'Working Parties' continued working in the Front-Line area. Casualties reported were: -

- **5 other ranks (O. R.) reported sick**

JULY 4th

42 other ranks (O. R.) joined the Battalion for duty from Divisional reception camp. 'Working Parties' continued to work in the Front-Line area, but work stopped at 11.45pm due to a raid carried out by the 7th Battalion Royal Fusiliers who were on the Battalion's left. The rest of the Battalion were still in reserve. Casualties reported were: -

- **6 other ranks (O. R.) reported sick**

JULY 5th

Two Officers and 52 other ranks (O. R.) of the 7th Battalion Royal Fusiliers had carried out a very successful raid on three enemy posts. Four prisoners of the 68th Reserve Infantry Regiment (R. I. R.) of the 16th Reserve Division were captured and many others were killed.
The identification of these prisoners confirmed that the 16th Reserve Division had taken over from the 21st Reserve Division. 'Advanced Parties' from the Hood Battalion proceeded up to the support lines to take over from Hawke Battalion. 'Advanced Parties' from the Drake Battalion came down to the reserve line to take over from the Battalion. The rest of the Battalion moved off from the reserve lines at 9am and relieved the Hawke Battalion in support. The relief was completed by 11.10pm.

The Hawke Battalion relieved the Drake Battalion in the Front-Line. Sub Lieutenant F. H. Kirkhouse returned to the Battalion for duty from the 'Gas Course'. Casualties reported were: -

- **1 other rank (O. R.) reported sick**

JULY 6th

The Battalion were in the support line. Three platoons per Coy were working on digging fire bays in Bovet Trench and wiring in front of the trench. 2nd Lieutenant Russell Rees and 22 other ranks (O. R.) reported for duty with the Battalion. Casualties reported were: -

- **1 other rank (O. R.) reported sick**

JULY 7th

The enemy artillery was more active on this day especially around the Battalion Head Quarters. Word was received that the Germans are expected to attack the Front-Line between Amiens and Arras between the 10th and 21st July, their objective being Abbeville. The information was received from the interrogation of the prisoner captured by the 7th Battalion Royal Fusiliers on the 5th July. The 'Working Parties' continued during the night, deepening Bovet Trench and making bombing blocks. Casualties reported were: -

- **4 other ranks (O. R.) reported sick**

JULY 8th

The Battalion were still in the support lines. 'Working Parties' continued during the night. 50 other ranks (O. R.) joined the Battalion for duty but remained in the transport lines until the next day. Casualties reported were: -

- **5 other ranks (O. R.) reported sick**

JULY 9th

At 7.15pm an enemy aeroplane dived out of the clouds and brought down one of the observation balloons, which burst into flames. The enemy aeroplane, flying extremely low, then attacked the Front and Support Line Trenches. It was heavily fired upon by the 'Lewis Gun Teams' and rifle fire from the men, but was not brought down. At 8pm three enemy aeroplanes attacked a British aeroplane and brought it down near Grandcourt. 22 other ranks (O. R.) joined the Battalion for duty. Casualties reported were: -

- **1 other rank (O. R.) reported sick**

Observation Balloons

The Royal Naval Air Service, The Royal Flying Corps and later The Royal Air Force deployed large numbers of fixed kite balloons for observation over enemy lines. They were usually either the **'Drachen'** or the **'French Caquot'** types. Beneath each canopy was slung a wickerwork basket that held two observers, typically an Officer and an N. C. O., although defended by anti aircraft guns sited on the ground. Most often, the observers went aloft unarmed, in the hope that the enemy aircraft would only shoot at the balloon and not at its crew. The balloons were tethered to a tender lorry by a cable that was unwound to allow the balloon to ascend to 6000 feet altitude. It could be rapidly rewound on a drum mechanism if attacked. Communication with the ground was by telephone along a separate cable.

JULY 10th

The Battalion were still in the support lines. Another observation balloon was brought down by enemy aeroplane. 'Advance Parties' from the Battalion moved up to the Front-Line to take over the position from Hawke Battalion. Sub Lieutenant Moon rejoined the Battalion for duty from rest camp.

JULY 11th

At 6.30pm the Battalion moved up to the Front-Line to relieve Hawke Battalion. The Drake Battalion took over the support lines from the Battalion, which was completed by 7.50pm. The relief of the Hawke Battalion was completed by 9.50pm. Due to heavy rain, all the trenches were in a bad condition and in some places, it was reported that water was knee deep. At 11pm the 115th Infantry Brigade on the Battalion's right carried out a trench raid on Hamel sector. 19 prisoners of the 11th/29th Reserve Infantry Regiment (R. I. R.) were captured along with 1 Machine Gun. Several of the enemy dugouts were blown up. Casualties reported were: -

- **2 other ranks (O. R.) reported sick**

JULY 12th

The enemy artillery consisting of trench mortars and high explosive shells fired on the Battalions Front-Line positions early in the morning. The barrage lasted 45 minutes and a certain amount of damage was done to the trenches at night. A trench raid was carried out by Drake Battalion which again proved very successful. 22 prisoners from the 29th R. I. R. were taken. 30 other ranks (O. R.) joined the Battalion for duty. The Battalion suffered the following casualties:-

- **4 other ranks (O. R.) reported sick**
- **3 other ranks (O. R.) wounded**

JULY 13th

The Battalion were holding the Front-Line Trenches. At 2.30am a German soldier of the 29th R. I. R. 16th Reserve Division surrendered to one of the

Battalion's posts. He complained of suffereing from gas poisoning. He was sent down to Brigade Head Quarters for interrogation but was admitted to an **'Advance Dressing Station'** (A. D. S.) where he died shortly afterwards. His gas mask was of poor quality. Over 600 gas drums were successfully projected by a special Coy Royal Engineers earlier in the morning. Ground observations reported seeing many motor and horse drawn ambulances on the roads near the German lines. At 8.45pm an enemy aeroplane flew over the Battalions Front-Line and dropped a bomb, whilst this was happening, another enemy aeroplane attacked two observation balloons and despite receiving heavy fire from the Battalions machine guns and anti aircraft batteries, the two observation balloons were brought down in flames. Sub Lieutenant Struthers and Sub Lieutenant Hollinsworth and 30 other ranks (O. R.) joined the Battalion for duty. Lieutenant H. T. Ely returned for duty from the Lewis Gun Course. The 2nd Battalion Royal Irish Regiment relieved the Royal Marine Battalion on the Battalions left sector during the night. The Battalion suffered the following casualties:-

- 2 other ranks (O. R.) reported sick
- 2 other ranks (O. R.) wounded

JULY 14th

The Battalion were in the Front-Line Trenches. Enemy artillery increased during the day with whiz bangs and 4.2's. A **'Whiz Bang'** was a light shell fired from one of the smaller calibre field guns referring to the sound the shell made when it came to explode. Three enemy Battalions were seen opposite the Battalion's Front-Line Trenches and they were attacked by British aeroplanes and were forced to retire. 'Working Parties' continued during the night wiring in the forward positions. Sub Lieutenant Hollingsworth joined 'C' Coy in the line. The Battalion suffered the following casualties:-

- 5 other ranks (O. R.) reported sick

JULY 15th

Between 2am and 3am the Battalions Front-Line positions was heavily shelled with 4.2's and **'Yellow Cross Gas Shells'** (Mustard Gas). The shelling was then followed by a 10 minute bombardment with light shells (percussion shrapnel). The shelling continued in 10 minute spells for most of the day. The French sector was attacked in the morning after suffering a hostile bombardment between the Chateau Thierry and Main De Massi area. The French repelled the attack. The Battalion suffered the following casualties:-

- **3 other ranks (O. R.) reported sick**
- **7 other ranks (O. R.) wounded (gas)**

JULY 16th

The Battalion was still in the Front-Line Trenches. The enemy artillery was very active during the day, again using gas shells. The Battalion suffered the following casualties:-

- **5 other ranks (O. R.) reported sick**
- **2 other ranks (O. R.) wounded (gas)**
- **1 other rank (O. R.) wounded**

JULY 17th

The Battalion was relieved in the Front-Line Trenches by Drake Battalion and took over from the Hawke Battalion in reserve at Mailey Maillet. The Battalion suffered the following casualties:-

- **1 Officer Sub Lieutenant John Andrew Mathison reported sick**
- **3 other ranks (O. R.) reported sick**

JULY 18th

5 platoons were used for 'Working Parties'. 'C' Coy went to have baths at Acheux. The rest of the Battalion were in reserve. The Battalion suffered the following casualties:-

- **1 other rank (O. R.) reported sick**

JULY 19th

The Battalion were in reserve. 4 platoons were used for 'Working Parties'. The Battalion suffered the following casualties:-

- **2 other ranks (O. R.) reported sick**

JULY 20th

The Battalion were in reserve. 6 platoons were used for 'Working Parties'. The Commanding Officer (C. O.) and Adjutant left on leave in the local area. The Battalion suffered the following casualties:-

- **2 other ranks (O. R.) reported sick**

JULY 21st

The Battalion were in reserve. 'Lewis Gun Training' was carried out in the afternoon. The Battalion suffered the following casualties:-

- **1 other rank (O. R.) reported sick**

JULY 22nd

The Battalion were in reserve. The enemy artillery fired gas shells close to the Battalions Head Quarters. The Battalion suffered the following casualties:-

- **2 other ranks (O. R.) reported sick**
- **1 other rank (O. R.) wounded**

JULY 23rd & 24th

The Battalion were in reserve. The Battalion suffered the following casualties:-

- **1 other rank (O. R.) reported sick**

JULY 25th

The Battalion was relieved by the 9th Battalion Kings Own Yorkshire Light Infantry (K. O. Y. L. L.) and marched to Acheau. The Battalion left Acheau at 7.30pm and marched to Puchevillers a distance of about 11.1km (7 miles) arriving at 10pm and took over the 'Prisoner of War Cage' at Puchvillers. The Battalion suffered the following casualties:-

- **2 other ranks (O. R.) reported sick**

JULY 26th

The Battalion were at rest and spent the day cleaning up. Sub Lieutenant Unwin and Lieutenant Flowers R. M. and 137 other ranks (O. R.) joined the Battalion for duty.

JULY 27th

The Battalion began training. The Battalion suffered the following casualties:-

- 2 other ranks (O. R.) reported self inflicted wounds (A. S. I. W.)
- 1 other rank (O. R.) reported sick

JULY 28th

A Church Parade was held in the morning on the Drake training ground. Orders were received for the Battalion to move to Vauchelles. The Battalion sent out 'Advance Parties' to Vauchelles a distance of 9.9km (6 miles). The Battalion suffered the following casualties:-

- 2 other ranks (O. R.) reported sick

JULY 29th

The rest of the Battalion left for Vauchelles at 2.20pm arriving at 4.15pm. The 63rd Battalion transferred from the V Corps to IV Corps. The Battalion suffered the following casualties:-

- 6 other ranks (O. R.) reported sick

JULY 30th

The Battalion continued training. 'A' and 'B' Coys were on the rifle range, 'C' and 'D' Coys provided 'Working Parties' of 100 other ranks (O. R.), each to the Royal Engineers. The Commanding Officer (C. O.) returned from leave.

JULY 31st

The Battalion continued training. The Battalion suffered the following casualties:-

- 2 other ranks (O. R.) accidentally wounded
- 1 other rank (O. R.) reported sick

AUGUST 1918

AUGUST 1st

The Battalion took part in Divisional practice of taking up assembley positions in the event of an enemy attack on the Corps Front-Line and also occupying the Red Line. 18 other ranks (O. R.) and the following Officers joined the Battalion for duty:-

- Sub Lieutenant Robert Harold Brewer
- Sub Lieutenant George Simpson
- Sub Lieutenant John William Moncur
- Sub Lieutenant Edward Charlton Barras
- Sub Lieutenant Lawrence Jackson
- Sub Lieutenant Harry Carr

AUGUST 2nd & 3rd

The Battalion continued training. Lieutenant Flower left the Battalion to join the Royal Marine Battalion. The Battalion suffered the following casualties:-

- **6 other ranks (O. R.) reported sick**

AUGUST 4th

Church Service was held in the morning and an 'Advance Party' was sent to Beauquesne. The remaining Battalion left Vauchelles at 10.30pm and marched to Beauquesne a distance of 9.2 km (5 ½ miles). The Battalion suffered the following casualties:-

- **4 other ranks (O. R.) reported sick**

AUGUST 5th & 6th

The Battalion continued training. 6 other ranks (O. R.) left for rest camp and 6 other ranks (O. R.) returned from rest camp. Sub Lieutenant William Ernest Bach was posted from Hawke Battalion to Hood Battalion. The Battalion suffered the following casualties:-

- **3 other ranks (O. R.) reported sick**

AUGUST 7th

The Battalion continued training. There was a shorthand class which was held at Battalion Head Quarters. 11 other ranks attended the course. The Battalion suffered the following casualties:-

- 1 other rank (O. R.) reported sick

AUGUST 8th

'Box Respirators' for the Officers and men were tested in the gas chamber. The billet at 14 Rue St. Antoine had to be evacuated by two platoons of 'B' Coy owing to 4 other ranks (O. R.) contacting **'Septic Pharyngitis'**, a contagious disease, also known as **'Strep Throat'**. An infection of the membranes of the oropharynx (back of the throat), common symptoms include fever, sore throat and enlarge lymph nodes in the front of the neck and a headache. Vomiting may also occur. It is spread by respiratory droplets from the infected person, spread by talking, coughing or sneezing. Symptoms last for about 7 to 10 days, some develop a sandpaper like rash, which is known as **'Scarlet Fever'**. The Battalion moved off at 6pm and marched to Bethencourt, a distance of 18.2km (11 ½ miles). The Battalion spent the night in the open. The Battalion suffered the following casualties:-

- 4 other ranks (O. R.) reported sick

AUGUST 9th

The Battalion moved into billets in the village of Bethencourt. 6 Officers and 107 other ranks (O. R.) left the Battalion as **'Battle Surplus'**. The Battalion suffered the following casualties:-

- 4 other ranks (O. R.) reported sick

AUGUST 10th

The Battalions Company Commander (C. O.) and Coy Commanders reconnoitered assemby positions for the practice attack. The Battalion suffered the following casualties:-

- 7 other ranks (O. R.) reported sick

AUGUST 11th

A Church Service was held on the lawn in the front of Chateau at 11.30am. In the afternoon the Battalion carried out practice attacks in conjunction with Hawke and Drake Battalions. The Battalion suffered the following casualties:-

- **4 other ranks (O. R.) reported sick**

AUGUST 12th

The Battalion continued training. 2 Officers and 14 other ranks proceeded to the UK for leave. The Battalion suffered the following casualties:-

- **4 other ranks (O. R.) reported sick**

AUGUST 13th & 14th

The Battalion continued training which included 'Lewis Gun Training' and taking part in Brigade practice attack. Sub Lieutenant E. C. Kenny left the Battalion. The Battalion suffered the following casualties:-

- **6 other ranks (O. R.) reported sick**

AUGUST 15th

The Battalion had 'Rifle, Bombing & Lewis Gun Training' during the day. There was a trench mortar demonstration held at 10am. Sub Lieutenant Struthers proceeded to the UK for leave. The Battalion left Bethencourt at 8.47pm and marched to Orville a distance of 25.1km (15 ½ miles) arriving at 2.30am. The Battalion suffered the following casualties:-

- **1 other rank (O. R.) reported sick**

AUGUST 16th & 17th

The Battalion continued training. There was a **'Feet Inspection'** carried out by the Medical Officer. The Battalion suffered the following casualties:-

- **1 other rank (O. R.) reported sick**

AUGUST 18th

There was no training for the Battalion today. Billets were inspected by the Commanding Officer (C. O.). A Church Service was held in the afternoon. The Battalion left Orville at 8.30pm for Vauchelles.

AUGUST 19th

The Battalion left Vauchelles and marched to Souastre a distance of 10.2km (6 miles) and bivouacked in the the Souastre Support Trench in the Red Line at 3am. The Commanding Officer (C. O.) was at Brigade Head Quarters and received orders for the impending attack.

AUGUST 20th

An 'Advanced Party' consisting of the Commanding Officer (C. O.), Adjutant and Coy Commanders went forward at 4.30pm to reconnoiter the Battalion's positions for the attack. The Battalion left Souastre at 10pm and marched via Fonquevillers and Essarts to their assembly positions at Leeds Trench.

2nd Battle of the Somme

The dispositions of the Battalions for the attack were; Hawke Battalion and two Coys of the Drake Battalion in front and the remaining two Coys of Drake Battalion in support. The orders were that at zero hour, the Hawke and the two Coys of Drake Battalion were to pass through the Blue Line which, by this time, should have been captured. The two Coys of the Drake Battalion were to capture the Southeren end of Logeast Wood and the Hawke Battalion was to take the next objective, the Brown Line, and consolidate their position with an artillery barrage as protection. The remaining two Coys of the Drake Battalion and the Hood Battalion would pass through the Brown Line led by the tanks and capture the railway at Achiet Le Grand.

AUGUST 21st

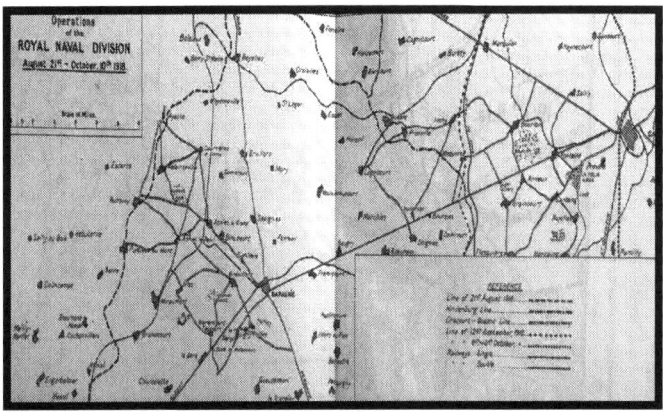

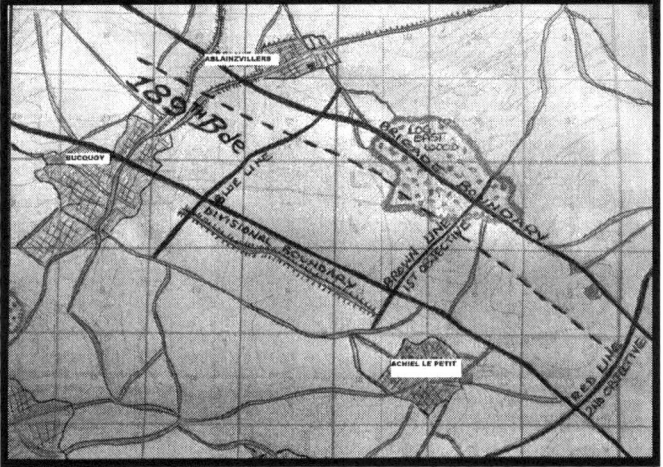

The Battalion arrived at their assembly positions at 3.30am and received a hot meal. Lewis guns were issued. Two grenades per soldier and S. O. S. rockets were handed out. The Battalion moved up the line and in position at 4.10am. At zero hour, 4.55am there was a heavy mist/fog over the area. A creeping barrage opened up and the Battalion's advanced. There was very little enemy resistance, but due to the now heavy fog, the Drake and Hawke Battalions became mixed up with the 37th Division and

with the Hood Battalion hard on their heels, as not to lose touch, the whole line was over the first objective with little enemy resistance. The fog was now even thicker and the enemy fired gas shells on Bucquoy without any effect. At 6.35am the Hood Battalion had advanced through Bucquoy and the Blue Line, even though they had lost touch with the other Coys. They continued the advance even though the barrage had ceased to be protective beyond the Brown Line. 4 tanks had arrived to continue the advance but with only 3 Coys of the Hood Battalion together at this time, each Coy was assigned a tank with the 4th tank following behind to mop up any machine gun nests. One of the tanks made good progress and reached Achiet Le Petit. The tank in the centre of the attack lost direction in the fog and ended up in the right sector with 5th Division. The missing Coy ('A' Coy) had joined the 5th Division in the attack on Achiet Le Petit. The tank on the left with 'C' Coy followed the trench down to the railway and took up position and got in touch with Drake Battalion on the left. 'C' Coy started to receive heavy machine gun fire from some old huts in Achiet Le Grand. The tank was put out of action amongst the huts, but 'C' Coy managed to take its objective. The fog was now lifting and as a result, enemy resistance was growing stronger. They dug in and prepared for a counter attack by the enemy. The 3 Coys had advanced across Archiet Le Petit and Archiet Le Grand roads and had reached their objective of the railway. They were counter attacked from the left and with tanks out of action and lack of ammunition, they withdrew to the South-East of Archiet Le Petit and dug in and remained in this position throughout the night.
My Taid Edwin, was wounded on this day.

AUGUST 22nd

At 5.15am the enemy counter attacked on the right, the enemy objective was to get through to Achiet Le Petit by using the valley running through the position. The attack failed due to the Lewis gun fire from 'D' Coy of the Hood Battalion. Similar attacks at 7am and 9am failed due to Lewis gun fire from 'D' Coy. There were no more enemy attacks on the Battalion's position during the day, although, enemy artillery was very active.
The Battalion was relieved at night and went back to trenches at Bucquoy.

AUGUST 23rd

The day was spent refitting and reorganising the Battalion.

AUGUST 24th

The Battalion received orders to move to an area near Achiet Le Petit. After a meal the Battalion marched to a position West of Loupart Wood and spent the night there. Commander Egerton left the Battalion to take command of the Brigade. Orders were received stating the Battalion should be prepared to move at once to attack Le Barque and Tilloy in conjunction with the New Zealand Division, who were going to attack Bapaume. Zero hour was to be at 7.30pm. The Battalion moved at 5.15pm and arrived at the assembly point at 6.15pm. The attack was postponed until 5am on the 25th August.

AUGUST 25th

Lieutenant Commander
S. H. Fish M.C. R.N.V.R.

At zero hour 5am the Battalion began to advance under Lieutenant Commander Fish. As on the 21st August, there was a very heavy mist/fog. When the Battalion reached Loupart Wood, it was found to be full of gas and many of the men were forced to return, suffering from the gas effects. The advance continued in a South-Easterly direction. The enemy machine gun fire was growing more intense and seemed to be coming from the flanks as well as from the front. Just after clearing the wood, Lieutenant Commander Fish was killed by an enemy shell. Commander Jones of the Drake Battalion was killed by machine gun fire shortly afterwards. The whole advance was checked by heavy machine gun fire and all ranks took cover in shell holes until steps were taken to deal with the strong point. Eventually, the strong point was silenced by the Battalion's Lewis guns and bombers and the advance continued.

The Brigade passed the village of Warlencourt and reached the road. There was some confusion for a time but an Officer took charge and organised the men back into units and they then continued along to the road. The Battalion proceeded South-East in the direction of Le Barque and formed a line along the Sunken Road known as 'Blue Cut'. Just South of the village the Battalion started to receive heavy enemy machine gun fire whilst in the Sunken Road.

Commander Beak

Commander Beak who had taken over command organised a meeting between Officers to decide whether to proceed with the attack as the enemy were seen in large numbers beyond the village of Tilloy. The Battalions next objective, after further discussion, was to continue the attack.

The Battalion left the Sunken Road and managed to get as far as the ravine known as **'Yellow Cut'**. Here again, the Battalion encountered heavy enemy machine gun fire and they found it impossible to advance further. Commander Beak decided to consolidate the position and hold the **'Blue and Yellow Cuts'**. During the rest of the day these positions were heavily shelled by the enemy aircraft who were active above the Brigades position. It was 10 hours after the Brigade had dug in along the 'Blue and Yellow Cuts' that the Brigades own artillery started to retaliate, but many of their shells fell too short and caused casualties amongst their own Battalion. After darkness had set in, there was a very heavy thunderstorm followed by heavy rain. The men had no shelter of any description and were just lying in mud and were soaked to the skin. The Battalion received word that their 'flanks' were unprotected and it was also discovered that the Battalion had advanced beyond the Butte De Warlencourt whilst it was still in the hands of the enemy.

This explained why the Battalion were receiving heavy machine gun fire from the right flank. A 'Reconnaissance Party' was sent out and it was discovered that we were in support of the Brigade on the left and the Marines and Artist Rifles and the 21st Division on the right.

AUGUST 26th

A further advance was contemplated but it was decided it would be impossible due to the fact the men were exhausted and support from the right and left was uncertain.

British soldiers resupplying a Gun Carrier Mark I tank, named Kingston, at Miraumont 26th August 1918

AUGUST 27th

The Battalion received orders for relief and were relieved in their positions by the 12th/13th Northumberland Fusiliers and marched to the Westside of Loupart Wood where the men received a hot meal and they spent the night in shell holes around the wood.

AUGUST 28th

The Battalion moved off from Loupart Wood at 6am and marched to an area near Miraumont and spent the rest of the day cleaning and resting.

AUGUST 29th

The Battalion spent the day reorganising and re-equipping and resting. Lieutenant Commander D. Galloway arrived to take command of the Battalion.

AUGUST 30th & 31st

The Battalion started training. Lewis Gunners, Signallers and Stretcher Bearers received specialist instruction. The Battalion moved off at 10.30pm and marched to Boiry Ste Rictrude where they bivouacked for the night in the field. The Battalion continued its training the next day.

My Taid, Private Edwin Roberts, service number 15736, 10th (Service) Battalion Royal Welsh Fusiliers attached to Hood Battalion 63rd Royal Naval Division was wounded between the 21st/22nd August 1918 during what is now known as the 2nd Battle of the Somme.

He was reported as wounded in the weekly casualty list issued by the War Office on October 1st 1918.

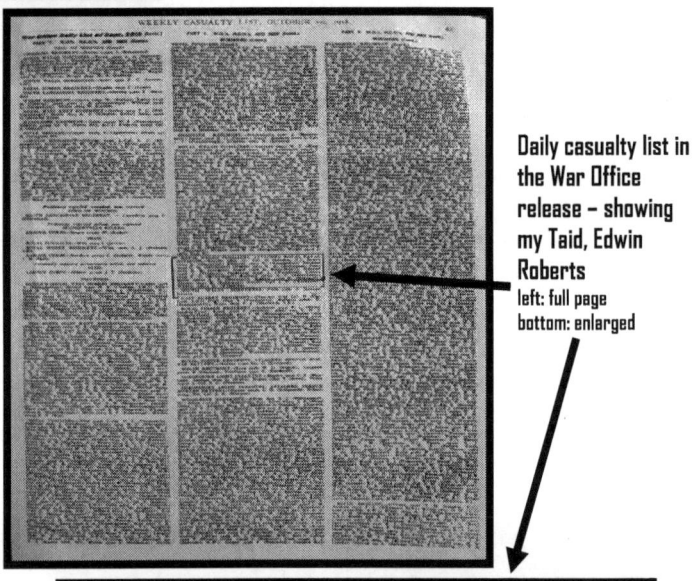

Daily casualty list in the War Office release – showing my Taid, Edwin Roberts
left: full page
bottom: enlarged

ROYAL WELSH FUSILIERS, ATTACHED ROYAL NAVAL DIVISION.—Bourlet 33899 Act. Cpl. G. (London, N.); Bowen 16115 L. (Aberavon); Edwards 38323 E. (Manchester); Forshaw 60337 C. H. (Stockport); Griffiths 33115 W. H. (Bodorgan); Jones 44213 R. R. (Corwen); Lloyd 57028 E. (Cefn-Mawr); Ormond 14319 J. (Trealaw); Parkinson 20558 J. (Wrexham); Pierces 60199 F. G. (Birkenhead); Radford 238101 A. E. (Abertillery); Reese 238100 A. E. (Stockport); Roberts 15736 E. (Holywell);* Thomas 69551 R. (Bodorgan); Wardle 60320 J. W. (Wilmslow); Whittle 238114 G. (Wilmslow).

My Taid Edwin was reported as suffering from a gun shot wound to the left hand. Machine gun bullets could fracture bones and pierce organs. The muddy and wet conditions of the Western Front, large portions of which had been well tended and manured farmland before the War, were ripe for infection.

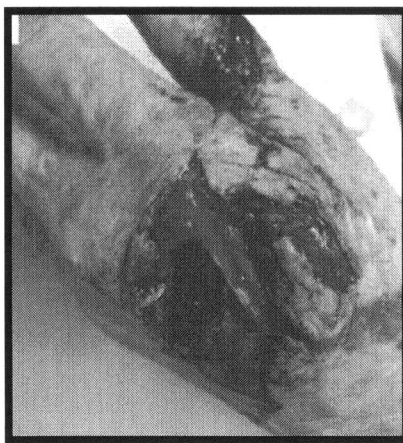

Gun shot wound to the hand

Gordon Highlander J. Reid described the effects of being hit by a machine gun, one of the most devastating weapons of the war:-

I had to go with my section between the second and third German lines to a machine gun post. Just as we got over out of the second line to go to this machine gun post, they opened up on us. Well, I said, 'Get down, for God's sake, or we'll all be killed!' We all flopped down, the six of us, I could feel something, a pain in my arm, then I felt something in my head. We shoved six bombs into this machine gun post and there was no more firing then. By this time, we were all wounded, the six of us were all wounded, but none of us was killed. And all in the left arm and the left hand. One chap had a bullet right through the palm of his hand, oh, it smashed up his hand. This bullet had gone into the muscle of my left arm, but it hadn't touched the bone, it had come right out the back of my arm. What had hit me on the front of the eye, the top of the eye, I don't know but it took all my eyebrow away and the skin, and it was bleeding, pouring down with blood.

German Machine Gun

The Maxim MG08 Machine Gun could fire 450 rounds per minute, belt fed and had an effective range of over 2500 yards and usually had a team of four to operate.

Gewehr 98 Bolt Action Rifle

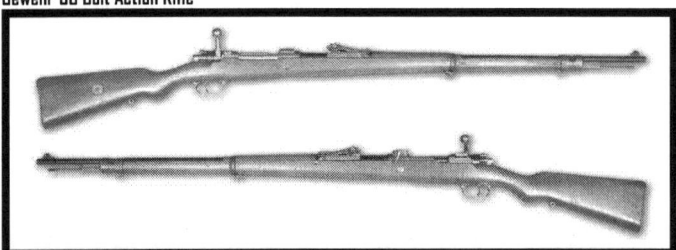

German Bullets

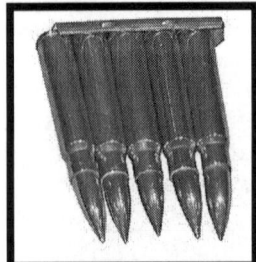

The Gewehr 98 Bolt Action Rifle was the standard German Infantry weapon of the War. The bolt and magazine system was designed by the Mausue Company.

It was forbidden for a soldier advancing in battle to stop and assist a wounded comrade, so my Taid Edwin would initially have treated his wound himself (if conscious of course). His **'Field Dressing'** would have been carried inside of his tunic and contained antiseptic pads and two bandages (one for the entry wound and one for the exit wound). The dressing would be applied by the Stretcher Bearer or the soldier himself.

If unable to walk he would have been carried by Stretcher Bearers to the nearest Regimental Aid Post. (R. A. P.) sometimes called the Battalion Aid Post and were usually situated in a dug out, in a communication trench or a deep shell hole.

The function of the R. A. P. was to assess the wounded and either patch them up and send them back to the line or pass them back to the

Advance Dressing Station/Field Ambulance. The R. A. P. was staffed by the Battalion's Medical Officer and several orderlies. This would have been located on the Bucquoy – Logeast Road.

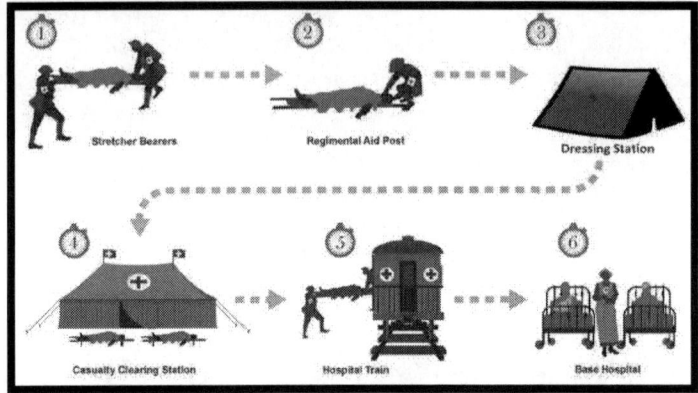

Once at the Regimental Aid Post (R. A. P.) my Taid Edwin would have been treated by the Medical Officer checking his dressing, overseeing the splinting or fractures and ensuring the patient does not go into shock. If Morphine is given or a Tourniquet applied, the soldier's forehead would be marked with an 'M' or 'T'.

The Medical Officer would also complete a **'Medical Field Card'** for each soldier and fix it firmly to the soldier, normally to a button with a string. The card would remain with the soldier as he moved down the evacuation chain.

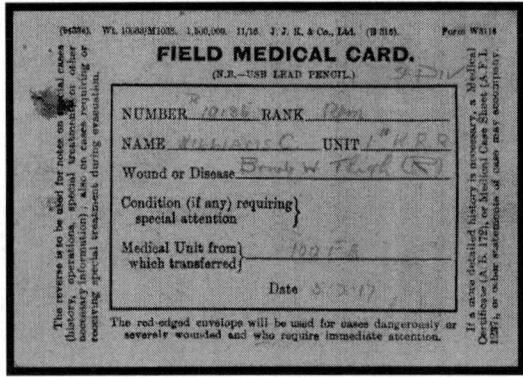

My Taid Edwin, would have been moved to 149 **'Field Ambulance'** at Fonquevillers. The Field Ambulance was a complete medical unit, when at full strength, comprised of 10 Officers and 224 men. The Bearer Division has 18 Stretcher Squads each of 6 men. The Tent Division was comprised of 9 Medical Officers and 1 Dental Officer, as well as Stores, Batmen, Clerks, Cooks, Dispensers and Nursing Orderlies and the Transport Division, which had 60 men attached from the Army Service Corps which made up the medical support for one Infantry Brigade.

One aspect of the duties of a Field Ambulance is to set up **'Advance Dressing Stations'** (A. D. S.). This would be in old schools, large houses or Churches, or if nothing else was suitable, tents. Each A. D. S. would have 3 Officers and 53 other ranks (O. R.), 36 Privates would be employed as Stretcher Bearers with 1 Officer supervising them. The other ranks would be employed as Cooks, Clerks and Dressers.

The Stretcher Bearers would collect the wounded from the R. A. P. and carry them back to the A. D. S. The soldier's condition would then be assessed to make sure bandages had not loosened or become too tight and to also make sure the soldiers were not haemorrhaging or going into shock. Surgery was not undertaken at the A. D. S. unless absolutely necessary as it had no holding capacity. Those that were deemed to be urgent cases were transferred to the **'Main Dressing Station'** (M. D. S.). The M. D. S. was based at Souastre. Those soldiers who were not deemed as urgent, were transferred straight to the **'Casualty Clearing Station'** (C. C. S.).

The Main Dressing Station (M. D. S.) were usually located about 1 to 3 miles behind the Advanced Dressing Station (A. D. S.) and closer to the Casualty Clearing Station (C. C. S.). The ideal location would have been in a large building where water, light, heating and drainage was already available. If no building was available, then tents again, were used.

Foncquevillers Aid Station – note the wounds to the hands and arms

Every M. D. S. was organised with six sections: -

SECTION	ORGANISATION
RECEIVING SECTION	which provided hot drinks, sandwiches and cigarettes
RECORDING SECTION	where clerks took patients information and examined field medical cards
RESUSCITATION SECTION	for warming and reviving those suffering from shock or the effects of haemorrhage
DRESSING STATION	Where dressings were applied and any urgent surgical treatment, adminstration of A. T. S. or Morphia, if not carried out already
GAS SECTION	To keep gas victims from any other patients
EVACUATION SECTION	Where the patients treatment was classified with whatever they were suffering from and how they were treated and then evacuated to the C. C. S.

Each M. D. S. had 1 Officer commanding, 2 Medical Officers and a Dental Officer, A Quartermaster and 59 other R. A. M. C. ranks along with 1 Royal Army Service Corps Officer and 44 A. S. C. ranks attached.

The M. D. S. could carry out urgent operations and better arrangements could be provided for resuscitation of thoes suffering from shock or haemorrhage or both.

Casualty Clearing Station

A Casualty Clearing Station (C. C. S.) was generally a large, fully equipped, often tented hospital. The C. C. S. was better equipped and staffed and were able to x-ray and perform major operations on soldiers. A fatal delay in treatment of infected wounds was one of the main reasons and causes of death for a soldier. Post mortems of abdominal cases had revealed that most of them had died of haemorrhaging which may have been avoided if surgery was performed earlier. Given the conditions at the time, over 43% of soldiers wounded in the abdomen, subsequently died. With huge numbers of more lightly wounded men flooding in, who stood a greater likelyhood of surviving, the available resources were allocated to them in preference to those most likely not to die.

A very harsh decision to make. Casualties arriving at the C. C. S. were received, assessed, then divided into 3 catagories, known today as triage.

SECTION	ORGANISATION
NON SERIOUS CASES	To be returned to duty after recuperation and rest
SERIOUS CASES – BUT STILL FIT TO TRAVEL	To be immediately sent to Base Hospitals
SERIOUS CASES	In urgent need of immediate treatments

Casualties were provided with food and rest and were prepared for the further journey to Base Hospital which could have been immediate or after recuperation. The main objective was to provide necessary treatment and move patients out as quickly as possible. Sometimes patients who were recuperating could be retained at the C. C. S. for up to four weeks before being returned to their units or transferred to a Base Hospital via ambulance train.

The conditions which determined the selection of sites for a C. C. S. were:-

- **PROXIMITY TO RAILWAYS**
- **GOOD ROAD APPROACHES**
- **ADEQUATE WATER SUPPLY**
- **REASONABLE SECURITY FROM HOSTILE ARTILLERY FIRE**

Early C. C. S.'s usually worked in groups of two or threes and in a relay. This meant that one would be closed and treating casualties for evacuation by train or ambulance to a Base Hospital, whilst the other would be empty and readying itself to receive new casualties. When the second site became full it would close, but by now, the first site would be empty and ready to receive new casualties again.

At the time of my Taid Edwin and his comrades being wounded, they would have been sent to either No. 3 C. C. S. or No. 29 C. C. S. Both were based at Gezaincourt. As you can see from the following figures, both

Casualty Clearing Stations were extremely busy during the period from August 21st to August 28th.

DATE	NO. 3 CASUALTY CLEARING STATION			NO. 29 CASUALTY CLEARING STATION		
21ST AUG		SICK	WOUNDED		SICK	WOUNDED
	ADMISSIONS	73	499	ADMISSIONS	82	782
	DEATHS		9	DEATHS		2
	SENT TO BASE HOSPITAL	172	390	SENT TO BASE HOSPITAL		499

DATE	NO. 3 CASUALTY CLEARING STATION			NO. 29 CASUALTY CLEARING STATION		
22ND AUG		SICK	WOUNDED		SICK	WOUNDED
	ADMISSIONS	123	574	ADMISSIONS	121	287
	DEATHS		20	DEATHS		7
	SENT TO BASE HOSPITAL	51	480	SENT TO BASE HOSPITAL		681

DATE	NO. 3 CASUALTY CLEARING STATION			NO. 29 CASUALTY CLEARING STATION		
23RD AUG		SICK	WOUNDED		SICK	WOUNDED
	ADMISSIONS	78	689	ADMISSIONS	78	717
	DEATHS		18	DEATHS		15
	SENT TO BASE HOSPITAL	86	542	SENT TO BASE HOSPITAL		765

DATE	NO. 3 CASUALTY CLEARING STATION			NO. 29 CASUALTY CLEARING STATION		
		SICK	WOUNDED		SICK	WOUNDED
24TH AUG	ADMISSIONS	69	421	ADMISSIONS	91	365
	DEATHS		43	DEATHS		24
	SENT TO BASE HOSPITAL	89	705	SENT TO BASE HOSPITAL		763

DATE	NO. 3 CASUALTY CLEARING STATION			NO. 29 CASUALTY CLEARING STATION		
		SICK	WOUNDED		SICK	WOUNDED
25TH AUG	ADMISSIONS	88	751	ADMISSIONS	65	316
	DEATHS		21	DEATHS		18
	SENT TO BASE HOSPITAL	55	537	SENT TO BASE HOSPITAL		337

DATE	NO. 3 CASUALTY CLEARING STATION			NO. 29 CASUALTY CLEARING STATION		
		SICK	WOUNDED		SICK	WOUNDED
26TH AUG	ADMISSIONS	79	412	ADMISSIONS	32	348
	DEATHS		37	DEATHS		22
	SENT TO BASE HOSPITAL	40	256	SENT TO BASE HOSPITAL		325

DATE	NO. 3 CASUALTY CLEARING STATION			NO. 29 CASUALTY CLEARING STATION		
27TH AUG		SICK	WOUNDED		SICK	WOUNDED
	ADMISSIONS	63	218	ADMISSIONS	37	218
	DEATHS		15	DEATHS		15
	SENT TO BASE HOSPITAL	31	308	SENT TO BASE HOSPITAL		500

DATE	NO. 3 CASUALTY CLEARING STATION			NO. 29 CASUALTY CLEARING STATION		
28TH AUG		SICK	WOUNDED		SICK	WOUNDED
	ADMISSIONS	63	119	ADMISSIONS	27	102
	DEATHS		12	DEATHS		12
	SENT TO BASE HOSPITAL	105	122	SENT TO BASE HOSPITAL		159

The Base Hospital was further back from the Front-Line than the Casualty Clearing Stations (C. C. S.). The British Hospitals were generally located near the coast, close to a railway line, in order for the casualties to arrive. They also needed to be near a port where men could be evacuated to England if they needed a longer term of care and treatment. The Base Hospital was very well equipped as it was permanent, not a temporary one like the C. C. S's. They had specialist equipment such as 'Operating Theatres', 'Laboratories' – to identify infections, 'X Ray Departments' and some had specialist departments to treat 'Gas Poisoning'. Hospital Ships evacuated the wounded to England on a daily basis. Around half of the soldiers admitted to a Base Hospital returned to their units after treatment and rest. Some were transferred to 'Convalescent Depots' to complete their recovery, whilst those who required further treatment, were evacuated to England. Some Base Hospitals could cater for over 2000 patients, they had proper hospital beds, unlike the C. C. S or A. D. S.

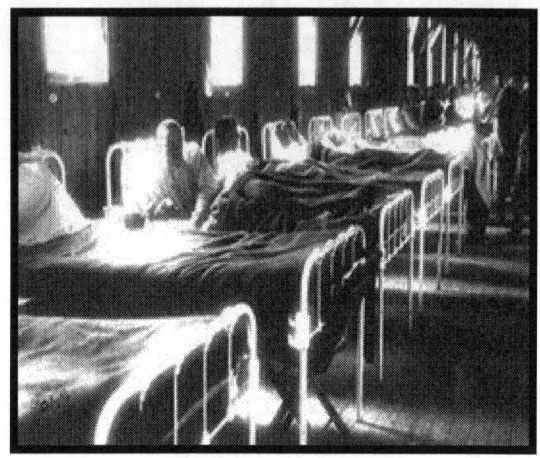

**HOSPITAL BEDS IN THE BASE HOSPITAL
&
A BASE HOSPITAL OPERATION**

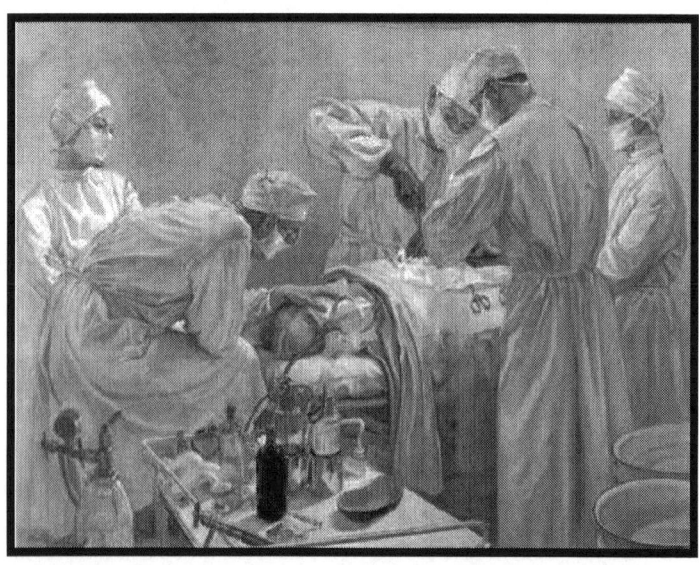

If further treatment was needed then the soldier would be evacuated to England on a 'Hospital Ship'. Large Hospital Ships could carry as many as 4000 wounded, but these were only used following large offensives. Medium Hospital Ships, with around 800 beds were more flexible and they could carry up to 1600 using the beds and sitting cases on the deck. The Medical Staff on board were split into teams; an Officer, two Nursing Sisters and ten Orderlies looked after 100 beds. They assessed each casualty during the crossing and tagged serious cases with red labels so they could be identified and unloaded first. Dover, Southampton, Devonport and Folkestone were the main ports in England used to receive the wounded from the Western Front.

H. M. H. S. Hospital Ship - Brighton

It now goes a little bit vague on my Taid Edwin. He was shot in the left hand and would have ended up, after going through the 'Casualty Evacuation Chain' at a Base Hospital. How severe his wound was, I don't know. His Service Records no longer exist because they were destroyed, like many others, in the Blitz on London in 1940. He always suffered in later life with Rheumitoid Arthritis in his hand and shoulder which I believe were because of his wounds.

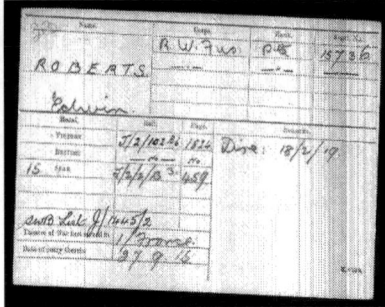 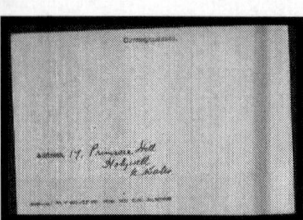

My Taid Edwin's Medal Card states that he was awarded the 1914/15 Star, The Victory Medal and the British War Medal. Also on his Medal Card is an award of a Silver War Badge. The Silver War Badge (S. W. B.) was awarded to Servicemen/women who were discharged from Military Service during the Great War. The most common reason for the award of the Silver Badge was the King's Regulations, Paragraph 392 (xvi) meaning they had been released on account of being permanently physically unfit, this was often as a result of sickness, disease or 'War Wounds'.

Soldiers discharged during the War because of the disabilities that they had sustained overseas in a 'Theatre of Operations' (an area where there was active fighting) could also receive a King's Certificate. The certificate was an ornate printed scroll in which the number, name and unit of the

discharged serviceman or woman was handwritten in calligraphic script and contained a facsimilie signature of King George V.

The Silver War Badge was first issued in 1916 when it was also retrospectively awarded to those already discharged since 1914.

On my Taid Edwin's Medal Card it states he was discharged on 18th February 1919 but on his Pension Records, his date of discharge was 7th December 1918 and his pension of 5 shillings and 6d commenced on the 8th December 1918.

His disabilities were noted as : -

1. G. W. S. Left Hand
2. Rheumitoid Arthritus

Both disabilities were attributed to his War Service. This seems to confirm that my Taid Edwin, after being wounded for a second time in August 1918, did not return to 'Active Duty' because of his injuries. If you look closely at my Taid Edwin's Pension Form, he is marked as being 'Single', which was an error as he was married in 1905. My Taid Edwin would have been 39 years old when he returned home.

Pension Form 1

Pension Form 2

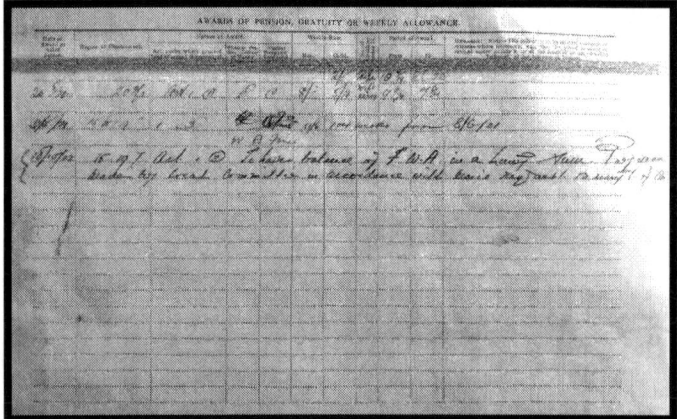

Pension Form 3

When the War ended and my Taid Edwin and his comrades had returned home to North Wales, the Lord Lieutenant of Flintshire, Mr Henry N. Gladstone, wanted a record of all men who had served from Flintshire in the Great War and appointed a committee of local ladies and gentlemen for the purpose of preparing a complete list of Servicemen for the county records.

Cards were sent to all addresses throughout the county of Flintshire for the men to complete. Cards were also sent to all of the families of the men who had been killed in the War.

The cards asked for the following information: -

- **FULL NAME**
- **ADDRESS**
- **SERVICE NUMBER**
- **WHAT PART OF THE ARMED SERVICE THEY SERVED IN**
- **DISTINCTIONS, MEDALS AND AWARDS RECEIVED**

The cards, once returned, were later kept in two categories: -

- **Category 1 – THE LIVING – marked with a letter 'L'**

- **Category 2 – THE FALLEN – marked with a letter 'F'**

The 'Fallen' also had the top right hand corner of the card removed. All these cards are held at Hawarden Records Office in Flintshire. Even though there is a large amount of these cards to view, not all were returned (for whatever reason), so this list is not complete, but still a very useful resource.

Hawarden Record Office

This is a copy of my Taid Edwin's card at Hawarden Record Office. As you can see from his card, he served for 4 ½ years and was wounded twice. It was this card that started me on the journey to research his Military Record.

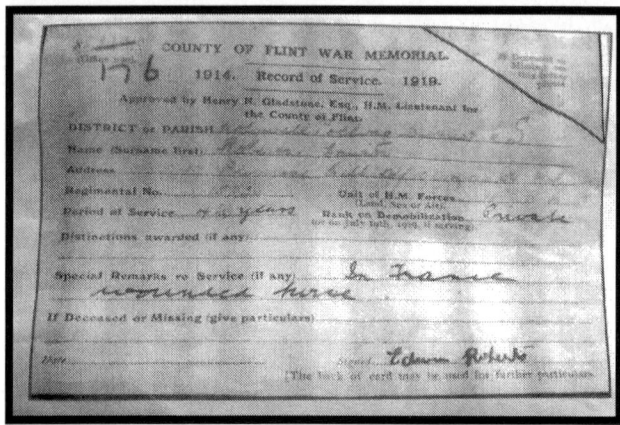

Record Card

A scroll was sent to all servicemen from Flintshire who served in the Great War by the H. M. Lieutenant for the County of Flint.

My Taid Edwin - Private E. Roberts' Scroll

Many men like my Taid Edwin, returned home to 'Welcome Home Parades and Parties' held in the local town hall and parades through the streets. The two pictures below are from my Taid Edwin's home town of Holywell, Flintshire on their return.

Holywell High Street Parade (above) & the Town Hall Party (below)

Life was expected to return to normal for the soldiers. They would return back to their families and the jobs that they had previously held, but life had changed and would never be the same. The promise of a 'Life Fit For Heros' for the returning hero soldiers soon disappeared for my Taid Edwin and for so many others.

Chapter 9
Battalion Honours

Out of the long **'Roll of Battle Honours'** won by the Battalion's of the Royal Welsh Fusiliers during the Great War, the 10th (Service) Battalion earned wholly, or in part, the following:-

- **Ypres 1917**
- **Somme 1916 Bazentin**
- **Delville Wood**
- **Ancre 1916**
- **Arras 1917**
- **Scarpe 1917**
- **Arlcux**
- **Polygon Wood**
- **France & Flanders 1914-1918.**

The following lists of Honours and Decorations won individually is also a fitting record to the Battalion as a whole. The lists do not include the long 'Roll' of Officers, Non-Commissioned Officers and men who were mentioned in Despatches for Special or Distinguished Services.

VICTORIA CROSS

The Victoria Cross is the highest Military Decoration awarded for **'Valour & Devotion to Duty in the face of the enemy'** to members of the Armed Forces, regardless of Rank, up to two bars may be awarded, this in recognition of further **'Acts of Gallantry.'**

First established by Queen Victoria on the 29th January 1856, to recognise **'Valour in the Crimean War.'**

Prior to this, there was no means of adequately rewarding the individual for their **'Gallant Services'**, be it Officers or the lower Ranks.

The Victoria Cross (V. C.) was awarded to just 633 individuals between 1914-1918.

Two men from the 10th (Service) Battalion Royal Welsh Fusiliers were awarded this prestigious Award. Both Victoria Crosses were awarded during the Battalion's engagement with the enemy at Delville Wood on the Somme on 20th July 1916.

CORPORAL JOSEPH JOHN DAVIES 34314

Joseph John Davies was born at 7 Nock Street, Tipton, Staffordshire on 28th April 1889. His Father, also John, served in the 7th Regiment of Foot (Royal Fusiliers) for twelve years. His Mother, Ann (Nee Bullock) was from Bilston, Staffordshire. Joseph was educated at Greatbridge Council School, Tipton. After leaving school, Joseph was employed as a 'Planer' at Old Park Works, Wednesbury. Joseph married Lucy Mason on the 8th June but sadly, their first born child died in infancy.

Joseph enlisted in the Welsh Regiment on August 19th 1909 and he was posted to the 1st Battalion at Bordon, Hampshire. He served in Egypt and became an 'Armourer's Assistant'. On 27th January 1914, he left Egypt with the Battalion for India, serving until November that year before returning to England, arriving on Christmas Eve 1914. Joseph's marriage had sadly ended in divorce due to Lucy's relationship with a Benjamin Andrews.

Joseph was posted to France with the 1st Battalion on 16th January 1915 and was wounded at Ypres on 10th March, the same year he was evacuated back to Britain.

He returned to France in May and was promoted to Lance Corporal and he transferred to the Royal Welsh Fusiliers.

He was promoted to Acting Corporal in January 1916 and then Corporal in April 1916.

Joseph was posted to the 10th (Service) Battalion Royal Welsh Fusiliers in France on 8th May 1916.

On 20th July 1916 at Delville Wood, Corporal Davies and eight men became separated from the rest of the Company. The men were completely surrounded but Corporal Davies managed to get his men into a shell hole and by throwing bombs and opening rapid fire, he succeeded in routing the enemy out and not content with this, he followed them up in their retreat and bayonetted several of them.

The London Gazette, 26th September 1916 reported his award and added the following comment: -

"Corporal Davies set a magnificent example of pluck and determination. He has done other very gallant work and was badly wounded in the second Battle of Ypres."

Joseph was promoted to Acting Sergeant on the day of his action. He was wounded on 8th August 1916 suffereing a gun shot wound (G.S.W.) to his left shoulder. He returned to Britain.

Joseph was presented with the Victoria Cross by King George V. at Buckingham Palace on 7th October 1916.

Joseph's arm was still in the sling and the Victoria Cross medal was placed on the sling by the King.

He later was awarded the Russian Cross of St. George 1st Class on 15th February 1917.

Article from The War Illustrated - Sergeant Davies leaving the Palace after King George V had placed his Victoria Cross on his bandages.

Joseph's wound meant that he was no longer 'fit for active service' and was discharged from the Army on 14th December 1918. Joseph re-enlisted in the Herefordshire Regiment (Territorial Army) on 13th November 1920. He was discharged in November 1922 aged 33.

He remarries on 23rd June to Elsie Thomas in Hereford Registry Office before moving to Birmingham. Joseph worked as a Commissionaire for the Birmingham Corporation Gas Works. Joseph and Elsie had two daughters and later moved to Poole in Dorset.

During World War Two, Joseph was not fit enough for service with the Home Guard and instead served as a Regimental Sergeant Major of Poole Cadet Force in Dorset. He was also Chief A. R. P. Warden at Oakdate, Poole and worked at the Royal Navy Cordite Factory in Holton Heath throughout the War.

Joseph died at Bournemouth Royal National Hospital in Dorset on 16th February 1976 aged 87. He was cremated and his ashes were scattered on 'Evening Hill' overlooking Poole harbour. His Victoria Cross and other medals are held by the Royal Welsh Fusilier Museum in Caernarfon Castle.

Medals Displayed In Caernafon Castle

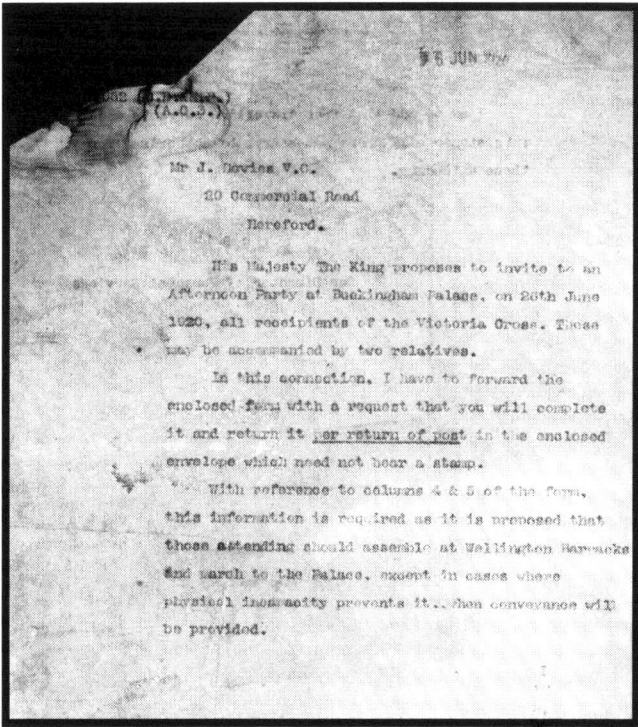

Letter sent to Joseph Davies in 1920, from the King, inviting him and two guests to the Palace

Plaque near his home in Tipton and the plaque in Delville Wood, Somme, France

PRIVATE ALBERT HILL 15280

Albert Hill was born in Hulme, Greater Manchester on 24th May 1895. Albert was one of nine siblings. His Father Thomas was a Coal Miner and his Mother Elizabeth was a Charwoman. Albert was educated at Trinity Wesleyan School in Denton Manchester. He then worked at Alpha Mill when he left school becoming an apprentice "Hat Maker" with Messers Joseph Wilson & Sons Ltd in Denton Manchester.

Albert enlisted on 3rd August 1914 joining the 10th (Service) Battalion Royal Welsh Fusiliers sailing for France on 27th September 1915 with his Battalion. Albert's Brother Joseph was also in the 10th Battalion R. W. F.

Albert, whilst fighting with his Battalion at Delville Wood on 20th July 1916, and whilst under heavy fire, performed the following acts which led to him being awarded the Victoria Cross (V. C.)

THE LONDON GAZETTE 26TH SEPTEMBER 1916

"No. 15280 Pte. Albert Hill R. Welsh Fus. For most conspicuous bravery. When his Battalion had deployed under very heavy fire, for an attack on the enemy in a wood, he dashed forward, when the order to charge was given, and meeting two of the enemy suddenly, bayonetted them both. He was sent later by his Platoon Sergeant to get in touch with the Company, and finding himself cut off and almost surrounded by some twenty of the enemy, attacked them with bombs, killing and wounding many and scattering the remainder. He then joined a Sergeant of his Company and helped to fight the way back to the lines. When he got back, hearing that the Commanding Officer and a scout were lying out wounded, he went out and assisted to bring in the wounded Officer, two other men bringing in the scout."

Albert was presented his Victoria Cross by King George V at Buckingham Palace on 18th November 1916. Albert received a hero's welcome on his return to Denton. Albert was also awarded the French Croix-de-Guerre on 9th December 1916.

Albert Hill's V. C. Home-Coming Article in The Manchester Evening News

Albert was demobbed on the 16th February 1919 and returned to his pre-war job. On 14th February 1920 he married Doris May Wilson at St. George's Church in Hyde. The couple decided to emigrate to the United States on 12th May 1923 aboard R. M. S. Scythia bound for Boston Massachusettes arriving on 31st May 1923. They settled at Central Falls for ten years before moving to Pawtucket, Rhode Island in 1933. In 1944 they became American citizens and the couple had four children. Albert was employed as a "Bricklayer's Labourer" with the H. M. Soule Construction Company. Albert tried to enlist during the Second World War, but due to his age, was advised to do defense work instead. He attended the Coronation of Queen Elizabeth II in 1953 and during his visit to the UK, he returned to Denton on 3rd July. Albert died at Pawtucket Memorial Hospital, Rhode Island on 17th February 1971, aged 76, and is buried in Highland Memorial Park, Pawtucket. His medals are held at The Royal Welsh Fusiliers Museum at Caernarfon.

Plaque at Memorial Gardens, Denton & Plaque at Delville Wood, Somme, France

His medals are held at The Royal Welsh Fusiliers Museum at Caernarfon

Albert Hill Article in the War Illustrated Magazine – 14th October 1916

*TEXT BELOW PHOTO * *Private A. Hill Royal Welsh Fusiliers, won the Victoria Cross by magnificent conduct. His Battalion had deployed under heavy fire for an attack , and when the order to charge was given he dashed forward and bayonetted two of the enemy. Cut off presently and surrounded by a score of Germans he killed and wounded many with bombs and routed the rest, afterwards fighting his way back to the lines. There he heard that an Officer and a scout were lying wounded outside, and he went back and brought in the Officer, the scout being carried in by two other men. In conclusion, he captured two Germans and brought them in a prisoners.*

MILITARY CROSS

The Military Cross was established by King George V on 28th December 1914.

"We are desirous of signifying our appreciation of such services by a mark of our Royal Favor we do by these presents for us our heirs and successors who distinguished and meritorious services have been brought to our notice."

The Military Cross is awarded for an act or acts of exemplary gallantry during active operations against the enemy on land, to Captains or Officers of lower rank up to Warrant Officers. (N. C. O.'s or other ranks instead, received the Military Medal).

The 10th (Service) Battalion were awarded a total of 15 Military Crosses to the following recipients: -

Captain Bernard Grellior – London Gazette Page 3425 - 30th March 1916

Captain Bernard Grellier, Royal Army Medical Corps (attached 10th Battalion, Royal Welsh Fusiliers).

For conspicuous gallantry and devotion to duty during operations, when tending the wounded under heavy shell fire. He helped to dig out wounded men who were buried.

2nd Lieutenant Albert Nevitt – London Gazette Page 4930 - 16th May 1916

Temp. 2nd Lt. Albert Nevitt, 12th Bn. (formerly 10th Bn.), R. W. Fus.

For conspicuous gallantry. When leading a bombing attack up a communication trench all but one of his men became casualties, but with this man he went on to within 10 yards of the enemy, when he was himself wounded. He had previously shown great daring on reconnaissance.

Captain Charles Albert Roy Follit - London Gazette Page 5460 - 31st May 1916

Temp. Capt. Charles Albert Roy Follit, 10th Bn., R. W. Fus.
For conspicuous gallantry on several occasions, notably when, during an enemy attack, he displayed great coolness and utter disregard of personal safety and was largely responsible for the repulse of the enemy. After daylight he went out and rescued two wounded enemy, although heavily sniped at the whole time.

Lieutenant Leonard Patrick Vernon - London Gazette Page 10193 - 20th October 1916

Temp. 2nd Lt. Leonard Patrick Vernon, R.W. Fus.
For conspicuous gallantry during operations. Previous to a bombardment by us of an uncaptured portion of the enemy's trench he went round and warned back our men who were lying in shell holes near the enemy parapet.

Captain Albert John Stanley James - London Gazette Page 36 – 1st January 1917

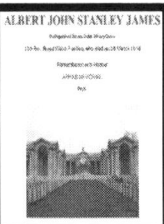

Temp. Capt. Albert John Stanley James, R. Welsh Fus.
At the time of his death he was in command of a battalion of the King's Own Royal Lancaster Regiment. In July, 1916, he was awarded the Military Cross for services at the Somme.

Captain Rev. David Cynddelw Williams - London Gazette Page 1021 – 26th January 1917

Rev. David Cynddelw Williams, Army Chaplns. Dept., attd. R. Welsh Fus.
For conspicuous gallantry and devotion to duty. He accompanied the battalion to the front line, and performed most valuable service in the rescue and tending of the wounded under an intense fire. He has on many previous occasions done fine work.

Temp. 2nd Lieutenant Harry Pritchard - London Gazette Page 1019 - 26th January 1917

Temp. 2nd Lt. Harry Pritchard, R. Welsh Fus.

For conspicuous gallantry in action. When all his men were wounded he remained with a Serjeant, and held his position. On another occasion he led an offensive patrol and bombed an enemy working party.

Bangor University Memorial
Harry Pritchard was born on the 24th May 1894, the eledest son of William H. Pritchard and Margaret Ann Pritchard of King Street, Cefn. He was on the teaching staff of the Cefn Mawr Council School and was preparing for a scholastic career at the University College of North Wales in 1914 when he joined the Army. He enlisted in September 1917 at Shotton, and received a commission with the 12th Battalion of the Royal Welsh Fusiliers. He was awarded the Military Cross in January 1917 (as Temp. 2nd Lieutenant) for conspicuous gallantry in action. When all his men were wounded he remained with a Sergeant who was badly wounded and held his position. On another occasion he led an offensive patrol and bombed an enemy working party. The University Student Registers record that he died in September 1924.

Captain Charles Gwyn Noel Morgan – London Gazette Page 7239 – 18th July 1917 &
Page 8805 – 25th August 1917

2nd Lt. (A./Capt.) Charles Gwyn Noel Morgan, M.C., R. Welsh Fus., Spec. Res.
For conspicuous gallantry and devotion to duty under an intense hostile bombardment, which practically obliterated his trench and caused his company to lose nearly 50 per cent. of its strength. He directed the operation of digging out those who had been buried, greatly inspiring his men by his splendid spirit and heroism.
(M.C. gazetted 18th July, 1917.)

2nd Lt. Charles Gwyn Noel Morgan, R.W. Fus., Spec. Res.
For conspicuous gallantry and devotion to duty whilst in charge of a working party in front of our positions. Though subjected to severe rifle, machine gun, and grenade fire he continued to work until his task was successfully accomplished, setting the finest example of personal gallantry and coolness under the worst conditions.

Great War Forum
Capt Charles Gwyn Noel Morgan - Born 1896 at Llanstephan, Radnor. Educated Llandovery. Served with an OTU. Commissioned 2/Lt 4th October, 1915. Attached 9/RWF and saw action with this Bn. Attached 10/RWF - 31st August, 1916. Awarded first MC for action around Louverval Trench area. Wounded 15th July, 1917 - awarded bar to MC. Returned to 9/RWF. Survived the war. Went up to Keble College and took MA degree. Called to the Bar. Died - Worthing, March 1939. His medals are on display at the RWF Museum. Caernarfon. LG 18/7/1917 & 25/8/1917.

Captain Morgan Watcyn Williams – London Gazette Page 7250 – 18th July 1917

Temp. 2nd Lt. (actg. Capt.) Morgan Watcyn Williams, R. W. Fus.

For conspicuous gallantry and devotion to duty. He led his company with great skill and courage. When held up by overwhelming fire, he reorganised his men under greatest difficulties, and held on to an advanced position under heavy shell fire for eighteen hours until relieved.

Captain Oscar Stanley Hughes – London Gazette Page 9574 – 17th September 1917

T./2nd Lt. (A./Capt.) Oscar Stanley Hughes, R. Welsh Fus.

For conspicuous gallantry and devotion to duty during an enemy counter-attack. Although twice buried by shells and severely wounded during an intense bombardment, he refused to leave his company, remaining at his post and inspiring them under terrible conditions by his splendid spirit and heroism.

Acting R. S. M. William Webb – London Gazette Page 49 – 1st January 1918

5796 C.S.M. (A./R.S.M.) William Webb, 2nd Bn., Suff. R, attd. R. Welsh Fus.

William Webb won a Distingushed Conduct Medal (DCM) whilst serving with the 2nd Battalion Suffolk Regiment at Le Cateau – 26th August 1914.

2nd Lieutenant David Charles Hunter – London Gazette Page 4216 – 6th April 1918

T./2nd Lt. David Charles Hunter, attd. R.W. Fus.

For conspicuous gallantry and devotion to duty in remaining to command his company, though himself wounded, in an attack in which all the other company officers had become casualties. He reorganised the company, established a post, and beat off a heavy counter-attack. In attempting to regain touch with the brigade on his left he and his orderly came upon an enemy post, rushed it and bayoneted one man, the rest escaping in the darkness.

Lieutenant Algernon William Fish – London Gazette Page 4212 – 6th April 1918

> T./Lt. Algernon William Fish. R.W. Fus.
> For conspicuous gallantry and devotion to duty in going forward with only fourteen men and occupying the furthest objectives until reinforced. When the brigade on his left were driven back by a counter-attack he gallantly held his line and brought heavy fire to bear on the enemy, showing great courage and cheerfulness throughout.

Lieutenant Arthur Patrick Comyns – London Gazette Page 8788 – 26th July 1918

> Lt. Arthur Patrick Comyns, R.W. Fus.
> For conspicuous gallantry and devotion to duty in action. When a considerable length of trench on both sides of him had been evacuated by the garrison, he held the trench with a Lewis gun and three men, keeping up a steady fire and inflicting many casualties on the enemy until reinforcements arrived.

Lieutenant Cyril Henry Elphick – London Gazette Page 10946 – 16th September 1918

> T./2nd Lt. Cyril Henry Elphick, R. Welsh Fus.
> For conspicuous gallantry and devotion to duty. He was indefatigable in rallying men of scattered units and leading them forward again. He was eventually wounded while so employed.

WESTERN MAIL, WEDNESDAY, SEPTEMBER 25, 1918.

FURTHER M.C. WINNERS.

In the eighth instalment of the new honours list appear the following Welsh recipients of the Military Cross, with a description of their brave deeds:—

Temp. Sec.-lieut. Cyril Henry Elphick, R.W.F.:

He was indefatigable in rallying men of scattered units and leading them forward again. He was eventually wounded while so employed.

DISTINGUISHED SERVICE ORDER (D. S. O.)

First established by Queen Victoria in September 1886, the first D. S. O. was awarded on 25th November the same year. The D. S. O. is awarded for meritorious or distinguished service by Officers during wartime, typically in actual combat, serving under fire, and usually awarded to those above the rank of '**Captain**' until 1943. The recipient must have been '**Mentioned in Despatches**' by the Commander in Chief of the Army. Between 1914 and 1916, the D. S. O. could also be awarded to Staff Officers when they were not under fire or in contact with the enemy, but by 1917, it was once more restricted to those who had served in the presence of the enemy.

On 23rd August 1916 a warrant allowed a '**Bar**' to be awarded as a way of formally recognising further acts of merit.

Five Distinguished Service Order's (D. S. O.'s) were awarded to the following recipients of the 10th (Service) Battalion Royal Welsh Fusiliers.

Major (Temp. Lieut-Col) George Rowlandson Crosfield - London Gazette Page 3428 - 30th March 1916

Major George Rowlandson Crosfield, 4th Battalion, The Prince of Wales's Volunteers (South Lancashire Regiment), Territorial Force (attached 2nd Battalion).
For conspicuous gallantry and good service. He repeatedly visited the front line under heavy shell fire, and during the successful assault rallied and led back to the attack men who had suffered much from artillery fire. Previously he had made an excellent and daring reconnaissance of the enemy's position.

Temp. Captain Charles Albert Roy Follit - London Gazette Page 1878 - 23rd October 1916

Temp. Capt. Charles Albert Roy Follit, R. W. Fus.
For conspicuous gallantry during operations. During our deployment in a wood the enemy twice attacked, and we came under heavy fire. It was mainly due to Captain Follit's fine work that the deployment was completed. He also did most gallant work reconnoitring the enemy wire.

Temp. Major Frederick Alfaro Samuel - London Gazette Page 29 - 1st January 1917 &
The North Wales Chronicle and Advertiser for the Principality – 5th January 1917

> Temp. Maj. Frederick Alfaro Samuel, R. Welsh Fus.

> **DISTINCTIONS FOR WELSH OFFICERS.**
>
> **NEW YEAR HONOURS.**
>
> The following are included in the list of naval and military honours published in the *London Gazette*:—
>
> Temporary Major Frederick Alfaro Samuel, R.W. Fusiliers.

Captain (Actg. Lt-Col.) Geoffry Lee Compton-Smith - London Gazette Page 7212 18th July 1917

> Capt. (actg. Lt.-Col.) Geoffry Lee Compton-Smith, R. Welsh Fus.
>
> For conspicuous gallantry and devotion to duty. He commanded his battalion with the greatest skill and determination. Immediately the objective was gained he moved forward to supervise consolidation and cover the advance of another brigade. Although wounded, he remained in the position, and his personal example was of the utmost value to all.

Temp. Maj. (A./Lt-Col.) Albert John Stanley James - London Gazette Page 6459 – 3rd June 1918

> T./Maj. (A./Lt.-Col.) Albert John Stanley James, M.C., R.W. Fus., now Entrng. Bn.

Postumusley Awarded as he was killed on the 28th March 1918

LEGION D'HONNEUR - FRANCE

The National Order of the Legion of Honour formerly The Royal Order of the Legion Of Honour is the highest French Order of Merit, both Military and Civil. Established in 1802 by Napoleon Bonaparte.

NAME	DATE AWARDED
Major Geoffrey Lee Compton-Smith	31st May 1916

CROIX DE GUERRE - FRANCE

The Croix de Guerre is a French Military Decoration. It was created to recognise French and Allied Soldiers who were cited for valourous service during the Great War.

NAME	DATE AWARDED
Private Albert Hill 15280	19th September 1916

CROIX DE GUERRE - BELGIUM

The Croix de Guerre of Oorlogskruis is a Military Decoration of the Kingdom of Belgium. It was established by Royal Decree on 25th October 1915. It was primarily awarded for bravery or other Military virtue on the battlefield.

NAME	DATE AWARDED
Captain Frederick Hughes Sewell	31st January 1918
Corporal Edward W. Hughes 55058	31st January 1918
Lance Corporal David Watters 15386	31st January 1918
Private John Edgar Marchant 13861	31st January 1918
Private Thomas Edward Profit 15092	31st January 1918

CROSS OF ST. GEORGE - RUSSIA

Established in February 1807 by Decree of Emperor Alexander I, it was intended as a reward for undaunted courage by the Lower Ranks.

NAME	DATE AWARDED
Sergeant Joseph Davies 34314	19th September 1916

ALBERT MEDAL

During the Great War, the Albert Medal was awarded for supreme bravery in the field and to honour people who died whilst saving the lives of others. Named in memory of Prince Albert, Queen Victoria's Husband, the medal was first awarded in 1866.

NAME	DATE AWARDED
Captain Albert Nevitt MC (awarded for staying to assist an injured Sergeant after an explosion at a bomb store)	31st January 1918

DISTINGUISHED CONDUCT MEDAL

First established by Queen Victoria on 4th December 1854 and is awarded for gallentry in the field. A distinguished award for bravery for N. C. O.'s and soldiers of the British Army, second only to the Victoria Cross for other ranks. The 10th (Service) Battalion R. W. F. were awarded 8 D. C. M.'s to the following recipients:-

Private J. Lloyd service number 15514

> 15514 Pte. J. LLOYD 10th Bn.
> For conspicuous gallantry. During operations he made three journeys with bombs under heavy shell fire and otherwise greatly distinguished himself. He had previously displayed great gallantry as a bomber.   (31.5.16)

Sergeant Major William E. Hewitt service number 11553

11553 CSM W.E. HEWITT
   For conspicuous gallantry in action.
At a critical moment he rallied men of
many companies and told them off in
parties as coolly as though he were on
parade, although under very heavy fire.
He shot two of the enemy himself, and
brought in a wounded officer under
heavy fire.   (20.10.16)

Sergeant William T. Jones service number 15722

15722 Sjt. W.T. JONES
  For conspicous gallantry in action.
When his officer had been wounded, he led
his platoon on with great coolness. When
ordered to retire, he reorganised the men
of the company in his vicinity and super-
inteded the digging of a trench. His
cool courage was very marked, and he never
faltered in his duty, although the handle
of his entrenching tool was blown away by
a shell.   (20.10.16)

Sergeant Arthur Punchard service number 15791

15791 Cpl. A. PUNCHARD
   For conspicuous gallantry and devotion
to duty in action. After receiving
three bullets in his side, he continued
firing his machine gun till the situation became less acute. He then handed
the gun to next man, and, although in
great pain, gave clear instructions as
to how the team were to carry on.
(20.10.16)

Private Edgar Ouldcott service number 15335

15335 Pte. E. OULDCOOT
   For conspicuous gallantry during and
after an attack. He rescued, under heavy
artillery and machine gun fire, many
wounded men, voluntarily remaining behind
when his battalion was relieved, and
assisting to carry in the wounded of
another regiment.   (20.10.16)

Sergeant Harry Hartley service number 15427

> 15149 Sjt. H. HARTLEY
> For conspicuous gallantry and devotion
> to duty. He organised bearer parties
> under heavy shell fire, and greatly
> facilitated the work of clearing the
> wounded.   (9.7.17)

Private M. Hughes Morris service number 15427
On the dedication below, his full name was not shown, it has been mistyped. His full name was Morris Hughes Morris

> 15427 Pte. M. HUGHES
> Conspicuous gallantry and devotion to
> duty on very many occasions. During an
> intense bombardment of our positions he
> was indefatigable in his efforts, digg-
> ing out buried men, assisting the wound-
> ed, rallying and bringing up ration
> parties; in fact, continually displaying
> heroism of the highest order. His fear-
> less example was invaluable in steadying
> the younger men, who were in the trenches
> for the first time under the most terrible
> and trying conditions, and no praise could
> be too great for his conduct under fire.
> (25.8.17)

Sergeant Frederick Gibb service number 15724

> 15724 Sjt. F. GIBBS (Birmingham)
> For conspicuous gallantry and devotion
> to duty. He has on many occasions led
> his pack train through heavy barrages to
> the front line, and has always succeeded
> in delivering his rations intact. His
> courage and resource, so frequently noti-
> ceable during a period of two years,
> shows him to be a splendid type of NCO.
> (17.4.18)

MILITARY MEDAL

The Military Medal is awarded to personnel of the British Army and also to personnel of other commissioned ranks for bravery in battle on land. The Military Medal was first established by King George V on 25th March 1916.

"It is ordained that the names of those upon whom we may be pleased to confer the Military Medal shall be published in the London Gazette and that a register thereof shall be kept in the office of our Principal Secretary of State for War".

The 10th (Service) Battalion R. W. F. were awarded 58 Military Medals to the following recipients:-

	RANK	NAME	SERVICE NO.	DATE
1	SERGEANT	DAVID M. MCSWEENEY	15137	9/10/16
2	PRIVATE	WILLIAM THOMAS	31172	10/8/16
3	PRIVATE	JOHN RICHARD BALLARD	15175	24/10/16
4	PRIVATE	MORRIS H. MORRIS	15427	19/2/17
5	SERGEANT	HENRY MOUNTFORD	23410	20/6/17
6	SERGEANT	PATRICK MURPHY	16298	9/10/16
7	LANCE SERGEANT	HENRY HARTLEY	15149	31/5/17
8	SERGEANT	ROBERT WHITE	15500	19/2/17
9	LANCE CORPORAL	FRANK PARSONS	24406	1/11/17
10	COMPANY SERGEANT MAJOR	ROBERT HEDLEY	15339	26/4/17
11	PRIVATE	JOHN O'PIERCE	14194	
12	PRIVATE	ARTHUR N. WILLIAMS	15728	9/10/16
13	PRIVATE	EDWARD ARTHUR POLIN	15483	12/5/16
14	PRIVATE	JOHN CASEY	25109	
15	LANCE CORPORAL	JOHN M. PRICE	15215	24/10/16
16	LANCE CORPORAL	HENRY WOODWARD	23397	
17	PRIVATE	DAVID HUGHES	15081	31/5/17
18	PRIVATE	ROBERT ALBERT WYNNE	4697	9/10/16
19	PRIVATE	JAMES ABBOTS	31114	
20	CORPORAL	HECTOR HUSSEY	24891	
21	PRIVATE	EDWARD A. ROBERTS	15084	19/9/16
22	REGIMENTAL SERGEANT MAJOR	EDWARD ROBERTS	15313	12/5/16
23	SERGEANT	JOHN T. JONES	14647	
24	CORPORAL	OWEN JONES	40940	1/11/17
25	PRIVATE	W. O. JONES	20731	10/8/16
26	PRIVATE	JAMES L. LEWIS	55034	
27	SERGEANT	JOHN MILLS	6614	19/9/16
28	PRIVATE	DAVID WATTERS	15286	19/9/16
29	PRIVATE	J. IVOR ROBERTS	31075	19/9/16
30	PRIVATE	JAMES BASSETT	15020	31/5/17

	RANK	NAME	SERVICE NO.	DATE
31	PRIVATE	JOHN E. PARRY	36978	31/5/17
32	SERGEANT	JOHN AMES	15042	31/5/17
33	SERGEANT	DAVID HUGHES	25394	31/5/17
34	CORPORAL	SAMUEL EDGE	57047	31/5/17
35	PRIVATE	FRANK JENKS	54408	31/5/17
36	PRIVATE	DAVID PHILLIP PARRY	54961	31/5/17
37	SERGEANT	ALBERT P. CARTER	235021	20/6/17
38	LANCE CORPORAL	FREDERICK BROWN	235031	20/6/17
39	LANCE CORPORAL	HARRY VICTOR MAJOR	35071	20/6/17
40	LANCE CORPORAL	JAMES A. LEEDER	54953	20/6/17
41	SERGEANT	JOHN EDGE	39204	1/11/17
42	LANCE CORPORAL	ROBERT JONES	20761	1/11/17
43	PRIVATE	WILLIAM HENRY HOLDEN	18534	1/11/17
44	PRIVATE	HARRY E. ELLIS	48879	1/11/17
45	PRIVATE	HAROLD SAMUEL EVANS	203336	1/11/17
46	PRIVATE	HARRY BAILIFF	16022	1/11/17
47	SERGEANT	JOHN HOLLIS	57030	1/11/17
48	PRIVATE	ALBERT DUTTON	60451	1/11/17
49	SERGEANT	JOSEPH HARVEY	4120	1/11/17
50	CORPORAL	JAMES H. SLOMAN	70158	1/11/17
51	PRIVATE	WILLIAM SMITH	32565	1/11/17
52	CORPORAL	WILLIAM SKINNER	34150	1/11/17
53	SERGEANT	SYDNEY SUTCLIFFE	15551	9/10/16
54	CORPORAL	MESHECK PETERS	15109	9/10/16
55	PRIVATE	JOHN PRITCHARD	15689	9/10/16
56	PRIVATE	WILLIAM THOMAS	15424	9/10/16
57	PRIVATE	LEONARD STEMBRIDGE	27575	9/10/16
58	PRIVATE	GEORGE W. ABLE	15589	9/10/16

BAR TO MILITARY MEDAL

A **Medal Bar** is a thin metal bar attached to the ribbon of a medal. It indicates that the recipient has met the criteria for receiving a medal in multiple. Three soldiers won the Bar to The Military Medal, shown below:-

RANK	NAME	SERVICE NO.	DATE
PRIVATE	DAVID WATTERS	15286	31/5/17
PRIVATE	MORRIS H. MORRIS	15427	1/11/17
PRIVATE	HARRY BAILIFF	16022	19/8/19

PRESENTATION OF COLOURS

The Colours of the 10th (Service) Battalion R. W. F. was presented on the 9th August 1921 at Wrexham Barracks and bore the numeral X in the centre of the roundel. The Battalion was one of those disbanded in February 1918 to make good shortages of manpower.

The Colours of the 10th (Service) Battalion R. W. F. was presented at Wrexham Barracks by Lieutenant General Sir Francis Lloyd, the Hon. Colonel of the Regiment and **'Laid Up'** the same day in the Regimental Chapel in St. Giles Church, Wrexham at the same time as the 8th, 9th, 11th, 19th, and 26th Service Battalions and three Garrisons.

The North Wales Weekly News – Thursday August 11th 1921

Royal Welsh Fusiliers – Presentation of Flags.

An impressive scene was witnessed on the Barracks Square, Wrexham, on Tuesday, when Lieutenant General Sir Francis Lloyd, the Hon. Colonel of the Regiment presented union silk flags to two Battalions of the Royal Welsh Fusiliers. One of the flags - that of 6th Garrison Battalion of the Royal Welsh Fusiliers which was raised at Aintree – will eventually be placed in Liverpool Cathedral. Another one – that of the 15th Battalion raised in London and known as the 1st London Welsh Battalion was subsequently taken to London and handed over to the custody of the London County Council for placing in their new County Hall. The remaining flags, those of the 8th, 9th, 10th, 11th, 19th, 26th and 1st and 2nd Garrison Battalions of the Royal Welsh Fusiliers – were taken to the Wrexham Parish Church and there hung in the private Chapel of the Regiment in that historic building. The Archbishop of Wales, accompanied by Canon Davies, Vicar of Wrexham, consecrated the flags on the Barracks Square in the presence of a large gathering.

Above: The colours hanging in St. Giles Church Wrexham

Left: Lieutenant General Sir Francis Lloyd, the Hon. Colonel of the Regiment

Below: St. Giles Church Wrexham

Officer Service Records

Please find below details of Officers mentioned in the War Diary with their '**Service Record Reference Number**' which are held at the National Archives in Kew.

I have searched the National Archives Online website for this information.

Hopefully the reference numbers are correct and correspond to the relevant names; there are so many variations of names and common surnames of some Officers that I cannot guarantee they are 100% correct. If you are unsure if someone listed is correct or not, please research the Officer further.

RANK	NAME	SERVICE RECORD NO.
LIEUTENANT COLONEL	JOHN HEATHCOTE FORRESTER ADDIE	WO374/396
LIEUTENANT	FREDERICK MARSHALL ARNOLD	WO374/2299
MAJOR	RICHARD ANTHONY ADAMSON	WO339/29900
LIEUTENANT CAPTAIN	CHARLES DEREK ALLTREE	WO339/47633
2ND LIEUTENANT	BERTIE MAVOR ALEXANDRA	WO339/29773
2ND LIEUTENANT	ARCHIBAL GEORGE WILLIAM BUCHANAN	WO339/3836
CAPTAIN	GEORGE PENDERILL BLAKE	WO339/22338
LIEUTENANT	STANLEY FLEMING BANCROFT	WO339/32591
CAPTAIN	ARTHUR DE BLES	WO339/16605
CAPTAIN	JOSEPH WILLIAM BLACKSTONE	WO374/6899
2ND LIEUTENANT	WILLIAM ARTHUR BOUETTE	WO339/33951
LIEUTENANT	ALFRED BERNARD BROTHERTON	WO339/39680
CAPTAIN	WILLIAM STANLEY BROCKLEHURST	WO339/26713
2ND LIEUTENANT	JOHN WILLIAM BROXUP	WO339/81452
CAPTAIN	HARRY BESWICK	WO374/6174
2ND LIEUTENANT	REGINALD PERCY BATTY	WO339/83289
MAJOR	GEORGE ROWLANDSON CROSFIELD	WO339/59140
LIEUTENANT	ADRIAN VICTOR CREE	WO339/5413
CAPTAIN	EDWARD HENRY CHAPMAN	WO339/36293
2ND LIEUTENANT	ARTHUR EDWARD CAPELL	WO339/4651
LIEUTENANT	WILLIAM ANDERSON COWIE	WO339/44984
CAPTAIN	BERTRAM MEYHEW CUTBUSH	WO339/44450
CAPTAIN	JAMES OSWALD CALDWELL	WO339/25912
2ND LIEUTENANT	HENRY CURRAN	WO339/64816
LIEUTENANT	FRANK CROSS	WO339/75416
LIEUTENANT	JOHN PERCY CARRINGTON	WO339/4918
CAPTAIN	JOHN OWEN WOODLAND CANDY	WO339/32382
LIEUTENANT	JOHN LLEWELLYN THOMAS DAVIES	WO339/17719
LIEUTENANT	PERCY TRUEMAN DALE	WO339/1881
2ND LIEUTENANT	WILLIAM NORMAN DAVIES	WO339/1936
LIEUTENANT	WALTER DANIEL	WO339/97402
2ND LIEUTENANT	JOHN FRANCIS DALE	WO339/38443

RANK	NAME	SERVICE RECORD NO.
2ND LIEUTENANT	ERNEST DIXON	WO339/57298
2ND LIEUTENANT	THOMAS MORGAN DAVIES	WO339/83855
LIEUTENANT	DAVID FELIX DAVIES	WO339/77698
CAPTAIN	CHARLES JOHN FREE DENT	WO339/27972
LIEUTENANT	ALBERT CHARLES DANIEL	WO339/52076
2ND LIEUTENAT	JOHN CHARLES DAVIES	WO339/95125
CAPTAIN/CHAPLIN	DAVID PICTON EVANS	WO374/54076
CAPTAIN	HARRY ELPHICK	WO339/113803
LIEUTENANT	THOMAS ALFRED EVANS	WO339/83778
2ND LIEUTENANT	JOHN WILLIAM ELLIS	WO374/22561
LIEUTENANT	ALGERNON WILLIAM FISH	WO339/2043
CAPTAIN	CHARLES ALBERT ROY FOLLIT	WO339/14938
MAJOR	EDWARD FREEMAN	WO339/56015
CAPTAIN	EILLIAM PERCIVAL GRIFFITHS	WO339/13540
2ND LIEUTENANT	LEONARD GEORGE GODFREY	WO339/60907
LIEUTENANT	SLURLEY AYLMER HAINES GRANVILLE	WO339/15766
LIEUTENANT	GEORGE WILLIAM GUTTERIDGE	WO374/29853
LIEUTENANT	DAVID CHARLES HUNTER	WO339/82279
CAPTAIN	ESME HUME HOWARD	WO339/26113
2ND LIEUTENANT	WILLIAM HUGHES	WO374/35496
CAPTAIN	TEGERIN HUGHES	WO339/24683
CAPTAIN	WILLIAM JOHN DOUGLAS HALE	WO339/42224
2ND LIEUTENANT	JOHN EDWYN HUGHES	WO374/35440
2ND LIEUTENANT	LOWARD LOCK HARRIES	WO339/42962
2ND LIEUTENANT	GEORGE ALFRED HALL	WO339/47952
LIEUTENANT	JONATHAN HUXLEY	WO339/100173
LIEUTENANT	DENNYS GODFREY ISAACS	WO339/29063
LIEUTENANT COLONEL	ALBERT JOHN STANLEY JAMES	WO339/34063
CAPTAIN	DUDLEY WILLIAM GERALD JACKSON	WO339/58394
CAPTAIN	BERNARD DIGBY JOHNS	WO339/20856
2ND LIEUTENANT	OWEN LEWIS JONES	WO339/34298
LIEUTENANT	EDWARD VAUGHAN JONES	WO339/57128
2ND LIEUTENANT	GOULDBOURNE HAYWARD JENNINGS	WO339/39675
2ND LIEUTENANT	JOSEPH AUBREY JAMES	WO339/70084
LIUETENANT	DAVID LEWIS JENKINS	WO374/37326
LIEUTENANT	WILLIAM THOMAS JONES	WO339/38580
LIEUTENANT	HAROLD MADAC JONES	WO339/26568
2ND LIEUTENANT	JOHN TREVOR JONES	WO339/103239
2ND LIEUTENANT	MORTIMOR JONES	WO339/103238
CAPTAIN	REES VAUGHAN JONES	WO339/15884
2ND LIEUTENANT	JOHN DAVIES JONES	WO339/82284
2ND LIEUTENANT	JOHN HAROLD JONES	WO339/126095
LIEUTENANT	SPENCER THOMAS JONES	WO339/30677
2ND LIEUTENANT	DAVID JOHN JONES	WO339/98858
LIEUTENANT	STUART CAMERON KIRBY	WO339/103241
LIEUTENANT	SYDNEY COURTNEY KIRKBY	WO339/57081
CAPTAIN	WILLIAM THOMAS LYONS	WO339/144028
MAJOR	CHARLES HENRY LORD	WO339/16631

RANK	NAME	SERVICE RECORD NO.
CAPTAIN	HAROLD JOHN KINGSLEY LEWIS	WO339/2946
CAPTAIN	CHARLES EDWARD LEATHAM LOCKE	WO339/3393
LIEUTENANT	FRANK ALLAN LAWSON	WO339/40366
2ND LIEUTENANT	DAVID EDWARD LAWRENCE	WO339/103242
CAPTAIN	CHARLES GWYN NOAL MORGAN	WO339/43538
MAJOR	HENRY HALL MORGAN	WO339/26849
CAPTAIN	JOHN GRAY MCKENDRICK MACAULAY	WO339/95921
CAPTAIN	WALTER BEVERIDGE MORGAN	WO339/25926
CAPTAIN	MENZIES MURRAY	WO339/5484
2ND LIEUTENANT	DONALD MCBEAN	WO339/11990
2ND LIEUTENANT	WILLIAM HUGHES MORRIS	WO339/43271
2ND LIEUTENANT	WILLIAM MACAWLAY	WO339/38002
CAPTAIN	EDWARD WILLIAM MAPLES	WO339/16594
CAPTAIN	ARTHUR ERSKINE HUMPHREYS-OWEN	WO374/35645
2ND LIEUTENANT	ROBERT TUDOR OWEN	WO339/83165
2ND LIEUTENANT	ROBERT GWILYM SMITH OWEN	WO339/79949
LIEUTENANT	JOHN OVERTON	WO374/51679
CAPTAIN	HARRY PRITCHARD	WO339/42688
LIEUTENANT	VIVIAN HENRY PIERCY	WO339/14353
2ND LIEUTENANT	HARRY PAGE	WO339/60932
CAPTAIN	WILLIAM EMERYS PARRY	WO339/59172
2ND LIEUTENANT	JAMES HYWELL PARRY	WO339/59173
2ND LIEUTENANT	WILLIAM THOMAS PHILLIPS	WO339/103256
CAPTAIN	DONALD GUY QUIN	WO339/43262
LIEUTENANT	HUBERT WILLIAM RAYNER	WO339/57516
2ND LIEUTENANT	TOM REA	WO339/57819
2ND LIEUTENANT	WILFRED ARTHUR RICHARDS	WO339/4329
2ND LIEUTENANT	WILLIAM ROWLANDS	WO339/59485
CAPTAIN	WILLIAM FERRIS RUDD	WO339/32557
LIEUTENANT	LEWIS EURON ROBERTS	WO339/43261
LIEUTENANT	GEORGE DEVEREUX SCALE	WO339/17823
MAJOR	FREDERICK ALFARO SAMUEL	WO339/37740
MAJOR	GEOFFREY LEE COMPTON SMITH	WO374/14983
CAPTAIN	SYDNEY GEORGE SHUTE	WO339/37033
CAPTAIN	JOHN AUBREY BERKLEY SPENCER	WO339/20602
2ND LIEUTENANT	FRANK ARCHIBALD SKINNER	WO339/68200
LIEUTENANT	EDWARD SWAINSON	WO339/82311
LIEUTENANT	BENJAMIN JOHN STEADMAN	WO339/33593
2ND LIEUTENANT	ROBERT OLIVER STANLEY	WO339/5730
LIEUTENANT	HOWARD DALTON TAYLOR	WO339/56988
MAJOR	GEORGE DANIEL TRUSLER	WO374/69627
2ND LIEUTENANT	GEORGE THOMAS	WO339/40663
2ND LIEUTENANT	JOSEPH THOMPSON	WO374/68199
LIEUTENANT	LEONARD PATRICK VERNON	WO339/113736
LIEUTENANT	HERBERT ARTHUR VERNON-MAYNARD	WO339/210
CAPTAIN/REVERAND	DAVID CYNDDELW WILLIAMS	WO339/102108
CAPTAIN	JOHN ARTHEUR WALKER	WO339/1068
CAPTAIN	MORGAN WATCYN WILLIAMS	WO339/57821

RANK	NAME	SERVICE RECORD NO.
2ND LIEUTENANT	HUPHREY EVAN WYNNE WILLIAMS	WO339/3649
CAPTAIN	DAVID JOEL WILLIAMS	WO374/74738
LIEUTENANT	LEWIS WILLIAMS	WO374/74974
LIEUTENANT	WILLOUGHBY CLEEVE WELLS	WO339/34103
LIEUTENANT	LEONARD WILLIAMS	WO374/74973
2ND LIEUTENANT	ARTHUR OWEN WILLIAMS	WO339/69826
2ND LIEUTENANT	EDWIN GORDON WILLIAMS	WO339/64275
2ND LIEUTENANT	CHARLES WILLIAM WILMORE	WO339/47663
2ND LIEUTENANT	ALUN TREVOR WORTHINGTON	WO339/98904
2ND LIEUTENANT	GEORGE HENRY WEBB	WO339/93732
2ND LIEUTENANT	RICHARD HENRY WILLIAMS	WO339/55409
2ND LIEUTENANT	PETER WILLIAMS	WO339/41719
2ND LIEUTENANT	EVAN WILLIAMS	WO339/70350
LIEUTENANT	JOHN REES WILLIAMS	WO339/73520
LIEUTENANT	ARTHUR GWILYM WILLIAMS	WO339/67377
2ND LIEUTENANT	THOMAS EDWIN WILLIAMS	WO374/75098

I was unable to find the service numbers of the following list of Officers on the National Archives site.

RANK	NAME
CAPTAIN	E. W. BELL
MAJOR	STUART SCOTT BINNY
2ND LIEUTENANT	E. H. BAYLISS
CAPTAIN	EDGAR WILLIAM BISHOP
2ND LIEUTENANT	FRANCIS ERIC CRANE
2ND LIEUTENANT	ARTHUR PATRICK COMYNS
LIEUTENANT	W. G. DANIEL
2ND LIEUTENANT	H. D. EVANS
MAJOR	CORNWALL COTTON GIBBINGS
CAPTAIN	BERNARD GRELLIER
LIEUTENANT	ROBERT KING HOLMES
2ND LIEUTENANT	CECIL WILFRED JONES
LIEUTENANT	E. T. LLEWELYN
2ND LIEUTENANT	ALBERT NEVITT
2ND LIEUTENANT	T. A. OLIVER
MAJOR	F. A. PHILLIPS
LIEUTENANT	WILLIAM R. REES
2ND LIEUTENANT	WILLIAM SIDDONS
2ND LIEUTENANT	RALPH CECIL SEEL
2ND LIEUTENANT	HERBERT GORDON THOMAS
2ND LIEUTENANT	OWEN EDGAR THOMAS
2ND LIEUTENANT	W. S. WYNNE WILLIAMS
2ND LIEUTENANT	ARTHUR FELIX WILLIAMS
2ND LIEUTENANT	JAMES MACALLUM WARDLAN

Chapter 10
Edwin's War In Map Form

Map 1 - The Journey from the Port

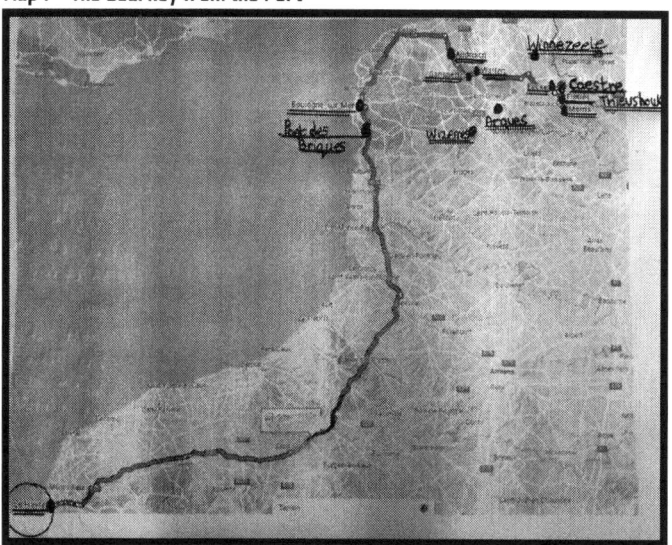

Map 2 - The Journey around Flanders

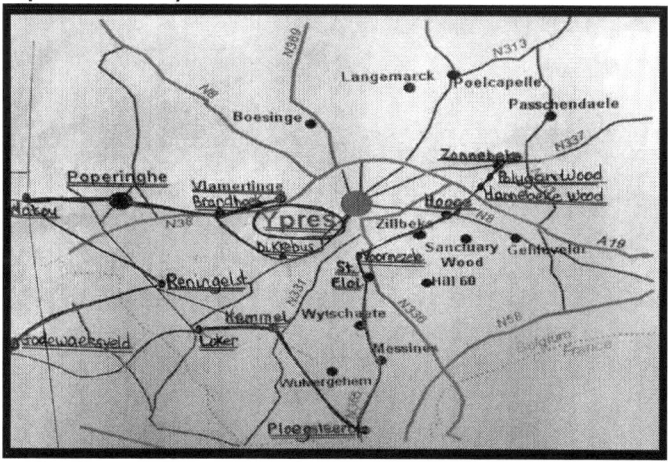

MAPS NOT TO SCALE

Map 3 – The Journey around The Somme

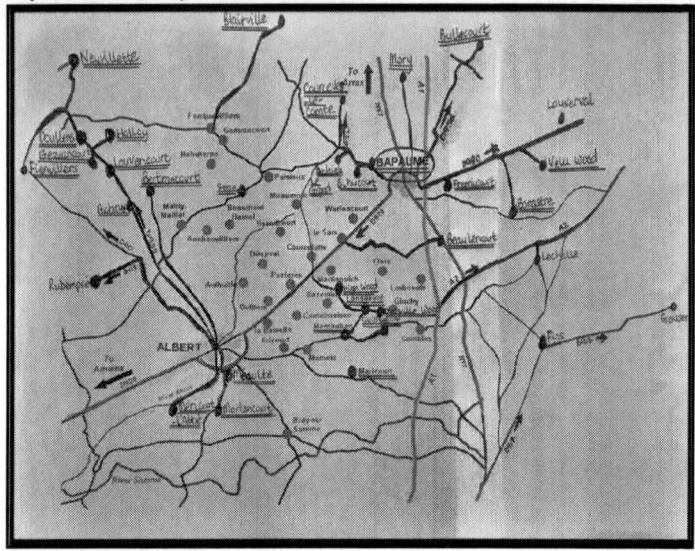

Map 4 – The Journey around Arras

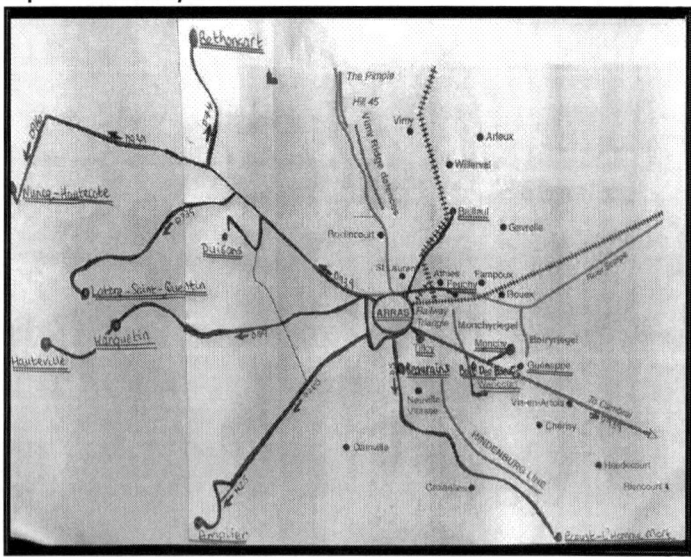

MAPS NOT TO SCALE

Map 5 - The Journey around Loos

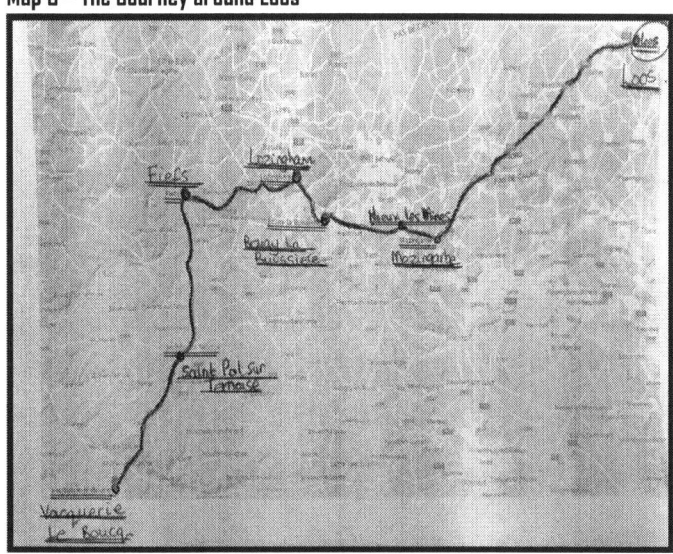

Map 6 - My Taid Edwin's Last Journey Before Home

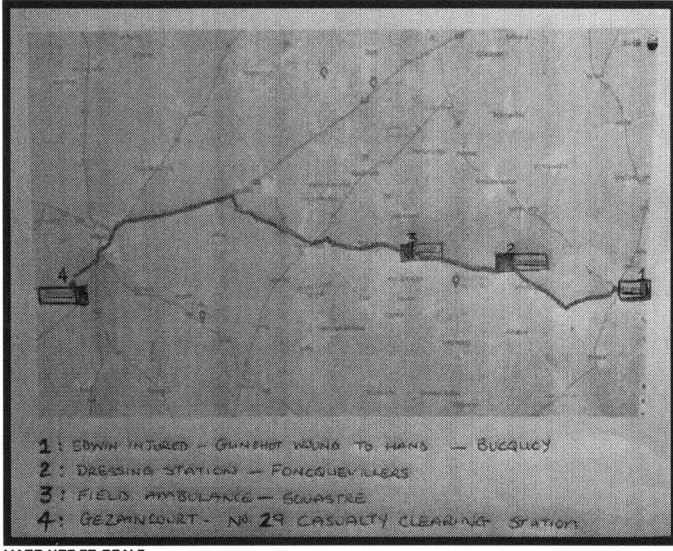

1: EDWIN INJURED - GUNSHOT WOUND TO HAND — BUCQUOY
2: DRESSING STATION — FONCQUEVILLERS
3: FIELD AMBULANCE — SOUASTRE
4: GEZAINCOURT - No. 29 CASUALTY CLEARING STATION

MAPS NOT TO SCALE

Chapter 11
The Later Years

My Taid Edwin returned home to his Wife Mary Ellen and their three children John aged 11, Tom aged 8 and Katie aged 4. They lived at 17 Primrose Hill, Holywell, Flintshire, North Wales. Times were hard and jobs were hard to come by; Edwin was 40 years old and still suffering from his wounds from years of serving on the Front-Line. The terrible conditions had taken its toll on him. My Taid Edwin, like thousands of other soldiers returning from the front, found that being a civilian again did not always match up to expectations. Many soldiers came home after they had served their country in it's hour of need, expecting to pick up their lives from where they had left them. Some were lucky and walked back into their old jobs but others spent years searching to find one.

The War was prolonged, brutal and an expensive conflict. Britain not only incurred over 700,000 deaths and more than twice that number wounded, but the destruction of 3.6% of it's human capital, 10% of it's domestic and 24% of it's overseas assets had seen the country spend well over it's 25% Gross Domestic Product (G. D. P.) on the War effort between 1915 and 1918 and the economic damage continued to accrue throughout the 1920's and beyond. The unemployment rate climbed to 23.4% in May 1921 and from then it never fully recovered, remaining over 10% in almost every month of the 1920's.

In 1920 many ex servicemen marched on Whitehall and 10 Downing Street in London to bring attention to their plight with banners and flags that read: -

Front page of 'The Daily Mirror' newspaper, reporting on a violent confrontation between police and the protesters on Whitehall. The flashpoint was near Downing Street and the cenotaph. The march-by had an estimated 10,000 people, many of them former soldiers, was organised to ask for aid to be given to the large number of post-war unemployed.

On the 1921 census my Taid Edwin and the family were still living at 17 Primrose Hill, Holywell, Flintshire, North Wales. Edwin's occupation was recorded as a 'Coal Hewer' but he was out of work at the time of the census. I wonder if he had been out of work since returning home from the War because of his wounds? Edwin was still receiving his 'War Disability Pension' up until the 18th of October 1922 when a lump sum was paid to him. On the 1921 census Edwin and his Wife Mary Ellen had two more children, Elias born in 1919 and Elwyn born in 1920. Mary Ellen was also pregnant with Myra, who was born later in 1921.

NAME	RELATIONSHIP TO HEAD OF FAMILY	AGE	OCCUPATION
EDWIN ROBERTS	HEAD	42	COAL HEWER OUT OF WORK
MARY E ROBERTS	WIFE	38	-
JOHN D ROBERTS	SON	14	-
WILLIAM THOMAS ROBERTS	SON	11	-
KATE ROBERTS	DAUGHTER	7	-
ELIAS ROBERTS	SON	1	-
ELWYN ROBERTS	SON	-	-

My Taid Edwin and my Nain Mary Ellen had their 7th child Gwladys May Roberts (my Mother), who was born on the 19th May 1925. On my Mother's birth certificate it states my Taid Edwin's occupation was a Coal Hewer.

Edwin's local pub in the town of Holywell was the 'Black Horse Inn'. It was situated at the top of Holywell High Street but is no longer there. The building had been knocked down after being empty for many years and replaced with a new building with a 'Boots Chemist' and 'Santander Bank' in it's place.

Black Horse Inn (left)

The story in the family is that my Taid Edwin, who did not suffer fools lightly, after a heated argument outside the Black Horse Inn, punched someone through the window of the 'Fruit and Veg' shop just up the street from the pub. The incident was talked about for years and people were very wary of upsetting the Robert's family.

Holywell High Street (2018) showing where my shop Ideal Lighting was in comparison to where the Black Horse Inn was located and Lodwicks the Fruit & Veg Shop was located

During the early 1930's, my Taid Edwin and his family moved to a new housing estate in Holywell called Coronation Estate. They moved into number 45, which is still there today.

On the 1939 register my Taid Edwin and his family were still living at 45 Coronation Estate, Holywell (photograph on the left).
Edwin was now 60 years old and was working as a General Labourer.

NAME	RELATIONSHIP TO HEAD OF FAMILY	AGE	OCCUPATION
EDWIN ROBERTS	HEAD	60	GENERAL LABOURER
MARY E ROBERTS	WIFE	55	UNPAID DOMESTIC DUTIES
ELIAS ROBERTS	SON	20	PAINTER'S LABOURER
ELWYN ROBERTS	SON	19	PAINTER'S LABOURER
MYRA ROBERTS	DAUGHTER	18	ARTIFICIAL SILK SPINNER
GWLADYS MAY ROBERTS	DAUGHTER	14	SCHOLAR
ALBERT EDWIN ROBERTS	GRANDSON	3	-

My Taid Edwin, like many others, fought in the **'War to end all Wars'** but 20 years later another storm was gathering over Europe and beyond. A storm which would bring great sadness to Edwin and his family.

It must have been so hard for my Taid Edwin and my Nain Mary Ellen to see their children go off to War. Edwin would have known what they would be in for. Did he try and talk them out of going? Would he want his children to live through the horrors he experienced only 20 years earlier? When his Sons and his Daughter joined up, all Edwin and Mary Ellen could do was to hope and pray they would all return home safely.

Elias Roberts was born on 11th October 1919 the 4th child of Edwin and Mary Ellen. On the 1939 register he was living at home with his parents Edwin and Mary Ellen at 45 Coronation Estate, Holywell, Flintshire, North Wales and was employed as a Painter's Labourer.

Elias enlisted on the 17th January 1940, joining the 8th Denbighshire Battalion Royal Welsh Fusiliers with service number 4198208. His height was 5' 10 ½ ". He weighed 144lbs. His eyes were hazel and his hair was black.

Elias attended S. E. C. No. 14 Course with No. 1 General Cavalry Tank Corps at Sunningdale from 24th January to 16th February 1941. Elias was transferred to the 13th Battalion Kings (Liverpool) Regiment in late September 1942 joining the Chindits Training at Saugor (now known as Sagar) in India with a small draft of men from the Royal Welch Fusiliers. He was placed into Northern Group Head Quarters (2 G. H. Q.) which was the organisational hub of the section of the Chindits, comprising of Columns 3, 4, 5, 7, 8 plus Major General Orde Wingates own Brigade Head Quarters.

Major General Orde Wingate

The Chindits were the largest of all of the Allied Special Forces of the 2nd World War, formed and led by Major General Orde Wingate D. S. O. They fought behind enemy lines in Northern Burma during 1943 and 1944 in the War against Japan. They were unconventional due to their total reliance on **'Air Drops'** for their supplies and complete dependance on **'Wireless'** for communication. Elias was part of the 1st Expedition in February 1943, code name **'Operation Long Cloth'** which marched over 1000 miles during the campaign. The Chindits would infiltrate deep behind the Japanees lines in Northern Burma. For many months they lived and fought the enemy in the jungles, their mission was to raid the enemys lines of communication, blowing bridges, railway tracks and disturbing supply routes. The Chindits were organised into 'Columns' each with a strength of about 340. Each column was strong enough to defend itself and capable of mounting surprise attacks on the enemy targets, yet small enough for concealment and for mobility to evade capture. Columns would combine to strike larger targets and then disappear back into the jungle. On the 8th February the Chindits commenced their advance into Burma from the Indian base town of Imphal. Operation Long Cloth had begun. Initially the columns met no opposition, but soon, some of the units were sighted by the Japanese, who initially believed them to be small groups gathering intelligence. It was not until there had been a number of engagements with Japanese outposts and patrols and the successful demolition of a railway bridge that the enemy realised the force opposing them was of Brigade strength. The Japanese had been caught by surprise and were confused not knowing the intent of the Chindits or how they were supplied. Three Japanese Regiments, each consisting of 3 Battalions were sent to the area to locate and destroy the invaders. The Chindits now became the hunted. By now the Chindits were deep in enemy territory on the 13th March 1943 an airdrop supplying the Chindits was interrupted and had to be aborted due to Japanese interference. Withdrawal would be hazardous as the return route to India required the re-crossing of two major rivers (Irrawaddy and Chindwin) which would now be guarded by the Japanese. Despite this problem, the Chindits continued their advance Eastwards attacking targets as they went. On 24th March Wingate was ordered to withdraw, by this time the Chindits had advanced so far to the East that they were almost out of range for the air drops. They also found themselves in an area short of water and heavily patrolled by the Japanese. Exhaustion and hunger took it's toll. Wingate gave the order to disperse into smaller groups, now essential equipment was dumped and mules that were no longer required turned loose. Out of the 3000 Officers and men that started Operation Long Cloth, only 2182 came back four months later, having covered between 1000 to 1500 miles in that time. The men that returned were in a very poor condition, suffereing from tropical diseases and malnutrition. Of those that had returned, only 600 were passed for further active service.

Elias was taken prisoner by the Japanese. He was reported missing in the Battalion's War Diary on the 10th July 1943 after the column was broken up into smaller units. On 30th April 1943, whilst attempting to cross the narrow, but fast flowing river, close to the village of Okthaik, they were ambushed by the Japanese. Many men were killed and others wounded. The survivors quickly formed up into small dispersal groups and headed off Westwards. It is very possible that this was when and where Elias became detatched from the group or when he was wounded. Three other soldiers from Elias's Battalion were also listed as 'Missing' on the 10th July 1943 and ended up 'Prisoners of War' (P. O. W.) in Rangoon Jail.

Number	Rank	Name & Initial	Casualty	Date of Casualty	Remarks
5413029	L/C.	Arries	M. Missing known to be wounded	30.4.43.	
3770656	Pte.	Almond	A. Missing	30.4.43.	
3780506	Pte.	Ashcroft	L. Missing	10.5.43.	
4201249	Pte.	Bradley	J. Missing	20.4.43.	
3780055	Pte.	Blay	T. Missing	10.7.43.	
3781629	Pte.	Brennan	F. Missing	8.7.43.	
3780118	Pte.	Callan	B. Missing	10.7.43.	
4194640	Pte.	Clarke	F. Missing	30.4.43.	
5922101	Pte.	Coffin	L. Missing	10.7.43.	
3777821	Pte.	Cocks	J. Missing	30.4.43.	
3781620	Pte.	Felber	H. Missing	8.5.43.	
3780694	Pte.	Holleran	P. Missing	30.3.43.	
3779055	Pte.	Holland	D. Missing	10.7.43.	
5620093	Pte.	Lee	G. Missing	30.3.43.	
5856210	Pte.	Leach	A. Missing	11.4.43.	
3780700	Pte.	Palmer	E. Missing	10.9.42.	
3778540	Pte.	Phillips	R. Missing	30.3.43.	
4198208	Pte.	Roberts	L. Missing	10.7.43.	
6627251	Pte.	Sewall	H. Missing	30.3.43.	
6827056	Pte.	Still	J. Missing	30.3.43.	
3854474	Pte.	Taylor	J. Missing	10.7.43.	
3719103	Pte.	Williams	E. Missing	10.5.43.	
2130546	CSM.	Wilson	J. Missing	30.4.43.	
3779449	Pte.	Moogat	P. Missing believed wounded, and died of wounds.	12.3.43.	

Elias Roberts on the 'Missing List'

Rangoon Jail

Elias Robert's name appears on the P. O. W. Casualty List for Rangoon Jail, which sadly shows his **'Date of Death'** in block 6 on the 27th August 1943. He was P. O. W. number 530 and he was buried in the English Cantonment Cemetery in Plot Number 32. Elias's Japanese Card is scant in detail and does not show either his date or place of capture, however, the reverse side of this card states the cause of death as **'Death was Malnutrition'** and that the prisoner died at 11.30am in Block 6 on 27th August 1943.

546	-	Pte	Stell A.	18.8.43	-
551	-	Pte	Phillips Bert	20.8.43	-
527	-	Pte	Lenihan J.	21.8.43	82
574	-	Sgt	Wyse K.	21.8.43	-
532	-	Pte	Ackerman J.	22.8.43	-
585	-	Pte	Holland G.	25.8.43	-
530	-	Pte	Roberts E.	27.8.43	32
494	3781435	L/cpl	Kay J.	2.9.43	53
576	378----	L/Cpl	Lee G.	2.9.43	-
577	1880658	Pte	Hunt S.R.	2.9.43	35

Block 6 Death Card

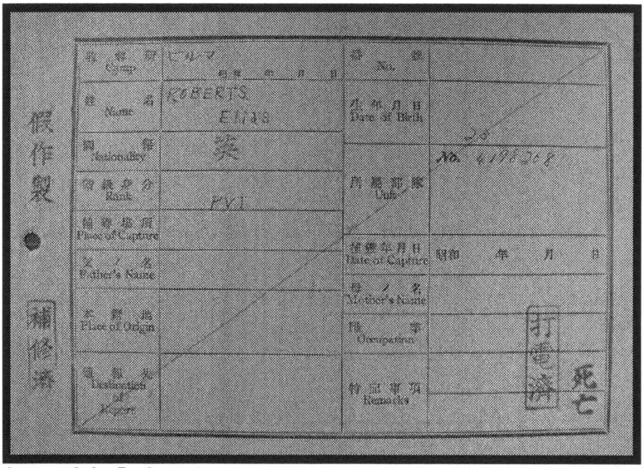

収容所 Camp ビルマ

番号 No.

姓名 Name ROBERTS ELIAS

生年月日 Date of Birth

国籍 Nationality 英

所属部隊 Unit No. 4198208

Rank PVT

Place of Capture

Date of Capture 昭和 年 月 日

Father's Name

Mother's Name

Place of Origin

Occupation

Destination of Report

Remarks

打電済

死亡

假作製

補修済

Japanese Index Card

My Taid Edwin and his family were informed by the War Office that Elias was **'Reported as Missing'** on the 25th July 1943 and were only told of Elias's death in the Japanese P. O. W. camp on the 2nd June 1945 nearly two years later. It must have been a terrible two years not knowing if you Son was alive or dead.

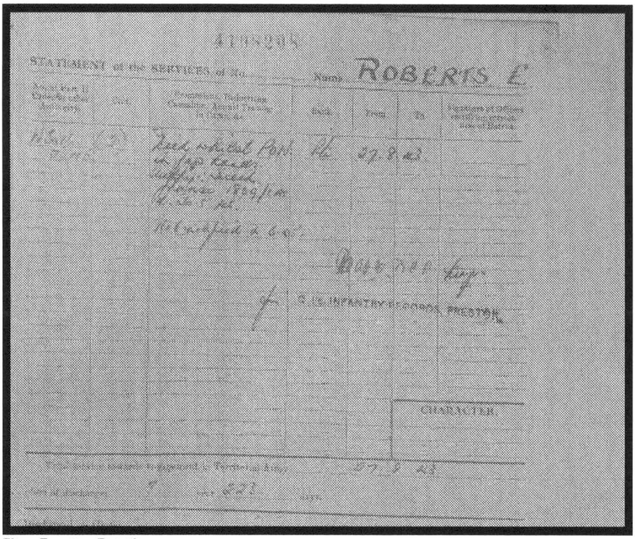

4198208

STATEMENT of the SERVICES of No. ... Name ROBERTS E

Rank | From | To

27.8.43

No. 4 INFANTRY RECORDS, PRESTON

CHARACTER

27.8.43

Elias Service Details

After the War, the story in the family, after speaking to other survivors of the camp, was that Elias had gone to the aid of a fellow prisoner who was being mistreated by the Japanese guards. Elias struck one of the guards, who then retaliated and beat Elias to death. I am not sure if this story is true, but this was the story that was passed down through the family.

After the War was over the Commonwealth War Graves Commission moved all of the British Graves from the Cantonment Cemetery over to the newly constructed Rangoon War Cemetery, where Elias is now at rest. Elias is also remembered on the local War Memorial in Holywell, Flintshire, North Wales.

Grave in Rangoon War Cemetery

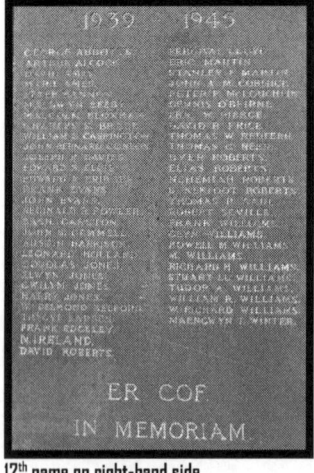

12th name on right-hand side

Elias (middle of photograph)

William Thomas (Tom) Roberts was born on 6th March 1910 in the Bagillt Parish, Flintshire, North Wales the 2nd child of Edwin and Mary Ellen. On the 1939 census Tom was living at 36 Coronation Estate, Holywell, Flintshire, North Wales and was employed as an Art Silk Worker (Viscose Department).

Tom enlisted in the Army on the 10th March 1927 aged only just 18, joining the Royal Welsh Fusiliers serving 4 years, until the 9th March 1931. Tom re-enlisted on the 13th February 1940 after the outbreak of the 2nd World War, joining the 2nd Battalion Welsh Guards as a Guardsman, service number 4187599.

The 2nd Battalion Welsh Guards was formed on the 18th May 1939 and was stationed at the Tower of London when Britain declared War on Germany in September of the same year. The Battalion remained at the Tower of London before it moved to Camberly in April 1940. At Camberly, the Battalion joined the 20th Independent Infantry Brigade (Guards) on the 21st May and then moved to Dover, where it embarked on board S. S. Biarritz and the Mona's Queen for Bologne, arriving at the port the next morning. The Battalion took up defensive positions. The Battalion suffered heavy casualties defending the port before being evacuated shortly before midnight on the 23rd May, on board the Destroyer, Windsor.

Tom was one of the many soldiers that was taken prisoner by the Germans and spent the next five years in prison camps in Poland. Tom spent his time in two camps:- Camp VIIIB (8B) at Lamsdorf & Camp XXI-A (21A) at Torun. His prison number was 5090.

Lamsdorf Camp   Torun Camp

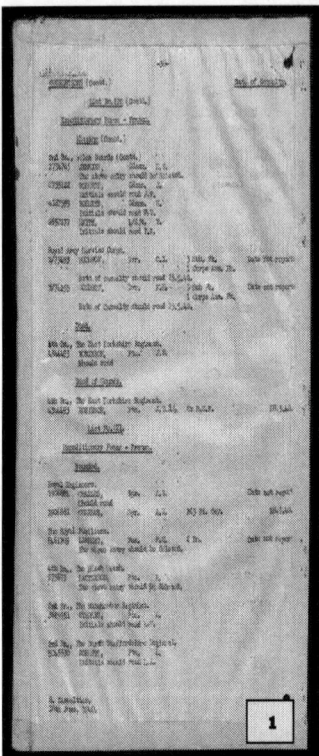 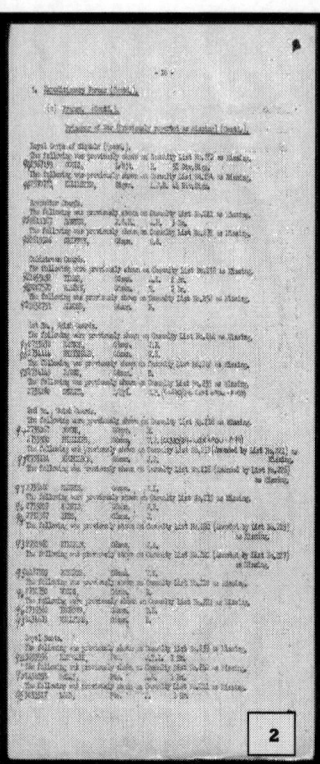

List 1 shows Tom is 'Missing (3rd on the list)   List 2 shows Tom a 'Prisoner of War' (19th on the list)

Tom returned home in 1945. Tom appeared in the local newspaper in 1980 telling of his campaign to receive his War Medals.

Tom holding his medals

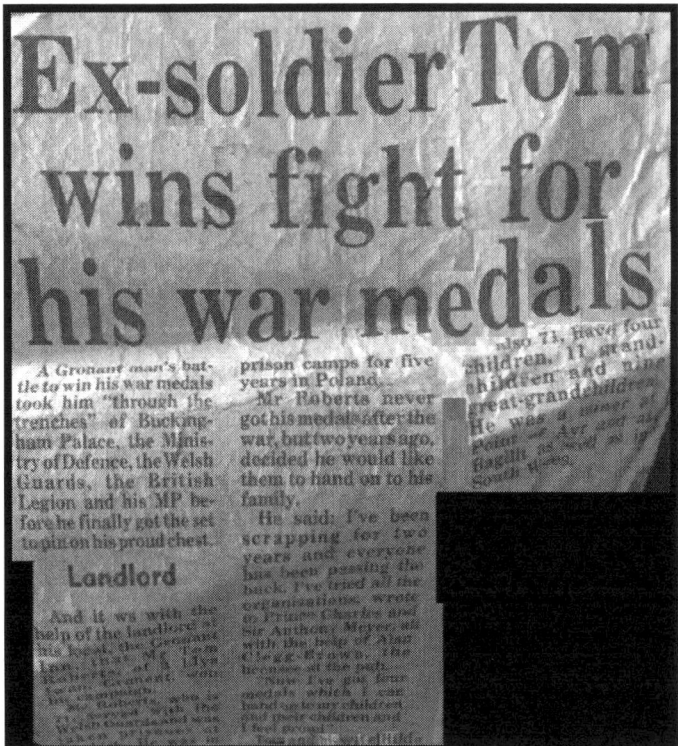

Ex – soldier Tom wins fight for his war medals

A Gronant man's battle to win his war medals took him "through the trenches" of Buckingham Palace, the Ministry of Defence, the Welsh Guards, the British Leigion and his MP before he finally got the set to pin on his chest.

Landlord

And it was with the help of the landlord at his local, the Gronant Inn, that Mr Tom Roberts of 3 Llys Iwan, Gronant, won his campaign. Mr Roberts who is 71 served with the Welsh Guards and was taken prisoner of war. He was in prison camp for five years in Poland. Mr Roberts never got his medals after the war, but two years ago, he decided he would like them to hand on to his family.

He said: *"I've been scrapping for two years and everyone has been passing the buck. I've tried all the organisations, wrote to Prince Charles and Sir Anthony Meyer, all with the help of Alan Clegg-Brown, the licencee of the pub. Now I have got four medals that I can pass onto my children and their children, and I feel proud."*

Tom and his wife Hilda, also 71, have four children, 11 grandchildren and nine great-grandchildren. He was a Miner at Point of Ayr and Bagillt as well as in South Wales.

Elwyn Roberts was born on 8th November 1920 the 5th child of my Taid Edwin and my Nain Mary Ellen. He married Sheila Edwards in July 1951.

Not much is known about Elwyn's War. All I have been able to research is that he joined the R. A. F. as an Aircraftman 2nd Class with service number 408713.

He survived the War and died at the age of 80 in March 2001.

Elwyn and Sheila's wedding with my Taid Edwin on the right of the photograph

Gwladys May Roberts (my Mother) was born 19th May 1925, the 7th and the last child of my Taid Edwin and my Nain Mary Ellen. She was born in Holywell and lived at 17 Primrose Hill, Holywell, Flintshire, North Wales.

My Mother served in the Auxillary Territorial Service (A. T. S.) and married for the 1st time to Patrick Fitzgerald, in Croydon, 17th December 1944.

I have struggled to find any 'Service Records' for her, writing to the Army Personel Centre in Glasgow without any joy. I often wondered why my Mother was in London at all, until I came upon details when I visited Bletchly Park and found a C. M. Fitzgerald and a Mr C. P. Fitzgerald both having served in Bletchly Park. When I researched further and I looked at her 1st marriage certificate, one of the witnesses, a Mr A. W. J. Hemmings, was also working at Bletchly Park in charge of Hut 6. Whilst visiting Bletchly Park I spoke to one of the women working there and she confirmed that over 10,000 people worked at Bletchly at it's peak, even her Father, who also had no records, so it was more than likely that my Mother worked there too. My Mother remarried in January 1968 to my Father Joseph Henry (known as Harry) Warburton. My Mother died in 1973 aged 47 when I was only a child of twelve, so I never got the chance to ask her what she did in the War and my Father Harry died two months later aged 50, so again, I was never able to ask the questions I would have loved to ask them both.

The documents at Bletchly Park showing all three names on the marriage certificate.

My Mam Gwladys and my Father Harry

I am unable to find any Service Records for my Taid Edwin's other children, John David Roberts, Katie Roberts or Myra Roberts.

John David Roberts was the eldest child born to Edwin and Mary Ellen, born in 1907 in Bagillt Parish. He married Elizabeth, known as Auntie Bessie in July 1938. He died in 1974.

Katie Roberts was the 3rd child born to Edwin and Mary Ellen on 12th March 1914 in Holywell, Flintshire. She married Thomas Griffiths in 1938. She died in 2000.

Myra Roberts was the 6th child born to Edwin and Mary Ellen on 16th October 1921 in Holywell, Flintshire. She married William Noal Pike known as Uncle Bill in July 1945. She died in 1970.

Katie Roberts

Myra Roberts

Uncle Bill & Uncle Tom at the back
Auntie Myra & Auntie Katie at the front

Between 1945 and 1954 my Taid Edwin and his family still lived at 45 Coronation Estate Holywell. Mary Ellen was now suffering with Cancer and sadly passed away on 2nd January 1954 aged 70.

Not long after this event, my Taid Edwin moved in with my Mother Gwladys and my Father Harry at 3 Mwdwl Eithin in Carmel, Holywell, Flintshire.

Edwin at 3 Mwdwl Eithin Carmel with my Sister Linda

57 Coronation Estate

My Mother and Father, with Edwin, my brother and two sisters moved back to Coronation Estate, Holywell, buying No. 57 in 1960. I was born in this house a year later in 1961. Edwin remained with the family for the rest of his life. His bedroom was downstairs in the front room (always known as the parlour – the best room). During the time he spent living with us he would spend his days talking to his friend Mr Cawper, who funnily enough, lived at No. 45, Edwin's old house. He used to walk to town somedays and stop outside the school railings to give us sweets during breaktime, but as he got older, he was unable to do this anymore due to his arthritis and old age; he was nearly 90 years old by then. I remember he fell outside and cut his head which needed stitches. The very next day, he pulled the stitches out saying he didn't need them! My brother Steve and myself used to play tricks on him, but he never really did anything to stop us, mainly because he couldn't catch us!

Back - Susan Pike (Myra's Daughter, Edwins Granddaughter) and Linda my Sister
Front - Taid Edwin, Me (Russ) and my Brother Steve

Towards the last few months of his life, my Taid Edwin, spent time in the local Cottage Hospital in Holywell. I remember walking home from Primary School, aged 8, with my friend and decided to go and visit him. When asked by a very scary Matron in the Hospital what we were doing there, I replied *"I have come to see my Taid."* The Matron asked *"What is your Taid's name?"* I had no idea what he was called, I only knew him as Taid! Luckily my Taid must have heard the commotion and recognised my voice and shouted to me telling me where he was. I sat with him for a while and when it was time to go (as instructed by the scary Matron!), he gave me a few pennies for sweets and waved goodbye. That was the last time I ever saw my Taid as he passed away a few days later on 2nd March 1970. He is buried in Holywell Cemetery.

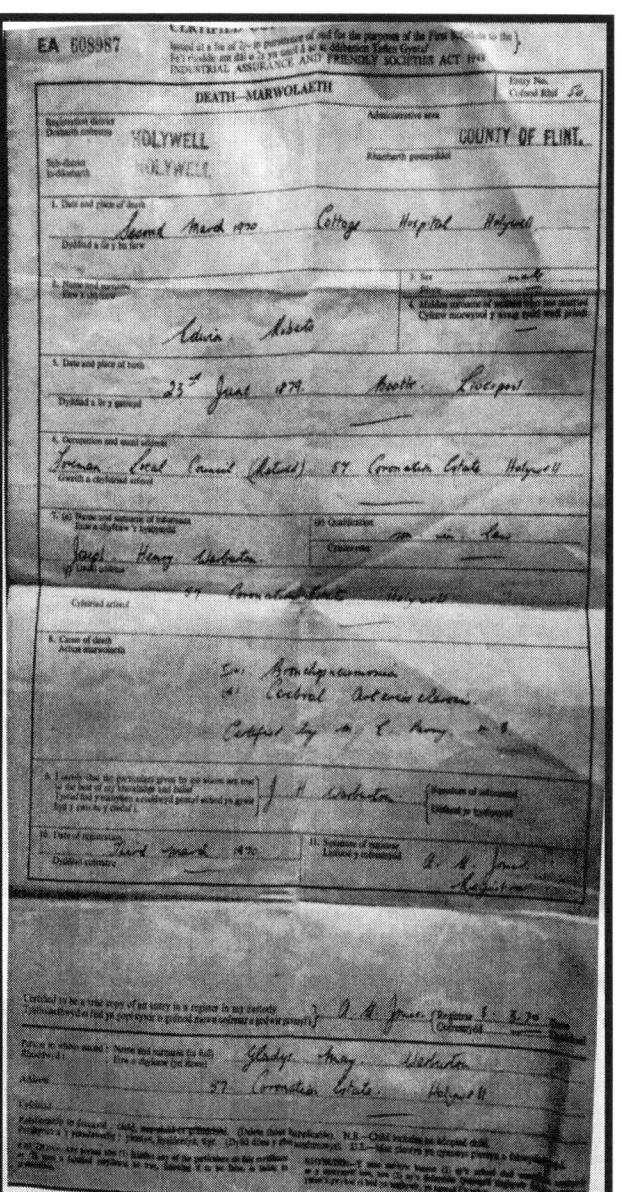

Edwin's Death Certificate

Holywell Cottage Hospital – demolished 21ˢᵗ May 2018

Taid and Nain's Grave - (the date of death is incorrect for Taid, it should show 1970 not 1969)

I visit Taid's grave regulary, at the same time as I visit my Mother and Father's grave who both passed away three years after Taid and are both buried in the same graveyard, quite close to my Taid and Nain. I had a brass plaque made with Taid's Name, Battalion and service number 15736 on it. This sits on his gravestone so not to forget that he served in the War.

Plaque I had made which sits on the stone underneath the flowers

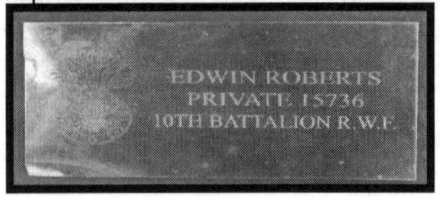

Edwin's Family Tree

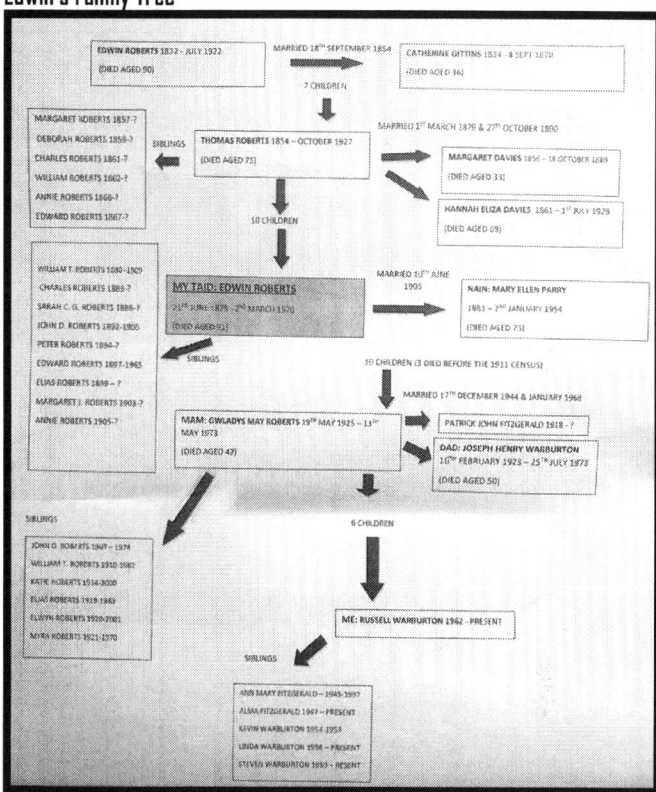

Our family is very proud of Taid's service in the Great War. Like so many others, he went through so much, but after doing the research I can now see how lucky he was to make it through at all. I wanted to write this book as a lasting tribute not only to him, but to everyone who fought with the 10th (Service) Battalion Royal Welsh Fusiliers in the Great War.

I hope we shall never forget them!

The Urban District of Holywell Roll of Honor - Line No. 53, My Taid, Edwin Roberts

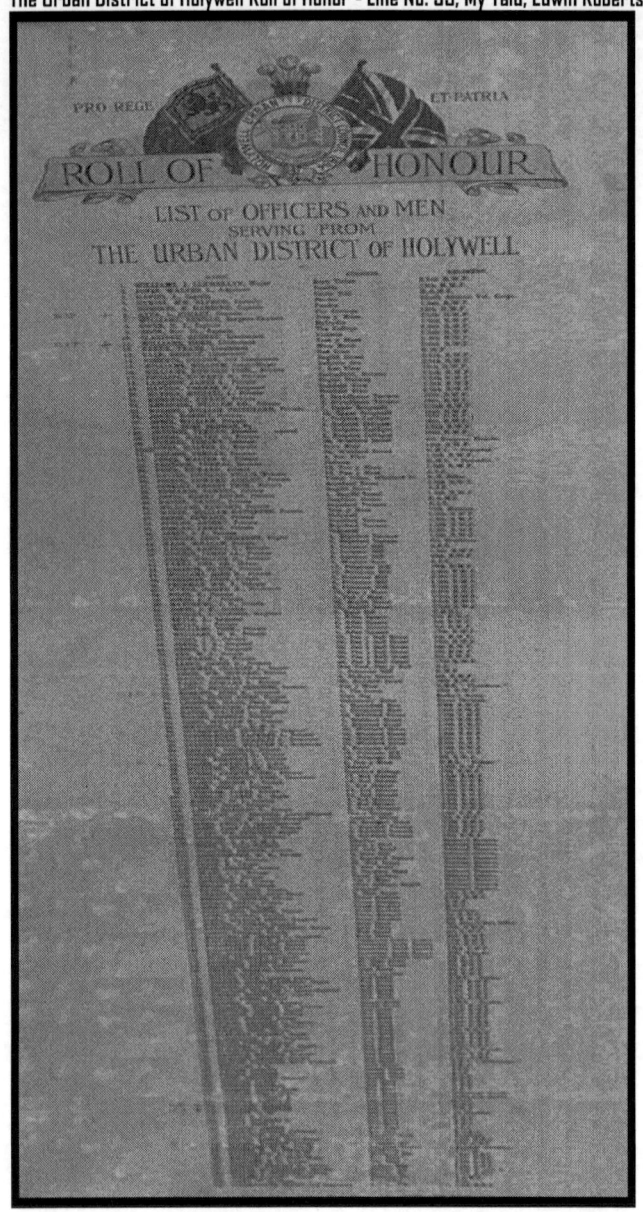

SOURCES AND PERMISSIONS

I would like to thank the following people who helped me make this book possible:

- Rupert Peploe – Grandson of Lieutenant Colonel Geoffrey Lee Compton-Smith Commanding Officer of the 10th (Service) Battalion Royal Welsh Fusiliers, who kindly allowed me to use some of the information from his excellent book "Last Letters", telling the story of his Grandfather

- Alan Culpitt – Grandson of Private George John Culpitt, 10th (Service) Battalion Royal Welsh Fusiliers, who kindly allowed me to use some of the information from his Grandfather's Diary about his time serving with the Battalion

- The Royal Chaplin's Museum

- Keith Jones and the Staff of The Royal Welch Fusiliers Museum, Caernarfon, North Wales for all of their help and guidance in sourcing photographs and information for my book

- Rosemary Wyeth (Romy) for all her help and supplying information on Codford

- Mark Thomson at Romsey War Memorial Archive

- Durham Mining Museum

- Library of Wales

- The Gazette

- The Opiham Society

- British Newspaper Archive

- Darryl Porrino for all your help and support and his excellent books on The Fallen of the R. W. F.

- "The Welsh at War" by Steven John
- "Wales on the Western Front" by John Richards
- From "Khaki to Cloth" by Morgan Watcyn Williams
- "The Great War Handbook" by Geoff Bridger
- "Kitchener's Army" by Peter Simkins
- Regimental Records of the Royal Welch Fusiliers by Dudley Ward
- "The Somme" by Peter Hart
- "1918" by Peter Hart
- "Amiens 1918" by Gregory Blaxland
- "Arras 1917" by Jim Smithson (Great War Group Publication)
- 10th (Service) Battalion R. W. F. War Diary – WO95/1436/2
- 8th Entrenching Unit War Diary – WO95/793/7
- Hood Battalion 63rd R. N. D. War Diary – WO95/3115/1
- 76th Brigade War Diary – WO95/1433/1/2/3 & WO95/1434/1
- Wrexham Museum
- Imperial War Museum
- The War Diary of the 10th (Service) Battalion 1914-1918 by Lieutenant F. N. Burton & Lieutenant A. P. Comyns M. C.

If this book has kindled an interest in the Great War for you, please consider joining the following: -

www.greatwargroup.com

Registered Charity Number: 1191846

MORE TITLES FROM THE AUTHOR: AVAILABLE ON AMAZON:-

For Our Town – For Our Country
The Story of the Men on the Holywell Memorial

ISBN-13 : 979-8766775188

Five Communities At War
Brynford, Caerwys, Rhes-y-Cae, Whitford & Ysceifiog Memorials

ISBN-13 : 979-8412458120

Printed in Great Britain
by Amazon